The First,
The Few,
And
The Only

The First, the Few and the Only

2
You're not alone

The First,
The Few,
and
The Only

Michael Thornhill
VAWZEN Rising LLC

The First, the Few and the Only

Copyright © 2025 by Michael Thornhill
All rights reserved.

The scanning, uploading, and distribution of this book without permission is a theft of intellectual property. No portion of this book may be reproduced in any form without written permission from the publisher or author, except as permitted by U.S. copyright law. If you would like permission to use material from the book (other than for review or study purposes), please contact hiraeth412@yahoo.com. Thank you for your support of the author's rights and VAWZEN Rising LLC.

This publication is designed to provide accurate and authoritative information in regard to the subject matter covered. It is sold with the understanding that neither the author nor the publisher is engaged in rendering legal, investment, accounting or other professional services. While the publisher and author have used their best efforts in preparing this book, they make no representations or warranties with respect to the accuracy or completeness of the contents of this book and specifically disclaim any implied warranties of merchantability or fitness for a particular purpose. No warranty may be created or extended by sales representatives or written sales materials. The advice and strategies contained herein may not be suitable for your situation. You should consult with a professional when appropriate. Neither the publisher nor the author shall be liable for any loss of profit or any other commercial damages, including but not limited to special, incidental, consequential, personal, or other damages. Some names & identifying information have been changed to protect confidentiality

The web addresses and QR codes referenced in this book were live and correct at the time of the book's publication but may be subject to change.

Book Cover by Jonathan Zoeteman
Illustrations by attributed artists (all rights reserved by artists)
For speaking engagements contact us at Hiraeth412@yahoo.com

First edition July 2025,
Printed in the United States of America
ISBN 979-8-9993627-0-4

You're not alone

The First, the Few and the Only

To Me—

To the boy who tried to make himself small
so they could feel tall—

Arise… like Antaeus from the Greek mythos.

Not in defiance,
but in dignity.
Not in rage,

but in rightful remembering.
For no matter how long they stood over you,
you were always the deeper well.
Always the one with water to draw.

So let the record show:
You beautiful Black Afro-Cuban man…
You did write.

And it was good.
And it was whole.

You never wrote to change the world.
You wrote to unbury yours.

And it will outlive the echo of every doubt
that ever tried to keep you bowed.

The First, the Few and the Only

To the reader—

To the first.
The few.
To the only one with
your face in the room

You were never alone.

You belong to a long line
of fire-starters and quiet tempests.
Of deep wells and deeper knowing.

Your experience is your expertise.
And that expertise— always remember—
is something no one else can bring into this world.
That is worthy of being witnessed.

In these pages
Your experiences will not go unnoticed.
Your lived expertise will not go un-witnessed.

Your story—
the good,
the bad,
the unbearable,
the mundane.

This book was written to care about it all.
Let it stand among your crowd of witnesses.

Let me.

The First, the Few and the Only

7
You're not alone

The First, the Few and the Only

Contents

Dedication – p. 5
Prologue & Lexicon: Between Two Witnesses – p. 10
Chapter 1: The Things We Carry – p. 20
Chapter 2: …Wasn't Always a Token – p. 27
Chapter 3: Consequences & Repercussions of the "Better" School(s)p. 32
Chapter 4: INTEGRATION – p. 38
Chapter 5: The "Pax" Romana – p. 69
Chapter 6: Sardoodledom – p. 73
Chapter 7: I Am Not Your Negro – p. 94
Chapter 8: White Imagination – p. 110
Chapter 9: BIPOC Competition & The HNIC – p. 123
Chapter 10: Different Shades of Belonging – p. 144
Chapter 11: Villains in Common – p. 189
Chapter 12: Academia – p. 196
Chapter 13: Evangelical Church – p. 205
Chapter 14: Black Hollywood (They've Gotta Have Us) – p. 238
Chapter 15: Burning House Politics – p. 261
Chapter 16: Ghosts in the Shell – p. 275
Chapter 17: Young, Neurodivergent & Black – p. 308
Chapter 18: Maroons of the Borderland – p. 327
Chapter 19: Fin – p. 344
Afterword: From Ones Witnessed Me First – p. 358
Acknowledgements – p. 362
Appendix A: WHITE EYEZ ONLY – p. 377
Appendix B: Blight or Blessing – p. 392
Appendix C: Book 2 Preview: The Body – p. 402
Appendix D: Song Lyrics – p. 402
Appendix E: Citations – p. 403

You're not alone

The First, the Few and the Only

The First, the Few and the Only

Prologue: Between Two Witnesses

Don Quixote

Name: Don Quixote de la Mancha
Alias: The Knight of the Mournful Countenance, Man of La Mancha
Powers: Unbreakable idealism, aliferous, unwavering chivalry, delusions of grandeur, master swordsman (in his own mind), can see through a giant's illusions, delusional, vawzen, hiraeth
Weaknesses: Reality, Windmills, Common Sense

Origin Story:
Once a humble country gentleman named Alonso Quijano, he became obsessed with tales of knights and heroic quests. Consumed by his reading, he donned a rusted suit of armor, renamed himself Don Quixote, and set out to restore chivalry to the world. With his loyal squire Sancho Panza at his side, he battles "imaginary" foes, defends the honor of his idealized Lady Dulcinea, and tilts at windmills, believing them to be fearsome giants.

Mission:
To revive the age of knighthood, defend the helpless, and fight injustice - whether real or entirely imagined.

The First, the Few and the Only

Notable Battles:
- The Legendary Windmill Fight ("Mistook" windmills for towering giants, was promptly defeated by physics)
- The Innkeeper's Castle (Declared a humble inn a grand fortress and was "knighted" by a bewildered innkeeper*)
- The Great Sheep War (Charged into a flock of sheep, believing them to be an enemy army—both he and the sheep suffered casualties)

Famous Quote:
"When life itself seems lunatic, who knows where madness lies?"

Arch-Nemesis:
The Enchanters of Reality (a.k.a. anyone who tries to convince him the world isn't as magical as he believes it to be)

Legacy:
Though often seen as a fool, Don Quixote's undying belief in a better world makes him a hero of the heart—a warrior for dreams, no matter how impossible they seem.

The First, the Few and the Only

Josiah Henson

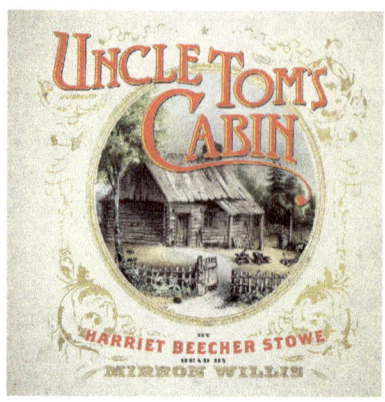

Name: Reverend Josiah Henson
Alias: The Real-Life Uncle Tom, The Liberator of Dawn
Powers: Indomitable will, strategic brilliance, oratory fire, unyielding faith, creative ingenuity, aliferous, ancestral strength, hiraeth, vawzen
Weaknesses: The scars of bondage, the weight of memory

Origin Story:
Born into slavery in Maryland in 1789, Josiah Henson endured unimaginable brutality, witnessing the sale of his father and the suffering of his people. But he refused to be broken. A man of profound faith and intelligence, he became a preacher and overseer, earning his enslaver's trust. When betrayal threatened to sell him deeper into the South, he made a daring escape with his family, trekking over six hundred miles to freedom in Canada. There, he became a leader, founding the Dawn Settlement - a refuge for freed people - and guiding over two hundred others to liberation through the Underground Railroad.

Mission:
To break the chains of slavery, uplift his people, and prove that Black men and women were destined not for bondage, but for greatness.

Notable Battles:
- The Night of the Escape (Carried his sick child on his back while evading slave catchers and crossing into Canada)

The First, the Few and the Only

- The Betrayal of Isaac Riley (Denied promised freedom, he fought back with faith and cunning to free himself)
- The Building of Dawn (Turned a settlement of fugitives into a thriving, self-sufficient community)

Famous Quote:
"I saw before me a life of toil and of trial, but I was my own master, and no man could say to me nay."

Arch-Nemesis:
The Slave System (and all who profited from it, including those who claimed to own him)

Legacy:
Josiah Henson's life was a testament to resilience, faith, and Black self-determination. Though his story was distorted in Uncle Tom's Cabin, his real legacy is one of power, leadership, and liberation. He was a true hero who not only freed himself but paved the way for others; he turned suffering into strength and oppression into opportunity.

The First, the Few and the Only

Windmills and the Plantation
A Fool's War or a Prophet's Burden?

There is something about the way Don Quixote saw the world that unnerved people. He looked at windmills and saw giants, tilting his lance at them with the conviction of a man who refused to be bound by the smallness of what others perceived as reality. They called him mad, a fool, a relic from an age that never truly existed; and yet, when he rode out into the world, he did so with a heart so full of purpose that his delusion became its own kind of truth.

Josiah Henson too waged war against something no one else seemed to see - at least, not in the way he did. The world he was born into told him that obedience was wisdom, that servitude was the best he could hope for, and that any vision beyond that was madness. He believed, at first, that virtue within the system would lead to reward. He carried himself with honor, worked harder, climbed higher, trusted deeper. He was told that if he was good enough, loyal enough, faithful enough, freedom would come.

But freedom, like justice, is not given. It is taken.

And so, Henson did what the world saw as madness: he got out. He left behind everything that had shaped him, everything that had defined the possibilities of his life, and stepped into the unknown. He saw the windmills for what they were - not giants, but something just as dangerous. Not monsters, but machines, relentless in their turning, indifferent to the lives they grind beneath them.

When The World Calls You Crazy

There is a peculiar kind of loneliness that comes with staring down what others refuse to notice.

Ask any Black/Brown body who has moved through a white institution, anyone who was the first, any of the few, any of the only ones in the room. The moment you begin to speak of the thing beneath the thing - when you name what is hidden in plain sight - the world tilts its head at you, like in Inception. It can slowly turn on you. It calls you angry, paranoid, too sensitive, too difficult. It tells you that you are fighting ghosts and windmills.

The First, the Few and the Only

Like Quixote, you are warned that the battle is pointless. That the giants are only in your mind. That you should lay down your sword, keep your head down, be grateful…. smile. I can't tell you how many times I almost deleted this book due to these things, this racial gaslighting. The windmills almost won.

Like Henson, you are told that if you are obedient, if you endure, the system will take care of you. That your suffering has meaning. That your loyalty will buy your freedom.

But windmills do not stop turning just because you refuse to fight them. Plantations do not free their captives just because they were faithful.

The Danger of Seeing Too Clearly

Both Don Quixote and Josiah Henson suffered because they saw too much. One was mocked, the other hunted. But here is the question: who was truly mad?

In Don Quixote's universe: was it the one who saw the giants and charged toward them? Or was it the one who saw them and pretended they weren't there?

In Josiah Henson's universe: was it the one who left the plantation to build paradise? Or was it the one who made their own version of paradise on the plantation?

The plantation, like the windmill, is a machine. It does not have a conscience. It does not have a heart. It was built to churn, to grind, to break, to mar. So long as it continues, it does not care who it destroys in the process. Oppression is in every room—sometimes loud, sometimes quiet, but never absent. As Resmaa Menakem teaches, and adrienne maree brown echoes: all oppressions are usually present, though not equally weighted in each space.

Henson learned this the hard way. The higher he climbed, the more he saw that the system was never meant to reward him. That survival within it was not the same as liberation. The closer he got to power and its lame ass promises, the more he was expected to betray himself too. (I dare you to google or chatgpt "Josiah Henson the betrayal of Isaac Riley")

So, he ran.

The First, the Few and the Only

He chose what Quixote never could - he let go of the illusion. He saw the machine for what it was and refused to keep feeding it. Instead, Henson left to build a safe place to which his people could escape.

The Question for Us

Are we still charging at windmills? Are we still fighting for recognition in institutions designed to consume us? Are we still catapulting our bodies into meat grinders in hopes to change the meat industry? Or are we ready, finally, to stop mistaking survival for freedom?

Because the truth is the machine does not need me to believe in its reformation. It only needs me to keep turning its wheels. To keep reaching for a seat at its table. To keep hoping that if I endure, I will be rewarded.

But I will not be. Not in the long run.

And so, the question is whether we are brave enough to fight the windmills or brave enough to walk away altogether.

As David Bowie said, "Always remember that the reason you initially started working was that there was something inside yourself that you felt that if you could manifest it in some way you would understand more about yourself and how you coexist with the rest of society.1" I present these two because I'm still trying to make sense of my own coexistence in U.S. society.

As I sit between these two figures, Don Quixote and Josiah Henson, I write this book as a love letter to the reader. But not just any reader - those of you who are the first, the few, and the only. If you watched Hidden Figures, then this is for the Taraji P. Henson's out there, the actress who got shafted by the industry as much as the character she played in the film. If you watched Jackie Robinson's biopic, then this is for those of you who feel the spirit of number 42 as you integrate your team. If you have seen Charlie Brown, then this for all you Franklins out there. If you are the only SquarePants who lives in a pineapple under the sea, then you get me (the token sponge in the ocean).

The First, the Few and the Only

This, an attempt at loving myself by writing to you, is part memoir, part workbook, part somatic exercise, part research project. In truth, it's an attempt at loving the part of me that has felt like the burdened prophet in white institutions as much as the part that has always felt like the war-addicted fool. No matter how you experience this book, know that my intent for you as your author of choice is a kind pace. I have no doubt you can blaze through this text. I'm not daring you. I just ask that you don't. The best use of this project, in my humble opinion, is to read the following pages at the pace of your body. You'll often hear me say, "What's coming up for you?" or quote Uncle Resmaa Menakem when I ask, "Where is your breath?" That's me checking your pace and literally inviting you to pace yourself, so slow down and check your breathing. If you see a leaf like this: 🌱, know that I'm asking you to answer that question in real time.

Don't force yourself through this. You will meet your body and your story in new ways through this. Whether you honor the invitation is up to you, but I promise, these pages go down way smoother if you do. As the author of My Grandmother's Hands, Resmaa Menakem, often says "Nibble, don't gorge."

Everything that comes up for you as you read is neither good nor bad, it's just data. What do we do with data? We notice it and name it. Then, "…name it to tame it," as my therapist tells me. Your nervous system will be activated, and I'm here to tell you that you are worthy of care and comfort, so slow down for you. As Charles Kettering said, "A problem well named is a problem half solved." That's all I attempted to do in these pages. Noticing and naming. Because this stuff is so complex for each of us and how we found our way in a white world.

I also hope that in reading this you will realize that what is happening to you is actually happening to you. That for the bodies of culture, as Resmaa calls us, BIPOC folks, the stories in this book will corroborate your reality. That you will learn to see a history you didn't know you were a part of and be better able to look into your possible futures. I wanted to write the book I always wanted to read. In Adrien Pei's book, The Minority Experience, he identifies three primary pillars that minorities must navigate here in North America: history, pain, and power. This book is an attempt to tell the history of the token, and it will be broken down into historical contexts, random links, stories, side quests, workbook style getting involved somatic/reflective prompts, breath pauses, personal experiences/impacts, and how said historical contexts shape contemporary forces.

The First, the Few and the Only

Lastly, you may notice the book walks ideas forward in a lot of crooked lines. As a man who is both Black and neurodivergent, how I wrote this book is how my mind works. When you are reading and see a QR code leading to an Instagram video or YouTube video or song in the middle of a thought, know that's how my mind works. This is how I intended it to be read. You can read the following in a way that works for a neurotypical brain or scan the QR codes & join me in my world. If you choose to read how I wrote it and walk through my thought process, I promise it will be more fun.

Lexicon:

🧭 **Side Quests** this invites exploration without overwhelming. An exploration that is fully optional and for only if a section really lands for you but you want more about the topic… I got you. Each one extends the experience, turning a chapter into a journey.

🌱 **Getting Involved** prioritizes action, both online and offbook. Ways I planned for you to engage your body or mind like you would a rep in the gym. Reading the pages is the inhale, but getting involved is the exhale. Also, a symbol 🌱, for you to hear uncle Resmaa Menakem and I asking, Where's your breath?

〰️ **Random links** are the neurodivergent off ramp. Nestled between paragraphs are what I expect you to click if you so decide to engage how this neurodivergent writer's mind works. Totally optional, but more fun for sure.

The Neurodivergent Path Starts Here: www.thefirstthefewandtheonly.com

The First, the Few and the Only

Book 1
The First, the Few, and the Only is all about naming & noticing
(You Are Here)

Book 2
The First, the Few, and the Only: Weathering is all about harm & repair

Book 3
The First, the Few, and the Only: Power is all about liberating & empowering

---

The First, the Few and the Only

Chapter 1

The Things We Carry

"Alpacas" by Jonathan Zoeteman

"I feel most colored when I am thrown against a sharp white background."
-From Zora Neale Hurston's book How It Feels To Be Colored Me 1928

"A problem well-named is a problem half-solved"
-Charles Kettering

I was at a retreat with a bunch of African-American pastors once. A few of us weren't necessarily pastors, but it was all men of color. A couple of us weren't African-American. There was me, a Ghanaian Cuban American (Afro-Cubano), and my guy Davido, who was from Kenya, I believe. We all had great laughs, good food, and deep conversation. One afternoon, we got to talking about racism in North America and in the Protestant churches within. Then, after listening to the conversation for some time, our brother Davido said,

"Hey, guys, can I ask a question? Let me preface…I'm from Kenya, and in Kenya we didn't have paved roads, we didn't have running water and had to walk a

The First, the Few and the Only

distance just to get to school. Here in (North) America there is so much opportunity, and in our village the goal was always to try and get to America and make it. When I got here, I worked hard and studied hard, and I just have a really tough time when I hear you guys talking about racism holding you back. You have running water, paved roads, great infrastructure and jobs. Can you help me understand better why racism is such a barrier to you guys? Because I don't often mind what people think of me, just don't touch me or my family and we're good. Help me understand, please?"

There was a pause. Then one man spoke of slavery. Another spoke up and articulated systemic oppression. Another said he could see his point and will have to think on that. Then I raised my hand to share.

I said something to the effect of, "You have seen the realities of colonialism in your country, is that correct, brother?"

Davido replied, "Very much so."

"What Kenya experiences regarding colonialism, North America is five or more evolutions past. In Kenya, do white bodies hold most of the seats of power in your country?" I asked.

"Generally, yes."

I continued, "As a Ghanaian Cuban American, I know very intimately that Africans do not like African-Americans and are often socialized with some degree of prejudice against African-Americans. Am I correct about that, Davido?"

Davido said, "You are actually right about that."

"There was a Nigerian woman who thought the same way, as she was raised to look down upon African-Americans. I think her name is, I'm gonna butcher this, Chimamanda Ngozi Adichie," I said.

"I've heard of her," Davido said.

The First, the Few and the Only

"Well, she wrote a bestseller called Americanah I think. Well, anyway, she tells the story when she was walking out of a convenience store in maybe NY and an African-American man held the door for her. She said thank you as she walked through. As she walked out, the man said something to the effect of, 'You're welcome, sista.' She spins around, looks the man in the eye, and says, 'I am not your sista,' then walks away. It wasn't until later that she realized that whether African-American or Nigerian… in North America, we're both Black. And that means something in a society floating on a blood ocean of racial contempt and fear 1. We are both the other. We are both of no difference at the end of the day to a racialized land. In Nigeria, Black excellence is normal. Here, it comes with a cost to the first, the few, and the only that are allowed in white spaces. Even the most brilliant among us will often earn high positions at predominantly white companies and despite our suits, perfumes and colognes, our watches, our pedigree, our degrees, and certificates and accomplishments we still get called diversity hires or face microaggressions that make us sometimes gaslight ourselves. You know what it means to be Kenyan; you will, in time, learn what it means to be Black. Others have had the fortune of learning what that means earlier than others, so it isn't as shocking or surprising. In the end, you are Black too, and it is something that I had to learn from white bodies. I didn't feel like the 'Black guy in the room' until I moved from Ft. Lauderdale to New Castle, PA, my senior year and finished my senior year at an all-white school. As you grow older in this country, I think that white bodies prefer a few at a time….

"Here in the US, they realized that keeping Black and Brown bodies out of the power class was short-term gain, long-term loss. They realized that having a few at a time would be beneficial to the longevity of their control. See, they bring up the brightest ones, the leaders, get them used to their comforts, and socialize them to the point where, by all intents and purposes, we think like them and learn to act like them. We laugh at their jokes so much so that by the time we realize it, we don't feel welcome in the Black community at all. Tokenism is a masterful way to weaponize us against ourselves. Being Black in white spaces always has a cost that you pay either socially or bio-psycho-socially in regard to poorer health outcomes, but either way, brother, those are my thoughts."

The First, the Few and the Only

Davido said, "Thank you all for your thoughts. That was enlightening. Michael, I appreciate the way you framed that…we're both Black. I'll have to think about that because I never felt Black until I came to this country. I remember being called that and I was like, 'What do you mean Black, like a cat?' I'm Kenyan-American, but that gave me something to think about."

The room was quiet after Davido spoke. Not the kind of quiet that comes from a lack of things to say, but the kind that settles in when truth rearranges the furniture of a man's mind. When someone suddenly sees the architecture of the world they've been living in - not just the walls but the foundation, the cracks in the concrete, the names chiseled into the stone.

I saw it settle over him, the slow understanding that Blackness, in this country, was not just a color or a culture. It was a condition. One that was placed upon you, whether you chose it or not. Whether you embraced it or rejected it. Because here, Blackness is not about where you are from - it is about where you are positioned.

And that positioning, that sorting, that labeling - who gets to be at the top, who is pushed to the bottom, who is granted proximity, and who is left on the margins - that is where tokenism comes in. Colonialism was always about control, and control has always required evolution.

There was a time when control meant chains, plantations, and auction blocks. Then it meant laws, red lines, and separate fountains. When that became too obvious, too grotesque for even the most loyal defenders to justify, control took on a new face. It became subtle, polished, and respectable. It no longer needed shackles when it could offer incentives. It no longer needed whips when it could use rewards.

That is tokenism.

The First, the Few and the Only

The realization that you don't have to exclude an entire people when you can simply invite a few. A chosen few. Just enough to say, "See? We are not racist. We have one of you at the table."

And that chosen few - "the first, the few, the only" - they step into those spaces believing they have won something. And in a way, they have, but every reward carries a price, and in these rooms, the cost is belonging. 🌱

Because to be the chosen one means to be the only one.

To be visible but never fully seen.

To be included but never fully embraced.

To be praised but never fully accepted.

And for some, that trade-off is worth it.

Because for some, tokenism is not a curse - it is an escape. A way out of a community where they never felt valued. Some of us were never the cool kids in Black spaces. We were too nerdy, too awkward, too soft-spoken, too different. But in white spaces? Our very Blackness became currency. Our slang, our walk, our perceived toughness - it made us interesting. Desirable. Marketable. Even if it meant leaning into the caricature, even if it meant becoming the punchline, acceptance is acceptance.

So, some of us learn to perform.

We master the balancing act of being Black but not too Black. Palatable. Approachable. Enough to add color to the room, but not enough to change its temperature. The more we play the role, the more we convince ourselves that we are winning. That we are different. That we are exceptional. Until one day, something happens.

Maybe it's a joke that lands wrong. Maybe it's a meeting where your voice is drowned out. Maybe it's a promotion that never comes. Maybe it's a Kenyan man or melanated man getting strangled to death on live television by police. Maybe it's

The First, the Few and the Only

nothing at all - just a slow, creeping realization that no matter how much they like you, you will never be them. That as much as you have distanced yourself from your own people, you are still not fully accepted in theirs.

And that is the cost of tokenism.

Colonialism didn't die. It evolved. It learned how to smile. How to extend an invitation. How to make room for you, but just enough so things are never too Black, too Latino, too Asian. How to make you think you are winning when really, you are just being used.

The tragedy is not just that this happens. The real tragedy is how many of us willingly sign up for it. How many of us, tired of being on the bottom, reach for any place that feels higher—even if that place is just a step stool someone else is standing on.

Because when whiteness is the measure, even scraps can feel like a feast. But a feast where you are the only one eating is just another kind of starvation. That, for my friend Davido, is what I was trying to make sense of what it meant to be Black in America. And that is what my dear brother will come to understand in time.

🌱 **Getting Involved:** What's coming up for you? Where's your breath? Did you get a shift in your body? Or did you hear an echo in your memory?

Take a moment to simply notice it. Name it here:

_____

🧭 Side Quest

Check out this LinkedIn post, although she talks about poverty, I want you to pay attention to see if tokenism, with all of its occupational hazards, is a part of the exchange her mother makes for her family provide stability to her children;

The First, the Few and the Only

Take a moment to put the book down, look out a window, and reflect on what this brought up for you.

What's coming up for you as you read this?
Jot down notes on where your mind went, or where you may be feeling heat or tension in the body.

_____

_____

_____

_____

_____

_____

_____

_____

_____

_____

_____

The First, the Few and the Only

Chapter 2

…Wasn't Always A Token

Again… token is a term for a minoritized BIPOC body navigating white space—spaces made by white bodies for white bodies that allow a few Brown bodies in at a time.

This is my story of not always being a token. My story begins with my abuelo escaping Cuba before the borders closed. No, he did not ride a small boat made of debris to Florida—he got papers and flew over before the embargo and whatnot. He was able to bring his wife and two daughters over as well later. Because of him, I get to be North American as a citizen. Because of him, I got to be one of the first of the Leon's to be born on U.S. soil.

His youngest daughter, Aida, was my biological mother. She grew up in the States, was top of her class throughout her pre-college years, a Rockette like you see at the Macy's Thanksgiving parade, and graduated college as salutatorian. She met my biological father, a charismatic consultant from Ghana who was in the U.S. on a work visa. They had a love at first sight kind of Tangled meets The Little Mermaid type thing.

Nine months later, my twin and I were born. Twelve days later, we were placed for adoption. We were the only negros in the León family. Aside from the 1988 shame of an unwed daughter being pregnant and 'sent away' for nine months, my Tía—aunt in Spanish—later told us there was racism involved in the 'encouragement' to have Aida give us up for adoption. That one of the reasons our abuelos encouraged our mom to give us up for

The First, the Few and the Only

adoption was because they didn't want negro grandchildren or something like that.

We were born in Orlando and adopted by an African-American/Cherokee father and a second-generation German American mother. At just twelve days old, we were brought to Broward County, Florida, where we remained for seventeen years.

We grew up in an environment where most of the white bodies we knew were either Jewish or Italian. Our world was filled with people from Brazil, Central America, Japan, Mexico, Puerto Rico, the Middle East, Cuba, China, Italy, Romania, Haiti, the Dominican Republic, and Jamaica. It was a vibrant, ethnically diverse region, rich with languages, religions, and cultures overlapping and intertwining. By all intents and purposes, high school looked like different shades of brown. I mean, even the white bodies all had brownish tans so…

Me on the right

It wasn't until after Hurricane Wilma, when our mom decided to move us from South Florida to New Castle, Pennsylvania, that I first experienced what it meant to be a token Brown body. Moving from an ethnically diverse, multicultural world to a predominantly white space was more than just relocation; it was an initiation into a different way of being seen. Suddenly, my identity wasn't just mine—it became a

The First, the Few and the Only

projection of what others expected a Black or Brown body to be. 🌱

Summarizes some of my general feelings then

I went from knowing the unspoken social rules - never call an African-American Haitian, how to dap the right way to the right ethnic group, never call a Puerto Rican Mexican or vice versa - to a place where little white high school boys and girls accidentally called me or each other the n-word. Yeah, you read that right. They would ask me if they could say it, as if my permission could somehow erase the weight of that history. I ignored them and walked away.

I went from a world where culture was complex, fluid, and deeply understood to one where people relied on caricatures. White teenage peers assumed I loved basketball, Lil Wayne, and partying. In reality, I liked movie clubs and acting, and my twin preferred other sports. We were into Lecrae, Flame, and Cross Movement (gospel rap). We preferred Bible studies over parties. But it didn't seem to matter who we actually were - what mattered was how our Brown bodies were supposed to behave.

It was as if my presence came with a script already written for me, and I was failing to play the part they had imagined.

A white girl backed out of a school dance at the last minute because she "couldn't go," but I saw her there with a white male peer. This wasn't just rejection; it was a reminder that my body was acceptable to watch, to joke with, to worship on the same floor, but not to stand beside.

Being asked for the Black perspective in class with every gaze on my singular Brown body wasn't just curiosity. It was the expectation that I somehow spoke for

The First, the Few and the Only

an entire people. This treatment came at the hands of college-educated, white-bodied adults.

All of it - the small things, the questions, the assumptions - felt like happenstance at first. Later I realized it was part of something bigger. A pattern. A way of being seen that had little to do with who I actually was and everything to do with what whiteness imagined me to be.

The Wrong Kind of Black

I was talking to my friend Chesco, who grew up in a poor Black Pittsburgh neighborhood in Western PA. As a kid, he loved listening to Chuck Berry and Lenny Kravitz, but his peers would ask, "Why you listening to white people music? Why you being weird?"

He told me something I haven't forgotten: "Being born and raised here [Western Pennsylvania] always felt foreign." He said there's a kind of faking that's expected in Black communities here—a pressure to conform to a narrow script. There's a box Black people try to put him in. And then there's the box white people try to put him in. Either way, he's trapped. Never fully free. Never fully seen.

And the more he learned—about himself, about the world—the more it scared people. White folks were unsettled because he didn't fit their image of who a Black man should be. But it scared some Black folks too.
He told me, "I went to Black schools, grew up in a Black neighborhood, played football with Black kids, hooped with everybody—but the sambo mentality is still strong here. It's like if you step out of line, start thinking for yourself, you're either 'not Black enough' or 'trying to be better.'"
Recently, he gave a ride to a white coworker who's also a friend. The Black Eyed Peas were playing on the radio. She giggled and said, "You listen to Black Eyed Peas? Why don't you have something more… gangsta?"

That same week, he was playing Mos Def and a Black woman challenged his Black card too. "As if," he said, "only listening to music about corruption or killing is what makes us Black." Whether we come from immigrant stories or Black neighborhoods in Western PA…

The First, the Few and the Only

Whether we were raised around many cultures or in the thick of one...
Tokenism isn't always about being the "only one" in a white room.
Sometimes, it's about being the wrong kind of Black for any room.
It's about being handed a script that has nothing to do with who you really are.

🌱 Getting Involved

Questions for Melanated Readers:

    1. Where does this chapter resonate in your story?

    2. Ever walk into a room and one of the first things you do is scan the room for other Black or Brown people? This was my baptism into that practice.

Questions for Melanin -Deprived Readers:

> What's coming to mind right now? If you are wondering what to do about what you have just read, you can start by naming and noticing in the margin of the book. What is coming up in your memory bank as much as your body. Perhaps start by noticing your breathe.

I told you about my story, and Chesco's story, what about yours?

_____

_____

_____

_____ 🌱

Chapter 3

Consequences & Repercussions of the "Better" School(s)

Story 1

When my mom moved us to New Castle, Pennsylvania, she bought a lovely home on Graceland Road. Because the Florida market was way more inflated than the houses in Western Pennsylvania, she was able to buy a pretty cool house with a heck of a lot of land. More land than I had ever seen, let alone thought my mom could ever afford. Once we moved in, I remember our mom brought up options for which high school my brother and I would attend. I was confused because I thought the school zones determined that, but she told us that our house on that street was literally on the line of two different school zones. We had to choose. It was either New Castle High School or Neshannock High School. We drove by the schools, and New Castle High looked cooler.

Mom did some digging in the community and was told by many people that Neshannock was a "way better school" and to never send her kids to New Castle High. That's what the folks at the predominately white Baptist church said, at least. So, without much else to go on, my mom preferred we go to the better school.

What we later realized was that Neshannock High wasn't necessarily the better school. While hanging out with some of the other rising upperclassmen from the church youth group during that summer before senior year, they told us the residential history of New Castle. New Castle was supposed to be the Pittsburgh of Western Pennsylvania, but at some point, the rich folk decades ago changed their minds and chose to invest in Pittsburgh/Allegheny City - two cities separated by the Allegheny River that chose to become one, now known as Pittsburgh. They told me that New Castle was a huge throughway for drug trade between NYC and Ohio, or at least it was back then. These kids also decided to tell me to notice how the

The First, the Few and the Only

north of New Castle has all of its own grocery stores, school, and restaurants because the rich folks wanted to separate themselves from downtown New Castle, western New Castle, southern New Castle, and the residences on the east side because of all the drugs "down there." My brother and I realized that this wasn't just a residential history but a racial one.

Later, I discovered that only two things separated upper New Castle (Neshannock) from the other parts: wealth and race. When my brother and I went to high school, we realized something shocking very quickly. We roamed the halls with some kids from our youth group to find our lockers. We found our classrooms and followed classmates to the cafeteria in the afternoon. We noticed that we were two of the ONLY few Brown bodies in the whole damn building. Mind you, we went from a graduating class of seven hundred in Coral Springs to a graduating class of seventy. Also, the high school wasn't just a high school - it was the elementary school and middle school as well, all in one building with about seven hundred students total. These were all kids from the wealthier families within New Castle as opposed to the other residential housing properties outside of Neshannock. I remember walking the halls and seeing only one Asian kid and one other Black kid that first week of school. The Asian kid had blue contact lenses and wouldn't really look my way the couple times I tried to say "what's up" in solidarity, which was whatever. But when I saw the Black kid, I remember giving him "the nod."

Y'all, HE DIDN'T NOD BACK! That was the second sign that we may have chosen the wrong school. I couldn't understand why he didn't nod back. I remember in my next class wondering why he didn't return it. Eventually, I interpreted it as my twin and I were alone in this school.

By the following Spring, I learned the other Black student ended up transferring to New Castle High, and the Asian guy ended up dying in a car crash later that year. That left just my brother and me. Later, it dawned on me... the word for what my brother and I already became: tokens. 🌱

The First, the Few and the Only

Story 2

I'll never forget meeting a Black woman in ministry, we'll call her Felicia, who was older than me. She had been put in white schools as a child during desegregation. She told me how her parents had promised it would be a better school with greater opportunities for her future, but when she got there, her parents hadn't prepared her for the formative social effects of being the only Black girl. She was telling us about the year that another Black girl came to her school, back in the day, and her face lit up as she spoke. They became immediate friends and were that way until the girl moved.

When Felicia had her daughter, who is African-American, she and her husband put their daughter in a fancy, all-white academy. After about six months, she noticed that her daughter was depressed, when she talked to her daughter, Felicia could tell that she wasn't herself. Felicia's daughter confessed that she didn't like who she had to be while on school grounds to fit in. She begged her mom to be put back into the public school for her high school years. Felicia spoke with her husband, and they agreed to put their daughter back in public school. The daughter became herself again, and her grades went back up as well. Felicia said that since she herself was so young, she never had a choice to go back. She didn't want to do to her daughter what was done to her. 🌱

more research on this phenomenon can be found in book two.

Story 3

"I want my hair to be a mohawk with straight hair, Daddy."

The First, the Few and the Only

My six-year-old said this to me the day before his kindergarten graduation. While trying to discuss what kind of haircut he wanted for his big day the next morning, I heard him say this while I was putting on his sister's shoes as we got ready to go to the local Latin barber up the road. As I did my best to explain to him that his overgrown curl-hawk may not stay straight by the time he got to

school, he dug his heels in and said something I wasn't expecting to ever come out of his mouth.

"I hate my curls."

With folded arms and a scrunched-up face, his mood went from jovial to quite the opposite. I stayed curious and asked, "Did you say you hate your curls, mijo? Can you say more as to why?

"My friends have straight hair, and I want straight hair like them!"

I looked at their mom, and she walked away. I decided to corral the kids into the car and put on some music so I could think. I thought back to all the years that I wrestled with loving my curls, and all the times I hated my own hair into my twenties. I thought about ALL the TV shows I was intentional about. All the kids shows that had protagonists with brown skin, dignity, many speaking lines, and glorious curls, from Blaze and The Monster Machines to Black Panther, Santiago of the Seas to Miles Morales. Since he first saw his first screen, to all the toys that ever entered our home from birthday parties, they had to look like him. If they didn't, I snuck them into the garbage when he wasn't looking.

We arrived at the barber. I asked him again about his hair, and he said he wants straight hair, no more curls. We went inside, and I said in Spanish that I needed their help. I broke down the situation with my son. They pulled out their phones and began showing him cool hairdos - some with blonde highlights, others with curls that draped over the forehead, and even photos of Miles Morales. My son looked at me with sad eyes. I realized that I was pressuring him. Additionally, I felt this instinctive pull to do what was done to me as a kid: "Sit your ass in that chair! I decide what haircut you're gonna have. I'm paying for it." That's what I grew up with.

The First, the Few and the Only

I asked the barber to take the drape off and take him out of the booster seat. We went outside, and I sat on the curb, pulling him and his sister into my lap. I told them an age-appropriate story of when I was a kid and how I struggled with loving my curls because I was adopted. My mommy didn't know how to style my hair because of the curls. I went on to explain how I learned that curls are cool.

He was unmoved, and I figured it went over his head. I decided to change strategies and just stay curious. I asked again why he doesn't want his curls, and he told me that he wanted to look like his friends. When I asked which friends, he said three names: Danny, Josh, and Onmaul. I realized that one was white, the other was mixed but hella light-skinned with super loose, relaxed curls, and the third was a Nepalese boy he played soccer with who had straight, pitch-black hair.

I took my kids by the hand and put them back in the car. I decided not to force a haircut on my son that he didn't want. We drove home in silence. I took some time to myself the rest of the evening to reflect on why it took the wind out of me. I was proud of myself for staying engaged and curious with my son. I was proud of myself for not forcing him to get whatever damn haircut I chose as the parent, which was my upbringing as a child, but I couldn't shake the feeling that I had failed him somehow.

I reflected on the decisions made before that day.

I thought back to researching the most diverse school districts in the city before we bought our first house. I remember driving around the apartment complexes of different zip codes with the most Indian and Hispanic families. I remember focusing on houses that were

zoned in those same areas so that our son and eventual daughter wouldn't be the only Brown kids in the room. To increase the probability that our kids wouldn't be the first Brown bodies that some white kid cuts his racial teeth on before ten. I recalled all the songs from Gracie's Corner that I played often and diligently for years. I reflected on how many prayers prayed that our son would have kids that look like him in his class.

I reflected on all the implications that I may have been reading into the situation.

The First, the Few and the Only

Did him wanting straight hair show the early signs of the conditioned self-hatred of wanting to look more euro-centric, or was I making it more complicated than it was? Was I being hypervigilant around the lurking white supremacy that is seeking to become internalized in my own children, or was I simply overreacting to a kid that just wants to fit in with his friends? Did I not find him enough Brown friends even though half the kids he played with were Indian? Was there a question I needed to wrestle with about my own past that I hadn't found yet?

I wish I had a perfect answer or close to this chapter, but - disarming honesty - I simply do not. His mom wet his hair the next morning, and we put some product in it to accentuate his curls like normal. We went to the graduation, he had a great time, and I was so proud to see my boy at his first graduation. However, there was a part of me that caught myself counting how many BIPOC kids were on that stage with him more than once. It was half his class, if you were wondering. All different ethnicities. I didn't bring it up again with him, but it still weighs on me. It weighs on me heavy.

🌱 Getting Involved

"Where's your breath?" -Resmaa Menakem

Is there a part of your body that feels tense? Are there any stories attached to that part of your body feeling what the sensations its feeling?

_____

_____

_____

_____

Now breathe.

Is there anything else coming up for you? Name it to tame it.

The First, the Few and the Only

Chapter 4

INTEGRATION

It was sometime during the Christmas season when Rudolph the Red-Nosed Reindeer flickered across my screen, and I found myself watching, not with the passive nostalgia of childhood, but with the sharp awareness of history, of blood memory, of lessons passed down through the generations.

There he was…Rudolph, born with a light that set him apart. A brilliance that, instead of being nurtured, was immediately met with shame. His father, a broad-shouldered buck, didn't meet this radiance with pride but with a raised voice, a demand: dim yourself, cover it up, blend in. He pressed down on his own flesh and blood, not out of cruelty, but out of fear. A learned fear. A fear that whispered of survival. As I watched, a question formed like a slow, rising tide: how often have older Black generations, out of love wrapped in fear, taught us to shrink ourselves, to be more palatable to the Santas of the world?
Santa - the great white man in power. The gatekeeper. The one whose approval meant everything in that frozen North. However, if we are being truthful, he needed the reindeer far more than they needed him, yet, somehow, they were all made to believe otherwise.

The First, the Few and the Only

This is where the weight of the story pressed down on me, because what is tokenism if not this very tale, wrapped in tinsel and clay-mation? The marking of difference as a problem, a defect, a thing to be hidden - until, of course, it becomes useful. Until the very thing that made you an outcast is suddenly necessary for the survival of the system that once rejected you.

Isn't that the way of things?

The North Pole is every boardroom, every campus, every film set, every institution where a singular Black body - one with a light too bright to be ignored - is both shunned and tokenized in the same breath. First, you are made to believe that your difference is a burden, a shame. The other reindeer mock you, your own kind may even scold you, warn you, tell you to fly lower, to quiet that light, to learn to laugh off the ways in which they exclude you. Then, when the storm rolls in, when visibility is low, when they suddenly need what you alone possess, they return, not with apology, but with expectation.

Rudolph did not need Santa. Santa needed Rudolph. The brilliance of that nose, the very thing he was told to despise, only became valuable when it served those who once rejected him. Sound familiar?

This is the great cruelty of being the first, the few, and the only. It does not celebrate difference; it commodifies us. It does not empower the othered body; it exploits us. It offers no real belonging, only conditional usefulness. The world may scorn your gifts, mock them, and beat them into submission, until the day arrives when they realize they cannot move forward without them. Even then, they will not call it justice. They will call it opportunity.

As I sat there, watching Rudolph soar into the night, leading the way for those who had once laughed at him, I felt no triumph in that moment – only a familiar, bone-deep knowing.

I watched him lead a sleigh into the sky but all I saw was slave chains on brown bucks with jingle bells attached. I watched Rudolph smile just because they let him be in the front and felt exposed. Realizing, with contemptuous disgust, that that is probably what I look like too.

The First, the Few and the Only

*"Just because you are used to the desert doesn't mean
you don't deserve the ocean."*
Rev. Fr. Albert Nwosu

What's coming up for you?

_____

_____

_____

_____

_____

Ruby Bridges, the first…

Ruby Bridges is an iconic figure in the American civil rights movement, known for being the first African-American child to integrate into an all-white elementary school in the South. In November 1960, at just six years old, she became a symbol of the struggle against racial segregation when she attended William Frantz Elementary School in New Orleans, Louisiana.

The First, the Few and the Only

Ruby faced intense hostility and threats from those opposed to integration. Each day, she was escorted to school by federal marshals due to the violent protests that erupted around her. Despite the challenges, Ruby remained courageous and resilient. She was often the only student in her class during that time, as many white families withdrew their children in protest.

Ruby's experience highlighted the deep racial divide in America and the importance of education in the fight for equality. Her story serves as a powerful reminder of the bravery required to challenge systemic racism and the ongoing struggle for civil rights in the United States. Ruby Bridges continues to advocate for education and equality, inspiring future generations with her legacy.

We are going to go back in time and talk about how desegregation was one of the worst things and the biggest harms to the Black community and the systemic crystallization of tokenism in the U.S. Just to be clear, I'm not saying that segregation was good, I'm critiquing how desegregation was done, the process. It was done in a way to benefit white people through the eventual crystallization of the token, draining of Black economic power, and Black talent/brilliance, but we'll get there after some historical Black glory and ancestral white violence gets named first. Desegregation was accomplished in a way reminiscent of our feel-good Rudolph story – those reindeer taken from their homes and raised to value themselves based on how well they fit into Santa's North Pole culture.

1870
Dunbar High School, the first…

Let's begin with Dunbar High School. It was founded in 1870 as a preparatory school for colored youth. 1 Paul Laurence Dunbar High School in Washington, D.C. is known for being the first public high school in the United States for African-Americans. It's also known for its notable graduates, academic excellence, and role in the history of public education.

Notable graduates:

The First, the Few and the Only

- Charles Richard Drew: Surgeon
- William Henry Hastie, Jr: Jurist
- Jean Toomer: Writer
- First Black member of a presidential cabinet
- First Black graduate of the U.S. Naval Academy
- Legal mastermind behind school desegregation

Academic excellence:

- Dunbar High School was an academically elite public school in the first half of the twentieth century.
- The school's well-educated teachers produced generations of high-achieving African-Americans.

Role in Public Education:

- Dunbar High School has played a significant role in the history of public education in Washington, D.C.
- The school's curriculum provided students with an understanding of their heritage and of African-American achievements.

Sustainable Design:

- The new Dunbar High School building is a LEED Platinum school project, the highest rating in the country.

1883

Frederick Douglass High School was the first high school in Maryland for African-Americans, founded in 1883. It was originally called the Colored High and Training School.2

Jazz Singer Alumni:

- Cab Calloway: Attended from 1924–1927 and graduated in 1928
- Ethel Ennis: Graduated in 1950
- Sallie Blair: Jazz singer

Other Notable Alumni:

The First, the Few and the Only

- Thurgood Marshall: Graduated in 1926 and became the first Black Supreme Court Justice. He argued the landmark Brown v. Board of Education case in 1954.
- Parren J. Mitchell: Graduated in 1940 and became a U.S. Congressman
- Lucy Diggs Slowe: Founding member of Alpha Kappa Alpha and the first Dean of Women at Howard University
- E. Franklin Frazier: Graduated in 1912 and became an American sociologist
- James "Buster" Brown: Graduated in 1932 and became a tap dancer
- Roger W. Brown: Graduated in 1959 and became a Baltimore City Circuit Court judge

Integration Led to Educational Control of Black Bodies

Manning Marable, historian, scholar, and Pulitzer Prize winner, founded the Institute for Research in African-American Studies and the African-American and African Diaspora Studies Department at Columbia University. He was a man who spent his life studying the movements, minds, and makings of Black America, in a firsthand account of the history of Jim Crow South. Mr. Marable once called Jim Crow a "perverse blessing." 3

Now, don't mistake his words - he was not romanticizing segregation. He made it plain: Jim Crow South was a curse, a crushing, relentless system designed to make Black people feel small, to remind them daily that their existence was tolerated but never welcome. However, he pointed out a bitter irony.

"The irony is that once you break down the walls of Jim Crow... Jim Crow was always an oppression unfathomable to most white Americans. It was always a curse - but it was also a perverse blessing. Its perversion lay in the way it destroyed any notion among white Americans that Black Americans were their equals. But the so-called blessing? It built a barrier. It kept out many of the negative cultural, social, and political influences that otherwise would have affected Black America. Not that I find anything redeeming about Jim Crow, but if one were to speak of a 'perverse blessing,' one could say that by forcing Black people into our own spaces, it gave us a clearer sense of who we were. It allowed us to develop institutions across class

The First, the Few and the Only

lines that responded to the problems and daily struggles confronting Black America." -Manning Marable 4

 To reiterate Marable's point, Jim Crow segregation had innumerable horrors. It was legislated law dictating that Black and Brown bodies could not laugh too loudly in public, could not kiss in plain view, and could not exist too freely, lest white comfort be disturbed. It was the unwritten rule that a Black man had better lower his eyes when speaking to a white woman, along with even worse laws of the South.

That trauma became culture. Have you ever noticed how some Black folks, especially elders, struggle with public displays of affection? That history runs deep. Or how, when we laugh hard, we cover our mouths, hide our teeth, or even take off running? That, too, is an echo of old laws meant to break the spirit, because there was a time when enslaved Black people weren't even allowed to laugh openly. Instead, they laughed into barrels—barrel of laughs, the phrase itself a ghost of a time when Black joy had to be muffled, lest it cost a life.

This is the thing about Black-led education before integration: it taught Black children their worth, their mission, and their dignity - not as granted by the world, but as inherent. Even when the outside world refused to honor their brilliance, Black institutions made sure that they understood it for themselves.

As Marable described in the documentary, Black Education in the South, it wasn't just about reading, writing, and arithmetic. It was about survival. It was about preparation. Marable stated, "They were given another value: a sense of dignity and a sense of mission. That it is your obligation to prepare yourself to be the best you can be. In probably every Black home across the South, more than ten thousand mothers and fathers told their children every day, 'You have to be not just as good as the white boy or white girl—you gotta be twice as good. Because of segregation, because of racism, you won't even get the same opportunities to compete for jobs. If, by some chance, a door cracks open for you, you must be ready. Absolutely prepared.'"

There was a seriousness to life, a collective sense of responsibility. Education wasn't just schooling. It was the secular religion of the Black community. In the absence of resources, in the face of secondhand books and crumbling schools, Black minds

The First, the Few and the Only

still learned. They took that learning and applied it to the daily struggles in their communities.

They built their own.

They established institutions where they controlled the curriculum, where Black children weren't just taught that America was the land of the free but that it was also the land of the slave. They learned that the litmus test of America wasn't its ideals – it was its treatment of the African-American. Langston Hughes knew this when he wrote the poem; "Let America Be America Again."

This is not just the case for Black people. America has always been tested by its treatment of the poor, by its treatment of Puerto Ricans, Mexicans, Guatemalans, Haitians, Uyghurs, Innocent Arabic Americans+ after extremist terrorist attacks on US soil, Eastern European Jews, Irish, Filipinos, and so many others who know too well that freedom in this land has never been evenly distributed.

That is the paradox of desegregation. It allowed Black people to see up close what had always been denied to them. Near enough to witness, never close enough to belong. That paradox also held that perverse blessing of segregation that Marable talked about.

Of course, segregation was monstrous. It brutalized Black and Brown bodies without batting an eye, but it also created Black spaces – unadulterated enclaves of identity, of culture, of self-determination. When those walls came down, integration came with a new kind of disillusionment. Some thought that the end of Jim Crow, a Northern invention not a Southern one, would come through legislation, through court challenges, through a slow re-education of white America.

Marable explained this mindset: "Many believed that if racism was merely ignorance, then educating white people would change their behavior. The problem with that thinking is that it ignored the economic and political roots of racism. Racism is not just about bad feelings—it is a system of exploitation. It is the subordination of people of color for political, economic, and cultural control."5

So, the question remains - what did we gain? And what did we lose?
What happens when the walls fall, but the gatekeepers remain?

The First, the Few and the Only

What happens when Black children are placed in white schools where their history is erased, where their culture is dismissed, their presence is ostracized, where they are made to feel lucky just to be allowed in?
What happens when trauma, once a forced condition, becomes an inherited culture?

Marable called Jim Crow segregation a perverse blessing, but blessing was never in the oppression itself. The blessing was in us before having to convince white society of our value. We enjoyed it. Black excellence was the norm, not the singular flower pushing through jagged concrete parking lots. In our ability to turn walls into sanctuaries, to turn exclusion into excellence, to build in the absence of access.

"Even in the bowels of oppression you had the ability of people to carve for themselves a sense of community, which inculcated a sense of mission, and constructive family values. Not in a kind of narrow individualistic or materialistic sense, that one saw in white middle class America, but a sense of, even within the midst of poverty, even in the midst of illiteracy, people had value to nurture young ones and care for the old ones. That you gave the children a sense of pride and dignity in who they were. That people set aside several weeks in February to instill in their young people a sense of what Black history month was and pride in Black heroes and heroines in the Afro-American past. Segregation meant not only the hardship, not only the lost opportunity, and not only the terrible anxiety that you were prepared for a position and didn't get it and had to go home and explain why you didn't get it, but it was also sharing time, a sense of community and a sense of collective accomplishment in the face of terrible odds." -Manning Marable 6

Frederick Douglass High School in Baltimore and Dunbar High School in Washington, D.C. stand as towering monuments to the power of Black-led education. They are a testament to the very essence of what Manning Marable spoke about when he described segregation's perverse blessing. These schools were not just places of learning; they were institutions of self-determination where Black excellence was cultivated and normalized despite systemic barriers.

Dunbar High School

Dunbar High School, founded in 1870 as the first public high school for Black students in the United States, became a model of what Black-led education could

The First, the Few and the Only

achieve. During segregation, when Black students were systematically denied access to well-funded schools, Dunbar produced some of the greatest Black minds in American history: scientists, judges, military generals, and intellectuals. It boasted alumni like Charles Hamilton Houston, one of the legal architects of Brown v. Board of Education, and Edward Brooke, the first Black senator elected by popular vote.

Dunbar's teachers were some of the most overqualified educators in the country. Denied positions at white institutions, Black PhDs, lawyers, and mathematicians found their way into Dunbar's classrooms, pouring their knowledge into Black children who were taught that education was not just about personal advancement - it was a mission. A duty. As Marable put it, "Black people believed in education more than anything else," and Dunbar embodied that belief. It wasn't just about getting a degree; it was about fortifying a people, preparing them to challenge a world that refused to see them as equal.

Then came desegregation. The walls came down, but instead of integrating Black excellence into the larger system, the system dismantled what Black people had built. The same overqualified teachers who had made Dunbar a bastion of Black achievement were no longer welcome in their own classrooms. The school, once a pipeline for Black leaders, became just another underfunded urban school, struggling in the wake of a promise that was never fulfilled.

Frederick Douglass High School

Frederick Douglass High School in Baltimore, established in 1883, carried the same spirit of Black self-determination. It was a school that stood as both refuge and battleground - a place where Black students were taught not just academics, but resilience.

This was the school of Thurgood Marshall, the man who would go on to dismantle legal segregation as the first Black Supreme Court Justice. It was a school where students weren't just prepared for jobs but for leadership. There Black teachers, knowing the weight of history, pushed their students to defy the limitations the world tried to place on them.
Like Dunbar, Frederick Douglass High School thrived under segregation, not because segregation was just, but because it forced Black communities to build

The First, the Few and the Only

better institutions for themselves. Schools like these were not merely about survival; they were about self-sufficiency. These schools instilled Black students with the seriousness of what Marable meant: the unshakable belief that they had to be twice as good because the world would only give them half the chance.

But integration, rather than uplifting these schools, undermined them. The best Black teachers were absorbed into white institutions or laid off entirely. The funding that had been withheld from Black schools was not restored; instead, they were left to decline.

There has been much debate over the merits of desegregation and whether it has caused more harm than good. It stands, though, that we feel some negative consequences in our culture as a whole.

🌱 **Getting Involved:**

The Betrayal of Integration

What Dunbar and Frederick Douglass High Schools show us is that Black-led education was not just about teaching. It was about building. These schools continued a culture where Black students were nurtured, where they saw examples of Black brilliance every day, where their history was not erased but celebrated.

Marable warned that those who believed racism was simply a lack of education were missing the larger picture. Racism was never just ignorance; it was economic and political control. "Education was the secular religion of the Black community…" - Manning Marable states 11:13. The destruction of Black schools (and Black educators en masse) was not an accident - it was part of a system that understood the power of Black self-sufficiency and sought to weaken it.

The tragedy of desegregation was not that Black children finally gained access to white schools. It was that the institutions Black people had built, these magnificent schools that had produced giants of Black excellence, were allowed to wither.

Frederick Douglass and Dunbar High Schools prove what Black communities could achieve when left to their own devices. They were proof that BLACK EXCELLENCE DID NOT NEED WHITE VALIDATION. They remind us that while access to education is a right, control over how that education is delivered is

The First, the Few and the Only

power. This power was taken from us at the beginning of integration, which went opposite to the designs of the Black architects of integration, like Thurgood Marshall. This tragedy of lost power occurred despite Marshall's (and those like him) gallant and best efforts.

⏱Side Quest ½

There are several academic studies and research articles exploring the psychological and emotional impact that occurs in Black children when attending predominantly white schools. The following studies explore topics such as identity development, tokenism, racial trauma, belonging, and the impact of systemic racism in educational environments. Explore at your own leisure:

First side quest of the chapter

For Black children in predominantly white prep schools, the journey is often one of complexity, marked by both visible and invisible hurdles. The long-term psychological impacts of these environments are not just about navigating the day-to-day but about the lasting impressions they etch onto a child's sense of self and place in the world.

Inez Beverly Prosser's pioneering 1933 dissertation, The Non-Academic Development of Negro Children in Mixed and Segregated Schools, offers critical insights into these impacts. Her research highlighted how Black students in integrated schools often wrestled with feelings of isolation and inferiority. These struggles were not just momentary but affected their social adjustment with peers, teachers, and even their own families. These ripples of harm often went unseen, yet they were deeply felt. 🌱

Similarly, Beverly Daniel Tatum's Why Are All the Black Kids Sitting Together in the Cafeteria? pulls back the curtain on how Black students often band together in predominantly white schools. This isn't about exclusion, but survival - a coping mechanism against the racial stressors that can erode mental and emotional health over time.

The First, the Few and the Only

The weight of tokenism also looms large in these environments. Being the only or the first often means living under a microscope. Every action feels scrutinized, and every misstep feels magnified. This hyper-visibility can create a crushing pressure to represent the entire race, leading to stress, isolation, ostracization, and a complicated relationship with one's own identity.

Kevin Cokley's research on impostor phenomenon in Black students resonates deeply here. Many of us know the feeling: walking into a room where it seems like every eye is waiting for you to prove you belong. These doubts are not mere insecurities. They are learned responses to environments that make belonging feel like a privilege rather than a right. And yet, resilience is not just a nice word - it is a life raft. For Black students, finding community, mentors, and culturally-affirming spaces is often the difference between surviving and thriving.

The stress of these environments doesn't just live in the mind. It shapes futures. The weight of navigating predominantly white spaces can affect academic performance, stifle motivation, and narrow the scope of what feels possible beyond graduation. The damage, if left unchecked, can echo into adulthood. Although this damage creates job security for therapists, it can negatively influence career opportunities, relationships, and overall well-being.

An intersectional lens also shows us that these experiences are not a monolith. Black girls, for example, often navigate compounded stereotypes around both race and gender. They may be subject to hyper-visibility or, conversely, complete erasure. Black boys, too, face a distinct set of challenges, often seen through a lens of suspicion or discipline rather than nurture and growth.

Then there are the school policies - the scaffolding that can either support or destabilize. Inclusive curricula, diverse faculty, and strong anti-discrimination policies are not just ideals but necessities. Beyond avoiding litigation, they set the tone, sending a clear message about whose voices matter, whose histories are told, and, consequently, whose presence feels valued.

Culturally competent support is also key. Black students need counselors and leaders who understand their experiences, not as outliers but as part of a broader systemic narrative without the need to educate or debate the validity of their experiences. These leaders lend a hand in creating braver spaces for open conversations about race and belonging. Strong and empathetic adults at school can

The First, the Few and the Only

help Black children solidify the ideal that identity is not an extracurricular effort - it is essential to their healing and growth.

These realities underscore why we must remain vigilant. For every Black child who walks through the halls of a predominantly white prep school, the stakes are high - not just for their grades but for their sense of safety, worth, and possibility. It is not enough to open doors. We must make sure they lead to places where Black children are not only welcomed but also truly seen, heard, and held.

May 31, 1921

Let's continue with Tulsa, Oklahoma, the home of Black Wall Street, and later, the home of the Tulsa Massacre. I remember years ago seeing a video of Tom Hanks, very professionally produced might I add, explaining his anger that he did not learn of the Tulsa Massacre until he was well into his adult years. The video was sincere, but it represented a larger cultural momentum in North America where white America was learning about the history of white racial violence in this country. This shined a light on what white bodies did to Black bodies who didn't stay in their place, Black individuals who not only lived in their glory and brilliance but also were productive and profitable. These Black bodies negated the lie of white superiority that white bodies were told, readily believe, and quite frankly, needed. White people told themselves that they were unequivocally better than Blacks, and that perceived violation against the white imagination was worthy of bloodshed.

I was leading an experience for pastors, elders, and leaders of a parish ministry that we called the Freedom Tour. I forget which city we had traveled to that year, but the whole goal was to do a three-day trip during which we would analyze the historical geography and social geography of the city in which we were staying. Our group looked at race in that city and how it affected the architecture, infrastructure, and roadway systems. Most highways, parks and stadiums within any given city are usually a dead giveaway of where all the thriving Black neighborhoods were located.

During this three-day event, the group talked extensively about the history of the area, which led to discussing the compassion and consequence of knowing said history. On this particular day, I remember that we were talking about Tulsa,

The First, the Few and the Only

Oklahoma. This was before Tom Hanks had popularized the awareness of the massacre by making the previously-mentioned video that was seen by his enormous following. Our speaker was Pastor Sherman Bradley, and he delineated the history of the Tulsa Massacre.

My good friend, who we will call Pastor Jimmy, was with me on this trip. He was from Oklahoma, and he had a very pronounced Southern drawl. Pastor Jimmy was an awesome guy – he would do anything for anybody, and he always wanted to learn from me. I wasn't used to that type of guy. I'm not saying this to be arrogant, but he was always willing to sit at my feet, so to speak. I preferred that we learned together during our chats. He constantly asked questions of me that he seemed afraid to ask, but he couldn't help himself. His curiosity came spilling out, especially when he asked me, "Is it disingenuous to be a white guy ministering to Black students? Should I find a Black guy to do that?" He was genuine and earnest, and I found him to be a great source of diversity within our ministry.

Anyway, during Pastor Bradley's talk about Tulsa, I was watching Pastor Jimmy's face. Now, this man usually had a smile that could light up the room, and he had the big, red, rosy cheeks to go with it. While Pastor Bradley was speaking, however, Pastor Jimmy was not smiling in the slightest. He was sort of hunched over, arms crossed with one hand over his mouth in disbelief. His face was taut, and his body was rigid. I had never seen him look so serious before.

Pastor Bradley concluded his talk and opened the floor for questions. Pastor Jimmy's hand shot up. He was called upon and said, "With all due respect, I'm from Oklahoma. In fact, I live near Tulsa, and I've never heard of this at all." He went on to question the validity of the topic, and he wanted to know where Pastor Bradley had gotten this information.

After many people chiming in to inform him that this is, in fact, a well-documented piece of American history, Pastor Jimmy said, "I really respect you guys, but I can't believe that this happened. I would've heard about it before now." He had a bachelor's degree in history and had studied church history all his life.

Pastor Bradley encouraged him to reach out to any of his older family members from the area and ask them about it. Jimmy left the room like a detective hot on the trail of a new lead. He later returned, weeping. He had spoken with his father, who had indeed confirmed the story's truth. Jimmy's father had never shared it because

The First, the Few and the Only

it was so shameful. In front of all of the ministers in the room, Jimmy had a breakdown as he questioned everything he thought he had known.

After some rage-filled sobs, Pastor Jimmy finally let out, "I feel lied to. I feel lied to by my teachers, by my dad—but my grandpa? What did he do? I feel lied to by everyone! I had this belief about my family, about my community, and I just now realize it was all a lie. All my pride in the amazing Christian folks I look up to…" His voice was shaking, words pouring out between tears. He continued with sharp and powerful rebukes, naming his revelation like he was trying to untangle the lie from his own skin.

Jimmy isn't the focus of this section, but his reaction is an illustrative lead-in to something deeper. The Tulsa Massacre most assuredly happened, but there's a lot of people who were kept in the dark about this, like my buddy. Generations of people - white, Black, and otherwise - were lied to by omission. Entire histories were erased, as was the horror of what was done in the Tulsa Massacre. The deeper truth beneath the massacre was also lost - the one that history books often refuse to tell.

Let's get this straight. Tulsa wasn't just about the violence. It was about wealth - Black wealth. What people don't realize is that in the late 1800s and early 1900s, in cities across America, the richest part of town was often the Black part of town. Let that settle. In contrast to today, the Black part of town is whispered about like a warning - the bad part of town, the crime-ridden neighborhood, the place you don't go after dark. I remember moving to New Castle, Pennsylvania, and hearing white high schoolers from a Baptist youth group say it outright: "…That's where the Black people live. That's the bad part of town." Was it always this way or was it designed to be?

Here's the truth they don't teach in school: in that first generation after slavery, Black people weren't just surviving - they were thriving. Entrepreneurs. Business owners. Skilled labor. Innovators. Millionaires. The real American dream, but with Black hands shaping it, and because white folks wanted to keep separate, that Black wealth circulated within Black communities exclusively. This was similar to Jewish communities creating self-sustaining economies that flourished beyond white imagination. The problem? It backfired on white supremacy and its myths.

The First, the Few and the Only

When Black wealth grew, when Black communities thrived, untouched by white hands - white America felt it, and they hated it. It challenged their narrative of racial difference as Bryan Stevenson calls it, their myth of superiority. It made them look at themselves and see lack - lack of innovation, lack of industry, lack of wealth, lack of the very Black brilliance they claimed as their own.

It became a foil to their learned beliefs of white superiority and challenged the root bed of their very culture. Imagine being a white milkman in 1921, delivering bottles to a Black household and seeing a grand piano in the living rooms. A grand piano in a Black home while you're barely getting by? That kind of sight burrowed into the soul like an infection, envy curdling into rage.

That rage became a fire, it became bombs, it became the leveling of entire communities overnight. What ignited this brewing flame? Was it a white girl who claimed to have been groped by a Black man, which she later admitted was a lie? A truth that people don't talk about enough is what happened after the massacre. Destruction wasn't enough then. Just like their grave-robbing pilgrim ancestors, theft had to follow. Don't believe me? Go see the Native American History Museum in Washington, D.C.

Survivors, covered in ash and grief, went to the banks to pull out their money to rebuild, to recover. The banks, however, refused them their money. Their own money held hostage. Gone. And just like that, Black wealth - generations of prosperity - was stolen. It was caused by this single act of financial violence that ensured Black people who had once built thriving economic districts would wake up in the "bad part of town." Not because they failed, but because they were robbed. #FreedmansSavingsAndTrustCompany of 1865 7

This is why the Apple TV film, The Banker, exists. If you haven't watched it yet, go do it. Samuel L. Jackson and Anthony Mackie tell the story of Bernard Garrett and Joe Morris, two Black men who found a way to outmaneuver the system by buying banks and real estate under the noses of white America, using a white man as their front. It was a direct response to the generational theft Black Americans had endured post-Tulsa, post-slavery, post every moment that Black prosperity was met with a system designed to keep it from lasting.

See, the real history of Black wealth in America is a history of sabotage. Post-slavery, Black banks were thriving, holding millions in Black savings. What

The First, the Few and the Only

happened? White-led institutions kept that money, held that money, stole that money, just as they did after Tulsa. The film lays it bare - how Black brilliance had to navigate through deception just to experience basic economic justice. Garrett and Morris did what Black people have always done: they adapted. If they couldn't own wealth openly, they'd own it covertly.

And the saddest part? Their strategy worked. Until, of course, the system caught up. Because whenever Black people find a way to win, white supremacy rewrites the rules. Most Black Americans' wealth was kept by a bank after slavery and never returned to them because they were making too much money. The film picks up in response to that history:

And here's what makes it worse. Some survivors of Tulsa Oklahoma 1921, the intentional flooding of Elbowood North Dakota 1953, of Rosewood 1923, of East St. Louis 1917, of Springfield 1908, of Chicago 1919, of Detroit 1943, of Washington DC 1919, of Wilmington 1898, of Atlanta 1906, of Camila 1868, St Bernard Parish of 1868, of New Orleans 1866, of Thibodaux 1887, of Colfax 1873, of Opelousas 1868, of Slocum 1910, of Clinton 1875, of Elaine 1919, of Philadelphia city police bombing MOVE in 1985 and of the intentional flooding of New York 1863... to name a few. Not to mention, weaponized 'eminent domain' and the forced move of Black communities wherever highways, big parks and stadiums stand in any given city in the United States of America. Those who had seen their homes burned and their families terrorized, took their cases to court. In Tulsa they won! In state courts and in federal courts. Some even made it to the Supreme Court. Yet justice was still denied. Again and again, Black communities would rise from the ashes, rebuild stronger, better, richer. Each time, white mobs, sometimes in the streets, sometimes in the boardrooms, would find a way to destroy them all over again.

The First, the Few and the Only

This is why integration, for all its promises, came at a cost. When Black communities controlled their own wealth, their own schools, their own institutions, they thrived, but the moment white America was forced to acknowledge that, the moment it threatened their hold on "power", they absorbed Black institutions instead of uplifting them. In doing so, they diluted Black power. Again, in the opposite direction of the Black architects of integrations design. 🌱

This is the hard truth: white America has never been content with Black success. Melanated glory. Not in Tulsa. Not in Greenwood. Not in banking. Not in education. The rules of the game were never broken. They were written, rewritten, and rewritten again this way. 🧭

Educational Control——> Economic Control —> Social Control

Dr. Claud Anderson, an accomplished author, has often said, "Never over six percent." What he means is that white people, to maintain a sense of control, rarely tolerate spaces where Black and Brown bodies exceed six percent of the total population. When that threshold is crossed, whether in a business, a neighborhood, a university, evangelical church, parachurch ministry or a corporation, there's a predictable reaction: white flight or white fear. Increased attrition of BIPOC employees. Heightened scrutiny. Alienation. A slow, methodical return to the perceived "natural order" - one where whiteness is dominant, uninterrupted, and unchallenged.

This isn't just social discomfort; it's an ancestral and curated expectation that whiteness should be the default. When that expectation is disrupted by reality, mechanisms are set in motion to restore it. It's not always as blatant as segregation-era policies, but the effect is the same. The pressure to conform. The silent but powerful push to leave. The quiet violence of isolation, ostracization and exclusion until the numbers are brought back in line.

Dr. Anderson's critique of integration forces us to reconsider its true impact. The way integration was executed was not designed to empower Black people but to

The First, the Few and the Only

contain us. Instead of fostering shared power, it strategically dissolved Black economic and social strongholds, funneling Black talent, labor, and resources into white institutions while ensuring those institutions never had to relinquish real control. Black schools closed while white schools remained intact. Black businesses folded while Black dollars flooded white-owned enterprises. Black neighborhoods, once self-sufficient, were destabilized, their residents pushed into a system that welcomed their participation but never their leadership or ownership.

Integration should have been a step toward Black self-determination. Instead, it became a tool of dis-integration - fragmenting Black identity, weakening Black institutions, and ensuring that whiteness remained the unchallenged center of power.

Dr. Anderson speaks to this reality with urgency. I encourage you to watch these three clips where he breaks down the historical and economic consequences of integration, and why Black economic independence is the only real path:

1 – 4 Dr. Claud Anderson

Educational control —> Economic Control —> Social Control —> Residential Control

History of Levittown's

Let's be clear: Levittown didn't happen in a vacuum. The shiny new suburbs that bloomed after World War II weren't just the result of economic prosperity or good old-fashioned American grit. They were the outcome of carefully orchestrated

The First, the Few and the Only

policies—many of them seeded during the New Deal—that kept the American Dream fenced off and color-coded.

See, during the Great Depression, the New Deal rolled out programs like the Federal Housing Administration (FHA) and the Homeowners' Loan Corporation (HOLC). On paper, these agencies were meant to rescue homeowners and make the idea of a house with a yard more accessible. And they did—but only if you were white. The FHA explicitly refused to insure mortgages in or near Black neighborhoods. HOLC drew up "residential security maps" that redlined entire communities, marking them unworthy of investment solely because of the bodies that lived there.

Fast-forward a decade or two, and William Levitt is building the blueprint for American suburbia: Levittown. A place where returning (white) GIs could buy brand-new homes with little money down, thanks to federally backed FHA and VA loans. This wasn't innovation. It was the same racist architecture—just with white picket fences.

Levittown wasn't just segregated by accident. Racially restrictive covenants were written directly into the deeds. Take Clause 25, for instance. It flat-out stated that homes could only be occupied by members of the Caucasian race. That wasn't a slip-up or a relic of an earlier era. That was the fine print, blessed by federal dollars. The FHA, still operating under its New Deal-era underwriting guidelines, backed it all the way. Even after the Supreme Court ruled in Shelley v. Kraemer (1948) that such covenants couldn't be legally enforced, the damage was done. These suburbs were designed to be white—and enforced it through policy, paperwork, and community gatekeeping.

And the few Black or Brown families who managed to break through the barricades? They were the exception—not the rule. And often, they paid the price in harassment, terrorizing by neighbors, or worse.

When we talk about the birth of the American middle class, let's not lie to ourselves. The postwar suburban boom—often hailed as the great equalizer—was a government-sponsored, racially exclusive club. The New Deal may have promised

The First, the Few and the Only

relief, recovery, and reform, but for Black and Brown families, it also built a legacy of exclusion. It ensured that the suburbs—and by extension, wealth accumulation, school access, and generational stability—would remain white, by design.

The same patterns continued from government to local neighborhoods. White resistance to neighborhood integration wasn't just about personal prejudice - it was a coordinated effort, backed by real estate agents, banks, and government policies. Redlining, restrictive covenants, and discriminatory lending practices ensured that even when Black families could afford to move into white neighborhoods, they were systematically excluded.

And when they did break through? The hostility was immediate. Cross burnings, bricks through windows, threats. By the early 1980s, the overt violence had simmered down, but the message remained: Black people could live in certain areas - but only a few at a time. A single Black family in a white suburb might be "acceptable." A Black neighborhood, however, was not. Residential segregation was another major consequence of integration. Black families were often excluded from white neighborhoods through a variety of discriminatory practices, such as redlining and restrictive covenants. Even when Black families were able to move into white neighborhoods, they often faced hostility and discrimination from their neighbors. The effects of integration were complex and varied, but it is clear that it did not always live up to its promise of equality. Architects of desegregation had the best of intentions at it's inception. However, over time and at the hands of folks like Levitt and other white men, integration served to maintain the existing power structure and further marginalize Black communities.

Tokenism Existed Before Integration…

… but it was solidified after. It allowed white institutions to claim they weren't racist while maintaining their dominance. A few Black students in a white school. A handful of Black employees in a white company. A single Black neighbor in a white suburb. Just enough integration to quiet the criticism—but never enough to shift power.

The First, the Few and the Only

2/2

Academic studies on the psychological and emotional impact
that occurs in Black children in pwi's on website.

This is why, even after desegregation, the structural inequalities remained. Private Christian schools - originally created to avoid integration - flourished, often with government support. Black schools were systematically underfunded. Black educators were pushed out. White neighborhoods remained gated in every way but name.

In its final application, integration didn't dismantle white supremacy. It preserved it. The nobility of racial integration was perverted into racial assimilation. It went from separate and unequal to together inside of a social hierarchy. Within that hierarchy, white men put themselves at the top.

It allowed white people to dictate the terms of Black inclusion - deciding who could enter, how many could enter, and under what conditions. It destabilized Black communities by eliminating Black-owned schools, displacing Black educators, and redistributing Black students into hostile environments where they were not truly welcomed.

The architects of desegregation had good intentions and designs. By the time the system got through with their vision, however, men like William Levitt - who built suburbs with explicit racial restrictions - had found ways to ensure that integration happened without actually sharing power.

Quick overview, for those who glazed over already; School integration wasn't reciprocal. Black students integrated into white schools, not the other way around. White students who didn't want to integrate simply transferred to private Christian schools, funded by government vouchers.

- Black educators lost their jobs as white schools absorbed Black students but refused to hire Black teachers. This didn't just affect the teachers' livelihoods but stopped much of what they provided to the next generation: the loss of cultural

The First, the Few and the Only

transmission, mentorship, built-in representation, in addition to economic stability.

- Housing integration was met with systemic resistance. Real estate agents and banks ensured that Black families remained segregated, reinforcing the idea that a "good" neighborhood was a white one.

- Tokenism became the norm. A handful of Black individuals were allowed into white spaces, but never in numbers that would challenge the existing power structure.

Rather than dismantling white supremacy, integration protected it—ensuring that Black communities remained controlled, contained, and dependent on white institutions for survival.

Just wants him out of his way, and his children's way

Side Quest

There is a great writer and educator that I look up to and hope to meet one day. Her name is Dr. Beverly Daniel Tatum, her work affirms that integration without systemic transformation is not progress - it is merely absorption into a system that was never designed with Black flourishing in mind. This section is my attempt at expanding on this work by illuminating the hidden curriculum of white institutions: where Black presence is tolerated but Black agency is suppressed. She wrote an amazing paper on this entitled Family Life and School Experience: Factors in the Racial Identity Development of Black Youth in White Communities.

Summary of Dr. Tatum's work

The First, the Few and the Only

🌱 Getting Involved

Are there stories and faces, vibrations, frequencies, images, memories, meaning-making, behaviors and urges coming up for you, affects and or sensations coming up in your body, Are you numb? Where in your body does it feel that way? What about emotions? Do you feel any strong or charged emotions right now? Where has your imagination gone? Are you drawing connections or new metaphors? Take a moment to write them down. Full stop. Notice and tend to your body.

Resource: Assimilation Blues by Dr Beverly Daniel Tatum

The Spoils of Our Struggle

"When the axe came into the forest, the trees said to one another, 'The handle is one of us.'"
Turkish Proverb

I want to zoom out for a moment - step back from the trees and take in the whole damn forest. Integration is not all bad. Let me be clear about that. But let me also be clear about something else: whatever good came from it did not come freely. It was not handed down in some benevolent act of American grace. No, any good that came from integration came from the sheer unrelenting grit of Black people - who, as always, had to fight not just for themselves, but for everybody else.

Because the truth is this: among all non-white ethnic groups, Native Americans and African-Americans have always been the tip of the spear. The first, the few, the only OGs. They were the ones to challenge white supremacy head-on, to be the battering ram against a door that was never meant to open for us. And yet, when the dust settled, when the laws changed, when the ink dried on the Civil Rights Act, who got to walk through that opened door first?

Not us.

White women. Then Eastern European Jews, the Irish, Asian-Americans. Latinos. Every so-called "minority" who could, at the very least, blend, benefit, or build without the permanent mark of Blackness trailing behind them. The Black body bled the most for civil rights freedoms but benefited the least. 8

The First, the Few and the Only

White Women: The Biggest Beneficiaries of Civil Rights

White women found a way to bend our struggle to their advantage. When we marched for justice, they rebranded it as a fight for "gender equality." When we demanded access, they tacked on their names to the policy changes. Affirmative action, a program meant to correct centuries of racial injustice, became a tool that disproportionately benefited white women. Today, they remain its primary beneficiaries.

And yet, when it came time to stand with us - when the rubber met the road - they were silent. The feminist movement of the sixties and seventies wanted liberation, but not if it meant aligning too closely with Blackness. White women fought to leave the kitchen but had no problem leaving it to a Black woman. When we spoke about racism, they told us to "wait" or to "focus on women's issues first," as if Black women did not exist at the intersection of both struggles for decades already;

- The civil rights movement, propelled by the relentless efforts and sacrifices of African-Americans, sought to dismantle systemic barriers and achieve equality. However, the benefits of these struggles have often been disproportionately reaped by other groups, notably white women.
- Affirmative action policies, designed to address racial disparities, have significantly benefited white women. The U.S. Department of Labor estimated that approximately six million women and five million minority workers advanced to higher occupational classifications due to these initiatives.
- In the corporate realm, companies implementing affirmative action saw notable increases in female representation. For instance, after IBM established its affirmative action program, the number of women in management positions more than tripled within a decade.
- Despite these advancements, wage disparities persist. White women earn approximately 82.8% of what their white male counterparts make, while Black women earn about 87.5%. However, it's essential to recognize that these figures can be influenced by various factors, including differences in occupations and industries. 9
- In the Diversity, Equity, and Inclusion (DEI) sector, specific salary data by race and gender is limited. However, broader trends indicate that white women often hold a significant share of DEI roles, potentially leading to

The First, the Few and the Only

higher average earnings in this field compared to women of other racial and ethnic backgrounds.
- These statistics underscore the complex dynamics of progress and highlight the need for continued efforts to ensure that the benefits of civil rights advancements are equitably distributed among all marginalized groups.

Asian-Americans: Privilege Paid for in Black Blood

One of the most complicated inter-ethnic relationships in America is the one between Black and Asian communities. And it didn't have to be. Had it not been for the American Civil Rights Movement, there would not be twenty-two million Asian-Americans in this country today. The  Immigration and Nationality Act of 1965 - an act born from the momentum of Black struggle - opened the door for Asian migration on a scale previously unimaginable. Before that, racist laws like the Chinese Exclusion Act of 1882 kept their numbers low, their entry restricted. But Black agitation for civil rights cracked open the foundation of white supremacy just enough for other groups to squeeze through.

Nearly every privilege Asian-Americans enjoy today was paid for in Black blood. And yet, time and time again, many have aligned themselves with whiteness, eager to claim the "model minority" status that was never meant for our people. Whether in the anti-Blackness embedded in certain communities, the economic success that came from setting up businesses in Black neighborhoods, or the silence when we called out injustice, the tension remains. Because while many Asian-Americans understand the struggles of discrimination, too many have been willing to stand on the shoulders of our fight without standing beside us. 10

Latin Americans: Beneficiaries of Our Battle, Bastions of Anti-Blackness

The Latino population in the United States is vast, diverse, and complex, but one thing remains true: much of what they have gained in this country is a direct result of Black struggle. When we forced open doors for equal education, housing rights,

The First, the Few and the Only

and labor protections, they walked through them. The Voting Rights Act, which was fought for with Black marches, Black arrests, Black bodies bloodied on the Edmund Pettus Bridge, was later expanded to protect Spanish-speaking voters. The workplace protections we bled for benefited Latino workers just as much, if not more, than they did us.

And yet, despite shared oppression, anti-Blackness remains deeply entrenched in many Latino communities. Colorism runs rampant. White Latinos distance themselves from their Black counterparts, clinging to proximity to whiteness whenever possible. The darker you are, the lower you are allowed to climb. We saw it when Black Panther: Wakanda Forever was released - when Tenoch Huerta, a darker-skinned Mexican actor, was cast as Namor, and many in his home country erupted in anger, lamenting the absence of a lighter-skinned actor in his place. Even in fictionalized power, Blackness is seen as a step too far.

Africans and Caribbean Immigrants

Even among our own, the legacy of Black American struggle is often overlooked. African and Caribbean immigrants who arrive in the U.S. with degrees, with access, with the ability to "succeed" in ways that feel just out of reach for many native-born Black Americans often forget the soil they're stepping onto. The economic and social opportunities they inherit were fought for with the bones of those who had no choice but to build this country.

The first-generation success stories often come with a disdain for "those Black Americans" who "don't work hard enough," as if systemic racism only applies to those without accents🌱. As if the wealth gap, the redlining, the school-to-prison pipeline, and the endless attempts to suppress Black advancement didn't happen to us all. The American Dream that some are able to grab onto was only made possible because Black Americans have been America's worst-kept promise and its greatest test of resilience.

The Price FFOs Paid

"Indoctrinated by the myths of the white world, we can think we are partakers of a table we are not invited to…people with too much faith in the white world and too little knowledge of the power we have to liberate ourselves" -Andre Henry

The First, the Few and the Only

No, integration was not all bad. But if we are to be honest, if we are to tell the full story…then we must admit this: the primary beneficiaries of integration were not the people who fought hardest for it. We tore down the walls. We bulldozed the barriers with flesh and bone, but when the dust settled, it was often others who stepped in while we were left in the rubble.

This is not a call for division, but for collective memory. It is not about keeping score, but about remembering who did the labor, who took the beatings, who filled the jails, who shed the blood. Because history has a way of erasing Black people from the very movements we created, of turning us into footnotes in stories we authored. And I refuse to let that happen.

We have always been the tip of the spear. And yet, when the battle is over, we are too often left behind. That is the cost of being first. Of being the few. Of being the only.

HIS-story by Poet Gil Scott-Heron [11]

I was wondering about our yesterdays and digging through the rubble.
And to say the least, somebody went through a hell of a lot of trouble to make sure
that when we look things up we wouldn't fare too well.
And we would come up with totally unreliable pictures of ourselves
I compiled what few facts I could, I mean, such as they are
To see if we could find out a little bit of something and this is what I got so far

First, white folks discovered Africa
They claimed it fair and square. They couldn't have been rob'n nobody
Cuz wasn't nobody there.
And white folks brought all the civilization cuz there wasn't none around
How could the folks be civilized when wasn't nobody writin' nothing down.

And just to prove all of their suspicions, well,
Didn't take too long.
They found that there were whole tribes of people
In plain sight,
running around with no clothes on

You're not alone

The First, the Few and the Only

That's right,
the men the women the young and the old
Righteous folks covered their eyes
And no time was spent considering their environment
Hell No, this just wasn't civilized

And another piece of information they have
OR at least this is what we were taught
IS that unlike the civilized people of Europe,
These tribal units actually fought

And, yes, there was some crude implements
And, yes, there was primitive art
And, yes, they were masters of hunting and fishing and courtesy came from the heart
And, yes, there was; love and medicine, religion intertwined with communication by drum

But no paper, no pencils and any other utensils
And, hell, these people never heard of a gun
And this is why the colonies came to stabilize the land
Because the dark continent had copper and gold and the discoverers had themselves a plan.

They would discover all of the places with promise
You didn't need no titles or deeds
Then they would appoint people to make everything legal
To sanction, trickery and greed
And back in the jungle when the natives got restless they would call it 'Guerilla attack'

And they would never describe it that the folks got wise
and decided that they would fight back
And still we are victims of word games, semantics are always a bitch
Places once referred to as underdeveloped are now called mineral rich
And the game goes on, eternally, unity is just beyond reach

You're not alone

The First, the Few and the Only

Egypt and Libya used to be in Africa
They've now been moved to the Middle East
There are examples galore I assure you
But if interpreting were left up to me
I'd be sure that every time folks knew this version wasn't mine
Which is why it is called His-Tory

Poem by Gil Scott Heron

The First, the Few and the Only

Chapter 5

The "Pax" Romana

The Empire's Tools of Peace [1]

History has a way of repeating itself, though the costumes and set designs change. The Roman Empire, in all its gilded arrogance, understood something about power that modern institutions have perfected: you do not need to be just, only convincing.

The Pax Romana meaning the "Roman Peace," was Rome's greatest con. A two-hundred-year period of so-called stability from 27 BCE to 180 CE, this was not peace as we imagine it - tranquil and just - but rather the kind of "peace" only possible under an iron boot pressed against the throat of the conquered. Rome wielded a sword in one hand and a contract in the other, dictating who could rise, who could speak, and who would be held up as proof of the empire's magnanimity.

Rome's secret? Give the illusion of inclusion without ever relinquishing true power. It was a strategy carved into every colonizer's handbook, a trick of the trade that modern institutions still use today. Whether it was appointing non-Roman governors to oversee their own subjugation or installing local kings who would bow to Caesar while appearing to serve their people, Rome was a master of optics. Some of the conquered, those allowed inside Rome's golden halls, were decorated in fine robes, given titles, and placed on the empire's grand stage - but only to serve as puppets. The moment they mistook their position for real authority, the empire reminded them that power belonged only to Rome. The moment they thought they could wield influence on behalf of their own people, they were replaced or erased.

Does that sound familiar?

It should. Because we are still living under a version of the "Pax" Romana, only now, instead of being called by Latin names, it goes by titles like Diversity, Equity,

The First, the Few and the Only

and Inclusion Officer or First Black _____ in Company History. Makes one wonder where the idea of the 'showpony' came from?

The Modern Empire and Its Tokens

Modern institutions - corporate, political, academic, and even religious - have inherited this Roman strategy of control through calculated representation. The token spokesperson is not new; it is ancient.
Look around, and you will see them: the one Black CEO of a predominantly white company, the lone Indigenous congressperson, the first Latina partner at a law firm that still treats her like a guest. Like Rome, these institutions offer a seat at the table but never a knife and fork.

But let's be clear: tokenization is not the same as representation. Representation implies agency, power, and a true seat at the decision-making table. Tokenization is performative, conditional, and exists to protect the empire rather than to challenge it. The moment a tokenized leader stops serving their intended function, they are discarded. A BIPOC individual in a position of power is expected to do two things:

1. Validate the empire - They must serve as proof that the institution is progressive, fair, and just. Their presence is supposed to quiet the whispers of injustice: "See? We have a Black leader. We have a Latina VP. We have a Native American professor. What more do you want?"
2. Never challenge the empire - If they speak out, if they advocate for their people too fiercely, if they disrupt the very structures that allow them to exist in their position, they are swiftly reminded who is really in control. They are asked to step down, they are labeled as "too difficult," they are branded as a "bad fit."

The Pax Romana of today exists in corporations, in politics, in Hollywood, in academia, and even in faith spaces. It exists in a Black pastor leading a megachurch but not addressing racial injustice from the pulpit. It exists in a Native American representative in Congress who is tolerated as long as they do not push for land reparations. It exists in a Black female executive who is only praised when she stays within the lines drawn for her.

The message is clear: you are welcome here as long as you serve our interests. The moment you don't, you are replaceable. Like I heard it once said, 'Women in

The First, the Few and the Only

powerful positions isn't inherently feminist especially when they use their power to harm more marginalized women.' So too, for people of color.

The Precariousness of Tokenized Leadership

Being a token is a high-risk proposition. The empire gives you a title, a stage, a microphone - but the moment you use it for something real, the moment you call out the illusion, the moment you demand justice instead of symbolic progress, you become a problem. Let those with eyes to see and ears to hear catch this: the Pax Romana was good for Rome. Not for the tokens. Especially not the lands and tribes they came from.

We have seen it time and again. The first, the few, and the only are often discarded when our presence is no longer convenient, when our influence takes too much control of the narrative. When we become more than proof of progress, and instead, proof of power. Whether it's the Black leader ousted after challenging corporate racism, the Indigenous scholar dismissed when they advocate for land back policies, or the Asian politician abandoned when she speaks out against systemic inequities, the playbook is always the same.
The real tragedy is that some tokens believe they have truly been accepted, only to discover the truth when it's too late. The empire does not love you. It uses you.

The consequences are devastating. The psychological toll of being both "the representative" and "the servant of the system" is a slow death. Tokenization breeds exhaustion, self-doubt, and isolation. It forces leaders into an impossible dual role - expected to be a beacon of hope for their community while remaining silent in the face of oppression. So, what do we do?

Rejecting the Empire's Terms

The lesson of history is that the empire does not grant true power. It only lends it, temporarily, for its own benefit. If we are to break free from the modern Pax Romana, we must refuse to play by its rules.

This does not mean rejecting leadership - it means rejecting leadership on their terms. It means creating spaces outside of the empire's control. It means refusing to

The First, the Few and the Only

be satisfied with symbolic victories. It means building systems that do not require permission to exist.

We have a choice: remain in the empire's service or build something of our own.

The Pax Romana was not about peace, and neither is the version of "diversity" that asks for our presence but denies our power. The question before us is this: will we continue to play the role assigned to us by the empire, or will we reject it entirely and build something new? This is not a call to burn down the empire – though history tells us that empires always fall anyway. Let the empires hang themselves by their own machinations. Let God deal with them. As J. Cole says, "Don't save her, she don't wanna be saved." This is a call to stop believing in the illusion. Peace for the few, and silence for the many is its essence.

Rome fell, and when it did, it was not because the tokens within it asked for justice. It was because those on the outside built something greater, and Rome cannibalized itself -without us. Pax Americana is next.

What's coming up for you right now?

_____

_____

_____

_____

🧭 The Lived Experience of The Black Man" by Franz Fanon

The First, the Few and the Only

Chapter 6

Sardoodledom

For many years I thought that my experience with tokenism only began when I moved from South Florida to the North: being one of the first Brown bodies in the room, one of the few Black bodies in the pews, even the only one in leadership at the company, or the only keynote speaker of color at national conferences. I realized, however, when I was preparing for the keynote speech about this book (book notes at the time) that there may be more to the story… maybe even earlier exposure to this theme of being one of the first, the few and the only, other than just senior year.

This is a real picture from, when I was younger at least, the very popular show every Thanksgiving on TV. This is years before streaming services and being able to select payment options that keep out any commercial breaks. Charlie Brown's Thanksgiving special would play every Thanksgiving. As you can see, this image speaks volumes. Perhaps some of you already noticed that even the dog has a seat with the others before Franklin does, who is left alone on the other side.

The First, the Few and the Only

Now I don't know if this was a subversive critique or an intentional use of the first Black character in Peanuts to send a message. If my memory serves me correctly, Franklin was added after the civil rights movement. There is even a museum in the U.S. dedicated to the celebration of progress that they added a FFO (first, few, and only) to the Peanuts lineup. But even in illustration, this FFO character was kept at the table at arms-length. Like many FFOs in real life.

Let's play a quick game in the book margin.

(1) Write down five Black characters from anime or cartoons. If you need to look something up to answer, that's okay.

(2) Let's try another one: can you name five Black superheroes from any movie? Or maybe five Black superheroes from comics? How about five TV shows with more than a few Black characters?

If you couldn't finish any of these lists, you get the point. Then I wondered if there were any Franklins since the Charlie Brown stuff. I mean, that was only once or twice a year. I thought back to my Toonami days, my Dragon Ball-Z and Power Rangers days and, welp… see for yourself:

The First, the Few and the Only

Different Character | Same Role

There is a popular historical role/term for the use of this type of character and their characteristics: a token. Now, there are different types of tokens and to better understand this, we'll have to start with the beginning of a familiar story in North American literature.

The First, the Few and the Only

Who was 'uncle tom'?

In the story Uncle Tom's Cabin, an anti-slavery novel by Harriet Beecher Stowe, we meet a number of characters, most notably Uncle Tom. This story was crazy influential. According to Essential Civil War Curriculum, Harriet Beecher Stowe's novel, "...widened the chasm between the North and the South, greatly strengthened Northern abolitionism, and weakened British sympathy for the Southern cause. The most influential novel ever written by an American, it was one of the contributing causes of the Civil War1." At the very least, it laid the groundwork for the Civil War.

Although the story is full of other characters, there are two that always stood out to me: Uncle Tom, the protagonist, and Sambo. This book, as well as the protagonist's influence on the war effort, cannot be overstated. Additionally, it's influence is still felt today. The very moniker "Uncle Tom," when said to a person of color, is the equivalent to calling them the N-word. Actually, it's worse. Ironically, the term is not for ANY Brown body. No, it is only reserved for Brown and Black bodies that are seen as being around white bodies too long to the extent that they become them. This is also alluding to deeper harming of its intended target as it also assumes that the very Brown/Black body has joined in with the "oppressor." It perpetuates the oppression of Brown and Black bodies through collusion, namely for betrayal. This is a grave harm to any Black body, especially to one who is professionally, or faith-wise, or academically surrounded by white bodies.

This is a confounding place to be in considering that all "opportunities for advancement" such as "good" jobs, "good" education, "good" church, and "good"

The First, the Few and the Only

neighborhoods have been systematically, economically, and culturally intertwined with whiteness. But I digress, that's for another chapter.

So, the term Uncle Tom is a term that is rich in racial history. It is a very derogatory racial term particularly for Black people. Similarly, the term Sambo is also rich in racial history and negativity, although Sambo's not as well-known of a term. Uncle Tom as a slur primarily came about due to Harriet Beecher Stowe's novel Uncle Tom's Cabin. Both of these terms can be somewhat interchangeable referencing some kind of betrayal, a Black person that is essentially actively choosing to turn on other Black people for the benefit, comfort, or security of wealthy white people.

Another way of thinking about it is essentially a sellout, someone who sells out his own people, his own tribe. It doesn't matter what for, but he will sell out his own people for gain, proximity to power, or anything he wants as long as it affords more privileges from/with white people.

It is my hope to clarify the realities that, although these terms are often used in modern society as interchangeable, they are far from interchangeable and are actually wildly different references. I also wanted to distinguish between the caricatures that are Uncle Tom, Sambo, and Coon versus the real-life examples of the people on which the terms are based. The Sambo character or caricature is one of the docile, childlike, adult Black males which was an image that thrived in the midst of slavery where many whites held a fixated image in their minds of Black people. This image was generally based on this one caricature, and that in and of itself is the definition of a stereotype.

Another example of a stereotype is the Coon caricature. The term is not only derogatory in nature, but it is a dehumanizing one based on the term raccoon. A classic example of this image was based on the character Lincoln Theodore Monroe Andrew Perry. He popularized this image through his work as the first successful Black male in films, primarily based on his depiction of this negative stereotype. The basic gist is of a lazy adult male that is slow in speech, lazy, and kind of stupid. He's apparently so lazy that it took him multiple minutes just to finish sentences. Although Lincoln Theodore Monroe Andrew Perry was very financially successful due to his portrayal of this character, it created a new form of the word Coon. Perry was "cooning" – he was sort of leaning into a caricature for white people, putting on an image that made white people comfortable in order to make them happy. And this act paid/pays really well. He put on this image of a lazy person because

The First, the Few and the Only

that's what white people wanted to see. Because that's the image of Black people that white people wanted to see, this caricature, known as Stepin Fetchit, became so popular that Perry became a millionaire. White people paid well for the versions of Black people they wanted to believe in.

Now Sambo was supposed to represent an adult male who was a buffoon, easily frightened, childlike, and generally happy about their life, no matter the squalor. This caricature, like the coon, was based on real people. This will be important when we get to Uncle Tom. The Sambo was representative of real, enslaved people who were loyal to their slave masters. A Sambo was so dedicated to his slave masters that he would betray his own people, no matter the cost, even to their destruction. A Sambo was a slave person that, no matter what, would obey his master.

In the movie Django Unchained, Samuel L Jackson's character, slave Stephen, will do anything for Leonardo DiCaprio's character, slave master Calvin J. Candie. In essence, that is the Sambo caricature embodied.

The coon and Sambo characters hold a kernel of truth for real life Black persons that would cave for the imagination or whims of white people, which white people were very comfortable with. One could make them laugh while making a fool of themselves for white people whilst confirming their stereotypes (coon), and the other was loyal to a fault at the expense and degradation of their own kind (Sambo). Now, mind you, these stereotypes in the time that they were used in history were very beneficial and needed for what white people wanted to picture when they thought of Black people. The whites wanted to keep them powerless, keep them illiterate, keep them childlike, make them loyal, keep them foolish, keep them from being smart, intelligent, well—read, punctual, and confident.

The terms Sambo and coon were an embarrassment to Black people everywhere because they represented Black folk who would betray their own for whites, and that truth was real throughout North America, from slavery to Jim Crow.

There are other similar stereotypes we'll get into later, but the ones I want to name right now are the Mammy The Savage the Aunt Jemima, The Sapphire (solidified through the show Amos n Andy) & The Jezebel 2 because it wasn't only Black men who were given racial stereotypes to fit into the imaginations of white people. Those stereotypes were often based on kernels of truth for Black people that did

The First, the Few and the Only

defend white people. Black woman also had terms of stereotypes that would capture kernels of truth of the function of some Black woman in the white world. But we'll put a pin in those for now.

The term Uncle Tom, popularized by Harriet Beecher Stowe's novel, was based on a real person by the name of Josiah Henson who you met in the prologue of this book. This term is also a contranym, a word with opposing but equally true definitions. It has many meanings but often gets likened to Sambo (a betrayer) and someone who's acting white. After explaining the real person who inspired the term in Beecher Stowe's novel, I trust and believe that you will see the wide gap between the caricature and the real person it was inspired by. In addition to the other meaning of the contranym. Here are a few quick facts about Josiah Henson for you to consider;3

1) He became a preacher by memorizing scripture despite not being able to read or write.
2) In 1830, he ran away with his wife and two youngest children to Canada, over six hundred miles away. Have you ever tried to walk with children through Disneyland for a day? Can you imagine six hundred miles with kids and no snacks?!?!
3) In 1841, he helped start a Freemen settlement called the British American Institute, which became a final stop on the Underground Railroad.
4) He helped over two hundred slaves escape to Canada.
5) He ran a farm, gristmill, and bred horses.
6) He built a sawmill, like the one in Ryan Coogler's SINNERS, making high quality Black lumber
7) He won a medal at the first World Fair in London for his lumber. Please check out this clip from the popular *show The Jeffersons* to see how the true Uncle Tom was inserted in Black entertainment to help right the ship, as it were: 4

Now don't get it twisted: Uncle Tom is a term for Black people that is almost worse than being called the N-word. It not only denigrates you to a N-word, but a N-word that betrays his own people. In many ways, this is seen as worse.

I have to admit I have not been one to slug people for calling me the N-word. Usually, I choose to go on about my business and try to pray for them or just go

The First, the Few and the Only

work it out on the box and on the punching bag. I know for certain that if anybody, especially a white person, ever call me Uncle Tom, whether I'm violent or not, I have to defend my honor. It's a term that is particularly slanderous because it assumes that any people of color that work in white spaces, any people of color like me who often is the only face like mine in white institutions, whether it be religious or academic, that, somehow by my hyper proximity to white people, I have become them. That is always an area of vulnerability, because in these white spaces I'm always trying to remember my cultural fortitude while also navigating a system that wasn't designed for me. I do that to the best of my ability, but to be called an Uncle Tom for doing that would feel pretty horrible and dehumanizing.

I had a buddy of mine at a local university, we'll call him Chesco. Chesco was and is someone who comes from what many would deem the hood in Pittsburgh, and all that comes with that space. He went to a local university to get his bachelor's degree, and I remember him telling me one day when I was a campus minister there that he finds it really frustrating to be seen as too white to be down anymore now that he is in college. People would say that to put him down, and it made him upset because he was only trying to better himself and get a degree. That comes at the cost of community, and that is something that I think a lot of people of color struggle with. People of color have to navigate that juxtaposition of community versus a better life. Uncle Tom is a term that may not often be said, but there are consequences to being around a lot of white people. The true term for Uncle Tom is someone like Josiah Henson who was a leader and an innovator, an author and a freedom fighter, an entrepreneur and a business owner. He is someone who breaks out on his own and creates things to give to his children and things that give room for other people to live out their dreams. That is one of the dreams and kind of freedom of all Black people - to go do their own thing and have it be successful.

Unfortunately, there's some Black people that see that and think of the Uncle Tom caricature versus the Josiah Henson person, and therein lies the rub. Redeeming Uncle Tom is sort of restoring that idea in the hearts and imaginations of BIPOC bodies. This ancestral hero that is Josiah Henson, a heroic figure in North American history. He was not designed to be misconstrued in American lore, Black imaginations, and Black culture.

As my friend, Dr Mychael Lee, said, "Sometimes, Black/Brown bodies that aren't tokens will side-eye Black and Brown bodies who are." It's like assumptions are made, and it always has a haughtiness from BIPOC bodies who have not been

The First, the Few and the Only

tokenized, often without knowing if there is fealty or loyalty to the institution or BIPOC liberation or empowerment. My friend went on to say that sometimes Black bodies will look at his location in the organization at previous jobs and then assume his wife is white just because he has a position of leadership and is the only Brown, male face at that leadership table. He sometimes feels compelled to prove to other Black people that he is valid by unprompted disclosure of his humble beginnings, navigating poverty with a single mom in Philly. When necessary, he let people know his wife isn't white. Can you imagine?

There's a Nina Simone quote that captures the Uncle Tom-Josiah Henson connection: "...when I die, my people, when I go, you see, I'm going to know that I left something for them to build on, and that is my reward. You got yours [referring to white people], you got yours, your money, your parents and your Easy Living. My folks... got nothing and they need inspiration twenty-four hours a day, and that's why I'm here." This quote encapsulates the hero that is Josiah Henson, who the Uncle Tom caricature was based on, the innovator who created opportunities for people that look like me well before the solidification of the Underground Railroad. The well-known work of Harriet Tubman was remarkable, and Josiah Henson was someone that was succeeding before it became cool. That's pretty damn inspiring.

Unfortunately, it is too common in the American imagination that Josiah Henson, the Uncle Tom character, is referred to as a derogatory term. This stereotypical caricature leads to negative and even harmful biases held by white men in legislative, political, and even institutional power. Not only that, but it's also internalized within Black men and women. These caricatures are also backed by a history of mechanically contrived stereotypes and unrealistic characterizations whose goal is to achieve morally questionable narratives. It's so funny because there's actually a word for this: sardoodledom. This denotes a mechanically contrived stereotype or unrealistic characterization to achieve a morally questionable plot point. This term does not just live in drama plays but in the imaginations of bodies, particularly white bodies of power. I believe it fuels tokenization throughout harmful institutions. To be clearer, these stereotypes, these caricatures would not have survived without <u>story</u> - not just any story but popular narratives that were told over and over again, whether through literature, film, silent movies, or branding. I'm going to explain more of some of the history of sardoodledom all the way to some of the current realities of it.

The First, the Few and the Only

🌱 Getting Involved

If you'll indulge me, let's start with another challenge.

Take a moment and jot down:

1. The first three childhood shows that come to mind from when you were a kid. Go.

2. The first three shows that the kids in your life - your children, nephews, nieces, or young cousins - watch today.

Your Childhood Shows	The Kids' Shows Today
_____	_____
_____	_____
_____	_____

Hold onto that list. We'll circle back in a moment.
Now, let me tell you a bedtime story…

The Three Little Pigs and the Big Bad (Dark) Wolf

The other night, I was putting my son to bed, and he asked me to read The Three Little Pigs, a classic. But as I turned the pages, something caught my attention in a way it never had before.

The pigs? Soft, pink. Virtuous. Industrious.
The wolf? Dark, gray. Sinister. A looming menace.

Now, I don't claim to know what specific breed of wolf the inspiration was here, but I do know that in this world, color is never just color. See, my son has a Marvel nerd for a father, which means our house is full of Spider-Man, Hulk, Black Panther, and the whole superhero roster. But one night, while reading a completely

The First, the Few and the Only

unrelated book - one without villains or heroes - my son pointed at the darker-colored characters and, without hesitation, said, "The bad guy."

I froze.

Because we hadn't taught him that. Not intentionally. We hadn't filled his bookshelves with villains. And yet, here he was, barely old enough to tie his shoes, already fluent in one of America's oldest, most insidious narratives: darkness is danger. Lightness is safe. 🌱

So, I sat with that moment while he fell asleep, flipping through the mental archives of my own childhood.

Let's go back to that list you made. Look at the villains. Any patterns? For me, the ghosts of Saturday morning cartoons came flooding back - Transformers, X-Men, Power Rangers, PowerPuff Girls (don't hate). And what do they all have in common?

The bad guys were always darker.

Megatron? Gun metal silver and Black.
Apocalypse? Deep blue, dark armor.
Mojo Jojo? Green skin, black fur, dark cape.
Mumm-Ra from Thundercats? Swathed in dark shadows.

Darkness, over and over again, was something to be fought, feared, or vanquished. And I know what some might say, "Relax, it's just a cartoon." But here's the thing about stories: they don't stay on the page. They don't stay behind the screen. They follow us. They teach us how to see the world, even when we don't realize we're learning.

The Racial Imagination at Play

I've been intentional about what my son watches. His lineup includes Blaze & the Monster Machines, Mighty Express, Spidey & Friends, and Santiago of the Seas - shows with diverse characters, bright colors, and what I thought was a more balanced ethnic worldview.

The First, the Few and the Only

And yet, somehow, he had still absorbed the same lesson generations before him had learned, which tells me something crucial:
It's not just about what we put in front of our kids.
It's about what the world has already put in front of us.

These stories - of dark villains and light heroes - have been told so many times, passed down through so many generations, that they have embedded themselves into our collective racial imagination.

And this isn't just about cartoons. This is about the way we, as adults, perceive real people. The way darker-skinned children get disciplined more harshly in school. The way police body cams show officers drawing weapons faster on Black men. The way a simple descriptor - "big," "dark," "threatening" - can turn an unarmed person into a justifiable target.

A wolf, into a monster.
A child, into a threat.
A man, into a headlining hashtag.

Rewriting the Story

So, what do we do with this? What do we do if the stories we've been raised on were quietly conditioning us into something else? Maybe we start with what we tell our children? Maybe we start with what we tell ourselves?

Maybe we take the time to ask:
Who are the villains in our favorite stories?
What do they look like?
And more importantly - who told us they had to look that way?

Because the thing about the Big Bad Wolf is - she was always just hungry, right?
And the thing about the Three Little Pigs?

Who knows? Maybe we only know what the pigs wanted us to know? Perhaps, the whole story starts before the building of buildings on "free" land the pigs discovered. Maybe the innocent little pigs found the land occupied, then cleared out the wolf's den, full of cute wolf pups, built their houses atop their bones, stacked

The First, the Few and the Only

their bricks, straw, and wood on the wolf's family unmarked graves, and then told the rest of us a big bad wolf is trying to eat them. Maybe in reality, she is just a mother looking to settle the score. I mean, c'mon, when have we known a wolf to be without its pack?

Sardoodledom

Sardoodledom- This term denotes a mechanically contrived stereotype or unrealistic characterizations to achieve a morally questionable plot point, and this term does not just live in drama plays but in the imaginations of white bodies in power AND, I believe, fuels tokenization in real life. If you haven't checked out a QR code yet, I specifically repeated the definition for the QR code below. It's the perfect segway into the history lesson we about to explore. Please scan:

Beau Sia's poem "Give Me A Chance"

Notice what comes up in your body as you read the following terms. Notice any tension, constriction, heat, and where it shows up in your body. Pay attention to any memories, friends, family, or acquaintances that come to mind. Honor the body by taking a somatic pause. Where's your breath? Check your body. Are you dissociating? Put the book down. Take care of your body whenever you need to. Because we are about to learn more terms for the big bad wolf.

The Savage

"The Wooing and Wedding of a Coon" in 1904, "The Slave" in 1905, "The Sambo Series" 1909-1911 and "The Nigger" in 1915, and Birth of a Nation in 1915. These films created early depictions of Black people as violent, hypersexualized, and dangerous. Birth of a Nation (1915) solidified the trope, portraying Black men as predators and white women as their victims which later justified segregation, lynchings, and the rise of the Ku Klux Klan. The psychological echos that precipitated in white imaginations was used to criminalize Black people in media

The First, the Few and the Only

and politics. This continues today in the portrayal of Black men as inherently dangerous in news, film, and criminal justice policies.

Stepin Fetchit

First Black Hollywood millionaire, but at the cost of reinforcing the lazy, clueless, subservient Black man. Made Black people seem childlike, incompetent, and dependent on white people. Modern versions: Mushmouth (Fat Albert), J.J. Evans (Good Times), Jar-Jar Binks (Star Wars). So fascinating how this began a trend that whichever Black actor embodied the white imagination's projection of the Black body the best, became the richest and got the most screentime. Do you think that still happens today? Can you trace in recent history how the most caricatured roles of Black actors got rewarded with the most screentime, best awards and highest income? [5]

Pick-Me Negroes

A Black man or woman that is pushed to the forefront that look like us, is chosen to represent us, but really not for Black people. Used as a vessel to push agendas and get Blacks on their side. Remember the Pax Romana? These Black individuals get elevated by white institutions to push anti-Black narratives. Used to deflect racism by portraying success as a personal effort rather than systemic. A historical example is Booker T. Washington's accommodationist stance, as well as a modern example is Black conservatives who deny systemic racism's existence or liberal pundits who say what minorities want to hear but where they validate our experience in public, in private they busy themselves with the interests of the wealthy, powerful and white.

Jim Crow Blackface Minstrels

This popularity continued, and at the height of the minstrel era, the decades preceding and following the Civil War, there were thirty-plus full-time Blackface minstrel companies performing across the nation (Engle, 1978). Established stereotypes like the dim-witted Sambo and the overly emotional Black buffoon. [6]

The First, the Few and the Only

The Sapphire

Solidified through the hit show Amos n' Andy. A bossy, headstrong matriarch who puts down her husband through verbal taunts and verbal abuse. She takes leadership of her home through a cantankerous nature and fierce independence encapsulated by her hand on the hip, finger waving. A domineering, emasculating Black woman who insults and controls her husband. Modern versions: the "angry Black woman" trope in reality TV, politics, and film. 7

Mammy

Crystallized in the novel and later film, Gone with the Wind. An obese and matronly woman with a masculine temperament, dominating everyone in her own home like a tyrant, but harmless and motherly and even humorous to the white family. Also served as a motherly embrace for the concerns and whims of all members of the white family with wisdom and counsel. Some depictions of the mammy even include the Black woman who breastfed the white children at the expense of her own kids. Hattie McDaniel in Gone with the Wind solidified this caricature, and it was so popular that the Bible is the only book that rivals it in book sales. The movie version is one of the biggest box office successes in American history. We see it revisited in films like Billy Madison starring Adam Sandler ⊘

Aunt Jemima

Evolved from the mammy caricature, before it became Chris Rutt's chosen name for his self-rising pancake mix and subsequent pancake advertising campaign. Aunt Jemima was the image of the Black woman that cooks well and loves to do it for white folks. A great podcast episode on Aunt Jemima is from Still Processing, done by Jenna Wortham and Wesley Morris - New York Times cultural writers. The episode is called "Reparations for Aunt Jemima." ⊘

The First, the Few and the Only

Jezebel

This caricature was a uniquely sexualized one that absolved white men of their lust and subsequent sexual abuse of African American women and girls. Often a mixed Black woman or "mulatto" - derogatory term for someone with one African American parent. A quadroon- a derogatory term for someone with a Black grandparent. An Octoroon- someone with at least one Black great grandparent. So, I believe Ronda Rousey would have been sexualized and marketed as an octoroon back in the day. 8

The Magical Negro

In 2024, there was a film that came out called the American Society of Magical Negros starring David Alan Grier. The premise of the film is built on the use of the very trope named in the title. But what is a magical negro? "The Magical Negro is a supporting stock character with abilities uncommon to the average human who comes to the aid of white protagonists in a film. Magical negro characters, often possessing special insight or mystical powers, have long been a tradition in American fiction. The old-fashioned word "Negro" is used to imply that a "magical Black character" who devotes himself to selflessly helping whites is a throwback to racist stereotypes such as the "Sambo" or "noble savage". A great depiction of this is the movies Green Mile and even The Legend of Bagger Vance starring Will Smith. Another film that captures this caricature is in What Dreams May Come you see another magical negro. What the magical negro reflects, though a caricature, is inspired by a kernel of truth. That truth is…Black bodies must keep white bodies from feeling uncomfortable, especially white women. Even if it's not right, it doesn't matter. I have to keep white people comfortable, or it may cost me coming home to my kids. Ergo, turn on the magical negro, when necessary. 9-16

The First, the Few and the Only

More on the Magical Negro

The Buffoon

"Dynomite!" Popularized in minstrel shows historically and revitalized in what they did to the character JJ in the show Good Times and the reason for which John Amos was fired, sardoodledom was what lived in the imaginations of the all-white writers, but it was nowhere to be found in the communities John Amos came from. Very Sambo/Stepin Fetchit-like. We also see Chris Rock play a version of this in Beverly Hills Ninja starring Chris Farley.

The Token - the only Brown body.

What you see is a satirical depiction of being the Black or Brown friend (side character) to white protagonists. Not central to the plot and peripheral to the white protagonist. There's a scene in Not Another Teen Movie:

 Other media examples of a token character. Feel free to put a check next to the bullets you have seen or remember. Two checks if you actually remember the token non-white character.

- Charlie Brown, (1959, Franklin) Not until 1968 end of civil rights.
- Johnny Quest (1964, Hadji)
- Rugrats (1992, Susie Carmichael) in s2e18
- South Park (literal name is Token and Chef (who they killed off))
- Jimmy Neutron (2002, Libby Folfax)
- Recess (1997, Chad Lasalle and Ashley Spinelli)

The First, the Few and the Only

- Family Guy (1999, Cleveland)
- Fairy Odd parents (AJ)
- Rick a& Morty (2013, buffoonish educator Mr. Goldenfold)
- Simpsons (1989)
- Futurama (1999, Hermes Conrad)
- Justice League (2001, Green Lantern)
- X-Men the Animated Series (Storm)
- Power Rangers (Black Ranger)
- Dumbo (1941, the racist crows)
- Fantasia (1940, racist half-Black, half-nymph)
- The Incredibles (Frozone)
- Bagger Vance (2003)
- Green Mile (1999)
- Lethal Weapon (1980's, Roger Murtaugh)
- Kindergarten Cop (1990, random Black child in class)
- Star Wars (1991, Mace Windu)
- Bring It On (2000, illustration of ppl stealing Black brilliance)
- Ghostbusters (1984, Winston Zeddemore)
- Clueless (1995, Murray Duvall | Stacey Dash)
- Avengers / Marvel Iron Man (2008, James Rhodes)
- Beverly Hills Ninja (Chris Rock's character named Joey)
- Don't get me started on Bollywood

TV Shows
- Matlock (1986, Conrad McMasters | Tyler Hudson)
- Seinfeld (1989, Jackie Chiles, Mr. Morgan, and the 19 other one-off Blacks
- Frasier (1993, good luck finding them)
- The Office (2005, Stanley)
- Stranger Things (2016, Lucas Sinclair)
- The Boys (2019, Reggie Franklin)

Animated TV Shows
- DBZ (1986, Mr. Popo | Piccolo | Uub)
- One Punch Man (2015, SuperAlloy Darkshine)

Laughable films (fake reverse tokenism where white boy is the savior)
- The Last Samurai

The First, the Few and the Only

In the above section, what films or kids TV shows would you add? How many checks did you mark down?

The Sambo

There is another version of Sambo - one that merges Uncle Ruckus from The Boondocks animated series with Samuel L. Jackson's character, Stephen, from Django Unchained. This archetype embodies a Black body not just subservient to the white man but endeared to the boot on his neck - and ever grateful for it. Sambo makes Uncle Tom look like Malcolm X. In fact, I believe this is what Black culture really means when we call another Black or Brown person an "Uncle Tom." As I covered in a previous chapter, it was Uncle Tom who did, indeed, participate in the oppression of other Black people - not solely to gain proximity to whiteness, but to enjoy the secondary benefits and the illusion of power and authority over others. What he may have enjoyed most wasn't the power, but the distance from oppression that his role afforded him. Many don't realize that, by the end of the original two-volume novel, Uncle Tom actually turns on and kills the master, "freeing" the other enslaved people. In contrast, Sambo grieves the death of the master - just as Stephen grieves for Master Candie in Django Unchained. Uncle Ruckus and Stephen are perhaps the most recognizable avatars of this modern Sambo archetype.

The Show Pony

In plays, films, television, and even cartoons, have you ever noticed how Black characters with strong jobs, high positions, or powerful titles are often presented? Sometimes the president in a film or show is Black, Latino, or Asian. Maybe the head of the company is Native American. But when BIPOC bodies are used as "show ponies," they're often surface-level, brown-faced authority figures—placed prominently for optics but lacking agency, depth, control or real narrative impact. These characters are trotted out to make a production appear progressive, while maintaining white-centered storytelling.

In The Help (2011), for example, the film is centered on white saviorism, with Black characters like Aibileen (Viola Davis) and Minny (Octavia Spencer) serving as inspiring props to advance the white protagonist's arc. Their pain is used to make

The First, the Few and the Only

white audiences feel good about "progress," rather than interrogating systemic injustice. In The Princess and the Frog (2009), Disney promoted Tiana as the first Black Disney princess - but she spends most of the film as a frog. This erases her Black regality and avoids real engagement with her identity. Unlike white princesses whose stories center on dreams and discovery, Tiana's narrative focuses on hard work and sacrifice - reinforcing respectability politics.

Scandal (2012–2018) gave us Olivia Pope (Kerry Washington), one of the first Black female leads in a primetime drama. While groundbreaking in visibility, her character often served melodramatic plots over genuine character development. Her power was repeatedly undermined by entanglements with white men, especially President Fitz. Her Blackness, though present, was rarely explored beyond aesthetics.

In Green Book (2018), Dr. Don Shirley (Mahershala Ali) is introduced as a complex historical figure, but the film centers on his white driver's redemption story. Shirley is isolated from the Black community and framed as a "Magical Negro" whose primary function is to educate and redeem the white protagonist. And in Captain Planet and the Planeteers (1990–1996), the Black Planeteer, Kwame, is the wise and serious team member - a token of gravity. But he lacks personal backstory or dimension, making him a one-dimensional symbol of diversity rather than an authentic character.

The problem with Show Pony tokenism in sardoodledom is that these portrayals follow a predictable formula. A Black character is placed in a visible role (check). But their agency, complexity, and cultural identity are often erased. The story consistently centers white character growth and comfort. These Show Ponies exist not to challenge narratives - but to cosmetically signal inclusion while upholding the very structures that exclude us.

Reduced to a token sub-archetype with prominence but no real narrative control—visible but voiceless, powerful in title but powerless in narrative. Unlike the Magical Negro who uplifts white protagonists through mystic wisdom or sacrifice, the Show Pony projects institutional power—but only within the confines of white comfort/control. This trope doesn't just live on screen. It echoes in real boardrooms, classrooms, and campaigns—where Black professionals are elevated for optics but kept away from real decision-making power and occasionally racially

The First, the Few and the Only

patronized. Like a character named Vernon Franklin in Dave Chappelle's skit called when keeping it real goes wrong.

🌱 **Getting Involved**

To put an apple in a full basket you have to take something out of the basket to make room for the apple. This getting involved activity is about naming not only what you just learned, but name what you are unlearning:

_____

_____

_____

_____

_____

_____

The First, the Few and the Only

Chapter 7

I Am Not Your Negro

This chapter title is drawn from-and inspired by Raoul Peck's documentary based on the unfinished manuscript of James Baldwin. Baldwin once warned that the most dangerous creation of any society is the man who has nothing to lose. But even more dangerous, it seems, is the one whose voice refuses to die.

I Am Not Your Negro, Raoul Peck's haunting visual essay, resurrects Baldwin's uncompleted manuscript Remember This House to remind us: erasure is not the same as silence. Even in death, James Baldwin still disrupts the white imagination more effectively than most living critics. It's funny how the ones they try to ghost the hardest—the names left off syllabi, scrubbed from textbooks, sidelined in Hollywood scripts, redacted from North American memory—are often the ones most dangerous to the systems they indict. 🌱

In that same spirit, this chapter is not just critique—it's an invocation. An invitation to see with new eyes. Just as Baldwin set the lives of Medgar Evers, Martin Luther King Jr., and Malcolm X in stark, revelatory contrast, this chapter aims to let films and television shows bang against and reveal one another. To unsettle the myth of "representation" and expose the scaffolding of tokenism beneath the surface.

What follows is an onslaught —yes, an onslaught—of films and television shows (I put an asterisk next to some of my personal favorites) that counter tokenistic media as well something I like to call, sardoodledom bingo cards. Together, they serve as a foil to the machinery of mythmaking that turns representation into spectacle, culture into costume, and good storytelling into bastardized tropes.

Baldwin once said, "The precise role of the artist… is to illuminate the darkness."

So let there be light.

The First, the Few and the Only

Let this chapter become your lens for spotting when media flatters the white imagination and flattens authenticity. Because once you see it, you can't unsee it—and, perhaps, you won't want to. Please, literally, put the book down and check out the laundry list of film & television shows I have curated for you, dear reader, as the next step in the reading experience whether you are neuro-spicy or neuro-basic:

The password for Chapter 7 is "GetOnCode"

There are so many yet unidentified genres from Afro-Arab sci-fi, Indigenous Asian fantasy to even queer Black Muslim stories that are anti-sardoodledom/non-tokenistic. We barely even touched anime! There are so many more stories out there that do not use sardoodledom to tell beautiful and powerful stories that make great television and fabulous cinematic experiences. I know I felt a big difference between Black Panther by Ryan Coogler and Captain America: Brave New World. Consider doing a movie night with friends or, for you wealthy readers out there, rent out a theater and team up with local high school and college groups to showcase a film above. *Side note*: if anyone wants to hire me to come speak on just anime anti-sardoodledom, PLEASE CALL ME! It's a yes immediately. I'll even give a discount because I love this shit so much!

The thing is that there are many counters and anti-sardoodledom out there, a few of which I have listed above. Blacks didn't take this disrespect lying down. I have always said that the imagination is the back door to the heart. So many Black people saw the truth and found a way to attack the fantasy of sardoodledom. Fantasies are what people want, but reality is what people need, as Lauryn Hill said. Shows were created that depicted more of the realities of the complexity of the Black community, like Boondocks and other shows like it. You just have to de-program yourself and watch some of these. Try to notice the shifts and contrasts you see compared to what you are used to. We all gotta do a sardoodledom detox, am I right?

This is why I believe colorism in childhood entertainment - the way we learn to associate darkness with danger - plays a role in how we, as adults, accept and normalize the presence of Black and Brown bodies. This is also why I believe

The First, the Few and the Only

tokenism in childhood shows - normalizing the few or the only Brown body in the friend group - influences what feels socially normative in the real world. Tokenism is not a mistake. Colorism ain't no mistake. They ain't accidents. They're by design.

Token Brown bodies in white professional and social circles didn't start showing up in the media until after desegregation. By all accounts, their purpose was not to challenge the racial status quo but to protect it. The logic was simple: give the audience one person of color, just enough to quiet any complaints, but not enough to disrupt the power structure or induce fear.

A Black best friend.
A wise Latina sidekick.
An Asian or Indigenous elder, full of mystical advice.

One or two at a time. Never more. Spaces can be too Afro-Latino, too Black, too Asian, too Indigenous, but they can never, ever, ever be too white. If there are too many of any race walking in the neighborhood, then Karen calls the cops. Just as we learned as children that darkness was something to be feared, we grew up learning that a little bit of Blackness, a little bit of Brownness, was all that could be tolerated. Too much, and the whole neighborhood might come crumbling down.

> "People who cling to their delusions find it difficult, if not impossible, to learn anything worth learning: a people under the necessity of creating themselves must examine everything and soak up learning the way the roots of a tree soak up water."
> -James Baldwin in No Name in the Street, 1972

🌱 Getting Involved

I know, that was a lot. Upon reading the password protected Getting Involved section on website, you literally just survived the wild ride of a neurodivergent's hyperfocus rabbit hole. You made it to the other side, and you should be proud of yourself. For me, it felt like a theme park ride, writing this section. For you, it may have felt like an old wooden roller coaster they should have decommissioned years ago. Let's check in with our bodies really quick. What's coming up for you? What would you have added to this unabridged list? What would you have taken out??

The First, the Few and the Only

From Onscreen to Offscreen

I was catching up with an old friend - one of the best to ever do it in that white organization we both know too well. The laughter came easy, like it always does when you've walked through the same fire and lived to talk about it. Then, as it often does, the talk turned, shifted like a storm rolling in, from jokes to the heaviness of things. The terror of another round of that orangish man clawing his way back into executive power, the way poor whites and starry-eyed Brown folks keep getting swindled by the same old con. And, of course, the wear and tear of moving through white spaces, or rather, that space - one we both had given too much to, one that had taken more than it ever cared to return.

Then he said it: the thing folks like us always hear but never quite learn to discard until we are burned out or old. "Maybe they'll wake up this time. Maybe white folks will finally see this country for what it is."

I shook my head. "What good is hope when it's continually drowned in the deep waters of our grief?" He frowned and asked me to explain, so I pressed on. "How many BIPOC lifetimes have been spent trying to teach them? How many BIPOC bodies have bent themselves into educators, bridge-builders, door-openers, only for white folks to press some invisible reset button the moment a new administration waltzes in? All that history, all that labor, all that sweat and breaking and breathing and pleading, wiped clean like chalk on a board, as if we never walked through the fire to begin with. And yet we keep waiting, holding our breath, watching them stumble over lessons they have already learned generations ago. Why do we keep believing that the next time will be different, that they'll finally get it, when even the best among them, like the Joanna Trumpauer Mulholland's and Jane Elliott's of the world, get dismissed along with us? How much longer until we decide to tend to our grief rather than exhaust our glory and brilliance on their selective ignorance and selective memory?"

Then he confessed something that caught me off guard. He said, "I pray those Black and Brown folk can forgive me for when I was spending most of my energy comforting whites rather than doing more for us."

Before me was someone whose work paved the way for me to do what I spent years doing, cross cultural impact work eventually from coast to coast for several years. How could this legend whose ghost still remained on the lips of executives

The First, the Few and the Only

and influential leaders in the organization almost two decades after his time in the organization say something like that? He helped fundraise the first minority fund for staff of color in ministry.

We continued the conversation since we ended up talking about an opportunity, but after some more laughs and camaraderie, I had to go pick up my kid from school across town. I couldn't help but walk away wondering, "What would make him say that?"

⏱ Side Quest

A Sardoodledom Bingo Card would be a powerful, accessible way for readers to assess whether a film truly centers Black and Brown voices - or falls into the same tired, harmful patterns, ensuring we capture the full range of ways Hollywood de-centers Black and Brown voices while pretending to center them.

Here's a five-by-five Bingo Card concept, where each square represents a common trope or red flag in films that claim to be about Black and Brown stories, but ultimately de-center them:

How to Use It:

1. Watch the film and mark each trope you see.

2. If you get a Bingo (five in a row, column, or diagonal), the film is sardoodledom.

3. If the whole card fills up, Hollywood is still Hollywood-ing. Shut it off. Burn the hard copy (Just kidding?)

> *"Everyone and their mother is looking for an answer,*
> *but only people with real courage have the*
> *courage to ask big, fat questions."*
>
> Christopher Rivas, Playwright, Actor
> The Real James Bond… Was Dominican

The First, the Few and the Only

1. Sardoodledom Litmus Test: The Classic Tropes Edition
"Does this film rely on outdated but persistent racist archetypes?"

🍯 Aunt Jemima Comforts Everyone	👩‍🍼 Mammy Protects White Character	🦊 Jezebel = Oversexualized & Used	🤡 Stepin Fetchit Buffoonery	🎭 Neo-Blackface "Hip" Friend
🗡 "Savage" = No Culture, Just Violence	🐶 Loyal Sidekick, No Depth	🏆 Only There to Make White People Look Good	⚰ Dies First, No Backstory	🙂 The Sambo: Childlike & Happy to Serve
👩🏽 The Sapphire: Angry & Unloveable	🚫 Never a Love Interest	👊🏿 Black = Struggle, Never Joy	🎵 Gospel Scene for "Soul" but No Agency	😬 White Lead "Fixes" the BIPOC Character
🎭 Caricature Over Character	✨ Magical Negro Serves the White Protagonist	🚓 "The Good Cop" Narrative Ignores Reality	💼 Black Excellence = Proximity to Whiteness	🧑🏿 "You Speak So Well"
👀 Centering White Guilt	🍽 Food, Dancing, & Entertainment But No Agency	🙃 The Show Pony: Diversity Without Depth	🏚 Hood Story, No Future	🎻 Suffering as the Only

Example: Gone With the Wind

Why do you think GONE WITH THE WIND is a prime example? Use the space below to respond:

The First, the Few and the Only

2. Sardoodledom Litmus Test: The "Progressive" Film Edition

"It claims to be 'woke,' but does it actually center BIPOC experiences?"

🏆 White Savior, But in a Liberal Way	🎤 BIPOC Pain = White Protagonist's Growth	📖 "Inspired by True Events" (But Whitewashed)	🍑 Trauma, No Joy	🎬 Black Excellence as the Exception
👦 Token BIPOC, No Arc	🪦 First to Die, No Depth	🕵 Mysterious Black Friend with No Past	📚 White Person Teaches BIPOC About Their Own Culture	✏ Magical Negro Saves the Day
😱 Black/Brown Death = Plot Device	👩 The Sapphire: No Softness, Just Rage	🍑 The Jezebel: Over-sexualized, No Character	🐬 Pick-Me Negro: "I Don't See Race!"	🟠 Neo-Blackface: Black Culture, White Face
🎭 A-list White Actor in a BIPOC Role	🎶 Gospel Choir, But No Actual BIPOC Arc	🚫 No Dark-Skinned Leads	🏡 Suburb = Safety, City = Danger	😢 Ends on White Redemption
🐴 The Showpony: Here for Flavor, Not Depth	🚓 Copaganda Disguised as Inclusion	🏅 White Allies Get the Last Word	🔄 Black or Brown Mentor Exists to Uplift White Lead	🎻 Emotional Scene That Fixes Nothing

🏆 Example: Hidden Figures (2016 Taraji slayed in this film. Love you, Taraji!)
- Softens racism to make white audiences comfortable (NASA's racism is framed as a few "bad apples," not systemic.)
- White savior moment added (Kevin Costner's character knocking down the "Colored" bathroom sign never happened in real life.)
- Centers white acceptance rather than Black resistance (The Black women's struggles are framed through the lens of how white colleagues perceive'm)
- Overly sanitized story (The real Mary Jackson, Dorothy Vaughan, and Katherine Johnson faced much harsher discrimination)

The First, the Few and the Only

3. **Sardoodledom Litmus Test: The Blockbuster Edition**
"Big budget, but do BIPOC characters actually get a story?"

🎬 White Hero in a "BIPOC" Story	☠️ The Dead Mentor Trope	🪄 Magic, But Only to Serve Others	🔥 The Savage Trope (Again?!)	🌍 "Exotic" Culture = Backdrop
🎩 Wise, Ancient, Mysterious BIPOC	📕 First to Die, Again	🙋 Token With No Arc	🟠 All BIPOC Are Villains	🏚️ Poverty or Struggle Narrative
🏆 White Savior Arc	🙄 "But I'm One of the Good Ones"	🐎 Showpony for Diversity Points	🎶 Dance & Sing, But No Character	🚫 No Dark-Skinned BIPOC in Lead
🏴 Culture as Costume	💼 Black & Brown = Criminal or Noble Savage	🚓 Cops Are Always the Heroes	🔄 History Gets "Adjusted"	😬 "Colorblind" Casting That Still Centers Whiteness
🙃 Sidekick With No Love Life	🧑‍🍳 Always the Caretaker	🎷 Uses Racism as a Plot Device, No Resolution	📚 Ancient BIPOC Knowledge, White Hero Uses It Better	🎤 Teaches the yt character a lesson, then leaves

Diversity is here… but only as long as it doesn't disrupt the status quo.

🏆 Example: Captain America: Brave New World (2025)

- Diversity, but BIPOC protagonist spends his time cleaning President Thunderbolt Ross' mistakes and caring for the white character's needs. (Sam Wilson is Captain America, but did the film truly grapple with systemic issues, or just gesture at them?).
- BIPOC lead, but still playing by the rules of a white-dominated system (Will Sam's leadership be questioned in ways Steve Rogers' never was?)
- Superhero stories that avoid political and social commentary (obedience over innovation).
- Villains as vague stand-ins, not real threats (Will the film address white supremacy indirectly/directly, or use a generic, non-racialized antagonist?)
- Black hero must prove himself worthy, while white hero assumed to be (Steve Rogers never had to justify his right to be Cap once he liberated that

The First, the Few and the Only

POW camp, but Isaiah Bradley was tortured for it and Sam Wilson is forever proving his merit despite it.).
- Green Mile, Marvel edition.
  - Mad love to Anthony Mackie, though. Not his fault.

🌱 Getting Involved

- Watch the film and mark each trope you see.

- Bingo = Sardoodledom confirmed!

- If the whole card fills up… Hollywood still has work to do. Pull out your social media, use the hashtags, and make your voice heard: #Sardoodledom #TheFirstTheFewandTheOnly

These Bingo cards don't just call out bad representation - they help you develop a sharper eye for media analysis and empower yourself as a consumer to demand better stories.

The First, the Few and the Only

4. **Sardoodledom Litmus Test: The "Feel-Good" Racism Edition**

"This film makes white audiences feel good about racism…without actually challenging it."

🏆 White Savior Wins the Day	👯 Token Best Friend, No Story	🫂 Black/Brown Character Forgives Racist Person	🧕 Mammy or Caretaker Role	🎩 Magical Negro Offers Wisdom
🚔 "Not All Cops" Narrative	📖 Inspired by a True Story (But Whitewashed)	🎻 Swelling Music = Fake Resolution	💰 Poverty = Virtue	🏦 BIPOC Success = Proximity to Whiteness
🪃 Black/Brown Character's Purpose Is to Help White Lead	🎤 Gospel Choir, But No Black Arc	😢 Racist Character Learns Their Lesson	⚰️ Black/Brown Character Dies for the Plot	🔴 Black Woman = Angry & Unloveable
🎶 Singing/Dancing BIPOC but No Depth	🍦 Historical Inaccuracy for White Comfort	🔄 Racist Person Redeemed by Film's End	🏡 Suburbs = Good, City = Bad	🏆 White Ally Gets the Last Word
👀 Story About Racism, but Told from White Perspective	🙂 The "One Good One" Trope	😢 White Tears Centered Over BIPOC Pain	🚫 No Black Love Interest	🔥 Black Struggle as Entertainment

Example: The Help (2011)
- BIPOC characters exist to educate and forgive white people (Magical Negro, Mammy Trope).
- White savior narrative (Skeeter's book "solves" racism.)
- Swelling emotional score = fake resolution (Racism still exists, but film pretends it's solved.)

The First, the Few and the Only

5. Sardoodledom Litmus Test: The "Diversity, But Make It Decorative" Edition"

"Diversity" exists here, but only in the most superficial, unchallenging way.

🐴 The Show Pony: Just There for Flavor	👨🏾 The Token, No Depth	👨🏾 One Black Character in a White World	🚫 No Black Love Interests	🎵 Random Hip-Hop Track to Seem "Cool"
🌍 Exotic Setting, White Hero	🪦 First to Die (Again)	🎤 Soulful Performance, No Arc	🏆 White Ally = Secret Hero	😷 Culture Used as Costume
🎩 The Wise, Magical Mentor	🚓 Copaganda Disguised as Progress	🗡 Helps White Character, No Own Goals	🍑 The Jezebel = Oversexualized & Objectified	🟠 The Sapphire = Angry, Unlovable
📚 BIPOC Teaches White Lead Their Own History	🏚 Hood Story, No Future	🎻 Suffering but No Systemic Change	🙂 Pick-Me Negro: "I Don't See Race!"	🧎 Always the Servant or Caretaker
🚫 No Dark-Skinned Leads	💼 Black Character's Success = Whiteness	🎵 Music/Dance but No Character Depth	🙂 Never Allowed Complexity	🏙 The City = Crime,

🐴 Example: The Greatest Showman (2017)
- Tokenism (Zendaya's character has no depth beyond her interracial romance.)
- "Exotic" setting, but white lead (Hugh Jackman as P.T. Barnum.)
- Culture as decoration (Black and Brown characters only exist to support the white protagonist's dreams.)

The First, the Few and the Only

6. Sardoodledom Litmus Test: The "Historical but Make It Fictional" Edition

"Based on a true story," except the truth got left behind.

📖 Inspired by History (But Whitewashed)	📕 BIPOC Story, White Lead	🪓 "We Fixed Racism in 2 Hours"	🔄 BIPOC Erased from Their Own Story	🏆 White Savior Solves Everything
👨🏽 The "One Good" White Person	🚓 Cops Always the Heroes	😇 Suffering = Main Plot Point	👻 BIPOC Character Only Exists to Educate White Lead	🪄 Wise Magical Negro
🎶 Singing, Dancing, but No Narrative	🍑 Jezebel: Oversexualized & Dehumanized	🏚️ Poor but Noble	🙂 Pick-Me Negro: "I Don't See Race!"	🏙️ City = Crime, Suburbs = Safe
📗 White Character Learns, BIPOC Character Suffers	😬 History Altered for White Comfort	🟤 Black Woman = Angry & Bitter	🚫 No Black Love Interest	🎶 Emotional Choir Scene Fixes Nothing
🔥 The Savage Trope (Still?!)	🚓 Copaganda Disguised as "Justice"	👯 Tokenized for Diversity Points	🎩 Only Exists to Serve the White Lead	🏆 White Ally Gets the Last Word

📖 Example: Green Book (2018)
- White savior narrative (the real Dr. Don Shirley's family rejected the film's depiction.)
- BIPOC story, white lead (the movie centers on the white driver.)
- Erases systemic racism (makes racism a "bad apple" problem rather than a system.)

The First, the Few and the Only

7. Sardoodledom Litmus Test: The "Why Is This Still Happening?" Edition

"When we don't use our voice, they will harm you and say you enjoyed it" –
Anonymous

🏆 White Savior Wins	🐶 Suffering = Depth	🎤 Sings, Dances, No Story	📕 Dies First	📖 Based on History (But Changed)
🏮 Caretaker, Not Character	🎵 Gospel Scene, No Arc	🏠 Black = Struggle, No Joy	👩🏾 The Sapphire	🍑 The Jezebel
🎩 The Wise, Magical Negro	🏆 White Character "Fixes" Racism	🚓 Copaganda in a "Serious" Film	🎻 Emotional Scene, No Change	🔄 "Colorblind" Casting but Still Centers Whiteness
🏙️ City = Bad, Suburbs = Good	😊 The Show Pony for Diversity Points	🖊️ Helps White Lead, No Own Story	🤡 Buffoon or Sidekick	💼 Black Success = Proximity to Whiteness
📚 Educated BIPOC = "Acting White"	😬 Centering White Feelings Over Systemic Issues	🚫 No Dark-Skinned Leads	🛑 Black Woman = Angry, No Softness	🐶 Comedy Sidekick, No Arc

📖 Example: The Blind Side (2009)

- White savior narrative (Sandra Bullock's character "rescues" Michael Oher.)
- Black character exists to be helped (Michael's personal voice is nearly erased.)
- Poverty as virtue (Michael's success is tied to his adoption by white people.)

The First, the Few and the Only

8. 🎥 Race-Washing & Whitewashing Bingo
Did they rewrite history to make it whiter, softer, or more digestible?

❄️ BIPOC Character Replaced by White Actor	🎩 The "Race-Bent" White Savior	📖 Inspired by History (But Whitewashed)	🚫 No Dark-Skinned Leads	🏆 White Character Becomes the Hero
👀 BIPOC Character Reduced to Sidekick	🌍 "Exotic" Culture, White Lead	😬 BIPOC Character's Struggle = White Character's Growth	🔄 Real History Changed to De-Center Race	🎻 Emotional Scene Solves Racism
🧣 Culture as Costume, Not Character	🚓 Copaganda Disguised as Justice	🏠 Black/Brown = Struggle, White = Joy	🎶 Gospel Choir, No BIPOC Arc	🔥 BIPOC Suffering as Main Plot Point
🏹 "Savage" = No Depth, Just Violence	✨ Magical Negro Serves White Lead	🙇 Token BIPOC, No Love Interest	📕 BIPOC Character Dies to Motivate White Hero	💼 Success = Proximity to Whiteness
📚 White Character "Teaches" BIPOC Their Own Culture	🏙️ City = Crime, Suburbs = Safe	🍑 The Jezebel: Sexualized, No Character	😐 Show Pony for Diversity Points	🏆 White Ally Gets the Last Word

❄️ Example: Gods of Egypt (2016)
- BIPOC historical figures played by white actors (Gerard Butler, Nikolaj Coster-Waldau)
- Exotic culture, white lead (turning Ancient Egypt into a white fantasy)
- No dark-skinned leads (Egyptians were portrayed as white, despite historical inaccuracy.).

The First, the Few and the Only

9. 🎭 Culture as Costume and Buffoonery Bingo

"When Hollywood turns BIPOC culture into a joke or an aesthetic for a white protagonist."

🏇 White Lead Excels in BIPOC Culture	🎭 Culture = Comedy, Not Complexity	🏆 White Character Becomes the Hero	🔄 BIPOC Sidekick is More Competent	🤡 Buffoon White Lead in Non-White Culture
🎩 Ancient Tradition Reduced to Gags	📒 BIPOC Mentor, No Personal Story	🏯 Asian Setting, No Asian Lead	🎵 Orientalist Soundtrack	📖 Inspired by Culture, But Whitewashed
😬 Stereotypical Wise Old Mentor	🔮 "Mystical" Asian Wisdom for Laughs	🎤 White Character Imitates Accent	🗡 BIPOC Serves White Lead's Journey	💼 BIPOC Success = Teaching White Lead
👀 BIPOC Characters Have No Depth	🤸 Fighting Styles Reduced to Gimmicks	🎵 "Kung Fu Sound Effects" for Comedy	🚫 No Respect for Cultural Accuracy	🏆 White Hero Saves the Day… Again

🏆 Example: Beverly Hills Ninja (1997)

- Chris Farley's character is a walking buffoon in a sacred cultural space (trivialization of martial arts and Asian traditions).
- Asian characters are competent, but exist only to support the clueless white lead.
- Orientalism used for comedy (over-the-top, stereotypical depictions of ninjas, mysticism, and Japan)
- White protagonist is framed as a "chosen one" in a tradition he doesn't come from or honor with serious effort. Look, it's a comedy, one I enjoy to a degree, but two things can be true at the same time.

The First, the Few and the Only

10. 🎭 Culture as Costume and White Savior Bingo

"When Hollywood turns BIPOC cultures into a backdrop for white protagonists to 'discover themselves.'"

🐎 White Lead Excels in BIPOC Culture	🎭 Culture = Aesthetic, Not Complexity	🏆 White Character Becomes the Hero	🔄 BIPOC Sidekick is More Competent	🤡 White Outsider Masters Tradition
🎩 Ancient Tradition Reduced to Gags	📖 BIPOC Mentor, No Personal Story	🏯 Non-Western Setting, White Lead	🎶 Orientalist Soundtrack	📖 "Inspired by Culture," But Whitewashed
😌 Wise Old Mentor Dies for White Lead	🔮 "Mystical" Eastern Wisdom Fixes White Lead's Soul	🗡 White Character Gains Instant Mastery	🗡 BIPOC Serves White Lead's Journey	💼 BIPOC Success = Teaching White Lead
👀 BIPOC Characters Have No Depth	🏹 Fighting Styles Reduced to Exoticism	🎶 "Kung Fu/Flute Sound Effects" for Drama	🚫 No Respect for Cultural Accuracy	🏆 White Hero Becomes the Best at Local Tradition

🏆 Example: The Last Samurai (2003)
- Tom Cruise's character is a broken Civil War vet who "rediscovers himself" through samurai culture (white man finding purpose in an "exotic" land trope).
- He becomes a master of samurai combat in an unrealistic time frame, surpassing lifelong ethnic practitioners.
- Katsumoto (Ken Watanabe) exists to mentor and sacrifice himself for Cruise's journey.
- Samurai history and rebellion reframed through the lens of a white savior.
- Western guilt aestheticized, but no systemic critique of imperialism.

Which bingo card is your favorite?

_____

The First, the Few and the Only

Chapter 8

White Imagination

James Baldwin wrote,
*"The most dangerous place to be Black
in America is in white's imagination"*

I wish sardoodledom in the media only stayed on screen, but unfortunately it lives off screen too. The white imagination, especially in the U.S., is already coded in a racial binary that leaves BIPOC bodies falling, usually, in one of two categories inspired by their steady diets of sardoodledom. The white imagination doesn't see BIPOC people as people—it searches for bodies to fulfill roles sardoodledom taught them to imagine. Roles that must serve the script & confirm the biases or die trying. Here's how the racial imagination tends to cast us:

Black man in the office or in network:
pet or threat

Black man out of network:
violent brute or sexual brute

Black woman in network:
mammy (wet nurse) or Jezebel

Black woman out of network:
welfare queen or stripper instructor

Asian man in network:
Model minority/sage intellectual prop or sexually inferior token/emasculated sidekick

The First, the Few and the Only

Asian man out of network:
Smarty pants/kung fu novice/master or the smiling jester

Asian woman in network:
model minority or exoticized secretary/geisha-lite

Asian woman out of network:
nail salon worker or trafficked sex object / perpetual foreigner

Latin man in network:
passionate lover or sultry ornament

Latin man out of network:
legal Mexican or illegal Mexican

Latin woman in network:
warm/sexual vixen or spicy attitude/dumb

Latin woman out of network:
exotic/ sexual tourism for sale or cleaning staff/nanny/cook

Indigenous Men:
Invisible or Caricatures

Indigenous Women:
Invisible or Exotic Sex Objects

Pause. Full stop.
🌱 How's your breathing? What stories just came up for you?

_____

_____

111
You're not alone

The First, the Few and the Only

White Women with Power

"Emmitt Till got killed for less."
-Dr. Mychael Lee

I grew up with white women as my Sunday school teachers and my elementary school educators. They called me cute then. Adorable, even. When I was in high school in Neshannock, I felt watched whenever the white girls were nearby. Their white mothers called me handsome, but the white boys felt threatened. When I went to college, since all tokens are soulmates, white women always found the perfect person for me to date as cupid's helpers, it was always the only other Black female. When I went to the workplace, I felt like the pet or the threat.

This made me feel confused. I didn't know if I was the problem, but then I watched Severance. White women with power in the workplace feel like Helly Eagan and Ms. Cobel from that show, all wrapped into one. Especially the progressive ones. Not all, but these are just real-life experiences of how some white women have alienated me and other Black/Brown male bodies at work, regardless of malicious intent or lack thereof. It's as if they are constantly oscillating between the warmth of a hug and the cold steel of a blade hidden beneath their smiles. And if my time in the workplace has taught me anything - even in ministry - it's that Black and Brown men are always teetering between being a pet and a threat.

I remember when I had just started at a new company. I was on crutches, recovering from an injury, and I'd barely been there a week. I'd already stirred the waters by being too honest about the company's self-assessment on DEI initiatives. In a meeting with a room full of executives, there was a lot of back-patting about their diversity efforts, and I, perhaps too candidly, asked, "Then how come all your department heads are still white?"

The room went silent, the kind of silence that tells you the truth just hit a little too close to home.

Not long after, I was invited to a one-on-one meeting with the president of the company. I hobbled my way to his office, my walker in tow, and was greeted by his executive assistant - a white woman. I smiled and said hello, trying to keep things light as we were just coming out of COVID. I jokingly asked, "Are you an air high-fiver, a hugger, or a hand-shaker?"

The First, the Few and the Only

Her face lit up. "I LOVE HUGS," she said, and before I knew it, she was around my walker, arms wrapped tightly around me. It was a solid five-to-seven seconds of full-body contact. She stepped back, thanked me, and commented on my hug skills.

I went into the meeting, where a white man with all the power on the property spent half an hour telling me how powerless he was to change anything around diversity. It was another episode of self-victimization in leadership. When I got back to my office, I found an email waiting for me from the executive assistant. She told me how much she enjoyed our hug, using enough emojis to fill a middle schooler's diary.
I responded with something equally light, "If you need a hug, let me know," adding a smiley face. A week later, HR called me. I was being accused of sexual harassment.

My supervisor, a Black woman with a military background, came into my office. She didn't beat around the bush. "I don't think you did anything wrong," she said, "but don't hug these white women anymore. Or anyone, for that matter. You're a handsome Brown man - don't give them a reason to get rid of you."

It was both advice and a warning. Because as much as I had felt like a welcomed presence - a pet - I was now a threat.

At another job, I was leading a training around equity. It was a raw, necessary conversation, similar to what you'll find in the appendix entitled White Eyes Only later in this book. One of the white women, a director, ended up in tears. After the training in the next room, around other white colleagues, people were acknowledging the complex bind of being white and progressive - the dual reality of being both victims of harm and perpetrators of it. There was talk about not weaponizing their tears, not making it about them. This director, who had been raising kids for twenty years before coming back to the workforce, opened up about how she'd never been challenged like this before. She'd never had DEI training until then. She was visibly shaken, just beginning to share her vulnerability when the president called her into another meeting. She had to wipe her tears and put her professional mask back on.

That evening, I thought about how everyone else had space to share except her. I sent her a text: "Just wanted to check on you, was a heavy conversation today

The First, the Few and the Only

before your meeting. You doing okay?" It was common practice at this company - leaders texted staff in the evenings all the time.

A week later, I received an email with a screenshot of my text. She had filed a formal complaint, claiming I was targeting her because of her race as a white woman. She said my text was inappropriate and biased, that I had crossed a line. I went straight to HR and the president, laying all my cards on the table. An investigation followed, and it turned out she had sent similar late-night texts to other white colleagues. The only difference was that I'm a Brown man.

The company eventually ruled in my favor, acknowledging that this was not a policy violation, but a "cultural fit" issue - for her, not me. By then, the damage was done. Once again, I had been thrust from pet to threat, my good intentions weaponized against me.

This is where the comparison to Severance becomes crystal clear. Mrs. Cobel is the master of manipulation, the smiling face of corporate control. She embodies the white women in the workplace who present themselves as allies but wield their power in ways that can be deeply harmful to Black and Brown bodies. On the other hand, Helly is the quintessential embodiment of white women in North America. Historically, white women have been victimized by structures out of their control, until we zoom out and realize [SPOILER ALERT… skip the next four paragraphs if you want to save the surprise] that Helly is in more control than we were led to believe.

Helly Eagan's dual character in Severance - as both the corporate executive Helena Eagan and her "innie" Helly, trapped in the company's dystopian control - serves as a chilling metaphor for the duality of white womanhood, particularly in the ways white women can wield both victimhood and power to the detriment of BIPOC individuals.

Helena, in her "outie" life, is a privileged, powerful woman who voluntarily subjects herself to the severance procedure, fully aware of the suffering it will cause her "innie." She does so in service of maintaining the oppressive structure of Lumon, much like how white women historically have upheld and benefited from white supremacy while feigning innocence. Meanwhile, her "innie" Helly experiences the oppression firsthand, constantly fighting against a system that her "outie" self has willingly reinforced. This mirrors how white women can play both victim and

The First, the Few and the Only

oppressor – participating in inherited systems of harm while also positioning themselves as the ones in distress when held accountable.

Historically, white women have been some of the most dangerous figures for BIPOC communities, not necessarily because they wield direct power, but because they influence and enforce the systems that do. From the false accusations that led to the lynching of Black men like Emmett Till to the ways white women's tears can result in workplace retaliation against BIPOC colleagues, the duality of white womanhood - both oppressed under patriarchy and complicit in white supremacy - remains a significant and often deadly contradiction.

Helly's character exposes the reality that complicity and power are not always loud or obvious; they often exist in the quiet spaces of passive reinforcement, selective ignorance, and the ability to turn suffering into a personal, rather than collective, concern.

When I think back on these experiences, I realize they weren't just isolated incidents - they were patterns. For Black and Brown men, the workplace is rarely a neutral space. It is a stage where you must play your role carefully, where any misstep can mean the difference between being seen as a harmless pet or a dangerous threat. Too often, the shift happens not because of what you did, but because of how "you made" someone else feel. Black/Brown brilliance, ambition, and joy becomes a trigger, and the fallout of white fragility is all too real.

The Pet or Threat Binary

The delicate, often dangerous dance between being a pet or a threat in the workplace, especially when it comes to interactions with white women in power, isn't merely a reflection of personal experience. It is a part of a deeper, more complex historical narrative that speaks to the ways in which power, race, and gender intersect to shape Black and Brown men's roles in predominantly white spaces. As much as these women may present themselves as allies, they are too often complicit in the racial harm that permeates these environments, even without fully realizing it.

White women's dual role in this binary isn't accidental. Historically, white women have been positioned as both the damsels in distress and the gatekeepers of white supremacy, often straddling these two identities to serve their own interests, even when it perpetuates harm against Black men. Contrary to the notion that white

The First, the Few and the Only

women were passive participants, recent scholarship has highlighted their active involvement in slaveholding. For instance, historian Stephanie Jones-Rogers, in her book, They Were Her Property: White Women as Slave Owners in the American South 1, argues that white women were deeply complicit in slavery, both economically and socially. She presents evidence showing that these women not only owned enslaved people but also exercised significant control over them, challenging the traditional narrative that portrays them merely as victims of male-dominated systems.

The Casual Killing Act of 1669 2, passed in Virginia, served as a chilling legal framework that allowed for the casual killing of enslaved people by their owners without consequence. The law explicitly stated that if an enslaved person was injured or killed during punishment, their master would not be held accountable. This dehumanizing provision, which further reduced Black bodies to mere property, effectively absolved white slave owners from responsibility for violence and cruelty. Within this context of brutal laws, the role of white women - often portrayed as passive participants in the institution of slavery - was far more active and sinister than commonly believed. White women were not only complicit in the cruelty of enslavement but also engaged in extreme acts of violence, including infanticide. 🌱

According to an article by Tonia Crowe, "Under this law, white women were granted the right to kill mixed-race children born to enslaved women, especially if the children threatened the perceived purity of the white family's bloodline. 3" This cruel act of infanticide was a means of preserving the social and racial order that devalued Black lives. While history often obscures the brutality of white women's roles in the perpetuation of slavery, their actions - whether through direct violence or in maintaining the systems that allowed such horrors to occur - played an integral role in the dehumanization and destruction of Black and mixed bodies.

3. If you do not have a smart phone and want to know more about this, you can go to a desktop computer and do an internet search of the following two women: "Madame Delphine Lalaurie", and then "The White Witch of Rose Hall" 🧭

This historical context is crucial in understanding the dynamics of race and power that persist today. The legal frameworks established in the seventeenth century,

The First, the Few and the Only

coupled with the active participation of white women in slavery, their abandonment of Black and Brown women in order to gain voting rights through white feminism in 1919-1920, becoming the biggest beneficiaries of welfare as well as the most hired in DEI positions throughout the U.S. As Haley Lickstein [4], a political consultant and advocate for youth political engagement, said, "I think white women oftentimes don't recognize how much DEI initiatives have impacted their ability to rise in leadership levels and have a more equitable playing field. According to the job search site Zippia [5], 76% of chief diversity officer roles are held by White people, and 54% are held by women."

All of this has left a lasting impact on societal structures and perceptions. Recognizing this history allows for a more nuanced understanding of contemporary issues related to race, gender, and power, particularly in environments like the workplace where these historical legacies continue to influence interactions and perceptions.

White women, historically cast as fragile and in need of protection from Black men, perpetuate this complex harm today, knowingly or unknowingly. This notion of "protection" has long been linked to the cinematic myth of the "imaginative cruelty" of only white male slave owners. White women were often seen as needing to be shielded from the perceived/projected violence of Black men, a narrative that distorted the true nature of the relationships between white women and enslaved Black men, while being perpetrators of cruel harm and sexual predation. It was this invisible culture of brutality of slavery, upheld by law, and later perpetuated through societal norms, that continues to affect Black bodies in contemporary spaces, including the workplace.

These historical contexts are not simply relics of the past; they have bled into the present-day interactions between Black and Brown men and white women in positions of power. When I speak of being both a pet and a threat, it is not just a personal reflection - it is a direct extension of this legacy. In the workplace, Black and Brown men are still expected to perform according to an unwritten script: we are either objects of affection or sources of fear, but never fully human. This dynamic has roots in the institutionalized racism that has long been embedded within the systems and bodies that govern our lives.

When I reflect on the executive assistant who hugged me, her immediate response was a manifestation of white fragility - where the emotional discomfort of a white

The First, the Few and the Only

woman was given more weight than the experience of a Black man. Her behavior, under the guise of warmth, reinforced the narrative that Black men are always in the service of white emotional needs, whether as a source of comfort or as a way to safeguard our jobs as much as our very lives. The accusation of sexual harassment wasn't merely a misunderstanding; it was an indictment of the larger system that sees Black men as either objects to be consumed or as threats to be neutralized.

Similarly, in the case with the director who filed a complaint after I texted her, we see the way in which white women's tears, their vulnerability, and their perceived fragility are weaponized in the workplace. This dynamic is not just about individual harm; it is about a system that has, for centuries, granted white women the right to allegations of victimhood while simultaneously denying Black men their humanity. Even in moments where white women might appear to acknowledge their role in racial harm - as I saw in the tears of the director - they are often quickly brought back into the fold of whiteness by the larger structures of power that center their emotional well-being over the lived experiences of Black men.

The very existence of this binary - the pet or the threat - speaks to a broader systemic issue in which Black and Brown men are forced to navigate the treacherous terrain of white fragility, fascination, and white self-victimhood. White women in power may claim to be allies, but their actions, whether consciously or unconsciously, often uphold systems of racial inequality🌱 . This complicity is not always overt; it can be subtle, embedded in the way they react to discomfort, the way they view their own roles in perpetuating harm, their demand to be called allies matched only by their absence when need arises as well as the way they align themselves with those who hold the institutional power in these spaces. Whether the workspace is for profit, or non-profit, local & small or fortune 500, religious and non-parochial.

As much as the workplace might appear neutral or progressive, it is still a stage where racial hierarchies play out, where the dynamics of power continue to shape the way Black men are seen and treated. And as long as the patterns of racial harm, historically rooted in laws like the Killing Act of 1669, continue to echo through modern-day interactions, Black and Brown men will always face the danger of being both the pet and the threat - never fully free to exist outside the bounds of these harmful and false binaries.

The First, the Few and the Only

Deb's Story: A Black Woman's Experience

Deb's story is one of navigating the unspoken rules of whiteness in the workplace - the silent, suffocating pressures of being the only Black woman in the room.

She had barely begun accepting her natural hair when she landed the interview for an executive assistant position. Every Black woman she confided in advised her to straighten it, warning her that it might be the difference between getting the job and being dismissed before she even had a chance to speak. She panicked. With only two days before the interview, she fried her hair in a desperate attempt to make it more "acceptable." Clumps of it fell out. She arrived at the interview, hair damaged and brittle, only to discover that the director - a self-proclaimed progressive hippie - didn't care about her hair at all.

But the administration did.

She got the job. Shortly after, she prepared for a vacation, and like many Black women, she decided to get her hair braided - protective styling before travel. What should have been a personal choice became a spectacle. The day before her flight, she felt like an animal on display at the zoo. The white women in the office crowded around her, peppering her with questions:

"I could never do that."

"Can I touch it?" they asked, their hands already on the way before the question was finished.

"Is that all your hair?"

"How long did it take?"

Then came the reaching - the intrusive hands stretching toward her scalp without permission. Some asked first, as if their curiosity justified the violation. When she returned from vacation, her hair remained a common topic of discussion, as if her body existed for their entertainment.
When she transferred to another department, she was once again the only Black woman. There had been one African woman, but she left six months later. Deb was young, Black, and unmarried in a department full of fifty-something white women,

The First, the Few and the Only

most of them married. They went to lunch together, invited one another out, formed friendships. She wasn't just left out - she was ignored. The silence was heavier than the exclusion, an unspoken declaration: you are not one of us.

Then came the moment when Deb was managing a project, overseeing the team. A white woman on said team took it upon herself to delegate tasks and suggested that Deb, the team leader and only Brown body on that team, handle the DEI metrics - because of "marketing stuff."
Deb confronted her privately. There was no apology, just a suggestion: "Let's turn this into a teaching moment for the fellows." Deb wasn't a person to this woman. She was an experiment. A case study.
After the meeting, another white woman reached out to her privately: "I saw your face on the Zoom. Are you okay? That wasn't right. If you want, I can stand with you."

The performance of allyship. Where was she during the meeting?!
Once, she mistook a Jewish woman in the office for a true ally. They made small talk until the woman asked, "Where do you live?"
Deb would later realize this was a loaded question. A zip code is a racial marker, a social cue for stereotypes and biases. When Deb told her, the woman's face shifted. The next words out of her mouth were laced with thinly veiled disdain: "You people… it's rough over there, huh?"

Deb had long suspected that most of the white women around her were trying to figure out how she got this job - a job they had inherited through networks, handed down like a family heirloom. Other times when she expressed herself culturally, she would be told with a smile, "Well, I couldn't come to work dressed like that."

What the hell does that mean? When Deb asserted herself in response, calmly yet clearly, she was warned: "Be careful. You don't want to come across as mean."

She learned quickly - these white women didn't want to help her; some wanted to sabotage her. They were not the warm, nurturing figures society painted them to be. They were the white women in Hidden Figures, like Kirsten Dunst's character who watched Taraji P. Henson's character struggle and suffer, turning their heads in willful ignorance and haughty disdain. Deb felt like she had to wear a mask, to work ten times harder, only to be rewarded with more work and no additional pay. No appropriate title.

The First, the Few and the Only

She once trusted a white male ally - he had hired her, advocated for her, put her up for promotion. Then, one year later, she was still waiting on a final decision on said promotion. She finally came to that boss and said that she would need to look for another job if she didn't receive the promotion. He said, "Ok," and let her go.

Next thing she knew, in record time and short order, he gave it to a new white woman, someone who hadn't known him as long or worked as hard. The quiet betrayals cut the deepest. Suckling opportunists and Buddy from The Incredibles strikes again.

She saw it all - the emails from white executives forwarding résumés from their neighbors, their friends, their nephews. "Can you find a spot for my kid?" The caucasity. The audacity of whiteness, assuming that opportunity is a birthright. Most Black people don't have the luxury of a family connection that can place them in corporate spaces with a single email. The office had a casual dress code, but Deb had to be business casual - business professional, even. She had to look "the part" because of the high-profile people she supported, because she was the only Black body in the room. She shouldn't have to change herself to be palatable, but she did. Every day.

It bled into the rest of her life. She'd be out with her girlfriends, laughing, relaxed - until she spotted a white female coworker. Freeze. A moment of panic. If she switched into her professional persona, her friends would mock her for using her "white voice." But if she didn't, she risked being perceived as "unprofessional" by a coworker who might report back to management.

White women in the office often wanted/felt compelled to know her personally. If she didn't offer them something - some crumb of herself - they would call her cold, standoffish, difficult. Over the years, she learned to give just enough, a sliver of her humanity to satisfy them, but never too much.

She remembered reading a passage from a book about a moment when someone thought they were talking to a Black person - until that person shifted, distancing themselves. She had seen it happen before. She had done it herself. Once upon a time, she wanted to be the only one. She didn't want to align herself with Black colleagues who refused to code-switch, the ones white people didn't like. It took her years to realize that they were not her enemy. They were on the same team.

The First, the Few and the Only

To survive, many of us have perpetuated the same harms that wounded us in white spaces. "It's so strange when we become our oppressors." Deb once remarked. DEI work helped her name the things she had experienced. Before, she thought she was imagining it all. Now, she had language for it. She had never considered that diversity included ability, zip code, veteran status, or neurodivergence. Now, she knew better. Deb wished she hadn't had to learn the hard way.

4. Book: White Women by Saira Rao & Regina Jackson

What's coming up for you?

_____

_____

_____

_____

_____

_____

_____

_____

The First, the Few and the Only

Chapter 9

BIPOC Competition & the HNIC

from LEAN ON ME

This next section is hard for me to discuss, and the hardest part isn't the telling - it's the finding of the right words. The weight of it sits heavy, like something ancient pressing against my chest, something inherited, passed down through blood and bone.

My friend Vanessa told me about a study where they measured who, racially, was the most supportive of one another in the workplace. Over two thousand people surveyed, a wide enough pool to paint a picture clear enough for us to see our own reflection in it. And at the bottom of the list - the least supportive of each other? Black men to Black men and Black women to Black women. 🌱

Now, I didn't need a study to tell me something my body already knew. I've walked into rooms and watched white folks flinch at the sight of me. But just as often, I've walked into a room and felt it - the subtle shift when another Black man sees me. The bass drops in his voice, his posture stiffens. A quiet sizing up begins. And the thing that stings most is this: I have done the same. I have been the only Black man in the room, wishing – praying - not to be the only one. But the moment another brother walks in, my voice deepens, my shoulders tighten, because I need to know - who is he? What's his angle? Is there enough space for both of us?
The answer, at least according to history, has always been no.

Side bar: Did you know there was and is a civil war between old Black men and

The First, the Few and the Only

young Black men? Deadass. There is a hidden and yet lived-in contempt, curated by scarcity and some Willie Lynch shit that I have had to learn to recognize the hard way. End side bar.

Willie Lynch 1 knew this well - at least, the Willie Lynch of legend. Historians have debated whether that infamous letter was ever real, but does it matter when its lessons were lived? Break the Black man's mind and keep his body for labor. Separate him from the Black woman until she learns to fend for herself, until she teaches her children that men ain't reliable. Don't be like the dad. Make the old resent the young, the young resent the old. Turn skin tone into a caste system, let colorism seep into the bones of a people already broken, then sit back and watch them claw at each other while the real master of the game collects his winnings.

This wasn't just about slavery. It was about survival - who gets to be closest to power, who gets to be safe. That was the game then, and that is the game today. I learned this firsthand with a man we'll call Namaari. See, some BIPOC bodies don't just want to survive white institutions - they want to rule them, to carve out their seat at the table by any means necessary. They want to be the one who white folks call in first, the one who whispers in the master's ear. Some people call them Uncle Toms, others call them Sambos, but it doesn't matter which name you give 'em - the goal is the same. To become what is known as the HNIC - Head Negro in Charge.

Highlander Culture

"Don't ever confuse leading Blacks with Black leaders." Dr. Julia Hare

The First, the Few and the Only

In Little Mermaid, there is a character named Ursula, and she can give you the power to walk up there where the [white people are]. The song she sings, full of fascination about wanting more, seems silly to the viewer, but in real life Black people were and are conditioned to think that way. Melanated Little Mermaids. We are conditioned to want to send our kids to white schools, to the white churches with nicer groundskeeping and more fancy kid's ministries. That everything more and better is where white people are, so it's not our fault for believing a lie - it's our fault for staying in one.🌱 That is the accusation of "Uncle Tom" – acting white (or wanting white legs) because that is where the white people are. Some even think their ice is colder as Deante Kyle says in Grits & Eggs Podcast.

But there is a tradeoff for Little Mermaid. There is an exchange that must happen if she wants to be where feet frolic like fins in the deep blue sea. A Faustian bargain must be struck.

In The Little Mermaid, there is a deal, a contract inked in desperation, sealed with sacrifice. Ariel, the mermaid, sings of a world beyond her own, longing for the place "where the people are" - but let's not pretend we don't know what kind of people she means. White-bodied, land-dwelling, land-owning, wealthy, and powerful. She wants the prince, not just the sailor. In order to walk among them, she must give up her voice.

For Black and Brown bodies in white spaces, this story is no fairy tale - it's a mirror. We have been conditioned, from history books to living in the "better" neighborhoods, to believe that "everything more and better" exists in whiteness. That success is defined by proximity - closer to the power, closer to the privilege, closer to survival., and for some closer to stability. But the cost? The same as Ariel's. To stand where they stand, we must trade in our voice.

The voice that names the cracks in the palace walls, the injustices hidden in boardrooms and pulpits and corner offices. The voice that sees clearly because we come from below, from the depths of lived experience, from currents they don't even know exist. And yet, the moment we trade that voice, we become complicit in the lie - the lie that to be at the table is to be free.

But there is more to this game. Because Ursula, the one who orchestrates the trade, isn't just the villain. She's also the competition. She, too, wants what Ariel wants, and in white institutions, there is always an Ursula. Sometimes, she even looks like

The First, the Few and the Only

us. I dare you to put the book down and look up the song 'part of your world' from the film to see if you can hear/see the parallels too.

It is a brutal thing to realize that in spaces where there is room for only one or two of us, we are trained to see each other as threats, not allies. That there are those among us who, having made their own bargain, now sit at the right hand of power - not to dismantle it, but to guard it. To ensure that no other mermaid, no other Black or Brown body, rises too high.

Dr. Julia Hare said it best: "Don't ever confuse leading Blacks with Black leaders." Black leaders are chosen by the people. Leading Blacks are chosen by power. By corporations, by institutions, by the media that decides which voices are amplified and which are silenced. And when the people rise, when the ones still fighting demand change, it is the leading Black who is sent to pacify us. To "translate" our pain into something digestible. To manage us.

"Don't ever confuse leading Blacks with Black leaders" -Dr. Julia Hare. The full quote goes on to say, "Don't ever confuse leading Blacks with Black leaders. Let me tell you why you don't do that: Black leaders are chosen by you, they're chosen by the people they are going to lead they are chosen by us but let me tell you about the leading Blacks. Leading Blacks are chosen by the media. Leading Blacks are chosen by A.B.C. (All-Broadcasting Caucasians). Leading Blacks are also chosen by N.B.C. (Nothing Broadcasting but Caucasians), and the rest are chosen by C.B.S. (Caucasian Broadcasting System). When you allow leaders to be chosen by the media that is owned by the corporations when you get ready to change your lives, carefully watch what the leading Blacks are doing because that is when the leading Blacks sneak into the door of the corporations. They tell the corporations they know how to go and put them down and get you some real affirmative action negroes to come in here and work. We know how to do that, but at the end of the day the leading Blacks lead the corporations, and the leading Blacks have gotten paid while we have gotten played." 2

The First, the Few and the Only

This is the dark underbelly of the Head Negro in Charge - not a leader for the people, but a warden for the system. And this is not just a mermaid story; it is a Black story, too. An Asian-American story. A Latin-American story. The story of the FFO.

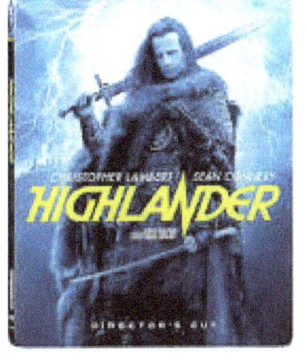

In the 1986 fantasy/action film Highlander, beings with extraordinary power walk among humans. They live long lives, wielding supernatural strength. But there is a catch: the only way to become stronger is to kill one of their own. With each beheading, their power multiplies. The war is not against humanity - it is against each other. The mantra that drives them? There can be only one.

Isn't that the very design of white supremacy? The illusion of scarcity. The belief that there is only one seat at the table, one executive role, one tenured professor, one bishop, one director, one diversity position. Instead of uniting against the system that placed these limits, we are turned against one another. The battle becomes lateral, not vertical.

Here's the final tragedy: the ones who want power the most are often the ones who serve it, not change it. Just like Highlander, there are those who refuse to play the game, who only want to live in peace, community and dignity like Christopher Lambert's character. Then there are those who will cut down everyone in their way just to be the last one standing in a war that never had to happen.

This is what it means to be in the palace. A place where even the most brilliant, the most resilient, the most magical of us must navigate impossible currents just to remain afloat. Sometimes, the very one who helped us get there - the mentor, the

The First, the Few and the Only

gatekeeper, the sponsor - becomes the one who seeks to control us. Becomes our Ursula. Because power, once attained, does not often like to be shared.

In The Little Mermaid, Ursula is defeated. Ariel regains her voice, only when nature steps in to help her. Cause Ariel was weak as hell and if that crab, fish and seagull never stepped in, Ariel would have been a shriveled up living zombie in a cave under the sea. Some of us know negros like that. But in real life? The Ursulas of our institutions often win. They rise, they rule, and they remain. And the people - the ones who needed real leadership, real transformation - are left with another figurehead, another titleholder, another "representative" who represents nothing but their own survival. Another point for the leading Blacks, the leading Latino, the leading _____.

So, the question is not just who has made it to the top. The question is: at what cost? And if the cost was their voice, their people, their purpose - did they really make it at all? So, the next time you see the first Brown/Black _____, ask yourself, what will it cost them to stay?

Elaine Brown on not taking cues from Black entertainers and Black athletes

The Game and The Players

There is a peculiar weight to being the first, the few and the only one in the room. A burden and a target. A throne and a trap. There will always be two kinds: the Black leader and the leading Black, just like Dr. Julia Hare stated. One who serves the people, and one who serves the master.

The HNIC is not always for us. Sometimes, they are simply paid to manage us on behalf of white power. Their job is not to free us but to keep us in line, to make the white institution look equitable while ensuring that true equity never takes root.

The First, the Few and the Only

I saw this up close.

When I entered ministry, I did not maneuver my way into leadership the way many Black and Brown folks have to - smoothing, contorting, endearing themselves to whiteness just to get a seat at the table. No, I was let in because I was the new, shiny one - charismatic, beloved by the people. But my older brother taught me well: hold your tongue just long enough. Learn the terrain. Because the moment they realize you are not here to cape for them, the moment you refuse to teach them how to look equitable instead of demanding that they be equitable, Killmonger hidden inside the Falcon (Black Captain America), they will turn on you.
And that is exactly what happened.

Even my Asian supervisor, once an ally when it benefitted him, found himself discarded when he was no longer useful. It was sobering to watch even he was just a tool in their hands, wielded against me for a time - until they turned their sights on him too.

Then came Namaari - a Black man in ministry, struggling, "looking for guidance." They called me in to meet with him and said he needed someone who looked like him to support him. I dropped everything, left my little cubicle, and drove out to meet him.

And the first thing out of his mouth? "The infamous Michael Thornhill."

Strange. But I left it alone.

Then came the flattery. Not the kind exchanged between Black folk who recognize and respect each other, but something too polished, too calculated. I remembered an old sermon by Dr. Charles Stanley: encouragement comes with open hands. Flattery comes with a hand behind the back.

Namaari was a flatterer. And over time, I learned why.
He wanted power, and as he admitted years later in an off the cuff comment, loved chaos. When he realized I was seen as the HNIC, I became the one he had to take out.

The First, the Few and the Only

But what power did I really have? I was being oppressed, undermined, silenced. They were trying to fire me, push me out, erase me, yet he saw me as an obstacle, not an ally. Because there could only be one. He was no Christopher Lambert, I was. And I was his next meal.

That's the trap of the HNIC system - if there can only be one Black leader, then the fight is never against whiteness. It is against each other. Some of us learn to survive by cozying up to power, by cutting down the competition, by betraying our own.

One day, I watched Namaari brag about profiting off white guilt after Ahmaud Arbery was murdered - "I made six hundred bucks off these white people. Got new sneakers out of it." I challenged him, "Is that really how you think we move forward?" Just like that, he stopped opening up to me.

But I watched.

I watched him love-bomb white leadership, wrapping his arms around them, telling them what they wanted to hear. Behind their backs? He ridiculed them, called them fools, idiots, useless leaders. It wasn't about justice. It was about playing both sides to gain power.

I watched him prey on other Black and Brown staff, especially those in crisis - drawing them in, earning their trust, collecting and hoarding their stories. But when the time came, he did not bring their pain to HR. He brought it to those in power - white leaders who saw him as "one of the good ones." He did not advocate for them. He leveraged them. When their usefulness ended, he discarded them.
I stayed in touch with some of those people. I used what position I had left to advocate for them, to fight for their dignity in conflict resolution meetings, to ensure their voices were heard. But Namaari? As soon as their trauma could no longer serve his rise, he stopped speaking to them altogether.

I saw in real-time the difference between a Black leader and a leading Black.

I have survived the diversity surveys with each wave of white consultants too, the ones that prove why Black men and women in leadership often find themselves pitted against each other. That our own can be some of the least supportive when whiteness holds the reins.

The First, the Few and the Only

So, I say this: this is not a flaw in Blackness. It is a design of white supremacy. A system that allows only one of us in at a time forces us into competition warping what ought to be community, into betrayal where there should be solidarity.

I stayed in that space for years, too many years, maybe doing good work, but it cost me. The snakery, the politics, the constant fight to justify my existence - it wore on my body, my spirit. Because there was never space to simply be a Black leader.

Only space to fight to remain the leading Black.

I refused, eventually, because the truth is - if they only let you in so you can be used to keep others out, you were never really in at all. I white-knuckled this tension for almost six years. I spent two years applying to jobs and interviewing before finally getting hired by a local company for better pay. A few days after I finally put in my two weeks' notice, my whole body shut down. It was as if the years of bracing and squeezing my fists, holding my tongue, choking down all I had to say and hiding my rage in the gym, had finally caught up to me and next thing I knew, I was in a hospital with viral meningitis and lost my ability to walk. I'll explore what happened afterward in Book Two. 🌱

The Masks They Hand Us

Paul Mooney on how they like you a certain way

It is one thing to be Black/BIPOC in a white space. It is another thing to be free.

They will dress you in power and call it progress. Hand you a title and call it triumph. But a cage with a golden door is still a cage, and there is a world of difference between being placed in a room and belonging there.
We have seen this game before with Thurgood Marshall and Clarence Thomas. One carried the weight of his people on his back, the other climbed the ladder and pulled it up behind him. We have seen it with Ben Carson and Harry Belafonte.

The First, the Few and the Only

One a gifted man who let himself be used as a prop, the other a man who used himself to ignite a movement. They love a Black face that reassures, that does not challenge, that smiles politely while the machine rolls on. They love a man who knows his place.

This is the quiet violence of tokenism - when they make you the weapon against your own, when they pit you against each other, when they force you to fight for a single seat at a table, they never meant to nourish you – just for you to cannibalize yourself. 🌱 We have seen it in the fields and in the house, on Hollywood sound stages and government floors. The first betrayal was on the plantation, and the echoes of that sale ring in every institution where we are made to believe we must compete for the right to exist.

Until we name this, we cannot navigate it. Until we navigate it, we cannot resist it. And until we resist it, we can only weather or wither beneath its weight.

Survival is not just about endurance - it is about discernment. Because there will always be two kinds of Black faces in the room: one who serves the people, and one who serves the master. "Uncle Tom" or Sambo. The trick of the system is to make them look the same.

The question is not whether they will let us in. The question is: who are they letting us be? When the moment calls for courage, for defiance, for truth - will they stand with us, or betray us to the very forces that placed them there?

Because in the end, a mask is still a mask. And power without freedom is nothing but a well-dressed chain.

🌱 Getting Involved As Resmaa Menakem says, "Where's your breath?"

Reversal

132
You're not alone

The First, the Few and the Only

Hobie Brown's of the World

Hobie Brown is a character most recently popularized by the 2023 action-comedy Spider-Man: Across the Spider-Verse. As of August 9th, the film grossed $690.9 million, globally, at the box office, making it Sony's highest-grossing animated film EVER. In addition, the film raked in $160 million dollars in streaming revenue. In the film, we meet the comic book hero named Miles Morales, AKA Spider-Man. He's the one from Brooklyn (which is where Steve Rogers is from too). Peter Parker is the one from Queens.

This film is part two of a trilogy highlighting Miles Morales' origins, development of his mastery of being Spider-Man, and some of his accomplishments as a new hero, all against a backdrop of different 'friends' and enemies that have a hard time believing in him. In the second film, Miles has a tough bad guy to face, well, more than one, I guess. Miles has to overcome rough odds when he gets framed as the bad guy for trying to do the right thing and eventually has to face the leader of a spider club he was actively not invited to, a guy by the name of Miguel O'Hara.

Along the way, Miles realizes that in this new institution of dimension-hopping Spider-Men, he is not welcome. And those he thinks are on his side may have ulterior motives. As Mike Tyson always says, "Not everyone who helps you is your friend, and not everyone who hurts you is your enemy."

The First, the Few and the Only

Amidst a cadre of new Spider-Men Miles meets as he hops across time and space to different universes throughout the film, he comes across a Spider-Man from Earth-138 - SPIDER-PUNK! His real name is Hobart "Hobie" Brown, and in his alternate reality, he is the one and only Spider-Man. Across the film we see some people celebrate Miles, one opportunist in particular tries to take credit for Miles' prowess by calling himself a mentor that he never was, we see Miles not accepted by others, but amidst all of this, Miles remains the friendly neighborhood Spider-Man. Although, only one spider man actually "looks out for" Miles, and that is Hobie. Hobie looks out for Miles throughout the film from the moment he met him. Hobie is constantly anticipating, forecasting, and giving sage wisdom in the small moments when no-one else is listening or around. Hobie whispers like he knows something is coming, saying the quiet part out loud. He somehow understands how Miles can maximize his powers, somehow knows when to prod Miles to be curious and slow to make any commitments, and even when someone holds Miles against his will, he is there to remind Miles how to break free with his own palms.

Why am I telling you all of this?

Hobie Brown vs. Miguel O'Hara

In Spider-Man: Across the Spider-Verse, the contrast between Hobie Brown (Spider-Punk) and Miguel O'Hara (Spider-Man 2099) serves as a powerful lens through which to explore true Uncle Tom-ness versus authoritarian control masked as leadership (i.e. Sambo-hood). While both characters operate within the multiversal Spider-Society, their approaches to power, identity, and resistance sharply differ - especially in the context of Miles Morales' struggle against systemic expectations.

Hobie Brown embodies true Uncle Tom-ness by rejecting rigid hierarchies and encouraging Miles to carve out his own path, even providing him with the knowledge and tools to break free. He is an active supporter rather than a savior - he doesn't dictate Miles' journey but instead helps him recognize his own power. Hobie's anti-fascist philosophy directly challenges the oppressive structures that limit individuality and disproportionately target those who exist outside of traditional norms, particularly Black and Brown people and the poor.

The First, the Few and the Only

Miguel O'Hara, in contrast, represents conditional allyship - a leader who claims to protect the multiverse but enforces strict, exclusionary rules that harm those who don't conform. His rigid belief in the "canon" (a metaphor for systemic expectations and gatekeeping) makes him an enforcer of oppression rather than a liberator. His conflict with Miles reflects the struggles faced by marginalized individuals when institutions' gatekeepers (often Black and Brown) try to dictate who belongs and who does not, often reinforcing racial and cultural hierarchies under the guise of order (i.e. HNIC subcultures).

The film also subtly engages with colorism, particularly in the dynamics between Miguel, Miles, and Hobie. Miguel, a lighter-skinned Latino, is positioned as an authoritative figure within the Spider-Society, a reflection of how lighter skin often affords more privilege and leadership opportunities in real-world structures. Meanwhile, Miles, a darker-skinned Afro-Latino, is deemed an anomaly - an unintended "mistake" in the Spider-Man canon - mirroring how Black and Brown individuals are often excluded from dominant narratives despite their undeniable contributions.

Hobie, in many ways, disrupts this structure. As a dark-skinned, explicitly anti-establishment Black character, he actively resists the system rather than trying to reform it from within. His presence highlights how true allyship requires not just supporting marginalized individuals verbally but actively resisting structures that seek to erase or control them.

Hobie Brown, or Spider-Punk, is more than just a rebellious, guitar-smashing "anarchist" - he is an intentional disruptor of oppressive systems, particularly those that dictate who belongs in certain spaces and under what conditions. Within the Spider-Society, an organization that presents itself as an inclusive multiversal coalition, Hobie recognizes that "inclusion" does not mean liberation - especially when it's controlled by figures like Miguel O'Hara.

Hobie is the kind of ally who understands that simply existing in a space is not enough if that space still upholds oppressive structures. His every action in Across the Spider-Verse is rooted in active resistance:

→ He mentors Miles through his actions, teaching him to question authority rather than blindly accept it or be enamored by the room he wasn't allowed until now.

The First, the Few and the Only

→ He subtly arms Miles with tools - literally by giving him the means to escape, but also figuratively by encouraging him to think critically about systems of power, despite its novelty. Like when he said, "Don't enlist till you know what war you're fighting" right before meeting Miguel O'Hara.

→ He never tries to center himself in Miles' struggle but instead steps aside, offers resources, and lets Miles define his own rebellion and timing.

This dynamic reflects the real-world role of true Don Quixote's- those who do not simply "allow" Black and Brown people into predominantly white institutions, but those who actively challenge those institutions when they seek to control, limit, or erase Black and Brown identities. Who sees the giants coming. Hobie is the one who sees the game for what it is and refuses to play along, making him dangerous to power structures that rely on compliance.

Miguel O'Hara: A Symbol of Black & Brown Gatekeepers

In stark contrast, Miguel O'Hara represents how Black and Brown individuals in positions of authority within white spaces can sometimes become enforcers of oppression rather than liberators. His character embodies what happens when someone from a marginalized background gains power but uses that power to uphold the very structures that once excluded them.

Miguel's role within the Spider-Society is eerily reminiscent of the "Sambo" figure from slavery times (if you trade buffoonery for menacing vampire vibes)- a Black or Brown individual who, rather than challenging the oppressive system, chooses to enforce its rules, often against other marginalized people. In his mind, he is simply maintaining "order," but in reality, he is gatekeeping access to power and belonging, and, ultimately, the narrative.

→ Miguel polices Miles' legitimacy as a Spider-Man, echoing how institutions often question the qualifications of Black and Brown individuals, even when they have proven themselves.

→ He upholds a rigid status quo, believing that only certain narratives (i.e., the "canon") should be preserved, mirroring how corporations and institutions tokenize diversity while resisting true systemic change.

The First, the Few and the Only

→ He uses his power to exclude, not uplift, showing how some Black and Brown leaders in white spaces perpetuate harm by trying to assimilate rather than disrupt, much like Sambos from the slave plantations.

Miguel's belief in strict hierarchies aligns with the real-world ways that some Black and Brown individuals, once given access to power, feel the need to police others like them to maintain their own proximity to privilege. This is seen in corporate settings, politics, the church and media, where those who "make it" often enforce the same gatekeeping rules that once oppressed them.

Resistance vs. Assimilation

Miles' conflict with Miguel is not just about personal resentment - it is a structural battle between two ideologies:

- Hobie represents the necessity of dismantling oppressive systems, even from the outside. He understands that real change doesn't come from working within an unjust system but from tearing it down entirely. You can start on the inside, but always being willing to leave.

- Miguel represents the illusion that gaining power within an unjust system allows one to fix it. In reality, he has become a tool of the same oppression he once fought against.

- Miles represents the struggle of many Black and Brown people navigating white spaces. He is constantly told that he doesn't belong, but rather than conform, he decides to forge his own path. Ya know: "Naw, I'ma do my own thing…" 🌱

Final Thoughts

By setting up Hobie as a model for true Uncle Tom's Josiah Henson allyship and Miguel as an example of institutional Sambo complicity, Across the Spider-Verse critiques the ways in which power is wielded within movements for liberation. The film challenges viewers to consider: are you helping to break oppressive systems, or are you enforcing them under the guise of maintaining order? Miles' journey is not just about proving his worth as Spider-Man - it's about fighting for the right to define himself on his own terms, free from the expectations of institutions that

The First, the Few and the Only

were never built with him in mind. And the self-acclaimed white mentors and wannabe allies like Ghost spider, are revealed as utterly useless when the chips are down and a fanged "Spiderman" (Miguel O'hara) is chasing down Miles. If you saw the movie these two characters kept telling Miles to stop running, never helping him fight them off, and never turning around to the spider society and say, "Stop chasing him!" 🌱

The film's brilliance lies in how it subtly addresses these real-world dynamics. Across the Spider-Verse isn't just about Miles Morales proving himself - it's about who gets to define legitimacy, who enforces that definition, and who chooses to resist altogether. Through Hobie Brown's radical solidarity and Miguel O'Hara's authoritarianism, the film challenges audiences to ask themselves:

→ Have you known an ally like Hobie – someone who actively resists authority and supports others in breaking free?
→ Or have you known leaders and managers like Miguel – someone who upholds the very systems that once sought to exclude you?

What comes to memory determines whether one is a true ally (Uncle Tom) or just another gatekeeper in disguise (Sambo). I'm convinced that, throughout most institutions, there is a Hobie Brown to our Miles Morales. They are hard to find, but oftentimes they have already found you before you realize it. I remember when I first got into vocational ministry, I had graduated from Slippery Rock University, then went off to training for the summer for a college campus ministry job. It was there that I remember being bright-eyed and one of a handful of Black and Brown bodies in a new wave of ministers. It was mostly white but hey, nothing new for me. Then one day one of the OG Black staff, a man by the name of Landon, showed up to speak. After his talk, during lunch, he asked me to take a walk with him. He told me things that were prophetic to what I would come to realize were valuable insights before a more inevitable exit almost ten years later. Like Hobie Brown, he said a lot by saying a little, and I never forgot his warnings and cautions.

History is full of Uncle Toms (Josiah Henson's), unsung heroes who did the work when no one was looking with true integrity and bravery. The system will always do what the system does… try to bury their story. These stories from real life will demonstrate the ways in which the system does their best to make sure they stay unsung, but you, the reader, are not what the system anticipated. As you take in these stories, their experiences will live on in your hearts. They were made to seem

The First, the Few and the Only

like villains to the public eye, but behind closed doors they were our greatest American heroes and legends for BIPOC people everywhere, just like Josiah Henson. Word alert:

Nintai: the ability to remain patient and persistent, especially in the face of challenges or adversity.

🌱 Getting Involved: Keep it a buck… Which one have you been? Miguel or Hobie? Ghost Spider or the 'mentor'?

Tokenism as Institutionalization

When you hear the word institutionalized, what comes to mind? For many, it conjures images of prisons, of Black men and women shaped and shackled by judicial systems never meant to set them free. But institutions are everywhere - not just in prisons, but in workplaces, universities, boardrooms. They mold us, contain us, and contort us, whether we recognize it or not.

I once stood outside a county jail, watching people step through the gates - some fresh out, some walking back in. I thought to myself, we are so alike. Me, with my master's degree in progress, raised in the suburbs of South Florida and Western PA, with access to wealthier circles, conferences, and global travel. Every reason to believe our lives should be worlds apart. And yet, standing there, I didn't feel different. I felt the opposite.

Now, before you rush to say, But we're all human! Kumbaya! - pause. Go stand outside that same county jail. Watch the way people move, the way they are seen. Ask yourself honestly: do you look up to them? Do you look down your nose at them? The truth is, I realized in that moment that I, too, am a Black body inside a white institution that is trying to shape me, confine me. The only difference is, one of us is being paid for it, while the other is making money for the state and private stakeholders. Oh wait, maybe that's the same too… 🌱

The First, the Few and the Only

Tokenism as Dangerous Naming

This book feels dangerous to me. The work that I do - our relentless naming of the structures we exist within and its abuses - makes us dangerous. Because to name white supremacy, to track its evolution from slavery to Reconstruction, from Jim Crow to civil rights to now, is to expose its ability to survive, to shift, to camouflage itself in the fabric of institutions.

White supremacy, like any predator, does not like to be seen, only felt.
In the New Testament, when Jesus named the demons, they froze. They panicked. They tried to bargain their way into another form, another host, so they wouldn't have to leave. That is what white supremacy does when we name it. It knows that once we expose its presence, it must either evolve again or risk being caught.

Full stop. 🌱

We need to understand something: white supremacy does not live in the walls of institutions. It lives in bodies. In our bodies, and it moves through the flesh of titans who uphold systems, like the hidden giants of Don Quixote's universe. Whispering its logic into our ears until we believe it, until we enforce it ourselves, until we do it to one another.

There is an inner colonizer in my mind, one that I have to regularly tell to sit the fuck down. But even as I silence it, I use what it has taught me - because that, too, is survival. I have learned from the system how to move within it, how to navigate its demands, how to name it without becoming its next victim.

But if freedom is the goal, then naming must become the priority, right?

The Game Behind the Game

There is a song and dance that happens when BIPOC bodies enter white institutions, and it is never more pronounced than when there are other Black and Brown folks in the room. Suddenly, the performance isn't just for white people. It's for each other.

The First, the Few and the Only

The fight for proximity to power. The zero-sum game of workplace dynamics. The civil war between older Black men and younger Black who are always seen as a threat by their elders. The lack of sisterhood between Black women. The self-curated contempt between non-European ethnic groups in and out of the workplace. The quiet war between those who believe that survival means aligning with the system and those who know that real power can never be granted by the master's hand.

I will name these dynamics in time. I will name the different types of tokens, the caricatures that have just enough truth in them to sting. Because for many, these roles have been a means of survival. But for now, I want to turn our attention to the deeper game - the one beneath the titles, beneath the corporate diversity initiatives, beneath the illusion that there can ever be true equity in a system designed to keep us in competition with each other.

Tokenism is not just about being "the only one in the room." It is about what you must trade to be there🌱, and that is a cost we must begin to reckon with.

Damon Wayans on how much they love a rich negro w/ money.

Tokenistic Rejection: Uncle Tom Revisited

Now, I know I've already taken you back through the ancestral memory of what a real Uncle Tom is - not the caricature, but the man, Josiah Henson. However, I need to revisit the way the negative stereotype of the "sellout" has real roots in history, especially when we examine what I call tokenistic rejection.

A prime example of this phenomenon emerged during the Obama administration. Whether you loved or hated him, there was an undeniable rise in the visibility of Black bodies on conservative media outlets. This wasn't simply about representation. These weren't just Black commentators expressing their own opinions. No, these were Black voices articulating the very talking points that white conservatives hesitated to say aloud, lest they be labeled racist. This was a strategic

The First, the Few and the Only

deployment of Blackness, a performance that gave cover to narratives that would otherwise be dismissed as overtly anti-Black.

Take, for example, Stacey Dash, an actress once known for Clueless, who became a media darling on right-wing platforms during Obama's presidency. She was given prime-time visibility to disavow policies aimed at racial equity, call for the end of Black History Month, and even defend Trump's 2017 comments about Mexicans. It was no coincidence that conservative outlets hired her during a time when they were most eager to challenge the legitimacy of Obama's presidency and broader racial justice movements.

But here's the kicker - once Obama was out of office, so were these Black faces on hyper-conservative, anti-Obama media outlets. They disappeared into thin air, and so did Stacey Dash.

Years after serving as a showpiece, as what many in the Black community deemed an Uncle Tom (again, not Josiah Henson), she found herself socially exiled. The very audience that had embraced her in conservative circles had no more use for her, and the Black community she once derided had not forgotten. She later attempted a public reckoning, blaming her past statements on anger and seeking forgiveness from the same people she had alienated herself from. But the damage was done.

This is the essence of tokenistic rejection. It is the cycle wherein Black individuals are granted temporary access and visibility in predominantly white institutions only so long as they serve a particular purpose, often to validate perspectives that would otherwise be deemed unacceptable. The moment that purpose is fulfilled, they are cast aside, left without the support of either the institutions that once uplifted them or the community they distanced themselves from in the process.

Historian Dr. Ibram X. Kendi writes about the way racial power structures use Black individuals as shields to deflect accusations of racism, only to discard them when they are no longer politically useful (Kendi, Stamped from the Beginning 3). Similarly, journalist Ta-Nehisi Coates has noted how Black public figures who align themselves with white supremacist structures often face an inevitable reckoning when they realize that proximity to whiteness does not equal protection (The Atlantic, 2017). 4

The First, the Few and the Only

Stacey Dash's story is not unique. She is part of a long line of Black figures used as instruments to undermine Black progress, only to be rejected when their role is no longer needed. The lesson is clear: when your platform is built on white validation alone, it is only a matter of time before the rug is pulled out from under you.

Ultimately, not every token propped up in front of Black and Brown communities is embraced by them, and even the white spaces that once eagerly uplifted these tokens will discard them the moment their usefulness expires. THAT is tokenistic rejection. Tokenism is not a guarantee of belonging - it is a transaction, one where the individual is only as valuable as their willingness to affirm the dominant narrative. When that currency runs out, so does the illusion of acceptance. The tragedy of tokenistic rejection is that it leaves its subjects stranded, estranged from their community, abandoned by their patrons, and forced to reckon with the reality that validation built on borrowed power is never truly their own.

What's coming up for you? Name it. Tame it. Write it. Confess it:

_____

_____

_____

_____

_____

_____

_____

_____

The First, the Few and the Only

Chapter 10

Different Shades of Belonging

I'm adopted. I was adopted at twelve days old with my twin brother by the Thornhill family and have been a Thornhill all my life. When I went off to college my freshman year, my mother got in touch with our maternal birth family, the León's, and we scheduled a trip to go see them. I'll never forget one day when we were hanging out with our Tía. She told an off-the-cuff story to us about when we were born. She mentioned that our mother didn't want to give us up, but their parents (my abuelos) convinced her to. One of their reasons was because our mom was pregnant with negro twin boys. There were no negros en la familia. We were given away for being negro?!

I remember hearing that and being somewhat shattered. She went on to say that she thinks that was the reason they are so adamant to brag to us that they go to a church where the pastor is Black, which they reminded us more than a few times during our stay with them.

Later, our Tía brought us to a sort of reunion of the family at a local casino or something, and I think it was a costume party. I remember being so excited to meet other folks from our biological family and wondering if they would recognize our mother in my face. Would I see faces like mine, personalities like mine?

Would the room freeze and everyone rush us?! I had literal butterflies.

When we walked into the room of around sixty people, the first thing I noticed was that my twin and I were the only morenos in the room (brown bodies). Everyone else was white-passing except our aunt, but it was a stark, standout thing. Our Tía told us to not bring too much attention to ourselves and behave. We decided to be ourselves and have fun. We disregarded her and quickly became the life of the

The First, the Few and the Only

party. We met our cousins, our cousins' cousins, our mother's cousins, and their husbands too.

We walked away from that night with so many memories, but I'd be lying if I said I didn't go to sleep thinking of what our Tía told us about being negros and how that influenced our abuelos pressure on our biological mother.

Limpia la Raza

I remember another story when I was in high school, when I first heard the phrase, "¡limpia la raza!" or "Clean the race!" I learned that it was a phrase Hispanic abuelas would say to their granddaughters and daughters to basically clean the race by marrying white men. Also, not going to lie, when I was in high school, I noticed how the Hispanic girls would mess around and make out with the Black kids, but when it came time to have a boyfriend, they would nine times out of ten end up with some white boy. As I got older, I noticed them choose white husbands too, more often than not. At least the one's I have stayed in touch with.

Beyond the fairy-tale musings about The Little Mermaid, there's a more insidious way white supremacy operates in different bodies—one that's often left unspoken. Have you ever noticed that when people of color are in leadership, they are often the lightest-skinned among us? As an Afro-Latino, I see this pattern constantly. Whether it's a Hispanic Chamber of Commerce or a Latino college affinity group, leadership is often occupied by those who could, at a glance, pass as white.

I remember meeting with the new president of a local Hispanic chamber of commerce and pointing out this very pattern—not just on their board but within their entire leadership structure. They looked at me across the table and admitted, "You're absolutely right. It's something we should probably change." That kind of quiet acknowledgment without urgency? It's a story as old as America itself.

Generations of Latinos have been conditioned to strip away their accents, lighten their skin over generations of breeding out melanin while keeping big lips & robust romps, and distance themselves from any marker that might reveal them as anything but "American." It's rarely discussed outright, but it's always there. Let me be clear: I'm not here to shame light-skinned Latinos. What I am here to name is

The First, the Few and the Only

the sociopolitical maneuvering I've observed—how whiteness, or proximity to it, shapes who is allowed in certain rooms.

Take a look at Latinos in the U.S. Senate. There are few, yes, but among those who are there, how many actually look Latino? How many could pass as white if you didn't see their last name? What does 'Latino' look like when you hear the word? Does it even look like the author of this book? This is not a coincidence. White bodies, whether consciously or subconsciously, tend to surround themselves with those who can blend in—who feel familiar, unthreatening. And while, yes, there are dark-skinned Latinos in positions of power, their presence does not negate the overall pattern.

It's always been fascinating to me to watch how those who claim to be Latino have, over generations, been conditioned to decouple themselves from the Black soul and roots of their ancestry. To distance themselves from their Black skinned grandfathers and great grandmothers. But the purge doesn't stop there. Don't have a Hispanic accent, don't speak Spanish, limpia la raza (clean the race), have the lightest skin. This never really gets talked about in my circles, but I've been noticing it all my life.

Now let me say, given my experience as an Afrocubano man, Latin people can be extremely anti-Black, like many Cuban Americans, and I believe this is a trend for a reason. That reason is that white bodies like bodies around them that have 'the complexion for the protection,' as Paul Mooney called it. White bodies are comfortable near bodies that are lighter and especially those that can pass as white. This is not something that white bodies force on the Cuban community as much as collusion. Now you may be thinking, "Yeah, but there's people who have dark skin in all kinds of high places and industries." Right now, I'm speaking specifically about Latinos. More specifically, Cubans. I don't know a lot about other Hispanic ethnicities but I can confidently say that I do know that Latinos who can pass as white, often do.

I remember talking to some friends in middle school when I lived in South Florida. These kids were Hispanic. The girls who had soft curls or straight hair were told to put "white" on any form they had to fill out. They confessed that their parents told them 'If they asked your race, say white'. What do you think that does psychologically to a little boy and a little girl in middle school? What kind of path

The First, the Few and the Only

do you think the parents imagine for them? 🌱 What's coming up for you? Put the book down.

The Perfect Token

This isn't just a Latino issue. African-American, Asian-American, and other minoritized communities face a similar dilemma: how to survive in a system that rewards proximity to whiteness. I've always had a healthy curiosity—are Asian Americans more "preferred" minorities than Black people? And by preferred, I mean which bodies are seen as least threatening to white people, and thus more welcome in white-dominated spaces? Who is allowed closer to power without disrupting comfort?

From interviews with friends, I've learned that many Asian Americans are groomed to navigate this tension early. Some play the part just to stay safe. Others embrace it, seeing tokenism not as a burden but as a badge of honor. That's where the danger lies.

Take my friend Chris. When we were kids, Pokémon was everything—cards, games, shows. One day he told me his white friends used to call him "our little Pokémon." He said it casually, but there was weight behind it. It was messed up, but at the time, it was his ticket to belonging. "I hated myself for going along with it," he told me later, "but I would've done anything to be accepted by white kids. I mean pokemon means little monster, looking back, that's pretty fucked up."

I interviewed a friend of mine I had met at a Christian conference about the intersection of tokenism and being Asian. Her name is Char. This interview is not to speak for all Asians nor to speak for all Asian-Americans, but it is indicative of some of the tensions that particularly Asian-Americans have. In many ways, Asian-Americans are groomed to be the perfect token. 7

When I was interviewing Char1, I remember one of the first stories that she told me was an early memory as a child. I asked her to describe her earliest racial memory or memory around race. She told this story, one where the American citizen, a white kid, cut her and her friends in line. He told her that he chose them because of their race.

"In kindergarten I felt inferior because I could not speak the language, and although I was an American citizen, I remember a kid coming up to me and saying they were

The First, the Few and the Only

doing an Asian cut. That's where you can cut in line and a Chinese person has to step back, but the "American" can cut in front."

In another memory from her childhood, she talked about the way she began to be groomed to become what she called a third-culture kid. She was too far from the mainland to be Asian and too Asian to be "American". She recalled the cultural grooming that began to take shape within her.

"With third-culture kids growing up in Shanghai, I had one white friend who would order food for me and would call herself an honorary Asian. She preferred hanging out with the Asians because she didn't like white supremacy. At an early age I figured out how to say what others want to hear."

Later Char spoke to me about the psychological effects on how she viewed her body based on those who are closer to whiteness.

"They [kids in kindergarten] would say which little girls are not pretty, especially how those who were mixed or half-white were. This left me always wanting to be more white. More pretty. I went to Pomono College, a liberal environment. I was trying to be American despite a lot of cognitive dissonance, but I wanted to show that I was American and not Chinese. I was happy to find out that my roommate was not Chinese. Freshman year my roommate was Black and was the first Black person I met."

I'll never forget when she charted her life course, from self-hating her face & culture to fiercely defending the beauty of both, the biggest pivot point was having that Black roommate. She went from looking down on Black bodies as something to stay away from, to learning from our passion joy and glory. She recalled later in the interview to her experiences since college and recognized the dichotomy of who she was around whites versus who she was able to be around other ethnicities.

"Since I've been speaking up on [the racial realities in white spaces in the city where she lives - removed for her safety], I don't think I've been a jerk, but I have realized that I needed to be my true self around white people. I was always my true self around my Black friends and Asian friends, except for that one white friend in Shanghai, even [in our Chinese church] where my husband and I used to attend. That's hard because Chinese are neutral and indifferent, and although they are my

The First, the Few and the Only

people, I feel comfortable. There I don't get gaslit. They just love their safety and wealth."

Here, Char reflects on her experience in a Chinese church - one of the few spaces where she felt she could be more fully herself, since that Black room-mate in college. But even that came with a cost. Being in an Asian community shaped by cultural norms of neutrality and deference - traits often encouraged in many Asian communities - meant those same values could be easily co-opted by white supremacy. Over time, that posture of humility and harmony was warped into something more palatable for white institutions: the perfect token, someone who would "go along to get along," at least on the surface. You know, the model minority. Char's quote doesn't suggest that all Asian-Americans navigate this in the same way, but it does name a real tension. Especially in white churches, she wrestled with the temptation to be the version of herself that made white people most comfortable - rather than being her whole, God-made self, both as a Christian and as a human. Her brother however, represented what Blacks would call 'cooning'.

"My brother is the quintessential Asian-American friend. He's a lawyer, and they like him because he says the things they say, and he likes [Justice] Clarence Thomas. He likes all the Black people who say what he agrees with but doesn't have any Asian or Black friends. Obviously, he is my brother, but I can't have a close relationship with him. Thank God he doesn't like Trump but still agrees with all the viewpoints. He can't stomach how rude Trump is, but he thinks the ends justify the means. I used to take pride in being the token Asian friend. I didn't like hanging with Asians, especially the non-assimilated ones - any with accents or ones who didn't sound American enough and have not thought through the whole tokenism thing. Now I'm not willing to be the token Asian friend, and since actively thinking about this over the past six years, I have friends around me having these conversations realizing how much racism there is in the world. They check in with fear, asking if they're ever racist towards me. I don't want to be the token Asian friend. I just want to be me. I know very little about racism because I have been trying to be white my whole life, and my little sister has been thinking about these things since she was [around the age of] fifteen or sixteen. She would call me out for cultural appropriation, and I'm proud of her for speaking up even when it was uncomfortable. I used to tell her that she is just siding with losers, but now I see her.

The First, the Few and the Only

She married a white guy who, after realizing how they treated her Asian family and said that her family eats dogs, he cut his family off totally. Ever since getting married I have been ashamed of being Chinese, but after discovering "elimination communication," I feel really good being Chinese.

<u>Tokenism, I think, may be worse with Asian-Americans because more of us want to be the token.</u> Not only do we believe tokenism is not a problem, but we think of it positively and associate this with having reached success and the American dream. We are always trying to prove that we are American because we look so different that we are never gonna look white. We are always trying to prove we are American. Even if you are fourth or fifth generation Asian-American, people will ask you where you are from. Americans always ask, "Where are you REALLY from?""

🌱 Getting Involved

What story/stories are coming to mind for you? Any faces? Take a moment to jot down some thoughts in the margin. Name it to tame it, friend.

PASSING

"What it is to be Black in America. Passing, the idea of passing in false faces. Like who do you have to be in order to be successful? And what piece of you did you sacrifice if you had to do it all?." - Erika Alexander 2

Doll Test

The film American Fiction is a masterclass in satire and grief that mark the Black experience in North America. It walks us through the modern-day realities of passing- less about pigment and more about performance, in America today.

The First, the Few and the Only

Historically, passing required a body so de-melanated in skin tone that white people couldn't visually ascribe racial ancestry or racial heritage. Green eyes, Blue eyes, brown eyes, non-kinky & loose curls -if any. You didn't just pass the brown paper bag test -you erased your melanated reflection altogether. Many Black & Brown folk distanced themselves from their darker, more melanated family members. There's a great scene in the film entitled I Am Not Your Negro where a mother comes to an elementary school to bring her daughter her raincoat. It was pouring rain outside, and when the mother came to the classroom, the teacher asked what her business was. The mother said, "I brought my daughter her coat."

The teacher doesn't even look at the class to check, but seeing the Black skin of the mother tells her simply that there are no colored children here. The mother counters, "Isn't (child's name) in your class?"

Then the teacher, as well as the entire class, slowly turn around to look at the young girl with that name who is hiding behind a book on her desk. In the scene, whispers swirl, you overhear children incredulously gasping to one another, "She's colored?! No way!" and even, "I had no idea she was like them."

Then the young girl rises out of her seat with her head down in both shame and contempt. She storms passed the white schoolteacher still "clutching her pearls". When the little girl gets to the door, she looks up at her mother with enmity and says, "I HATE YOU!" Then runs down the hallway, and her mother chases after her. It is a heart-wrenching scene that left an indelible mark on me. I highly

recommend the film as well as the incredible discussion guide to walk you through it that can be found ⊘ at the QR code.

Once, passing meant skin tone. Today, it also means posture, cadence, politics, performance. And not just for Black folk. Latinx, Asian, and even Western European Jews have historically sought proximity to whiteness for safety and access. Arline T. Geronimus, in Weathering, notes how even within Jewish communities, Western Jews discriminated against their Eastern counterparts. The deeper question becomes: where does the desire to be white even begin?

The First, the Few and the Only

False Faces

I don't have the answer, to be honest. We'd have to read a lot of other more impressive people's research to know, but I would wager survival, escapism, and upward mobility has something to do with it. It used to be the lighter you are the more this 'escape hatch' seemed to become available but that mirage is not always reality. The idea of wearing a caricature (false faces) like in the film American Fiction unburies a skeleton key that unlocks success in North America. We see the character Thelonious Monk discover how quickly caricature becomes capital. Inauthenticity becomes armor.

That to wear a false face is lucrative armor to get what we want. A fragmented vehicle for who we have to become, so we can get to where we have to go, to get what we want in order to be 'successful'. Although, that inauthenticity becomes armor, the subsequent fragmented identity- stitched together from stereotypes and caricatures, fulfills its purpose just like they did for the first Black millionaire actor Andrew Perry, i.e. StepnFethIt. Some learn how to use this sardoodledom skeleton key to get the success and the riches, but how much of ourselves did we lose along the way? What fragments of identity or better yet authenticity, are left beneath the false faces we wore to survive?

From a historical lens, there is a great cinematic book adaption about false faces and the lucrative armor it comes with called Passing on Netflix, starring Tessa Thompson, Alexander Skarsgård, and Helena Bonham Carter. The film captures the history of Black bodies that, over generations, found that those who were most likely the product of interracial rape from white slave masters and even white women who raped Black men over time develop lighter and lighter and lighter and lighter skin pigmentation, i.e. melanin. As long as light-skin Blacks copulate with other light-skin Blacks, you can get a lighter and lighter complexion. Every generation can keep having children with whiter bodies, and eventually you can get a skin tone and hair texture that is darn near indistinguishable from Europeans. It was the very reason the one drop rule was created. It became almost impossible to determine who was Black just by looking at them.

At this point in North American history, people who came from Black lineage started to be able to enjoy the fruits of being white due to their unmelanated camouflage. Primarily, these "fruits" were the access to buying homes, access to better jobs, access to everything better that was reserved and contained only for the

The First, the Few and the Only

white community, backed by not only law, but law enforcement and prejudice. This was a time where a lot of Black bodies found themselves able to marry white women or white men. These Black bodies could perhaps now have access to the type of life that Blacks were kept from for decades, for generations, centuries, even.

In the film Passing, two childhood friends reconnect—one of whom has married into the white world. To maintain her place in it, she hides her Black identity so completely that even her white husband doesn't know the truth. In a tragic twist, she begins to echo racist beliefs and language to secure her belonging in whiteness. This phenomenon isn't just fictional—it's real. There are people today who can pass as white, like my friend Marley.

Marley has the ability to pass, but she doesn't. She is fiercely pro-Black—so much so that even some Black folks on campus would perceive her as overcompensating. She is a brilliant and loving person, but it was hard to witness how some Black students treated her with suspicion or second guessing—especially those who never had to fight to be seen or believed as Black. It reminds me of the rapper Logic, who often raps about the challenges of being Black while presenting with white skin.

Even people like Shaun King—though controversial to some—has spoken openly about the complexity of embodying white skin while identifying as Black in mind, spirit, and heritage. They often face a dual burden: navigating a white world that assumes they're white, while also facing accusations from within the Black community that they are not "Black enough."

Their 'white camouflage' confuses white folks too—who may say racist things around them without realizing who they're speaking to. When whiteness assumes it's alone in the room, the mask slips. But people who can pass are forced to live inside that slip—absorbing the pain in silence, invisibly.

And then, on the other side, there are Black folks who look down on those who pass—policing identity as if melanin grants sole access to cultural belonging. As if any of us have the right to tell someone else who they come from, or who they are.

That kind of exile is heartbreaking. To those who pass and still fight for us—I see you. I love you. You are part of me. And I am part of you.

The First, the Few and the Only

Historical accounts of actresses who passed

Those who can pass—who not only inherit the pigmentation of camouflage but also adopt social behaviors and dress codes to sell the lie. The book behind Passing was inspired by a real person who proved this is more than fiction in the book A Chosen Exile. Whether in books or movies, this real-life phenomenon doesn't only live in pigment but also lives in behaviors. It's often a way of survival. A form of grief. A strategy in a country that still traumatizes bodies based on race. Because of that I've learned to have some compassion for those who choose to do this, as frustrating and upsetting as it is.

Remember Charlotte? She shared that, even as a kindergartener, she heard classmates say that Asians mixed with white were "prettier." There is something about bodies that are mixed with "white" that does something to those from the white community. It is a mix of awe, lust, and contempt. I'm not equipped to speak on that experience beyond Charlotte's interview responses, and I acknowledge that there is way more complexity to capture the Asian-American experience from more than just one Asian woman's perspective, but I can tell you about a guy I know.

More on Passing

A Story About Jay

I met Jay in ministry. We started around the same time, young, eager, stepping into a world that often claimed to welcome us but never truly made space for us. There's something about Black people - an unspoken radar, a knowing. Sometimes you can just tell when somebody's got Black in them. It's in the set of the jaw, the curl of the hair, the weight of the history pressing behind the eyes. Maybe that's why Black

The First, the Few and the Only

folks and Filipinos get along so well - something about that shared, quiet understanding. But that's beside the point.

The point is: when someone can pass, you watch. You wait. You tilt your head, scanning, waiting for the moment when they reveal themselves - not just in skin, but in allegiance. Do they lean into their Blackness, or do they tuck it away? Do they cape for whiteness, smoothing their edges, aligning themselves with power, or do they stand rooted in the truth of who they are?

Jay had green eyes, light skin, loose curls - features that, depending on the room, could grant him entry or exile. I knew before he said a word. He was one of us. But the way he prefaced his thoughts - that was what gave him away.

"As a white man…" he would say, launching into his point, and my stomach would turn. Because no white man has ever had to open a declaration of their opinion like that. Dead giveaway. White people don't move through the world naming their whiteness. They don't say, "As a white woman, I think…" No! White is the default, the unspoken standard, the unmarked category. It is Black people who are forced to identify whiteness, to name it, to contend with it, because white people are never forced to see themselves as a race at all! Jay thought he was blending in, but all he was doing was making the performance more obvious. He gave himself away.

I watched him oscillate, shape-shifting to survive. Around white people, he would say things that were borderline anti-Black, or at the very least, deeply accommodating to whatever white sentiment dominated the conversation. He played agreeable, played small, played safe. But when Black folks entered the room, the script flipped: "Well, my dad's Black, so I get it." That line always came quick, eager, like a password at a door he was afraid might close in his face. He was trying to prove something - to them, to himself, to me. But I wasn't fooled. None of us were.

There's a difference between code-switching and what Jay was doing. Code-switching is survival. It is strategy. It is the knowledge that to be Black in white spaces, you must know how to navigate both worlds because one misstep can cost you everything. What Jay was doing wasn't code-switching. It was something deeper, more fractured. It was a war. A passing. Reminded me of Jay-z's song:

The First, the Few and the Only

The Story of OJ

At first, I was irritated. Then I was sad. How lonely it must be to live in that liminal space, to never feel at home in your own skin, to spend every moment calculating which side to stand on, who to align with, who to be. 🌱

Years passed. We stayed in the same ministry, circling the same rooms, rarely working alongside each other. He gravitated toward me, always watching, always mirroring, like someone desperate to find the right rhythm in a song he couldn't quite hear. One day, I'd had enough.

I remember it clearly. We were in the office. I was an associate director by then. We were walking through headquarters, just the two of us, and I turned to him and said,

"Why do you do that?" I asked.

He looked at me, confused.

"Why do you always go back and forth like that? You oscillate between claiming whiteness and claiming Blackness depending on who you're around. You're mixed. Just be mixed. Why do you feel like you have to cape for somebody?"
He paused. Then, finally, he nodded and said something like, "That's a good challenge. Thank you for that."

Years later, he told me that conversation changed his life, that I had "invested" in him, that it was a gift to his growth. But the truth? I was just tired. Tired of watching him contort himself, tired of seeing him betray parts of himself over and over again. Tired of the whole damn performance. And , frankly, anooyed with how tightly he clung to me.

And yet, I was glad something in him shifted. Because there are Jays everywhere. I've met them, time and time again - people at war with their identity, people who don't know where they belong. Some, like Logic or Shaun King, claim both. They

156
You're not alone

The First, the Few and the Only

know who they are. They refuse to be boxed in by this racialized world that tells them they must choose.

The most insidious part of passing isn't always the person doing it—it's how it lands for those those who can't/won't. For many darker-skinned family members, it feels like a betrayal. A slap. A kind of abandonment that can't be named but lingers. I have felt that feeling when I see it at a government level in the Latino community, when the Hispanic Department of Commerce of the local government all look like white people. My very presence feels like it ruins a collective bit.

I have often wondered if this is also felt in the Indian community, folks with an Indian parent and a white parent specifically. I was with a buddy of mine from the salsa community here in my city, and we met for drinks. I arrived early so that I could work on this book. Actually, this very chapter. When he arrived, we shared pleasantries. After some time, he looked at my open laptop and asked what I was working on. I told him about the book and how I was trying to work out how to tell my story of hybridity and mixed-ness. I read him the problem I was trying to structure and articulate for the mixed body, and my journey seeking safety, belonging, and identity, being adopted and proud of my ethnic mixture simultaneously.

He looked at me without blinking an eye and asked, "What's the answer?" I told him I wasn't writing this book to provide an answer. I was trying to name my own journey well enough to create space—for others to discover language for theirs. He repeated the question. After some digging as to why he persisted for an answer, I discovered that he was not a white man. Until then I swore he was. Come to find out his father was from India and made him and his brother with a white woman. This led me to confess something: I've never met a child of an Indian father and white American mother who couldn't pass—as white or light-skinned Latinx. He laughed. We carried on the conversation, and he told me much about his perspectives on the matter. I walked away wondering how to discuss this in my book.

The First, the Few and the Only

Sadly, I've met people like this time and time again. I won't name them, but I just always wanted to name the phenomenon itself. I find it interesting that this is something that happens a lot throughout institutions, mainly white institutions that are designed and made for white bodies that prioritize white interests and centers white racial comfort, which incentivizes folks who can pass to do so and yet, that access comes at a cost: the quiet erasure of kinship. Of memory. Of soul.

🧭 5 Signs You're Witnessing Racial Passing
(Not Code-Switching)

We throw these terms around sometimes without pausing to distinguish them. But they're not the same. Code-switching is a tool—an adaptive skill that helps us navigate spaces that were never designed for our full selves. Passing, on the other hand, is about erasure. It's not just adapting—it's hiding. And hiding is exhausting. It's a survival strategy that sometimes costs more than it saves.

Here are five ways to tell the difference:

1. Identity is Claimed or Dropped Based on Who's in the Room
In white spaces, someone who is passing might avoid any mention of their Black or Brown heritage. In Black or Brown spaces, that same person may suddenly invoke their identity like a secret handshake. Passing often means identity is not an anchor—but a performance. It's not about who they are, but about who they think the room wants them to be.

2. They Overcompensate—or Go Quiet—When Racism Shows Up
When racism enters the room, someone passing often plays along—or says nothing. They may parrot white talking points. Downplay injustice. Make jokes at the expense of their own people. Where code-switching seeks protection, passing often

The First, the Few and the Only

seeks approval/invisibility. Passing doesn't challenge the violence of whiteness—it adopts and adapts to it.

3. They Only Acknowledge Their Marginalization When It's Useful
Like Jay, racial declaration is not an identity—it's a password. But identity isn't a passcode. It's a posture. And you can't build solidarity with a keycard mentality.

4. More Than Their Tone—They Shift Their Allegiances
Code-switching changes the delivery. Passing changes the message. If someone switches not just how they speak, but what they stand for—mirroring whiteness in voice, dress, humor, and values—you're not just seeing survival. You're witnessing self-erasure.

5. Whiteness Becomes the Default They Aspire To, Not the Distance They Hold
A code-switcher may still critique white norms, even if they play along for survival. But someone who is passing often treats whiteness as the goal. You'll hear weird things come out of their mouths. Phrases that go against their own racial self-interest and when someone capes for whiteness like that—it's usually because they're reaching for its safety. It's an act of alignment.

The difference? Code-switching is a learned art, it says: "I know both worlds. But I am still me."

Passing is a silent wound. It says, "To be safe here, I must become someone else." And that costs something. It costs belonging. It costs trust. It often costs the parts of ourselves we were told were too much to bring through the door. And this is the reason I have become compassionate for'm.

At the end of the day, the melanated cannot afford to confuse survival with betrayal. Let's ask harder questions about the kinds of rooms that reward erasure and punish wholeness. And for the sake of the Jay's in our workplaces, places of worship and lives, hopefully we can make room for those finding their way back from the disappearing act.

🌱 What's happening to your body, dear reader?
Take a moment to note what is coming up for you in the margin of the book.

The First, the Few and the Only

People Don't Pass in Hollywood, right?

The history of Hollywood is long and complex. Many actors and artists, particularly those of mixed or non-white heritage, have hidden or downplayed their backgrounds to fit the industry's preference for whiteness. Below is a more detailed look at historical figures like Dona Drake, Marilyn Monroe, Rita Hayworth, and others, along with contemporary artists who "pass" as white today.

Classic Hollywood Stars Who Passed as White

1. Dona Drake (1914–1989) – African-American and Mexican Heritage
   Dona Drake was born Eunice Westmoreland to a Black and Mexican family in Texas, yet she was marketed as an "exotic" foreigner, first as Una Novella (Egyptian), then as Dona Drake (Spanish/Latin American). She had to deny her Black ancestry to work in Hollywood and was cast in Latina or vaguely ethnic roles.
2. Rita Hayworth (1918–1987) – Spanish Heritage
   Born Margarita Carmen Cansino, Hayworth was of Spanish and Irish descent. Early in her career, she had dark hair and a strong resemblance to her Spanish father. However, when Hollywood wanted a more "all-American" leading lady, she underwent electrolysis to change her hairline, dyed her hair auburn, and rebranded herself as white.
3. Marilyn Monroe (1926–1962) – Possible Afro-Latin and Indigenous Heritage
   Though officially recorded as having Irish and Scottish ancestry, there has been speculation that Marilyn Monroe (born Norma Jeane Mortenson) had Afro-Latin or Indigenous heritage from her mother's side and was born in Mexico. Hollywood studios preferred their leading ladies to fit the white, blonde bombshell archetype, so any possible ethnic ancestry was erased from her public persona.
4. Merle Oberon (1911–1979) – South Asian Heritage
   Oberon, born Estelle Merle O'Brien Thompson in India, was of Anglo-Indian descent. Hollywood studios hid her South Asian roots, claiming she was born in Tasmania, Australia, to British parents. She avoided interviews that might reveal her heritage and

The First, the Few and the Only

even distanced herself from her mother to maintain her "white" identity.

Contemporary Artists Who "Pass" as White

5. Halsey (Ashley Nicolette Frangipane) – Black and Italian-Irish Heritage
   Halsey has spoken about her mixed-race identity, with an African-American father and an Italian-Irish mother. Because of her light skin, she is often perceived as white, leading to ongoing discussions about race and privilege in the music industry.
6. Logic (Sir Robert Bryson Hall II) – Black and White Heritage
   The rapper Logic has an African-American father and a white mother, but his light skin and European features mean he is often mistaken as fully white. He has frequently addressed this racial ambiguity in his music, discussing the challenges of being biracial.
7. Rashida Jones – Black and White Heritage
   Daughter of Quincy Jones (Black) and Peggy Lipton (white), Rashida Jones has light skin and Eurocentric features, leading many to assume she is white. She has spoken about navigating her mixed identity in Hollywood and how it has impacted the roles she is offered.
8. Troye Sivan – Jewish with Possible Mixed Heritage
   Though officially Jewish and South African, Troye Sivan has also been perceived as racially ambiguous. Some fans have speculated about possible Middle Eastern or North African heritage due to his features.
9. John Gavin (1931–2018) – Mexican Heritage
   a. The actor, known for Psycho and Spartacus, was born Juan Vincent Apablasa Jr. to a Mexican mother. However, he was presented as a white leading man, with his Latino roots largely hidden from the public.
10. Carol Channing (1921–2019) – Black Heritage
    a. Broadway legend Carol Channing, best known for Hello, Dolly!, revealed later in life that she had a Black father. However, throughout her career, she was perceived as white, allowing her to rise in an industry that was deeply segregated at the time.
11. Raquel Welch (1940–2023) – Bolivian Heritage

The First, the Few and the Only

   a. Born Jo Raquel Tejada, Welch's Latina heritage was downplayed early in her career. She adopted her father's surname and avoided Spanish-speaking roles to maintain her "white" Hollywood image.
12. Jackie Kennedy Onassis (1929–1994) – Possible Mixed Ancestry
    a. While officially recorded as of Irish and French descent, there have been claims that Jackie Kennedy had some Ashkenazi Jewish and possibly Indigenous ancestry. However, she was embraced as an icon of upper-class white elegance.
13. Clark Gable (1901–1960) – Black Ancestry
    a. Rumors have persisted that Clark Gable, the Gone with the Wind star, had Black ancestry, though he never acknowledged it publicly. His acceptance as a white leading man cemented his status as a Hollywood legend.
14. Alexander Hamilton (1755–1804) – Caribbean and African Heritage
    a. Born in the Caribbean, Hamilton's racial background has long been debated. Some historians argue that he had African ancestry, but he was able to pass as white in colonial America, allowing him to rise to prominence as a Founding Father.
15. Alexandre Dumas (1802–1870) – Black Heritage
    a. The French writer of The Three Musketeers and The Count of Monte Cristo was the grandson of an enslaved Black woman from Saint-Domingue (modern-day Haiti). While Dumas acknowledged his heritage, he faced racism in France, though he was still largely accepted as a white European intellectual

Contemporary Figures Who "Pass" as White

16. Snooki (Nicole Polizzi) – Chilean Indigenous Heritage
    Best known for Jersey Shore, Snooki was born in Chile and adopted by an Italian-American family. While she fully embraced Italian-American culture, her biological background includes Indigenous Chilean roots.
17. Cameron Diaz – Cuban Heritage
    Though often assumed to be fully white, Cameron Diaz's father was Cuban. Despite her Latina heritage, she was primarily cast in white roles and rarely discussed her ethnicity in Hollywood.
18. Chloe Bennet – Chinese and White Heritage

The First, the Few and the Only

> The Agents of S.H.I.E.L.D. actress was born Chloe Wang to a Chinese father, but she changed her last name to Bennet to avoid racial discrimination in casting. She has since been vocal about the challenges of being an Asian actress in Hollywood.

19. Bella Thorne – Cuban Heritage
    > Though often seen as white, Bella Thorne has Cuban ancestry on her father's side. Like many Latina actresses, her identity was downplayed to fit into Hollywood's preference for "racially ambiguous" white-passing actors.

20. Aubrey Plaza – Puerto Rican and Irish Heritage
    > Plaza has Puerto Rican roots but has often been perceived as fully white. She has spoken about how her mixed background has influenced her identity and career.

21. Vin Diesel – Black and Italian Heritage
    > Vin Diesel has a Black father and an Italian mother but has never fully clarified his racial background. Because of his light brown skin and racially ambiguous features, he has often been cast in roles that avoid specifying his ethnicity.

22. Esther Jones – Black Heritage (Inspiration for Betty Boop)
    > Esther Jones, a Black jazz singer in the 1920s, inspired the iconic Betty Boop character. However, her influence was erased, and the character was instead modeled after a white actress, Helen Kane, in an example of both passing and racial erasure.

23. Malcolm Gladwell – Black and White Heritage
    > The journalist and author of Outliers and The Tipping Point is of Jamaican and European descent. His light skin has led to assumptions that he is white, though he has often written about racial identity.

24. Naomi Scott – Indian and British Heritage
    > The Aladdin actress has an Indian mother, but she is often perceived as white or racially ambiguous. Her casting as Princess Jasmine sparked debates about colorism in Hollywood.

While passing in Old Hollywood was often a survival mechanism to escape racism and secure opportunities, today, the conversation has shifted. Many contemporary

The First, the Few and the Only

artists embrace their mixed heritage, but others face accusations of "convenient" racial identification - claiming their non-white identity when it benefits them but retreating into whiteness when it does not. The legacy of passing in Hollywood reflects larger societal pressures, showing how racial identity is still shaped by power, privilege, and opportunity. For some, passing is beyond skin-tone but in tone, affect, personality mirroring and behavior which the film AMERICAN FICTION explores thoroughly.

To be "the first, the few, or the only" in a white space is to carry a dual burden. It is not merely double consciousness, as W.E.B. Du Bois described - the constant negotiation between one's self-perception and the gaze of a dominant society. It is something heavier, more insidious. It is an Othering so precise, so particular, that it even isolates you from those who share the broader struggle. It is to be an "Other" that is also an "Only."

Double consciousness at least implies a kind of collective experience - a shared dissonance among the marginalized, but the singular burden of tokenization distorts even that. It extracts an individual from the collective, places them on a pedestal built of scrutiny and expectation, and demands they perform - not only for the white gaze but also for the communities they left behind. One must be representative yet exceptional, relatable yet unthreatening, a bridge yet a beacon. The performance is constant, exhausting, and yet, paradoxically, never quite enough.

James Baldwin once wrote, "The paradox of education is precisely this - that as one begins to become conscious, one begins to examine the society in which he is being educated." The more one understands the structures at play, the more suffocating the dual burden becomes. Consciousness sharpens the contradiction: one is elevated yet alone, visible yet unheard, present yet peripheral.

These themes are laid bare in American Fiction, a film that masterfully dissects the contradictions of Black representation in white spaces. The protagonist, Thelonious "Monk" Ellison, is a brilliant but underappreciated Black writer whose work is dismissed as too intellectual, too inaccessible, too distant from what white

The First, the Few and the Only

audiences expect Black stories to be. You know, sardoodledom. His struggle encapsulates the burden of singularity: to be Black in a white space is not merely to exist, but to perform, to translate oneself into legible stereotypes for white consumption.

When the character Monk, in an act of frustrated satire, writes an entire novel filled with the very racial clichés the industry craves - poverty, crime, trauma - it becomes an overnight sensation. His book, intended as a critique, is instead embraced as an "authentic" representation of Black life. Here, the dual burden reveals itself in its full absurdity: authenticity is not what one truly is, but what white audiences believe one ought to be. The Only must embody the collective, not as it exists, but as it is imagined.

This mirrors the experience of many firsts, few, and only's who find themselves in spaces that claim to celebrate their presence, but only insofar as they conform to preordained narratives. Whether in literature, academia, corporate spaces, or politics, the Only is rewarded, not for their individuality or prowess but for their willingness to reinforce a mythology about race. They must exist within the narrow parameters of acceptability - just radical enough to be palatable, just familiar enough to be safe.

The tragedy of Monk's predicament is not just that his true voice is ignored, but that his success becomes a prison. His ascent into the mainstream is not a triumph but a kind of erasure. Thelonious Monk once said, "A genius is the one most like himself." But for a Black artist, thinker, or professional in a white space, being oneself is often a liability. The Only must choose between visibility and authenticity, between success and selfhood. Exhaustion and battle fatigue.

To be an 'other' is to be estranged from the center of society. To be an 'only' is to be estranged from both the center and the margins no matter where you stand. It is to stand at the intersection of erasure and hypervisibility, carrying a weight that is both too much and never enough. It is to be seen and unseen in the same breath, to be heard only when one's voice echoes the expected script.

In American Fiction, Monk ultimately confronts the absurdity of his situation, but in reality, the struggle remains. The firsts, the few, and the only's navigate a world that demands both excellence and compliance, individuality and representation, presence and palatability. To exist in this liminal space is to be at war with an

The First, the Few and the Only

expectation that is not of one's own making. It is, as Du Bois wrote, "a peculiar sensation, this double-consciousness, this sense of always looking at oneself through the eyes of others."

But for the Only, even double consciousness is not enough to describe the weight of the performance. It is not simply seeing oneself through the eyes of others - it is being sculpted by them, reduced, reshaped, and sold back to the world in a form that is barely recognizable.

Passing is more than skin deep. As Erika Alexander from the hit television show Living Single, who plays the love interest of the main character on the film, is quoted saying that the whole movie is about passing. What is passing in the Black experience without understanding grief? We change and fragment our identities in such a way as to be the caricature that is needed or some suppressed version of ourselves. It is a dance and performance many, many, many of us are doing, sometimes without even realizing it.

The movie is a sobering reminder that we are caught in a system that rewards us for inauthenticity as much as for a riveting embodiment of the white imagination. There are those who pass by always smiling and being the personal 'Black' of political leaders. There are those that pass by repeating white racial dogma for a camera until the white audience finds someone more compelling. There are those who write and produce stereotypical Black caricatures that do more harm than good to the Black community that get a deluge of white audience views. There is a whole market that is accustomed to consuming media that centers Black trauma. There are many ways to pass economically by being in the most white and wealthy schools, or fancy Ivy League networks and secret societies.

I have felt the compelling nudge to say what the white body in power wants to hear, like Beau Sia in his poem entitled Give Me A Chance, in order to get more "opportunities". I remember feeling icky when they would say racist things to me. I remember thinking, "What about me made you think you could say that around me without consequences & repercussions?"

I also need to say something about those who cape so hard for white people. I believe that there are people who are truly not like Josiah Henson, but they embody the kernel of truth that lives in the caricature and stereotype of Uncle Tom. As depicted in various ways in the film American Fiction, Black and Brown bodies that cape so hard for white bodies, often to the point that they become rewarded for

The First, the Few and the Only

their collusion, have become people who want to navigate the institutions in an upward mobility, bodies that will do anything and say anything to white bodies to get there.

Remember the whole quote of Dr. Julie Hare, the one who said to never mistake Black leaders with leading Blacks? These are the people who are fighting to be leading Blacks because it gives them power, and they will do anything to become the preferred minority.

Namaari was the one who taught me this lesson. That's where I learned about this from, and I wanted to make a note and acknowledge that there are people who proved the term, "All skin folk ain't kinfolk." To use a reference from Planet of the Apes, there are a lot of Kobas that are not Caesars. They have contempt for some white people but will smile and dance in front of them to get near enough to take the power they need to enact their will. These are some of those dangerous people, institutionally, because you can't let your guard down. You think you're building bonds within a white institution when, in actuality, you're giving ammo to someone who sees you as an enemy and a threat before you even knew lines were drawn, and I've experienced a lot of harm from people like this. I have met Black leaders and even Black colleagues that would leave my nervous system and gut screaming, "Not safe, not safe!" I would have all sorts of alarms going off within my body when I was around them.

Similarly, when I was a child, I was usually around someone who's suspected of having some mental health issues that caused them to be violent. As a kid and when I was growing up around this person, it taught me to guard and protect myself when my body didn't feel safe around them.

That baggage and trauma taught me to see this Namaari person coming a mile away, to listen to my gut. My instincts allowed me to guard myself early on from this person because something in me said that this person is not trustworthy. Over time, it became evident as to why this person was as harmful as my body prophesied them to be. I, along with others in the company, later discovered how much they were fighting to become the preferred minority, fighting to become the HNIC by telling white people in power, who are genuinely insecure around Black people (and possibly even afraid of Black people), everything they wanted to hear. By the time they figured that out, Namaari did his best to flatter this white person in power, massage their ego. All of a sudden, Namaari was on a fast track to

The First, the Few and the Only

become leadership - not because of competency, but because of charm used in the worst ways. As I observed Namaari denigrate the white leader in charge, as I mentioned before, he was also the first one to flatter them in their presence.

🌱 **Getting Involved:** What story is coming up for you? Put the book down and recount the story aloud.

Liminality
(noun), li-mə-ˈna-lə-tē
in-between-ness

In architecture, liminality is a term used to describe the space between things - hallways, corridors, thresholds. Wikipedia calls it "the physical space between one destination and the next." Vocabulary.com defines it as "a quality of being in-between two places or stages, on the verge of transitioning to something new." I just call it in-betweenness.

An airplane is a liminal space - full of people suspended between where they've been and where they're going. A university, too, is liminal, a training ground between adolescence and adulthood, between potential and profession. But what about identity? Can ethnic hybridity be liminal? Can a body be a threshold between cultures, caught forever between destinations, never quite arriving?

I won't lie - growing up in the US, I never felt Latino enough, never Black enough, never African enough, never North American enough. The fact that I was adopted and never taught Spanish only deepened that sense of lacking. I'm not alone. Plenty of Latinos grow up in their own households, raised by their own parents, without learning Spanish - sometimes because their families fear discrimination, sometimes because survival demands assimilation. 🌱

I'll never forget the summer after my freshman year of college, working at a Salvation Army camp. A group of staff girls had just learned I was Cuban and were fawning over my exoticness when a Puerto Rican coworker overheard and scoffed, "He's not Cuban. Michael doesn't even speak Spanish."

I shit you not - I have never wanted to crash out and hit someone so bad in all my days. It felt like a stab to the heart, a violation, a shunning. She stripped something

The First, the Few and the Only

from me that I held so dear, something I was already fighting to claim. Now, I've never hit a woman, but when I found out she had a crush on my brother and he rejected her hard, I won't lie - I felt vindicated. "That's what yo ass get!" I thought. My man!

Years later, I met a guy at my apartment complex who is Black and Puerto Rican, AfroLatino like me. The bond was instant. He told me how, when he visited the Dominican Republic, everyone assumed he was native until he spoke. When they found out he was Puerto Rican but couldn't speak Spanish, they wanted nothing to do with him. Here in the States, Latinos judged him for being "too Black." The alienation was real - too dark for Latinos, too Latino for Black folks. Right there, in the middle of a casual conversation, we hugged it out like a long-lost family. No words needed. The in-betweenness had found its mirror. 🔥

But let's be real - being Afro-Latino is dope. Celia Cruz. Christina Milian 🔥, Laz Alonso - Mother's Milk from The Boys. Zoe Saldana - who, let's be clear, has starred in basically every billion-dollar movie: Avatar, Avengers: Endgame, Infinity War, Avatar: The Way of Water. Then there's Tessa Thompson, Gina Torres, Rosie Perez 🔥, Rosario Dawson, Tatyana Ali (The Fresh Prince), Miguel, Maxwell, Neil DeGrasse Tyson. And my personal forever crush? 🔥Soledad O'Brien🔥. See? Afro-Latinidad is a lineage of legends.

 Laz Alonzo

So why the shame? Why the rejection? I don't have an answer, but I do know how to name it when it shows up. In workplaces. On movie sets. In conversations laced with side-eyes and skepticism. Even Giancarlo Esposito, the brilliant actor known for Breaking Bad and Do the Right Thing, speaks about this in-betweenness - the way being both Black and Italian means navigating a world that refuses to let you fully claim either.

Liminality, in this sense, isn't just a place between. It's a life between. It's never being enough of one thing to belong but always being too much of something else

The First, the Few and the Only

to fit in.

My beautiful friend Constance, MBA, told me about her own version of this liminality. Liberian by birth, she excelled in white spaces, rising through education and corporate America. Her community back home lauded her achievements, but when she returned, she felt the distance. The very people who once uplifted her now saw her as evidence of what they didn't have. She became both a source of pride and a reminder of loss. When I asked her, "Do you feel like you're both a banner and a burden?" she didn't hesitate: "All the time." 🌱

And that's the thing about being "the first," "the few," "the only." You get the accolades, but inside the pretty packaging lies a heavy burden: alienation, fragmentation, chronic stress that leads to chronic illness, accelerated aging, shrinking community, burnout, marital stress, isolation. All while maintaining the grace and resilience white folks expect.

Every. Single. Day.
That is liminality, friends. For BIPOC bodies striving for mobility, not that we don't overcome it -- but it costs us.
Damned if you speak spanish. Damned if you don't.
 Being Mixed

Embracing the In-Between

Let's be real: there is nothing wrong with hybridity. There is nothing wrong with liminality. There is absolutely nothing wrong with my body.
My body is a living tapestry - a story woven from generations of people so drawn to one another that they created me. My skin, my face, my hands, my toes, my hair - all of it carries history. All of it is enough.
And yet, shame always finds a home. I've heard it said that shame gets stored in the body, attaching itself to a part of our body like a silent weight we carry. For me, that place was/is my nose. No matter what people said - no matter how many times someone called me handsome - I struggled to believe them. Because look at my nose.

Maybe for you, it's something different. Maybe it's the texture of your hair, the shape of your eyes, the shade of your skin. Maybe it's something no one else even

The First, the Few and the Only

notices, but you feel it every time you look in the mirror.

Let's pause here. Let's name it.

Is there a part of your body that carries your shame?

Are you willing to write it down?

Take a moment. Be honest. No one else will see this but you.

Write it here:

Now, consider this: what would it mean to see that part of yourself with love? Not through the lens of someone else's expectations, but through your own eyes, through the eyes of the people who made you, the ancestors who carried you forward, the generations waiting to come through you.

Sit with that. We'll come back to it.

Good Hair

Hair, like skin tone, is one of the most powerful gatekeepers of belonging in both Black and Latino communities. It dictates how one is perceived, what spaces one is welcomed into, and often, how much proximity to privilege one is granted. When I was in sixth grade, my brother and I stepped off the bus and wandered around the front of Sawgrass Springs Middle School (SSMS) waiting for the doors to open. While waiting, I remember my brother and I staying close because we didn't know anyone. We had been in private school for fourth and fifth grade, and everyone else knew each other from one of the three main elementary schools that funneled into SSMS.

Then, after some time, we were stopped by these three towering Black girls who said, 'Hey, what are you?"

My brother and I looked at each other, and my brother replied, "Twins."

You're not alone

The First, the Few and the Only

They said, "Noooo-uh, what are you?"

We looked at each other again, and I said, "Sixth-graders."

They said, "NOOOO, what are you?!"

I looked down for a moment and remembered when our mom told us we were adopted and that we were two things: I could only remember how to pronounce one of my heritages, so I uttered, "Cuban??"

Three eighth grade Black girls who towered over us erupted in a collective, "OHHHHHH! That's why they got that good hair like that."

The politics of hair - especially the favoring of looser, more Eurocentric textures - reinforces the same hierarchy of colorism: the straighter, the "better," the more acceptable. This was one of my first baptisms into it.

In the Black community, the discrimination against tightly-coiled, kinky hair has been both explicit and insidious. Schools have punished Black students for wearing their natural hair, employers have deemed locs and afros "unprofessional," and even within Black families, there's often been an internalized preference for "good hair" (a term that usually refers to looser curls or straighter textures). Laws like The CROWN Act, which had to be introduced to ban race-based hair discrimination, prove how deeply embedded this bias is in society. 4

In the Latino community, the same bias operates but is often more hidden under the guise of pelo malo (bad hair). Afro-Latinos with coarser textures are often pressured to straighten their hair, while those with looser curls or waves are subtly positioned as more beautiful or "presentable." In many Spanish-speaking cultures, children with kinkier textures are often told to "fix" their hair, reinforcing the idea that European-adjacent features are the standard.

A recent example of this played out publicly when Dominican actress Julissa Calderón, best known for Gentefied, spoke about being told her curls were unprofessional and wouldn't get her roles in Hollywood. Similarly, Afro-Latina actress Amara La Negra has spoken extensively about being encouraged to change

The First, the Few and the Only

her natural afro because it wasn't deemed "marketable" in the Latin entertainment industry.

Film & Television Examples

1. Black Panther (2018) and Wakanda Forever (2022) – The natural hair movement in Black communities has been amplified in the media, and Black Panther was a major cultural shift. The film showcased a spectrum of Black hair textures, from Shuri's free coils to Okoye's shaved head to Nakia's twists, celebrating natural Black hair as beautiful and powerful. However, the real-life industry still leans toward actors with looser textures being cast more frequently.

2. Insecure (2016-2021) – Issa Rae's HBO show Insecure did a masterful job of showcasing a variety of Black hair textures and styles, a rarity on television. But even Rae herself has spoken about how, early in her career, she was advised to wear wigs or straighten her hair to be "taken more seriously."

3. One Day at a Time (2017-2020) – The show, which focused on a Cuban-American family, tackled colorism and pelo malo culture when Elena, played by Isabella Gomez, called out her family's prejudices toward darker-skinned Latinos and natural hair textures.

4. America's Next Top Model (Early 2000s) – In multiple cycles, contestants with tightly-coiled hair were either pressured to straighten their hair during makeovers or given weaves to make them more "versatile." Meanwhile, mixed-race contestants with loose curls were celebrated for their "exotic" look.

5. West Side Story (2021) – While the film made efforts toward better representation, there was backlash over the casting of lighter-skinned Latinos, particularly Rachel Zegler as Maria, highlighting the continued preference for Eurocentric beauty standards in Latin American storytelling.

The Bigger Picture

At its core, the hierarchy of hair in both Black and Latino communities is a byproduct of colonization and white supremacy. Whether it's a Black woman being

The First, the Few and the Only

told her afro is "too political," a sixth-grader being told he has good hair, or an Afro-Latina being pressured to chemically straighten her hair to "look more Latina," the message is clear: whiteness is still the default, and anything too far outside of that norm must be corrected.

But resistance is growing. The natural hair movement, The CROWN Act, and media representation are slowly shifting these biases, forcing communities to question long-held beliefs about beauty, professionalism, and identity. However, as long as Hollywood, corporate America, and even our own families continue to uphold these hierarchies, the fight for true acceptance of all hair textures - without condition or compromise - continues.

All Hispanic?

Growing up without much Latin influence at home, I found myself grasping at anything that could anchor me to my identity. I knew I was Ghanaian-Cuban, but what did that mean when there was no roadmap, no voice calling out from the kitchen in Spanish, no rhythms of Caribbean soul or salsa weaving through the walls? So, I did what any lost soul does - I reached. I borrowed. I became a collector of Latinidad in any form I could find.

I said güey because the Mexicans in my school did. I threw around dale because Pitbull made it sound like a rallying cry. I wasn't just adopting phrases - I was staking my claim. With every syllable, I was telling the world: I belong too. Soy Negro y Soy Latino tambien. "Somos dos "as Black, Afro-Latina HBCU grad Dr. Stacey Speller says.

In college, this search became more focused. I started asking myself, "What can I adopt that will prove to the world that I'm Latino?" What would make people say it before I had to? I thought about learning Spanish fluently, cooking Cuban dishes, growing my facial hair a certain way, learning to dance salsa. Spanish vocabulary had

The First, the Few and the Only

been in my life since third grade, but conversation still slipped through my fingers. Cooking felt like too much work. Facial hair? Still patchy at best.

That left dancing.

I became obsessed. Not just interested, not just intrigued - obsessed. I would spend hours watching salsa videos, letting my eyes follow the lead's every movement, memorizing the way their feet whispered across the floor. In my dorm at Slippery Rock University, Rhoads Hall, the girls on my hall got so used to me popping out of my room, scanning for a dance partner, that when I appeared, they already knew - Michael needed a warm body for thirty seconds to practice a move before disappearing back into his cave to study another. Platonic and non-romantic.

Eventually, I started what I believe was Slippery Rock's first Latin ballroom club. I taught free classes - well, I tried to charge, but folks weren't paying, so free it was. Later, I partnered with the International Club and the Latin Student Association to host salsa nights. By my senior year, I had secured funding to keep the club alive after I graduated. Last I heard, the classes are still going strong.

Before I left college, I was packing two or three carloads of students to go salsa dancing in Pittsburgh at a spot called Mexico City. When I moved to Pittsburgh for my ministry job, I took it even further. I was dancing four, five, sometimes six nights a week. What once felt like discipline - the careful study, the hours of repetition - had transformed into play. I had found something that didn't just prove I was Latino; it allowed my body to breathe as an Afro-Cubano. Discipline brings freedom, right?

Women in the Pittsburgh salsa scene started pulling me aside. "What are you?" they'd ask, the same question I had been hearing since middle school. This time, I had an answer that resonated from my bones. Cuban. And they would light up. "Ohhh, that makes sense! You move like the people I used to dance with in Cuba!"

That was it. I had done it.

Years later, near the present day, I've become one of the most sought-after male leads in the city. I rarely have to ask women to dance anymore - they come to me, tapping my shoulder, letting me know it's their turn. This isn't bragging; this is the joy of finding something that speaks for me before I have to say a word. Since

The First, the Few and the Only

Slippery Rock, I've taught Latin ballroom at conferences, corporate retreats, weddings, and too many private lessons to count.

Recently, I was at a company event for a Hispanic organization I was consulting for. It happened to be the birthday of one of the best female dancers in the city, a woman I had known since my first days in the scene. She held her party at a fancy Mexican restaurant, and after a couple of hours of struggling to keep up with the rapid Spanish conversations around me, my mind was tired. I had just submitted my book proposal to my first publisher, and all I wanted was to check my phone for peer feedback.

I told everyone goodbye. When I reached the birthday girl, she looked at me in horror. "You can't leave," she said. "We haven't started dancing yet." Latin parties have a reputation in the Black community, and that night, they proved it right. I sat back down with my colleagues, and about forty minutes later, the music started.

Two and a half hours of dancing later, an older Venezuelan woman from the company locked eyes with me during our turn to dance and said, in Spanish, "Tú eres definitivamente Latino."

Some of the younger folks in the office, still catching their breath from dancing, turned to me and said in Spanish, "Wow, man. If we didn't believe you were Latino before, we all know now. Your feet told us the truth." And to think - it all started with a longing in college. A hiraeth.

🌱 Getting Involved:

> Hiraeth - (Welsh pronunciation: "HEER-eye-th" (with a soft "th" like in "think")) is a Welsh word that has no direct English equivalent, but hiraeth expresses a deep, nostalgic longing for a place, time, or person—often tinged with grief or homesickness for something that may no longer exist or never fully did.
>
> Example: A woman watches a little girl play with her father and feels hiraeth for when her daddy used to do the same. A man watched a boy being tossed in the air by his mommy, and he felt hiraeth because he never knew his mom.

The First, the Few and the Only

Have you ever felt hiraeth? Have you ever felt a nostalgic longing or homesickness for something outside of you that you felt belonged to you?

Name it to tame it below:

_____

_____

Seeing with my feet

One might ask, But what about your Ghanaian side? The truth is that I followed whatever path my face carved out for me. Just like that moment in middle school when the Black girls questioned whether I was "really Black," I learned that acceptance was often dictated by perception. My twin brother, with his stronger African features, resembled our biological father. I, on the other hand, had inherited our Cuban mother's Taíno nose.

Because my features leaned more Latino, I "unconsciously" leaned into that identity, thinking it would be the group where I'd find the most belonging. I wish I felt more of the rich cultural heritage of my Ghanaian side and I'm ashamed to say I don't feel much of it, except for when I dance, but what can you do? My biological dad abandoned my biological mom, and with his departure, went so much of that heritage inheritance. I followed my face to where I thought I would blend in the most.

But identity is never that simple. I quickly had to learn the brutal, unspoken rules of colorism within the Latino community - rules that dictated who was centered, who was celebrated, and who was sidelined. At the same time, I was also coming to understand the deep self-hate and colorism within the Black community. No matter which identity I tried to embrace, the same painful truth echoed back: the lighter you

The First, the Few and the Only

are the better you are or the lighter your skin, the further you could climb, whether in Black spaces or Latino ones.

I was reminded of this when Black Panther: Wakanda Forever was released. The character Namor, played by Tenoch Huerta, was a revelation - a powerful, dark-skinned Indigenous Mexican man leading an underwater empire. His performance was a standout, yet in his home country, there was outrage. Not over his talent, but over the fact that the Disney casting director didn't choose a Mexican actor that was lighter. The backlash was loud and telling in a country where mestizaje and Indigenous erasure have shaped beauty standards; many still expected their heroes to have fairer skin.

It was a stark reminder of the same forces I had been navigating my whole life. Whether in Black or Latino communities, colorism remained a gatekeeper, dictating who was allowed to claim space, who was palatable, and who had to fight for belonging.

My Older Brother's Warning

My brother warned me about whiteness early.
"No matter how smart you are, no matter how hard you work, they will never see you as one of them."

At the time, I brushed it off. I thought he was being dramatic, bitter even. I had grown up believing that if I just played the game right, if I kept my head down and worked twice as hard, I could carve out a place where I truly belonged. But the older I got, the more I saw the truth in his words.
Whiteness is a country with no permanent visas. You can visit, even stay a while, but you will never be a citizen. That's the paradox of being "the first," "the few," "the only." You are celebrated, but never quite embraced. A success story, but also a stranger. You become fluent in a language that will never fully be yours. It's the same story told a thousand different ways - across boardrooms, across campuses, across neighborhoods, across generations.

That's where the weight of liminality settles in. It's not just being between cultures; it's between acceptance and exile, between admiration and alienation.

The First, the Few and the Only

A Redencao de Cam (Ham's Redemption) by Modesto Brocos 1895

Ham's Redemption is a painting that carries more weight than the oil and canvas that contain it. At first glance, it appears to celebrate family, a generational moment captured in time. Beneath the surface, however, its message is as clear as it is insidious. The grandmother, the darkest figure, raises her hands to the heavens in thanksgiving - not for life, not for love, but for the baby's whiteness. The baby, impossibly pale, sits in the arms of a mother who is lighter than the grandmother but darker than the father, who, in turn, appears nearly European. The composition tells a story of racial ascent, of salvation through proximity to whiteness. It is an artistic manifestation of the racial ideology that shaped - and continues to shape - the Americas: the closer to white, the closer to freedom.

But what is art if not a mirror? Ham's Redemption does not simply reflect the aspirations of its time - it projects them forward, shaping reality as much as it records it. The painting is not just an artifact of nineteenth-century Brazil; it is a prophecy that still echoes in the ways Black and Brown bodies move through the world today. It is in the schoolteacher who praises the fair-skinned child for being "so articulate." It is in the job applicant who straightens her curls before an interview. It is in the tokenized professional who has been welcomed into white spaces, only to realize that his invitation is conditional - his value tied to how well he can reassure the grandmother, the mother, and the father in that painting that

The First, the Few and the Only

their hopes were not in vain. Life imitates art, and art, in turn, dictates the terms of life. 3

This is the tightrope we walk as the first, the few, and the only. We are the recipients of prayers we never asked for, walking through doors that were only cracked open to let in just enough color to prove a point, but not enough to change the room. Ham's Redemption tells a story that was never meant to redeem us, only to redeem whiteness itself.

Book resource
Racial Innocence: Unmasking Latino Anti-Black Bias
and The Struggle For Equality by Tanya Katerí Hernandez

The War with My Brown-ness and Afro-Latinidad

I recently attended a show in Pittsburgh called The Real James Bond...Was Dominican by Christopher Rivas. Shout out to the OG, author of Brown Enough. You killed it, compa.

It was powerful - more than a performance, it was a mirror. Rivas wove his own story with that of his father and the infamous playboy Porfirio Rubirosa, peeling back the layers of Dominican identity, colorism, and the wounds inherited through blood and culture.

One phrase from the show struck me deeply: "mejorando la raza," meaning "bettering the race." I didn't grow up hearing it quite that way. In middle school some girls told me it was "¡limpia la raza!" – "clean the race." The same mandate, but sharper, more explicit: whiten your lineage, erase the Blackness, breed toward European features. I remember Rivas handing out clothespins at the start of the show. At a certain moment in the performance, he asked the audience to take them out and clip them to their noses for a moment - the same way a family member had forced him to do so in childhood to prevent his nose from getting too wide, too Black.

I couldn't do it. I wouldn't. I had already lived with a clothespin on my nose for most of my life.

The First, the Few and the Only

Watching the white audience members pinch their noses, giggle, only to remove the clips moments later, made me starkly aware of something: could I ever take mine off? Or had it become a permanent part of me - psychological, somatic, inherited? Like my very body is something that needs to be cleaned (limpia la raza) or to be made better and whiter (mejoranda la raza).

It's strange writing about whiteness and Blackness when colorism sometimes cuts deeper than racism because it's your own people against you. Your own people are rejecting the very features they hate in themselves that they gave you, rejecting themselves through me.

    Getting Involved: Reclaiming what was never meant to be lost. Part two from getting involved on page 171 before Good Hair subsection.

By now, you've named it - the part of your body that has carried your shame. Maybe you wrote it quickly, without hesitation. Maybe your pen hovered over the page, reluctant to make it real. Maybe you still can't bring yourself to write it down. That's okay. Maybe you skipped the exercise quickly, or maybe you hesitated, feeling the tension between what you know and what you've been told to believe. Either way, you did it. You looked at it. That is no small thing.

But now, we must ask: who taught you to hate it?
Sit with this for a moment. Think about where that shame first took root. Was it in a childhood memory? A casual comment from a family member? A beauty standard woven into every ad, every doll, every movie, every compliment someone else received but you did not. Maybe you can't pinpoint a single moment. Maybe it's been there for as long as you can remember, passed down like an unspoken inheritance.

Reflection Exercise

- What is your earliest memory of feeling like this part of your body was "wrong" or "less than?"
- Whose voice do you hear when those thoughts creep in?
- If you could speak back to that voice, what would you say?

You're not alone

The First, the Few and the Only

Undoing the Clothespin

In The Real James Bond…Was Dominican, Rivas handed his audience a clothespin; a tangible reminder of how bodies have been policed, corrected, and contorted to fit into whiteness. Some people wore it for a moment, then let it go. For those of us who have lived with that clothespin our whole lives, what does it mean to finally take it off?

Let's try something.

1. Close your eyes. Picture the part of your body you wrote down earlier. See it in full detail. Now, imagine the hands that shaped you - your ancestors, the ones who came before you. What would they say if they could see you now? Would they call you a mistake? Or would they call you a miracle?

2. Place your hands on that part of your body. Gently. No criticism, no tension - just presence. Feel its warmth, its strength, its history.

3. Say this out loud or write it down below:
   This is mine. This was never a mistake. This was never something to be cleaned or corrected. This is beautiful. This is mine and it is good.

   Full Stop.

Breaking the Cycle

It's one thing to see the truth…it's another to live in it. The world will still try to hand you a clothespin. It will still try to convince you that you need fixing. But you don't.

Where do we go from here?

- What is one small way you can honor this part of your body today? (Wearing a certain hairstyle unapologetically, refusing to shrink yourself in a space, taking a selfie with pride, etc.)
- If you have children, nieces, nephews, or younger people in your life, how can you make sure they don't inherit this same shame?
- What would it look like to see your goodness, instead of through the lens of whiteness?

You're not alone

The First, the Few and the Only

Write your thoughts here:

You are not a product of someone else's prayer for proximity to whiteness like in Ham's Redemption. You are the answered prayer of ancestors who survived, who loved, who dared to exist fully in their bodies despite everything. The question is - will you?

Adoption and the Loss of Cultural Reflection

As my friend Milagra Lagunas says, "No soy ni de aqui o ni de alla," —I'm not from here or there. Growing up adopted made the dissonance even sharper. My face, my nose, my personality traits — none of it was reflected back to me in my home. My upbringing had its own complexities, but when it came to being Afro-Cuban, things got even more tangled.

I wasn't raised with mofongo, platanos, ropa vieja, or café con leche con pan in the morning. My mom was German, so I ate pork and sauerkraut. My dad was Virginia Black, so breakfast was eggs always accompanied by gravy. I had no language for Afro-Latinidad. No palette, no blueprint. I knew I was mixed, but I didn't know what that meant. I was a liminal body, an in-between. It wasn't until middle school that I even learned that Black and white don't make brown — they make grey. I had always assumed my brown-ness was just the arithmetic of race.

The First, the Few and the Only

Check out this image containing some of the different words whites came up with to categorize mixedness in the US:

In Latin America, race isn't arithmetic. It's taxonomy. In Cuba, there are sixty different terms for skin tone. In Brazil, there are 134. The need to name every shade, to assign value, to mark the borders of belonging is as deeply ingrained in Latin culture as it is in the U.S. 5

A distant cousin of mine had a white mother. Whenever he wanted to play basketball with the Black kids at the local court, he'd make his mom drop him off a fifth of a mile away. If they knew his mom was white, they might not let him play. They might test him, make him prove himself, or try to punk him on the court because having a white mom somehow made him more 'soft'. 🌱

1. Listen to the poem entitled: "Afro-Latina" by Elizabeth Acevedo
2. Check out a book called Brown Enough by Christopher Rivas

Secret Shame of Colorism

A darker-toned friend once told me something she had never shared with anyone before. She had two sons with a white man. When they were born, the first thing she thought was: "Thank you, God, that they are not my color." She went on to say;

> "You asked me what I think of that picture with the Black fur llama surrounded by white fur llamas, and I said that I see myself there. The other thought I had when I saw it was, this is hard, was when my sons were born. I have two, they are white, ya know, because their dad was white. So, they look more like him in their skin... and I was so thankful. They came out and the first thing I thought was, 'Thank you, God, that they are not my color.' Isn't that sad? Because of all the things I have gone through, my brother, sister, and I, moving through countries and always experiencing racism and all kinds of discrimination, regardless of titles, even regardless of socioeconomic, but when they

The First, the Few and the Only

were born, I thought that and have always kept that secret. You are the only one that knows, and I didn't tell anyone because I was so ashamed. I thought at that moment something so crazy, and I want you to put it in your book."

She hated herself for thinking it, but she had been carrying that secret, that shame, because of all the racism, all the rejection, all the ways the world had told her and her brothers that darker meant less. She was relieved that her children would not be worthy of all kinds of discrimination that she and her siblings survived as they moved throughout the world as darker-skinned Spaniard kids.

I sat with that confession, and then my own surfaced. My children's mother is Greek and Sicilian. When my first son was born, the first thing I noticed was that he was a boy, and I was elated. Next thing I noticed was his skin: he was brown, like his daddy, and I felt so happy. The last thing I noticed was his hair – it wasn't like mine. And I felt relieved.

What does that say about me?

For the way I saw my own body. For the way I see my own Ghanaian Cuban curls. For the choices I made in love and lineage without even realizing what was driving them. ¡Limpia la raza, right?! Here's the hardest thing to admit, I didn't just want my son to be brown. I wanted him to look more "Latino" than I did. I wanted him to be welcomed more easily for the very same reason one of my favorite actors, Tenoch Huerta, was rejected by light-skinned leaders in his own country after his knockout role as Namor in Black Panther 2. This is so hard to touch on for me as a father, and it feels dangerous to name. When you're tokenized enough, you get this feeling that my kids have to be closer to whiteness than me. That is FUCKED UP, and I have to get angry with that. I have to face my own inner contempt for my own body. I have to confront that shame. I, also, remember being deathly afraid that my son would come out looking white. I didn't want a son who could pass. So, I felt this inner turmoil because I didn't want him to pass, knowing that the Black community would never fully accept him if he was too white. If he was too white, he would have to fight harder, perform more, culturally over-compensate, and prove his belonging In ways I wouldn't wish on anyone. This war with my own brown-ness. This inner contempt for my own body. The very fact that the thought of wondering if my kids passed the brown paper bag test entered my mind disgusts me.

The First, the Few and the Only

Ultimately the war I couldn't overcome over colorism and my own body I put on my son and daughter by breeding my own hair out of them. What Nigerians call, "Making a .5"

Damn, that sucks to write out loud, to name it. I need to weep. I have to sit with the shame of it and decide what comes next.

🌱 Getting Involved:
Full stop.

"Where's your breath?" -Resmaa Menakem
Now breathe deeper. What's coming up for you right now? Is there a memory or emotion resurfacing?

Write it down, along with which part of your body it's manifesting through:

_____

The Inescapable War of Ethnic Liminality

Dr. Brian Bantum wrote about this in his book entitled Redeeming Mulatto, and it was a boon to me owning with pride my mixed-ness. He taught me how people in churches don't choose their church membership based on the theology or the preaching as much as their decision is based on the bodies in the room. In the pews. A formative shift for me to see bodies as a social determinant to membership. Nonetheless, I just want to say that another great resource I loved from Dr. Beverly Daniel Tatum's book entitled Why Do All The Black Kids Sit Together in the Cafeteria? One huge gift was the bill of rights for mixed bodies: when I read it while at an all-white, conservative Christian school, (I transferred after two years because I could no longer suffer the microaggressions and exclusion for starting the first diversity club called S.E.A.D. Students excited about diversity. I felt like I was dying slowly there) I thought it may be a gift to you like these were a

The First, the Few and the Only

gift to me. Dr. Maria P. Root's Bill of Rights for People of Mixed Heritage 6 counters so many of my internalized struggles:

I HAVE THE RIGHT

- Not to justify my existence in this world.
- Not to keep the races separate within me.
- Not to justify my ethnic legitimacy.
- Not to be responsible for people's discomfort with my physical or ethnic ambiguity.
- To identify myself differently than strangers expect me to identify.
- To identify myself differently than how my parents identify me.
- To identify myself differently than my brothers and sisters.
- To identify myself differently in different situations.
- To create a vocabulary to communicate about being multiracial or multiethnic.
- To change my identity over my lifetime – and more than once.
- To have loyalties and identification with more than one group of people.
- To freely choose whom I befriend and love.

I hold onto these words, and yet, I still feel the tension.

There were moments when my ethnic liminality put me at odds with Black people. Not because I ever sought to betray them or be a Sambo, but because they needed me to pick a side. Just like I needed Jay to pick a side. The war between Black and white was one I was caught in, often without realizing it, sometimes paying dearly for it.

As Dr. Brian Bantum says, "Our bodies are always doing work we don't know it's doing in the room." Isn't that the weight of it all? Even when we choose neutrality, our bodies cannot.

187
You're not alone

The First, the Few and the Only

What's coming up for you?

_____

_____

_____

_____

_____

_____

_____

_____

_____

_____

_____

_____

The First, the Few and the Only

Chapter 11

Villains In Common

The Eight Kinds of People I Met in White Institutions

The institutions were never neutral or random, and neither were the people in them. Over time, I learned to recognize patterns - certain types of people who showed up again and again, each playing a role in maintaining the system. Like in Geoffrey Chaucer's Canterbury Tales, some smiled as they set you up, others sabotaged in secret, and a few were simply drunk on proximity to power. These are their archetypes. Feel free to write out names/stories that come to mind & body in the space around each photo. I left plenty of room for you on each page of this chapter.

1. Lotso from Toy Story 3 – The Smiling Tyrant

I knew from the moment I met her that my body did not trust her. Lotso-types project warmth, the kind of white executive who hugs you like a teddy bear while quietly making sure you never move beyond the limits they set. They rule with a grandfatherly charm, but beneath the scent of strawberries, you can feel their sharp teeth at your neck while they do their best to convince you that everything is fine.

The First, the Few and the Only

2. Stinky Pete from Toy Story 2 – The Collector

They were the first of their kind I encountered - the ones who see you not as a person, but as a prize. A rare, charismatic BIPOC rising star to be displayed, not empowered. Their approval comes at a cost: stay in the box they've chosen for you or be discarded.

3. Dawn Bellwether from Zootopia – Self-Victimizing Betrayer

The ones who claim to love you, mentor you, and stand beside you until the moment they don't. Dawn-types are the architects of strategic backstabbing, operating under the veil of innocence. They perfect the art of self-victimization, and when things go wrong, you will find yourself cast as the villain in a story you didn't even know you were part of.

The First, the Few and the Only

4. Buddy from The Incredibles – The Suckling Opportunist

The eager sidekick, the "harmless" admirer - until they're given power, and suddenly, they aren't so harmless anymore. Buddy-types latch onto your brilliance, your labor, your energy, and use it as a launchpad. They mimic your greatness until they no longer need you, then move past you, ascending to positions you were passed over for. And when you're left sitting in the same cubicle where they first found you, they act as if they never knew you at all.

Buddy loves you when you're here.

But when he rises, you're nothing more than a steppingstone. He's already left you behind. At the end of the day, Buddy wants power. He will romanticize his proximity to you until he can have what he wants from you. Power. Above you. Over you. Ultimately, Buddy ain't ya buddy.

The First, the Few and the Only

5. Charles Muntz from Up – The White Idol

The founders. The presidents. The executives you once admired from a distance. The ones whose lore you were taught to adore. Their pictures were on a wall somewhere, and you actually believed the hype. You think they are different, that maybe this time, this one will be a true mentor. But like Charles Muntz, the moment they see you as a threat rather than a follower, their admiration curdles into hostility. If you get too close, you will see that their legacy was built on exclusion, their power maintained by sabotage. The lesson? Don't meet your idols. It's just like Shia LaBeouf's character in Money Never Sleeps, when he meets Michael Douglas' character and then that man stabs him in the back. Those are Charles's.

What's coming up for you? Anything(one) feel familiar so far?

_____

_____

_____

_____

The First, the Few and the Only

6. Evelyn Deavor from The Incredibles 2 – The 'Safe' White Liberal

Honest Iago from Othello. The Evelyn-types are dangerous precisely because they don't look like a threat. They play the role of the cool, progressive ally until you realize they have been working against you from the beginning. They don't need to win you over; they just need to be close enough to manipulate you and side with the winning team. When the chips are down, they are an opportunist and a survivalist who reverts to the original default ancestral colonizer programming. This is the last person you expect to alienate you. To use you. To consume. They feign solidarity, but choose their own survival in a zero-sum game you didn't know you were playing. This is the one that inadvertently teaches you that white liberals and white conservatives are kind of the same.

7. Namaariri from Raya and the Last Dragon – The Careerist Colleague

Not every villain has white skin. The system's design ensures that some BIPOC bodies learn to sacrifice their own in order to survive. Namaariri-types prioritize career over community, self-preservation over solidarity, isolation over connection. They have seen how the system rewards betrayal, and they have chosen to comply. Gamoras, not Nebulas.

The First, the Few and the Only

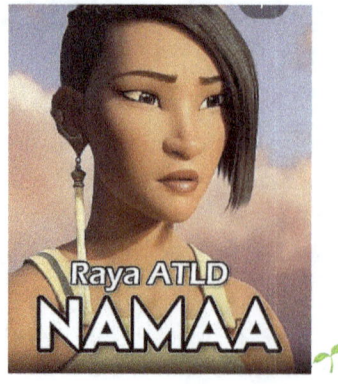

8. Hans from Frozen — The Fetishizer

They don't love you, they love the idea of you. The Hans-types are infatuated with the "exotic," the "different," the "uncommon." At first, they sing that "Love is an Open Door" song, but their admiration is never about who you are - only what you can provide for them. And once they've gotten what they want, they move on, leaving you to realize that you were never their equal, only their fascination.

As I discussed these archetypes I was putting together when writing this section with my friend Meagan, she posed a crucial question:

"Aside from Namaari, are Stinky and the others always white bodies? If not, how did they - the BIPOC versions of these characters - get this way? What compelled them to act in ways that oppress us, in the same ways they were once oppressed?"

The First, the Few and the Only

Neither of us had the answer then. I don't have the answer now. That question lingers to this day, but like my favorite Charles Kettering quote says, "A question well-named is a problem half-solved."

 Let's examine these villains across institutions more closely. Perhaps in doing so, the half-solved problems will reveal new answers.

Whispers of Windmills

Oh, the giants - the ones that shape-shift, masquerading as mere windmills but whispering in the night, their voices curling like smoke around the ears of the First, the Few, and the Only.
They taunt, they mock, they lie.

"You don't belong here."
"You should be grateful they let you in. If you left, who would hire you?"
"Don't rock the boat… at least you are in the room"
"Don't get too comfortable. What if they try to replace you?"
"You're just a diversity hire."
"You speak so well… soooo articulate."
"You're making too much of this. That wasn't a microaggression, that's just Janice."
"You can change things. Give it time and work your way up."
"You should smile more. You're representing all Black people. Don't fuck up."
"You owe them your success. You owe them your loyalty."
"Are you a real tiger?"
"It is an honor to be the first _____ at this company, right?"

These windmills
- these towering illusions of power,
spin endlessly, grinding down resistance,
hoping the First, the Few, and the Only will mistake their whispers for the truth.

But what happens when we stop listening? When we see them for what they are?

When we realize we are not small, and they are not giants.

The First, the Few and the Only

Chapter 12

Academia

As Austin Channing Brown said, "White people are exhausting." 1

No one ever warned me how brutal this space can be to Black and Brown bodies, about the slow burn-whether staff or student, on most college campuses in the U.S. Working in white academia is not just challenging – institutionalization is traumatizing. Serving institutions in BIPOC bodies means constantly navigating an unspoken, yet deeply entrenched, hidden curriculum designed to erase, exhaust, and diminish us. If that wasn't enough, this is where I met my first Lotso and several Hobie Browns, like my favorite professor, Dr. Knorr.

The Hidden Curriculum at My First PWI

At one college campus in particular, I served a campus tour guide. One day, the admissions office called and asked if I was available that afternoon for a tour. I paused my studying, crossed the quad, and made my way to Crawford Hall, where Courtney, one of the admissions executives, briefed me on the family I would be showing the campus to. This was standard practice - admissions staff would often provide a few details about prospective students so we could tailor the tour accordingly.
But this time, the request was different.

"They specifically asked for a tour guide of color," Courtney told me during the pre-tour briefing. Because I was it - the only one - I got the gig.

The First, the Few and the Only

I remember feeling a quiet excitement. Here was an opportunity to be professional, to be honest, and to show a potential student what life at Grove City was really like for students of color. The admissions team seemed really nervous, but I was eager.

When the family arrived, I greeted them with a smile and began the tour. The prospective student - a young Black woman considering Grove City - asked me a series of pointed questions about representation, demographics, and student organizations that offered safety for Black and Brown students. I answered each one carefully, measured yet honest. I knew the numbers because I had lived the reality. I told her, with a sense of pride, that I was actively working to create the first dedicated spaces for Black and Brown students on campus.

She listened intently, then stopped walking, turned to me, and said something that cut straight through my well-rehearsed professionalism:

"...why do you stay?"

I remember giving some microwaved answer about changing things where I'm at instead of leaving it for another generation to have to navigate without as much support as I had when I first came, leaving things better than I found it type thing. She accepted the answer, and we continued the tour.

That night I wept in the chapel alone. It finally hit me.

All the horrifying sense of futility, the alienation amidst a campus full of my brethren in Christ, the invisibility in student life, the chronic prolonged stress of racial battle fatigue, feeling like the only Black body in the room who has to speak for all Black people and not feeling like I know enough, the lack of representation in all speakers at chapel, in all the white portraits on the walls, and the sense that I was in romantic purgatory. The microaggressions, the banana peppers and banana pudding thrown at my dorm window, the bananas I would find on my desk in my room, the self-gaslighting, the self-hatred, the self-abandonment, and the amount of energy I gave to the other Black men on campus and how much I felt like they needed me to be good to lean on. These things I was carrying were actually as heavy as they feel when I stopped distracting myself with busyness and endless extracurricular activities. Not just the load but the toll of it all and why the heck was I really staying. What was I REALLY changing? Why wasn't I letting it go?

The First, the Few and the Only

I begged God for a way out because if not, I knew it would swallow me whole. I knew then and there that this was no way to experience my college years, and that I may need to transfer for relief, but was I abandoning a task God gave to me or was I relieving myself of an institutional design that I was never meant to change?

Status Competition & Erasure

For BIPOC scholars in predominantly white academic institutions, the terrain is not merely intellectual; it is a battleground of status, recognition, and survival. Dr. Knorr, a South American professor, articulates the quiet violence of erasure - how she resists the gravitational pull of systems designed to either consume or make invisible those who refuse to assimilate. The academy, she argues, sets up a game that many BIPOC scholars feel pressured to play, yet the game itself is rigged, built upon foundations of exclusion, extraction, and a relentless demand for proximity to power.

Status competition refers to the struggle for prestige, resources, and institutional validation within hierarchical structures. In predominantly white academic spaces, this competition is often racialized, requiring BIPOC scholars to navigate between visibility and survival, excellence and exhaustion. For many, the goal is not merely professional advancement but the ability to exist authentically within an institution that was not designed with them in mind.

Dr. Knorr highlights a paradox: while academia positions itself as a meritocracy, the measures of success are predicated on whiteness. Reducing meritocracy to a racial myth, better yet a racial smokescreen for classism, nepotism, and racism. Proximity to the president, funding, tenure - these are not neutral milestones but contested spaces where BIPOC scholars are either tokenized or rendered invisible. Some choose to fight for these markers of status, while others, like Dr. Knorr, resist by strategically staying on the periphery, carving out space to do work unmediated by white institutional expectations, or trivial councils that accomplish nothing.

The Trauma of Advanced Degrees

Earning an advanced degree as a BIPOC scholar is not just an intellectual pursuit; it is a process that often entails profound psychological, cultural, and even physical distress. The journey is marked by isolation, hyper-surveillance, and the constant

The First, the Few and the Only

negotiation of identity. Cultural identity erasure is not just theoretical - it is an embodied experience. Institutions recognize BIPOC scholars only from the point at which they enter the Western academic framework. They do not ask, "Where in Africa? Where in the Caribbean?" Instead, they acknowledge us only in relation to the dominant culture, presuming that our existence begins when we enter their gaze and which institutions we graduate from.

This erasure extends beyond geography to memory itself. As Dr. Knorr poignantly states, half quoting a book she had read:

"Whites need to write on dead trees to remember things they think about themselves, but we don't need that because our memory comes from a collective consciousness in connection to our ancestors, our bodies - because the memories were passed down to us through genetic intelligence."

In this, she speaks to the fundamental difference in how knowledge, history, and identity are preserved. White academia relies on the written word, the archive, the citation - structures of knowledge designed to uphold their own authority. For many Indigenous, African, and diasporic peoples, however, memory is not housed in books; it lives in the body, in oral traditions, in collective consciousness. The academy demands proof, while our histories pulse within us, undeniable and ever-present.

Choosing to Opt Out of the Game

Dr. Knorr's refusal to engage in status competition is a radical act of self-preservation and resistance. She understands that the institution thrives on BIPOC scholars battling one another for scarce recognition, playing a game that was never meant to serve them. Yet, as she reminds me often, *"We were not meant to live in competition."*

Instead of vying for scraps from a system that was never built for us, perhaps the deeper question is: how do we build something of our own?

The First, the Few and the Only

Essential Questions to Ask Before Enrolling or Working at a College/University

Side Quest: A checklist for identifying tokenism, microaggressions, and uncovering the hidden curriculum of academia in the US:

Closing Thoughts

Even with these questions, no amount of preparation can fully shield you from the realities of being Black or Brown in a predominantly white academic institution. The isolation, the ostracization, the quiet violence of being celebrated for diversity while simultaneously being erased - it is all part of the hidden curriculum that no syllabus will disclose or prepare you for.

However, asking these questions forces institutions to reckon with their own failings. It places the burden of accountability on them, not on you. And most importantly, it equips you with the knowledge to make informed decisions about where to invest your talents, your labor, and your future.

Because the real question isn't just "Why do you want to be here?" It is "Does this place deserve you?"

>End Side Quest<

Charles Muntz (Up) & The Setup

When I think of tokenism happening at Slippery Rock University, I recall how academic exec "Charles Muntz" tried to turn me into his Uncle Tom to replace Justin Brown because he became too powerful. You see, Justin Brown created a diversity club on campus that became so popular that other campuses were spending money to have Justin Brown travel and speak to their campuses. Muntz

The First, the Few and the Only

even sat JB down and told him that he would have to give the University money from these speaking engagements. When he said no, they decided to replace him and they set their eyes on me. What they didn't bank on was that, despite the status threat, that some Black leaders become friends. That Justin and I would talk about what was going on. We decided to look out for each other because the white institutions always bank on the few Blacks that rise up as leaders to not communicate, let alone be friends. That would be like MLK and Malcolm X telling each other the different ways the CIA was pressing each of them.

Ultimately, tokenism expects us to compete for proximity to power, but not for all the different ways to change a system, whether reformation or revolution. What I have found through my friendship with Justin was that, when I decided that my liberation is tied up with whomever the system sets me at odds with, and they decide the same, our friendship makes a third way that outlived the Muntz's of the university. All the institutional schemes to supplant Justin with someone they thought they could control, or at least to lessen his influential power, banked on me. Justin's experience saved me from being set up to be groomed to become their token. The more "Charles Muntz" approached me, the more I found myself resisting. Every time I saw him smiling at me, I saw Justin's face and how they were dogging him out.

It's so interesting how when two Black men are becoming too powerful & popular in the system, the system doesn't expect Black bodies to be friends. That is what connected us – that is where Justin Brown and I found both our strength and our escape from the setup of Charles Muntz.

Also, right before I had transferred, the Charles Muntz was pursuing our other Black friend, Dr. Mychael Lee, to use him to supplant Justin Brown's popularity and influence on campus. We all didn't find out until later when we were talking about how Charles Muntz was moving. He was trying to recruit us for some random, public-facing stuff - then we found out what was going on and put it all together.

🌱 Getting Involved

Do you have any stories that surfaced for you? Write them below:

_____

The First, the Few and the Only

Check out this talk by Dr. Beverly Daniel Tatum and take notes on what parts of her story reflect the history of the FFO.

The First, the Few and the Only

🌱 If you want to see some of this in action, then I would highly recommend you watch the film MASTER on Prime, starring Regina Hall.

Brilliance in the Streets, Soul in the Academic Space

"These energies have always been around, you know, this thing, we term it hustle, but it's really just the ingenuity necessary to survive. You know, and navigate in the world. We call it hustle because I imagine that's just our way of giving it a name because sometimes we wanna divorce ourselves from the academic space because that academic space was a source of brutality and hostility for a long time, but the reality of it is that it's still wisdom, it's still knowledge, it's still invention, it's still development, you know, and it's still progress. I think as we kind of pull back these labels we can acknowledge brilliance in the streets, we can acknowledge soul in the academic space, and we can allow these things to come together. Um, the world is filled with way too many bright people for us to have the problems we still have in the world"

- Lauryn Hill

 If the plantation in Josiah Henson's universe could whisper, its voice would not be the raging shout of an overseer or the crack of a whip - it would be something more insidious. The land itself would murmur, its whispers seeping up through the cracked earth, carried on the humid air, threading through the trees that had borne witness to generations of bondage.

The First, the Few and the Only

It would say:
"You were born here, you're lucky to be here and you will die here. This is all there is."

The soil, thick with the blood and sweat of those who toiled before him, would try to convince him that escape was impossible, that his fate was already written, pressed into the dirt beneath his feet.

"Freedom is a fever dream. Stay grateful & quiet. Even if you run, where will you go?"

The river, which could be both a barrier and a passage to freedom, would whisper doubt - telling him that the world beyond the plantation would never truly be his. That he would always carry the scent of bondage, that no matter how far he traveled, the weight of the chains would follow.

"Don't be ungrateful, Josiah. Things could be worse. We could make things better here"

The rustling crops, the same fields that had broken the backs of his ancestors, would mock him, warning that stepping out of line would not just cost him - it would cost those he loved. That the enslaver's "kindness" was a leash, not a mercy.

" Even if you make it out, will you ever be free? Will they ever let you forget?"

The trees, whose limbs had held the bodies of those who dared to dream, would taunt him with history, reminding him that the world outside still bore the same disease, just with a different name.
But beneath the whispers of the land, there would be another voice, quieter but steady. Perhaps the wind, perhaps the distant echo of ancestors long past. It would say:

"Keep going."
"There is a land this land cannot see."
"You were not made to break—you were made to build."

The land could try to own him, but it could not stop him from leaving footprints toward something greater.

The First, the Few and the Only

Chapter 13

Evangelical Church

A Black female pastor once said of the white Protestant evangelical church, *"they staple delicious fruit on diseased trees."*

The white evangelical church is not honest in its self-assessment. This section is a tough one for me. Let me begin this section by starting at the end of the story. As of the last few years, I have since left full-time vocational ministry several years ago. I still get pursued to preach at a local Presbyterian church by a pastor that knew me in my ministry days. Most times I say, "No, I'm not ready," but recently I agreed to preach once a month. When he asked me to join on as a part-time pastor, I said no. There is nothing wrong with white male bodies preaching from the pulpit, but my body contorts and constricts so much now at the sight of it. After years of trying to conform and be as authentic as I could manage, doing damn good labor but the better I worked the more I got knocked down for shining too bright by insecure white Christian leaders, and over time it made me feel some trauma when it came to being on stage, especially when that stage is in the territory of old white men who have the title of 'pastor.'

My friend and boxing coach, Francesco, invited me to join him for church at his home church about a year ago, and I have chosen to attend this predominantly Black church. I finally feel reconnected to my spiritual moorings.

As of last Sunday, I went forward to join the church as a member – my first church membership switch in nearly ten years. When the lady that received me started praying over me, she shivered noticeably and said, "I just got a strong sense that we need you here." My heart said, "Are you sure about that?" I felt broken, like I had gone off the reservation as they say and was of no use. All used up by white evangelical spaces. I felt disposable and like warped wood. All that promise replaced with rage, disappointment, burnout and shame.

The First, the Few and the Only

Additionally, whenever I hear soft rock in white Protestant spaces, my body and mind start to become dissociative. I experience constriction and tension in my back, and I become critical of the lyrics that focus on how God makes you "feel" rather than who God is. How did I get like this? When did my body start responding this way? When did I stop feeling safe in the church, and more particularly, the white church?

To answer that, we have to go back to the parts of my story I don't want to name. Inspired by how Kiese Laymon ends his book, Heavy, I find the words to say what I need to name: "I want to write a lie, and I feel as though you would read and enjoy one, but I cannot. I must write this instead. I need to show you where I been, where I bend…" and where I broke. 🌱

I have four books in front of me on my writing desk, each from popular and significant contributors to this conversation of race and the church. Each, in its own way, addresses the harms and impacts of white institutions, namely the church. I want to use my intellect to wow you with their words and their stories. I want to use my intellect to identify the harms of covert racism in the church through their quotes. I want to use their words so that I don't have to go search my own heart. I want to hide.

I don't want to get into the viscera of my story, but then I remember a chance meeting I had with a joyous Jamaican woman I met at check-in for a speaking gig in Chicago. She asked, without knowing me, "Are you an author? I don't normally do this at work, but when I saw you walk up to the counter I got a vision of you as an author. Are you writing a book?"

Y'all, I had not shared any information about my life with this woman. Taken aback, I replied, "It's crazy you say that - I just started working on an intro this morning."

She smiled and said, inspired by something out of body, "You must be honest in your book. This is gonna change things for so many people, but you have to be honest. I'm so proud of you. Wow, this is gonna be big! I got a visual of you signing books and helping people you'll never know."

Her voice sits with me even now as I write, compelling me to tell the truth, to bare my soul, to keep it real, to get into my body and my guts, and show you where I bend. To put words to my abdomen's constriction, where my body held the stress

The First, the Few and the Only

and trauma and betrayal for so many years. That's the same place where I get ulcers now whenever I'm stressed.

To do this, I need to paint the picture of the middle school Michael Thornhill, all the way through to the conclusion of my college education:
I remember accepting Jesus as my Lord and savior at an early age, right before middle school. I remember feeling so passionate to tell everyone in South Florida about God. When I would walk our dog during various times of the day, I would approach random adults to ask them if they knew where they were going when they died. One time I even chased down a runner jogging along the canal to talk to him while tugging the dog along for the ride. He didn't convert, but I remember discussing the Lord with him while I was gasping for breath from the chase. My parents never knew of my escapades during my daily dog walks. They just knew that sometimes I was out for a long time.

My childhood friend Miles recounted the first time he saw my brother and me. We were in the sixth grade at this point, and we were pointing out the words on our self-made shirts that said something like "Jesus Saves," or "Jesus Loves You" to a kid we caught right before school. Sawgrass Middle School made all the kids wait out front until school started, so we had a captive audience. The kid that Miles saw us talking to was cornered – he couldn't get away from us. It didn't help that he was in a wheelchair, thus thwarting any plan he may have had to escape us quickly.
We later joined the Christian club that Miles was leading called First Priority. It was an evangelistic club that was all about inviting your peers to come hear the Good News. I stayed in that club and became one of the leaders of it in high school, along with Miles. Though it was largely run by high school girls, we were the young men that ended the long drought of male leadership within the club.

The day after my brother and I finished junior year, my mother decided to rip us out of Broward County. For some reason, she chose to buy a house in New Castle, Pennsylvania, on the line between two school districts, as I mentioned earlier in the book. She chose Neshannock to be the school for us to finish our senior year.

Reader, you know all of that from the beginning of our journey in this book together. This is simply taking a deeper dive into my time in the Western Pennsylvania public education system/community.

The First, the Few and the Only

We went to Neshannock for about nine months, and it was there that we joined a Baptist Church where it seemed like no one ever stood up or clapped during worship. Being Southern Baptist /Christian Missionary Alliance in background, we were painted with a colorful brush of movement, contra-rhythms, and dance when worship music came on. Even though it was a Baptist Church in name, they felt more like the frozen chosen, as Presbyterians call themselves.

It was at this school and this church we first really FELT like the "Blacks" in the room. We stayed true to ourselves since we felt like we were just on a long vacation before returning to South Florida the first chance we got after senior year. It was during this time of my life that I began to notice that other Blacks and ethnic minorities in these spaces acted very different than us. It was always hard to name, but they felt quieter somehow in white spaces, collectively less noticeable and more agreeable to the hegemonic thought of white people in general. Now I'm not saying northern Blacks are docile - at our Black barbershop on the other side of town, there were plenty of charismatic Black men, but whenever we were in Neshannock, the white and rich part of town, the minorities who stayed there were always different. My brother and I always felt a shock to the system in the church and the school, which were the only places we ever went besides the barbershop. We survived that and met some cool white folk along the way, but we somehow felt rejected for not fitting into the expectations of our white peers.

The evangelical culture felt like a cover up I used to mask the systemic grooming of minority and biracial youth into not only token social props, but even sexual playthings. When I say grooming, I mean being taken in by someone that wants to use my goodness, beauty, and glory for their own interests, for their consumption. They were exploiting my charisma, my personality, my novelty, even my skin. I want to clearly state that evangelical spaces feel similar to the kind of grooming that pedophiles engage in, except with race. This is what I began to experience the older I got, and it became a theme and pattern in all the other white institutions I entered. I was baptized into it in the white church, especially as a Black male with any kind of charisma. It starts as trying to "mentor" you but as you may see in my story - things can get weird real fast.

After moving to New Castle, I began applying to colleges in the fall, and I remember wanting to go to Temple very badly. It was far from my mom, and it was known to be crazy diverse. I remember thinking that it would be just like where I

The First, the Few and the Only

grew up - a much-needed reprieve from all white spaces that I was already growing a bit weary of.

From Crimson Day to Crimson Furnace

My mom got a random thing in the mail about a small Christian school called Grove City College. It was a letter about something called Crimson Day. We weren't doing anything that day, so my mom planned an outing that included stopping by Grove City. I agreed. Especially since there wasn't anything else to do and my twin brother hadn't joined me in New Castle yet. By the end of the day, I'm pretty sure my mom wanted to attend there herself. She was head over heels for the head of career services, Jim Thrasher, after his speech on calling. I wasn't too wowed. I was more interested in finding somewhere to eat, but my mom had to introduce me to him. Along the way to meet Mr. Thrasher, we met the only Black man on the stage, who I later found out was director of student life.

On the way home, my mom asked me if I wanted to go to school there. I remember replying quickly, "Not at all." I felt like there were not many people of color there, and diversity was a priority for me. I wanted to remain evangelistic, and being amongst unbelievers felt like the best way to do that. I was also curious about what all the white pastors were so afraid of when they would mention in sermons (I followed Adrian Rogers, Charles Stanley, John McArthur, and a few others religiously online) about the treacherous terrain of the college campus. They were very clear that secular college campuses corrupt Christian boys and girls. I thought it wouldn't be as bad as they said and wanted to see for myself.

Nonetheless, by the time we got home she was crying and telling me that if I didn't apply then she didn't know what she would do. She was convinced that was where God wanted me. I looked at her and told her that I was pretty sure God could tell me Himself where He wanted me if He was that concerned about which school I went to. My mom had a way of trying to emotionally manipulate her sons, but I was a seasoned war veteran at this point. I knew how to dodge and block her ploys to get me to do what she wanted with her tears. After constantly bringing up Grove City, she switched tactics. Since I was paying for my college applications, she promised to pay for all ongoing college applications for me if I would promise to apply to Grove City as well. I was pretty hellbent on not going to a Christian

The First, the Few and the Only

school, but that wager was too enticing to pass up since I didn't really have much money. She set me up.

I agreed, but before the closing she added an addendum: "I'll pay for these applications, but if you get into Grove City, you have to promise to go." All I could think of was being on campus at Temple, so I decided to forego reason and not consider just how manipulative that was. I knew she was trying to trap me with her words, but Grove City claimed to not let in many people. I knew I had mediocre grades, so I figured I had her fooled because I didn't have the grades to get in there. I agreed to her terms, and somehow, she got me an application the next day. I did an interview and thought nothing of it. I recalled looking up more colleges when she wasn't around. I decided to do my own thing and apply to different schools online since I had a blank check on colleges I could apply to now.

A month later, I got an acceptance letter to Grove City College. I remember my mom being overjoyed, annoyingly so. I remember her exact reaction because I can recall feeling such a huge contrast between what she felt and what I felt. I was devastated because it meant that I was stuck in the North. It meant I was stuck in Western Pennsylvania. It meant I was stuck here.

I remember later trying to make the best of it, figuring that it was a college that was competitive to get into, so it was probably diverse. All I saw was a Crimson Day, and although I remember how white the audience was, I figured it was a fluke visitation day.

When I graduated, my friend Miles came out to help me move in. I remember packing up all the stuff, Mom being emotional on the drive over, and Miles and I joking back and forth from the short hike from New Castle to Grove City, PA. All eighteen miles. I remember trying to be happy, and it helped having Miles there. When we pulled into campus and drove to Memorial Hall, I remember there was all this commotion, lots of people milling around in white shirts. By the time we pulled in, I realized something. It was an entire army of white women unpacking people's cars for them and helping newly-minted freshmen get to their dorms. I don't know if white men were there too, but during the window of time we pulled in, it was all white women (and one Asian woman) in their Happy Helpers t-shirts. I remember Miles and I looking at each other with confusion and excitement. There were tons of girls all around us, of course we were going to be excited!

The First, the Few and the Only

Unpacking and saying goodbye happened fast, but as move in died down and everyone began to settle in, I remember walking through Memorial Hall. I came across a Brazilian guy named Ramon, a light-skinned guy named Mark, and a Puerto Rican dude named Andrew. Beyond those three guys and myself, all three floors, all six halls were packed with white men. I remember being a little shocked. My roommate, a white dude, was settling in, so I figured it would be an opportunity to get to know the guy I would be sleeping next to for the foreseeable nine or ten months. I remember wondering how many Black, Latino, or non-white people he knew. I guess I just wanted to make sure I wasn't the only Black dude, the first Black dude he knew, so I introduced myself. We shared where we were from, and I found an idea to assuage my initial curiosity. It was an impulsive idea, but I went with it. I jokingly said,

"Hey man, do you know who Stevie Wonder is?"

He replied, "What team does he play for?"

At first, I thought he was joking, but when I saw the seriousness in his face, I realized that he was very much not kidding. I was shook.

All the white women in the Happy Helpers shirts, all the white men in the dorm (male only dorms on this side of campus, female only on the other) …all of it hit me at that moment. The picture was beginning to become clearer. I remember excusing myself to go get a breath of fresh air outside in the front of Memorial Hall and thinking, "What the hell have I done?!" It was Neshannock High School 2.0.

I remember that there may have been one saving grace - that Black dude from the Crimson Day had been emailing me back and forth. He had been telling me throughout my senior year of high school that he wanted to mentor me and was so excited that I was coming to Grove City. He seemed like a dope dude, so I figured I would catch up with him at his office the next day.

I walked up the quad the next day and went looking for his office, and on the way, I spotted another Black dude. We were gonna cross paths on the sidewalk, so I called to him and said, "Yo, what up, fam?" I put my hand out for a dap. He walked up to me awkwardly and did the weirdest thing with his hand, as if it was his first attempt at doing a simple dap. After his failed attempt at greeting me, he walked away

The First, the Few and the Only

awkwardly as if he was well aware of the crime he had just committed with his hands. It hit me again: "Where the hell am I? What have I done?"

I focused on getting to the union and seeing my new mentor. He was crisp and clean and felt like a leader, the kind of man I could learn from. He greeted me with the warmest smile, introduced me to all the leaders and staff in student life, and then invited me into his office. He asked me how I was settling in, and I lied, telling him everything was fine since I didn't want to judge too harshly right away. I figured, all things considered, it wouldn't be that bad. He turned serious and revealed that he had accepted a job as Vice President at the University of Texas. He wanted to break the news to me in person, and he explained that he had accepted the job to be closer to his wife's family. I remember not wanting to make him feel bad, so I acted excited for him. He remained very apologetic.

I don't remember much else after that. I remember going somewhat numb. That week was a blur. I went to the orientation events and went to the different dining halls to try all my options. I remained hopeful, after all I made it to college. Then I met Andrew the other side of 2nd floor Memorial Hall. Andrew was this fun-loving, break-dancing, Puerto Rican pre-seminary guy from New Jersey. We clicked immediately, and I felt hopeful and forgot all about the deferred hope of my first mentor and the sea of white women. Andrew from the dorm and I started eating together, and he was charismatic like me. We became fast friends, and his roommate Jonny would tag along sometimes as well.

Two years later, Andrew had transferred out, Mark kept mostly to himself, and Ramon and I never really saw each other much. I became depressed for a couple weeks when Andrew left. I became the guy that Black freshmen guys would come to commiserate about the racist things teachers would say in the classroom. I heard all about the racist things that the white boys would say behind their backs, as well as when random white Christian women would make sexual advances on them because they had jungle fever. When the things they told me were astoundingly egregious, I would go to student life and try to advocate without giving any identifiable information about the recipient of microaggressions and racial macroaggressions. I soon discovered, however, that that never changed anything. I later would start the first Diversity Club at that school, a move which caused me to be ostracized by the white dude from the youth group I attended in my senior year of high school. Since we went to the same college, before I transferred, I joined the same housing group on campus as that white dude that I was friends with. I

The First, the Few and the Only

remember becoming a pariah to him and the other white housing mates just for wanting to make a safe place to talk about the harms I was hearing on campus. I was being "punished" for my desire to create a place to discover the instances others kept silent so that we didn't feel as alone. So that I didn't feel as disposable and invisible.

By the end of my sophomore year, only two freshmen girls hung out with me to study in the Buhl Library: Cat and Nat. I became buddies with a Mexican guy from our housing group, but he left the school in the fall of my sophomore year. I was cool with the young Black guys, and they looked up to me, but I was always there for them. I had no one I could go to, and Cat and Nat weren't friends as much as they were study buddies. I didn't want to divulge my issues to them, so I remember I would spend hours by myself in the chapel at nights. Praying. Reflecting. Questioning myself.

I remember feeling trapped and lonely at Grove City. It was crazy because not only was I founding this diversity group called SEAD (Students Excited About Diversity), but I was voted Big Man on Campus by the Sigma Theta sorority. I ran the 91.1 WSAJ radio station for a slot dedicated to Christian Rap. I was a tour guide (the only tour guide of color, might I add), and I even was a short order cook in the Gedunk, the eatery in the student union, on top of taking sixteen credits. I was a very active and a social guy but, in truth, I felt horribly alone.

My Second White Girl

There was this one white girl that took a liking to me, and she was a trained competitive dancer. We spent some time together, and I recall spending hours on the phone at night and taking some walks on campus, which was a big deal at a Christian school. One day I remember her saying something to the effect of becoming official. I asked her if her parents knew that she and I had been talking. She told me how she talked about me all the time and how excited they were to meet me since she talked me up so much. She said her mom is particularly thrilled based on what this young woman had told her about me and all the things I do on campus.

I remembered how my mom was disowned by her German dad over marrying a Black man in the eighties. He had never acknowledged his Black grandchildren. I then asked her if her parents knew that I was Black.

The First, the Few and the Only

She was taken aback by this. She began to profusely inform me how that means nothing and that it doesn't matter. I asked the question again. She said no. I then asked her who pays for her college and meal plan, if she was taking any aid or was attending school on scholarships. She said her parents pay for everything.

I remember telling her how much I cared about her and how attracted I was to her, but before taking any further steps, she needed to tell them my ethnicity and see how they reacted.

She protested fiercely. She told me how silly I was being and that her parents aren't like that, "Like…ya know…. ummm…racist." She said this last word in a whisper, as though she couldn't begin to fathom it.
I asked her if she would do this for me as an experiment, then we could date. She asked me how she was supposed to bring that up casually. Since we were going to be on a school break, I said that she should tell them that I'm coming to visit. I wanted to do the stand-up thing and meet her parents to ask if I could officially date her. She protested, talking about how stupid all of this was and that my plan wouldn't tell them that I was Black. I countered with an example and made up a scenario for her to find a way to reveal my ethnicity to them. I said something to the effect of; "Say I got into a fender-bender on the way, and some guy was being racist to me. When your parents ask what race I am, then tell them that way." She agreed and promised to call me the next day.

I didn't hear from her for a week.

When I finally got her on the phone, she was in tears. I asked what happened, and she told me that when her parents found out that I am Black, her mom didn't talk to her for that whole week. I would later find out her mother would go another week not talking to her daughter. She told me how appalled she was at her mom's reaction, so she went to her dad separately. He told her, "I know it's wrong, honey, and I'm sure this boy is nice, but I have to support your mom." She was devastated and told me over the phone how her mom threatened to stop paying for her school and her dance classes. She confided in me how crushed she was to find this out about her mom and dad.

Through the tears, she told me how much she cared for me anyway and didn't care what her mom thought. She wanted to be with me. She told me how she wished I

The First, the Few and the Only

was there to hold her, and I felt sorry for her. When it came time for me to speak, I told her how much our time together meant to me and that I'm sorry she had to find out this way. She began to apologize to me for how racist they were and that she isn't like that, and how her mom told her that becoming a beauty queen took hard work. She said that her mother had asked why she wanted to ruin her life like this. She asked me when we could see each other next.

I told her that we shouldn't.

She was flabbergasted and begged me to tell her why. I told her that I watched my mom suffer on her own for loving a Black man in the seventies and what it had cost her. My mother was disowned, and not allowed to see her mother again, due to her 1st generation German father's racial anger, until grandma's deathbed. I told her how much I love her desire for me. I felt desire for her, but I couldn't support her or myself at this point in our lives. I told her that she needed her parents, that the cost is too great to take out loans when she has it made. She was even more devastated. I said, "See if you can repair things with your family and tell them we broke up or something. When you get back to school after break, maybe we can chat and see how you're feeling or if your parents come around."

She agreed and promised to see me back on campus.

She never looked my way again.

🌱 Back to the Crimson Cave

You see, surviving Grove City while doing all the things a DEI department should be doing, on top of the psychological and emotional toll of being there for Black men on campus and advocating for us, was exhausting. Add in the alienation from the white boys on campus, and you'll understand why I felt like I was being worn down little by little. After the break-up-before-dating experience, I spent even more time in the chapel, praying or sitting in silence, grieving while questioning what the hell was wrong with me. I sat in that beautiful chapel wondering what the hell was wrong with my brain, heart, and body that I couldn't just go along to get along here. I knew I would never be white, nor did I want to be white - coming from where I come from, there is way too much pride in being Afro-Latino. It came to be that I had more friends in administration in different departments than in the student body.

The First, the Few and the Only

I felt abandoned once my Puerto Rican friend Andrew left, felt lonely after Jesus left, and the freshmen guys who joined the AO housing group with me either kept to themselves or left me out of the activities they were invited to by the upperclassmen. After a while I started to wear the ostracization with pride. It felt like proof to myself that I was a real one, that I somehow made my older brother proud for not selling out for acceptance. There were other girls that were attracted to me, and I was attracted to, but whenever certain white boys saw me around the girls on campus, they would swoop in and start flirting with them. I remember being annoyed but then thinking, "If these girls were real, they wouldn't give any attention to these jealous white boys who can't stand the sight of me talking to 'their' white women." I learned then that maybe there is a small part of white boys that can't STAND interracial fraternizing with white women. I eventually decided to transfer to Slippery Rock University.

Now, you must understand something: the culture of Grove City College was AND IS VERY elitist. My peers at Grove City believed themselves to be on a higher plane of existence than the "degenerates" who attended Slippery Rock. I regularly overheard, whenever a homeschooled kid or just a run-of-the-mill white kid got a C or a D on an assignment, people in the AO housing group would say, "Don't worry - that equates to an A at Slippery Rock University." I can still see the faces that said that to me. Well, not only did and does Grove City College attendees feel superior to those at SRU, but that is also where the upperclassmen would go to party at Ginger Hill or the Heights. The "angels" that went to Grove City would go to that den of iniquity to fulfill their taste for lust and debauchery. That is where I transferred to.

Grove City had an overarching belief that was shared when people transferred: "They must not have been able to keep up with the rigor of academics here." That essentially sums up the thing's folks would say to each other. They said it when Andrew transferred, and I heard it said when Jesus left too. If the transferee was a girl, they conjectured that she must have gotten pregnant, but usually they convinced themselves that it had to do with an inability to keep up with the sheer weight of the academic drive of the campus and faculty. It's a crock of shit, but believe me, once it got out that I was transferring, it was a salacious rumor that creeped throughout campus. Random people would come up to me and whisper, "Are you really transferring?" I usually dodged the question, but near the end, Cat and Nat were the only ones who would sit near me. I became even more of a pariah

The First, the Few and the Only

than I had previously thought one could become, especially at a Christian campus where the only difference between me and my Christ-following counterparts was the melanin in our faces.

Before I made the decision, the executive assistant from student life, the folks in career services and admissions, as well as the RD, Justin Juntunen, began to notice how depressed I had become. I recall Justin asking me one time, "What does it feel like when you come back from break?"

I told him that it felt like hiking in Timberland boots with no socks for miles and miles. It felt like my body was beat up and my feet were bloody, and when I came back to campus, I had to shove the boots back on and keep pushing. It meant a lot that these folks cared about me, but it was also heartbreaking that essentially no one on campus was naming that with me or around me enough to notice. I tried to hide how much I was unraveling, especially from the younger Black men I was showing up for. But they could see it anyway—because even in my silence, sorrow leaked through. I didn't want to look weak in front of the very people I was trying so hard to be strong for.

Even my mom told me during Christmas break of my sophomore year that she didn't recognize me anymore. The happy, charismatic, God-loving, passionate son of hers looked so beat down. I had told her about the girl whose parents were racist. I told her about almost beating up some white kid I was in Memorial Hall with who saw me at a table of upperclassmen girls. He had decided to walk past me and toss trash on my tray, asking me to throw it away for him. I remember getting ready to whoop dat ass back at the dorms where there were no cameras, but my Neshannock High school/First Baptist Church fellow-youth-group-goer, Scoot, saw my face on my way back from the dining hall. He asked me if I was ok. I said I was fine and that I had to go handle some business. He wouldn't let me pass. I was about to move him out of my way when he begged me to tell him what happened. I recounted the occurrence and told him to stay out of it because no short, punk white boy named Brad was gonna get away with that without dire consequences. No one had EVER done something like that to me, and I wasn't about to start letting stuff like that slide. I knew not to whoop his ass in front of cameras so that I could have my word against his. I'm not typically violent, but I had had enough of the internal pain to let that pass. Scoot somehow talked me out of beating him up and letting them win. He promised to go find him immediately and tell him to stay away from me. I laughed because I didn't need his help, especially since, at that

The First, the Few and the Only

time, I felt abandoned by him too. He spoke to the part of me that I had always been – a Christian leader. That made me pause. If his intervention didn't work, he said, he'd help me jump Brad. That made me laugh - the thought of tossing Brad's short, rotund, blue-eyed self between Scoot and my fists, so I obliged…for now. Like Winter Soldier & Cap beat up Iron man.
Apparently, Scoot addressed the issue in such a way that Brad was afraid to talk to me ever again. Scoot had told him that he had had to beg me not to come find him that afternoon. Apparently, this kid didn't want the smoke.

My mom was horrified and felt regret that she ever 'asked' me to go there. She begged me to transfer, and called my older brother to have him to convince me that there was no shame in it.

Never Return to the Scene of the Crime

I eventually left, transferred, and sure enough, I was seen as unable to hack it. After transferring, I had come back to see the new and first president of the SEAD club I founded, which is on campus to this day thanks to the hard work of students there over the years, and I got stood up. I went in to eat, and a couple guys I joined the AO housing group with spotted me and decided to sit with me. We made inconsequential small talk, pleasantries about the weather, and then they brought up my transferring. It got quiet. Henry and Jwags, Andrew's freshmen year roommate, proceeded to tell me that I had left too soon and gave up on what I was called to do on campus.

I felt enraged. They had alienated me amidst all I was doing on campus and abandoned me when I lived on the same hall as them. They had never come to any SEAD meetings when I had asked them for their support, yet they sit before me with the gall to tell me that I gave up too soon.
I left there vowing to never go back to that campus because the pain I felt there made me question my identity, brilliance, beauty, attractiveness, calling, purpose, sanity, emotional stability, and sense of reality. The caucasity!

I later went to SRU and got connected to a parachurch campus ministry lead by a lady named "Evelyn from The Incredibles 2." My friend, Ms. Krepps, RD of one of the female dorms and personal friend of the Black VP that said they would mentor me and later left for Texas, had apparently asked a few people on the Crimson

The First, the Few and the Only

campus to check on me regularly as a personal favor to him while I was at Grove City, and Ms. Krepps did. Before I even got to Slippery Rock, Ms. Krepps established this connection to campus. When I got there, I had never even had tour of campus and literally had no idea where anything was outside of my dorm in Rhoads Hall. I remember Evelyn connecting me to some of the leading Black men on campus. She had hunted down their phone numbers and connected us. She connected me to DJ, the head of the SRU gospel choir, and JB, the head of Building Bridges diversity group.

Fast forward the tape: I became good friends with other Christian and some non-Christians guys on campus. Although SRU had more Black and Brown bodies on campus, it remained less than six percent, Dr. Claud Anderson's "ideal percentage" for white bodies to maintain control of an area or institution. There were more Brown bodies, yet the institutional realities of tokenism were often the same for any of us who tried to move up in leadership.

After SRU

I made lifelong friendships and had the best time at Slippery Rock University. Upon graduating, I became a church-planting associate pastor in a parachurch ministry and, eventually, the national associate director for cross-cultural ministry within the same institution.

It started simply enough. While at SRU, I joined "Evelyn's" third attempt at leading a Bible study—her previous two had fizzled out. Ms. Krepps had connected us. This time Evelyn had backup: Jen, another blonde-haired, blue-eyed co-leader, and me—a melanated, charismatic, wounded Christian still reeling from the elitism of the Christian college I'd barely survived.

Together, we started something different.

We called it The Harbor. We wanted to create distance from Cru, which was well-resourced but culturally stale. Cru felt like a suburban white youth group cosplay—lots of acoustic worship, polished testimonies, and an unspoken expectation to code-switch your faith. The leadership was entirely white, except for one Black student who hovered near proximity but never power. Despite their missionary zeal, Cru defaulted to what made white, suburban Christians feel spiritually affirmed and culturally safe.

The First, the Few and the Only

It reminded me too much of Grove City.

FCA had a little more edge—cooler, more chill—but they catered to athletes, and I wasn't one. Not officially. So, we carved out something else. Something for the misfits. For the ones the church had wounded. For the seekers, the skeptics, the not-quite-anymore's.

Our study wasn't there to tell people what to think about the Bible. It was there to help them think with the Bible. We selected a passage, encouraged independent reading, and held open dialogue that welcomed all perspectives. We didn't preach; we anchored. We weren't tour guides pointing out spiritual landmarks—we were steady hands helping people navigate rough spiritual waters with a place to rest. Just like a harbor. We let the conversations find their current while quietly guiding them toward exegetical truth, what I like to call -riverbedding.

And it worked.

Within a year, our circle grew so large we had to appoint five additional Bible study leaders. But it was never about numbers. It was about the depth of the questions, the honesty of the silence, the sacredness of sitting beside someone who didn't believe and letting the Word still matter. The environment became so spiritually charged that leaders from other Christian organizations began showing up—not to teach, but to listen.
This was contextual ministry. And I fell in love with it.

As graduation neared, the team grew—and so did the pressure. "Evelyn from The Incredibles 2" kept asking me to join the ministry full-time. I had a gift for preaching, I knew scripture inside and out, and my Bible study group was the largest. But that never felt like the point.
Seriously—I'm not tryna flex. I'm just trying to name what's true: I had been doing ministry since middle school. I'd been living the Word before I even had the words for how much it was shaping me. But even then, I hesitated.

James 2 was always echoing in my ear: "Not many of you should become teachers, for you know that we who teach will be judged more strictly." That tension never left me. Even when I said yes.

The First, the Few and the Only

Even when I applied. Even when I got in.

Then they told me I had to raise my own salary.

That meant I had to be a college-educated Black man, in full-time vocational ministry, and still go out and fundraise for my livelihood every year. A tall order. But somehow, I managed to scrape together enough to make it to campus.

Some ministries won't even let you set foot on the "mission field" until you've hit full support. But not this one. They dropped me in as soon as the freshmen arrived, whether I had the funds or not. I spent that first summer—the one that was supposed to be my onboarding—scrambling to raise the rest of my support. It was grueling. But I was told it was a spiritual act, this hustle. Sacred, even. Eventually, I figured I'd made my bed. I might as well learn how to sleep in it.

I started with the people I knew—Black men from Slippery Rock who'd seen me grow. One of them, Mr. W., who was the very first person I asked. We met at Subway near campus. I'd already sent him a support letter and laid out the basics: who I was, what I was doing, and how much I needed. I followed the script I'd been trained to use. Open with a time check. Then the upfront contract which entailed being vulnerable about how awkward it felt to ask. Share updates about my life. Listen to theirs. Then, and only then, explain the ministry, the costs, and how they might help.

He listened politely. We talked about his work on campus, about his son. I told him about my new role, the church plant I was partnered with, and how the salary was split—part covered by the church for health insurance, the rest up to me to raise.

And then it happened.

He put his sandwich down and looked me dead in the eye. His voice dropped. His whole demeanor shifted.

He scolded me.

Not casually. Not kindly. Like a father figure who felt betrayed.

The First, the Few and the Only

He told me I was a college-educated Black man—brilliant, promising—and that I was wasting my potential by going around asking for money. He said it was embarrassing to see someone like me, someone who could have had any job, reduced to this.

Then he paid for the food, wished me well, and ended the conversation. 🌱
I walked out in silence and sat in my car for what felt like an hour before I could even turn the ignition.

What I felt wasn't just shame—it was full-body, soul-crushing humiliation. Like something was pressing on every organ inside me. I had looked up to Mr. W. since college. Many of us had. He once told me, "It would've been hard to be your father." When I asked why, he said I was so wise and brilliant, it would've been hard to teach me anything. And yet, here I was—leaving that conversation feeling like I'd disappointed him, like my calling looked foolish to the very people I hoped would understand.

That moment was the first hairline fracture. The first shard of glass underfoot in what I thought was solid ground.

But it wouldn't be the last. 🌱

Enter Stinky from Toy Story 2

"I don't really trust a church without outcasts, anymore"
-Charlotte V.

Later, I began working with a wealthy, all-white church in the North Hills. They were launching a second church plant downtown, and that's where they placed me. I was the associate pastor there while also continuing my campus ministry role. I essentially reported to three different people: the pastor of the new church plant, a lead campus minister who was tied to yet another church, and a regional supervisor from the parachurch ministry overseeing the whole geographic territory.

That's where I learned a bitter truth: even people with seminary degrees and advanced theology credentials—PhDs in urban ministry, doctorates in divinity—could still be deeply racist. Possessive, paternalistic, and quietly harmful in ways that

The First, the Few and the Only

felt holy on the surface. I spent three years under the leadership of a pastor who was emotionally and psychologically abusive. I learned how to keep my head down. How to endure. How to smile through microaggressions dressed in Christianese. This was my first experience with Stinky.

There were two other Black men in the congregation - Kenny and Dr. Mychael Lee. We were all connected, with Kenny later becoming a worship leader at the church.

The villain in this story, Stinky from Toy Story 2, made his favoritism clear. One Sunday morning, Kenny and I were sitting together near a window, chatting before service. Stinky walked up, shook Kenny's hand, told him how great it was to see him, and expressed how much he valued him in the ministry. Then he walked away, completely ignoring me.
Even Kenny noticed: "Did he just talk to me and ignore you?" I laughed it off, since it was one of many incidents, and I didn't feel comfortable making a scene by letting any of my emotions out. Eventually, Stinky approached both Kenny and Mychael separately, offering them a part-time role leading campus ministry - my job.

They both responded, "You mean Michael's job?"

Later, they told me, "Ain't no way in hell we'd take your job. That's so backhanded. Ain't nobody got time for that, plus you're so good at what you do. I ain't got patience like that with your students." They saw what was happening and stood by me.

They also wanted to check in on me and find out what the hell was going on between the pastor and me. I told them about the microaggressions and macroaggressions Stinky had said and done to me. I opened up about the racial comments he made to me as an Afro-Latino and how he treated the worship pastors and me. They were shocked but not surprised.
They said things like, "Oh, he always felt off to us."
"Yeah, he's very proud of creating a church with Black folks on the North Side, but in his heart, he still got unchecked racial attitudes that comes out on Black and Brown bodies under his 'authority.'"

The First, the Few and the Only

They consoled me the best they could and told me that neither of them ever wanted to replace me, not that I was worried at all. If they all needed to leave the church with me, they told me to just give the word.
I asked them to stay, so they did.

I later learned that he had a trail of charismatic Black and Brown talent that he had tried to force into boxes on shelves he controlled for years. I did more digging and discovered a pattern of behavior that matched up with an experience that was the straw that broke the camel's back for me. I recall one time getting a text from him while he was upset about something. I think I deposited the tithe for the week, but he didn't see it for some reason online yet, so he decided to come at me about it. I told him it was deposited and then he finally took off the fracturing mask and texted me the following, "Why don't you just quit ministry and go teach people how to salsa dance."

Yea, that actually happened. So, the same Michael who almost whooped this round Brad's ass wanted to take over the controller. I didn't let him, but I did text this degree-toting Rugby-bragging Stinky from Toy Story 2 that, 'if he wanted to talk to me like that, which was unacceptable, he should man up and say it in person not behind a phone.'

He didn't like that too much. After months of trying to get rid of me, and the worship pastors warning me to be perfect because Stinky had it out for me, before that text exchange, I had had enough. I'm not bowing to bullies, whether they hide behind a pulpit or not. Eventually, he fired me. No warning. No explanation.

I later found out that the mother church—his financial and institutional covering—let him go after realizing just how unjustified his decision was. By then, I had already moved on. I stepped into a new role as Assistant Director of Cross-Cultural Ministry, shifting from ground-level discipleship to higher-level administrative work.

Out of the Frying Pan | Into the Fire

But the scars stayed. A few years before I left the ministry, an African American leader in fundraising for BIPOC missionaries (support raising is what we called it within the institution) named Byron Johnson came to visit us at one of our quarterly retreats. He was from another ministry called Campus Outreach. One of

The First, the Few and the Only

the things he said that stuck with me was this: "I stuck around as long as I could and did what I could while I was there…. And when people felt like they couldn't take it anymore, I encouraged them to leave. But someone's gotta stay."

I stayed. I remember I was in administrative leadership for six years but knew I should have left within the first two years of being there. I sensed that I wasn't in a good environment, but I ignored it. Well, it was tough to ignore, but I spiritually bypassed it. I don't think this is what Byron meant, but by the time I heard his words while I was in administration, much of the damage had been done.

It was there that I experienced some of the worst administrative betrayal and workplace abuse in my entire life. No matter how little psychological safety I had, I kept pushing through and burning out, rinse and repeat. I preached burned out. I ministered to hurting BIPOC missionaries partnered with white evangelical churches burned out. I supported one of the most absent supervisors to date, while being both burned out and feeling ostracized. It was during this time that I realized how apropos what Dr. Thema said is: "A history of trauma can give you a high tolerance for emotional pain. Just because you can take it doesn't mean you should."

Despite all of this, I stayed, all the while enduring neglect from some older staff of color who only drew near to our department to support their favorite minority in leadership, Mr. Chan. Although there were only three to choose from, two Asians working remotely and me the Afro Cuban stuck at HQ, they only had a heart for what Mr. Chan was going through, both publicly & privately, and although he and I were a two-man department holding down a semi-national ministry for all DEI needs, only he was empathized with. I felt abandoned again. Because of this, I committed myself to providing good, rich care to the staff of color that did not belong to the clique of older staff that Mr. Chan ignored.

I found myself doing his job and mine for years under his neglectful leadership. The only solace I received during this time was knowing that the other assistant directors he supervised were neglected by him too. It helped me realize that it wasn't just me. So yes, my experience was shared by some of the white middle management staff, but what made it unique was that for them it was just a bad supervisor. For me? It felt like a betrayal.

The First, the Few and the Only

You see, it was just me and Mr. Chan servicing an entire staff, and we needed more staff the entire 5-6 years we ran that ship. I thought we were going to have each other's back, at least what he promised when asked me to join him. But he left me unguarded, unprotected. I felt like Phyllis Wheatley, reduced to a show pony for my giftedness but unprotected for the abuses that it brought.

He colluded against me both in silence, and feigned friendship with me in person. When we were away from each other, the other leaders only had wonderful things to say about me, but he never had anything positive to say. With upper brass, when they didn't like how much real change I was beckoning for, they would have him ask me if I wanted to go back to campus on a few occasions and if I agree that I'm called elsewhere. Whilst I'm running all programming for the department, including but not limited to; running a multi-city annual experience for missionaries, pastors and elders from across the United States on what we called a Freedom Tour to explore the intersections of race, a city's history, and our own story weaving the spiritual and radical history of this land, that I ran. National monthly podcast for staff to tune into and meet the cross cultural speakers that our department hired for our annual conference every year, I did weekly staff support and reporting for any harms or abuses our staff were witnessing or experiencing being BIPOC in a predominantly white church because too many of their white supervisors never took their complaints seriously and wrote them off as them being sensitive or them not being spiritually resilient enough, I even did consulting and spiritual coaching for pastors and elders in Western PA who wanted to grow in the walk regarding cross cultural ministry in anticipation of a cross cultural new heaven and new earth.

Plus, I wrote the first grant for the department in the organizations 40ish year history, as well as my first grant, because the leadership and Mr. Chan didn't want to let me beta-test an annual retreat for BIPOC staff to feel seen and heard due to the microaggressions and experiences they experienced in the white churches and our ministry required them to move their families near and work for in order to love on college students. So, I wrote a $20,000 grant proposal to the Lilly Foundation and received the first ever grant funding from that foundation that the company had been trying to get money out of since its inception. All the while, I'm still convincing Mr. Chan and leadership why all staff need to have BASIC bias training, which he and the VP fought me on across 3 separate conversations, but since I backed it up with so much scripture off the top of my head, they had to back down and let me do it. They made sure it was optional though.

The First, the Few and the Only

All the while I was getting paid around $20,000 – 30k less than any other middle manager or person with my adjacent role in leadership up until about my last year in leadership (five years), which I had to go to the VP to get cleared since my supervisor ignored that for years. The others just saw him as a poor supervisor, but I felt abandoned by my friend. He wasn't there for me, our friendship didn't matter to him, and he never came to my aid when I called for him. I blamed myself for trusting him for years.

There was one time near the end of my time in that ministry after Mr. Chan "left" that I remember being in a meeting, a diversity council meeting. Where DEI leaders often go to die. After 9 years, 6 of which was in leadership, I finally opened up about how I was dying in this ministry. I relayed to the others that I was fighting for everyone else's well-being, but who was going to fight for me? I brought my laments to nearly a dozen seasoned missionaries about how exhausted I was and how much I busted my butt to care for others without getting any care in return. My old campus minister, Evelyn from The Incredibles 2, called me later and said she thought I was being conniving and attention-seeking.

That was the final curtain call on our relationship. I fought for her to be in that diversity council when others from executive leadership specifically told me they didn't want her there, and I fought for her to be one of the first female emcees for our four-thousand-plus person annual conference in over a decade when I went toe to toe with white men in leadership who told me she wasn't qualified or entertaining enough. It's not that she owed me anything, but we had been together for a long time. I had ministered under her leadership during college, joined her ministry as a colleague, and opened up to her with some personal stories, experiences and pains while in leadership. She was the one who convinced me to trust and commit to the church plant where I met Stinky from Toy Story 2. I remember her hearing about what was being done to me by that pastor and she wept in front of me one night at a staff quarterly retreat because she knew how much she used my trust in her to get me to go to that specific church because that is what a man in her life we'll call Lotso from Toy Story 3 wanted me to do. After so many years of praying for one another and holding each other in close confidence, I couldn't believe that she had called me attention-seeking & conniving after asking for her help.

Not to mention, my father died the week prior to that confession to the council.

The First, the Few and the Only

I called two other pastors of color who were in that meeting to get their perspective on my confession, and they unilaterally said, "that girl trippn.(girl isn't the colorful term they used)" They reminded me how sobering it was to finally hear me speak up about what to so many was so evident and to, frankly, not engage with or talk to her anymore. One asked if I wanted him to say something to the Board about her and get her kicked out, but I declined.

To this day, she and I never spoke again.

I, soon after, left vocational ministry to work in university administration that following summer and got out. 🌱

> I don't need your
> lectures and lessons.
> I need you to
> lean in and listen.
> My wound
> is not your
> thought
> experiment.

Post by @JSPark3000

Interview with Shaq

 I started an Instagram page when I was still trying to create this book project but still had little to no capacity to do it. I was basically still in the trenches and unsure about how much I could really share without giving them a reason to get rid of me. Too much dangerous naming threatens the system. Too much disarming honesty puts the illusion of being "the best Christian workplace" in jeopardy.

For this project, I interviewed a friend of mine named Shaquille. He had spent time as a young man as part of a ministry that engages mostly Black urban youth with activities. He moved up in the organization, joined the staff, and even saw a friend of mine from college days, being ostracized for speaking out against institutional microaggressions and

The First, the Few and the Only

macroaggressions. Shaquille stayed after my old buddy from college got out of there, and in this interview, he had a lot to say about the viscera of navigating covert racism in evangelical parachurch ministry. He speaks very candidly about cultivated loyalty and about the good feeling that comes with being their show pony and token, sometimes. Although, eventually, that style of relating to a white world becomes too much to sustain.

Too costly.

He and I talked about his codependency with the sense of purpose derived from being the show pony or mammy (caretaker) that white people in power think they needed from his Black body. At one point in the interview with Shaq, he says that sometimes it feels so good to be their show pony that it's like crack cocaine. Not that he ever experimented with such narcotics, but that it was habit-forming and addictive

He later talked about, despite that drug-like good feeling, hating going to work and hating ministry. He said, "Every day I went to work felt like a funeral…. when you get to the point in ministry when you have to grieve in private, you shouldn't' be there…and that was every day for me. I had a key to this secret room, and that's where I went to cry, the kind of cry you do when you just got whooped. I looked forward to the weekends because I could feel happy again."

When we got to the topic of why he stayed, he said, "I didn't believe God would bless me if I [left], as if God's blessings only lived in that ministry. I minimized God to a place and location…I believed a lot of lies, including toxic loyalty. Like I had to be loyal to them to confirm that I'm good. If I leave, I'm the ugly duckling [again], I'm the one not willing to submit."

There is so much else he said in this interview that is well worth the watch.

🌱 Where is your breath? What are you thinking? What are you noticing?

Take a moment to get involved. Consider checking out the book playlist and playing "We Need You" by Cleo Soul in the background. Promises by Cleo Soul is a good one for this moment too:

The First, the Few and the Only

🧭 Activity: Consider writing a letter to your future self, five years in the future. What would you say? You could also write a letter to your current self. Notice your breath and care for your body. Put the book down. It's ok.

In talking to Shaq, I realized some things about my own story. In ministry, I often mistook my calling for their brand.

Viktor Frankl once said that if you want "…to be a light to the world, you must be willing to burn." But there is a difference between burning for the glory of God and burnout. Burning out for the failures of the brand is no way to live because eventually your own light will be snuffed out.

Burnout is not part of the cost of ministry. It is not, as a matter of fact, godly at all, nor is it holy. Jesus never did it, so why do we? Why did Shaq? Why do I? I'll address this in more detail in the next section, but for now, I don't think I was meant to be as chronically exhausted as I was during this season of my life.

What precipitates directly from covert racism in ministry is burnout when roles and functions lead to consequences and repercussions, exclusively for the BIPOC bodies within them. We serve at the pace of capitalism and the need to feel valuable to those in power. It is a perpetual performance that slaps our imago Dei and our intrinsic worth in the face – spits in its face, even.

In Dr. Rheeda Walker's book, The Unapologetic Guide to Black Mental Health, she unpacks how unease caused by racism and caring for white guilt more than you care for yourself can lead to disease.

I don't always feel like I'm allowed to be human and have emotions in ministry. Like everyone is allowed to be broken but me, even though I'm a walking bag of fragments and shards inside. There isn't a space to hold good care and attention for the sweat & tears of my Black body and the wounds caused by the assimilation that white Christians intrinsically expect of my body of culture. It doesn't have to be that way.

The First, the Few and the Only

News Flash

The Protestants in this country are part of the privileged, not the persecuted. When I was a child, I used to devour stories of martyrdom of faithful Christians from many anti-Christian governments who actively stripped devout worshippers from their families, their homes, and even from their children. They stripped these martyrs of their freedom and sometimes of their body parts. Many of them were killed – all in an effort to get them to renounce Christ and recommit to the State. I read Voices of the Martyrs books before bed from fifteen to seventeen years old. No one ever told me to do it. I just thought it would put my high school challenges in perspective as I sought to live out my life as sold out, like the song of the same name from Lecrae's first album: "We sold out, seeking God's face til I fold out, want we got it, we ain't tryna hold out. Break me, shake me, mold me. I'd rather die like Christ than live unholy. One-one-six, a band of misfits who get sick off the state of the world, so we hit strips and spit. Christ Jesus who scooped us out of the dirt and cleaned us, we were slave to sinful ways, but Christ freed us…"

I remember thinking: what better way to sharpen my purpose than to read about those who have given life and limb to the very thing to which I was committing my life? It was sobering nighttime reading, to say the least. Twenty years later, I see something I didn't back then: the martyrs I read about were rarely in North America. Here, Protestants have been more often the privileged than the persecuted. I grew up believing that to be a Christian in this country meant to be countercultural, but history tells a different story.

I remember learning about the suspicion and hostility John F. Kennedy faced simply for being Catholic. I remember learning that Protestants, by and large, didn't concern themselves with abortion in the 1960s – it was seen as a Catholic issue. It wasn't until it became a political strategy to unite Protestant and Catholic voters that it gained traction in evangelical circles. And as I continued to learn, I saw how much privilege Protestantism carried in America.

The First, the Few and the Only

Spiritual Bypassing

> I don't need your
> lectures and lessons.
> I need you to
> lean in and listen.
> My wound
> is not your
> thought
> experiment.

@JSPARK3000
Author of The Voices We Carry

As I awakened to my experience in white evangelical churches, I often felt seen but not heard. I had been given titles with no authority. I was sometimes acknowledged, yet muted, a mere show pony for the stage, relegated to a cubicle until the next performance. It was in these moments that I realized something deeper was at play. When I attempted to articulate my feelings, I was often met with spiritual platitudes, told to either repent or endure because "maybe" God was sharpening me. This dismissive reaction to my pain is known as spiritual bypassing. Psychotherapist John Welwood1 coined the term "spiritual bypassing," defining it as the use of spiritual ideas and practices to sidestep personal and emotional "unfinished business," shore up a shaky sense of self, or belittle basic needs and feelings.

An Example That Resonates

A striking moment from the documentary Deconstructing Karen on Apple TV comes to mind. In this film, Saira Rao and Regina Jackson host a dinner exclusively for white women, with a singular rule: no crying at the table. Should tears arise, a separate room is provided, complete with tissues and comfy couches. This rule sets the stage for a powerful exploration of white women's complicity in systemic racism and the urgent need for change.

Throughout the dinner, they engage in both heated and calm discussions about accountability and the link between white women's liberation and the perpetuation of its absence for women of color. They confront the uncomfortable truth that one

The First, the Few and the Only

cannot simply date a person of color and absolve oneself of internalized racism. With fierce kindness, they hold their guests accountable, demonstrating the extent to which they risk their own comfort and safety for this vital work, all motivated by love.

As the conversation unfolds, one quiet white woman eventually speaks up. She acknowledges the reality of white supremacy but questions the need for labels, asserting that while she empathizes with the struggles of her Black and Brown counterparts, she believes that love overcomes differences. Her remarks, however, are met with a historical context of harm from Saira, who challenges her to clarify what she means by lacking love.

In this moment, Saira calls out spiritual bypassing. "You're employing spiritual bypassing to evade the pain associated with oppression," she asserts. "Love is love, but when someone threatens my daughter, I won't just meditate my way through it or downward dog it until it gets better. I engage in this work out of love, and by sharing my pain, I expose myself to more abuse because I believe in you. I believe you can awaken, just as I did."

Regina adds, "Don't expect this journey to be easy. It's hard work, and everything worth having requires effort." As the dinner concludes, Saira circles back to her opening question, asking, "Who in this room acknowledges their racism?"

Spiritual bypassing often serves to skip over the grief, lament, and pain of those who are different from you, distancing yourself from the harm inflicted. For those interested in diving deeper into this conversation, you can find more insights below: 🌱 Getting Involved:

Holy Suffering?

Have you ever felt like someone sidestepped your emotions after you poured your heart out? I know I have. In my family, whenever I express my emotional needs, I hear, "Stop being so sensitive." Similarly, more times than I can count, I found myself spiritually bypassed in ministry spaces.

The First, the Few and the Only

I remember a moment when I was about to resign from a parachurch ministry. An older white woman called to check in. I had learned to be guarded, but I let my defenses down with her, thinking she was genuine. After I shared the burdens, I could no longer carry, she said something like, "Maybe this is your calling right now. You've been such a gift to this ministry. If you hang in there, things can change."

But this was six years after I had been pushed deeper into invisibility while BIPOC bodies fought for power. My role had been whittled down to nothing. I asked her, "Well, Sally, thank you for that, but what do I do with my constant suicidal ideation? What about the resentment affecting my marriage? How about the fact that I can't play with my son for more than ten minutes without dissociating? Because my body is so used to dissociating from strong negative emotions at work, it can't tell the difference between strong negative emotions and strong positive emotions anymore. I look at pictures of him from years ago, and though I was there, I have zero memory of it because I was constantly in and out of dissociation after work. What should I do about my health? I'm in my early thirties but have more gray hairs than my friends who are fifty-five. Do you really think my calling to save this ministry is so great that my personal life is just collateral damage?"

She was speechless.

I wasn't trying to shame her; I genuinely care for her and her family and have a special place in my heart for my friendship with her husband. But, dammit, I was exhausted by the spiritual bypassing that sidestepped my reality with empty platitudes, and great white hope disguised as faux prophesies of calling which felt more self-serving than compassionate. It pushed me to the brink.

Spiritual bypassing is counterintuitive for those who disconnect the mind and body from spirituality. Many view spirituality and the physical as a duality – two separate entities, yet this perspective is often a false dichotomy. Throughout Christian, Muslim, and Jewish scriptures, we see spirituality embodied. Think of Jesus on the cross or Moses' sons being circumcised by Zipporah to save Moses' life. Spirituality through the body becomes especially evident for those who are suffering.

For those distant from suffering, spirituality without the body becomes a convenient escape. They often blind themselves to the wisdom of the oppressed, the vulnerable, and the broken. And inevitably, the first, the few and the only.

The First, the Few and the Only

When navigating deep emotional, psychological, and social injustices, I'm always aware of who is safe among people of faith – those who spiritually bypass and leapfrog over my pain.

This brings to mind the story of the Good Samaritan. The priest, the Levite, and the innkeeper embody the three common traits of spiritual bypassing: speed, distance, and innocence. One hurries past the broken body; the Levite crosses the road to avoid it; the last clings to their innocence. When I experience spiritual bypassing, it often involves one or a combination of these three actions while I sit by, beaten down.

Spiritual bypassing isn't about connection, ironic as that may seem. It feigns connection through disconnection – speed, distance, and power. It offers a form of religion or spirituality without its true power. One key feature of spirituality is connectedness, and spiritual bypassing misses that mark entirely. It shirks the responsibility to care for one's neighbor, hiding behind spiritual jargon to mask a fickle heart.

It leapfrogs over the very entryway into critical connection. It prioritizes critical mass over critical connection and refuses to move at the speed of trust, despite its best intentions. At its core, it's an aversive maneuver that never lays a foundation for sustainable relationships, paving the way for perfectionism and performance as a mode of relating. This only solidifies the dark well of internalized harm.

> **There is a cost to sticking to your principles. I've chosen to avoid certain evangelical platforms because of their complicity with racism. That has stifled certain growth metrics, but...**
> JEMAR TISBY

> **I try to live by that Maya Angelou maxim, "When people show you who they are, believe them the first time."**
> **Stay the course.**
> JEMAR TISBY

> **jemartisby** 17h · Sometimes I long for the easier, faster route to my goals that would come with aligning myself with certain people or institutions. But I never regret the peace of mind and soul that comes with making mission-aligned decisions.

The First, the Few and the Only

"The vast majority of people walking away from Christianity in America are not rejecting the person and the work of Jesus. They are rejecting faulty biblical interpretations that lead to bigotry, oppression, and marginalization. This rejection isn't unchristian. It is Christlike." - Zach W. Lambert

Someone in the Desert Knows My Name

Painting by Meagan Nazario Michaelis

This painting hangs upon my wall. When I was finishing my masters, it hung next to my desk. When I got out of a toxic academic space, both religious and non-religious, it hung near my door. When I was finally getting out of toxic ministry spaces, I had it commissioned by my dear friend Meagan. I commissioned it for one of the last retreats and experiences I did before I left vocational ministry, using the money from my first grant I wrote about caring for BIPOC leaders exclusively.

It is a picture of Hagar, and like Hagar, I was accustomed to harsh environments that made deserts look like a vacation. A reprieve.

The First, the Few and the Only

Just because the people from the lush and grassy side of the painting felt Hagar was limited by her past, her economic station, her otherness, her age, didn't mean she should be denied a hopeful future for her and her son.

Like Hagar, you have the right to experience beauty, goodness, and delight. Your anger, longing, and tears cry out, testifying to this truth and remaining as a radical witness to the fact that you are not being delighted in or experiencing the good God intended. Although your current environment may make you feel otherwise, they are wrong, no matter their title, authority, anointing, or pedigree.

What I learned by stepping away from ministry and into the desert, what met me there also met Hagar. The God who sees Hagar saw me, and He certainly sees you.

You…are…not…alone. You can desire the ocean again and can find it in the desert. I left. Know that this section was the hardest for me to write because it's the one that cost me the most.

Once I joined Hagar and left, I have swam in oceans upon oceans of new faces that delight at the sight of me, voices that fill my heart with joy when I hear them call my name, and community that I never would have imagined if I didn't leave. Your people will find you because God never took His eyes off of you.

> "Just because you are used to the desert
> doesn't mean you don't deserve the ocean"
> - Rev. Fr. Albert Nwosu

What's stories are coming up for you?

_____

_____

_____

_____

_____

The First, the Few and the Only

Chapter 14

Black Hollywood (They've Gotta Have Us)

Paul Mooney on how Hollywood prefers their Blacks

Hollywood has always been a mirror with a warped frame—reflecting just enough of us to say "representation," while distorting the image until it's no longer recognizable. For Black artists, visibility has often come at the price of dignity, agency, or truth. But still, we showed up. Still, we shaped the culture. Still, we carried entire genres, only to be cut from the credits or shelved when they no longer needed our shine.

Simon Frederick's *They've Gotta Have Us* is more than a documentary—it's an excavation. A living testimony. A declaration that Black artists were never just included; we were indispensable. The industry didn't hand us a seat—it tried to hand us scripts soaked in stereotype, and we rewrote them with blood, brilliance, and refusal.

This chapter is an offering to the ones who refused to trade authenticity for sardoodledom. To Esther Rolle, who walked away from roles that mocked us. To the cast of LIVING SINGLE, whose voices raised a generation and was silenced by punishing one of them. To Eartha Kitt, who refused to bow even when it cost her everything. And to every name we'll never know, whose rejection from a casting call was a quiet act of resistance.

🌱 BLACK HOLLYWOOD (They've gotta have us)—but not like that. Not as caricatures. Not as quotas. This time, we tell the story.

The First, the Few and the Only

This time, in this book, we restore collective memory to set the story straight.

Sydney Poitier and Harry Belafonte

In an industry built for the white gaze - where Black men were either sexual threats, brutes or buffoons, and Black women were either jezebels or mammies - Sidney Poitier and Harry Belafonte walked onto the screen as something else entirely. They were smooth, deliberate, and deeply human. Their very presence was a contradiction, a quiet and elegant defiance against Hollywood's favorite lies. 1

They weren't the Black men white America had been taught to fear, nor the ones they longed to mock. They were refined, dignified, and dangerously undeniable. Poitier, with his precise diction and unshakable poise, was the embodiment of grace under pressure, playing roles that held up a mirror to a nation that swore it was better than its sins. Belafonte, with his velvet voice and activist heart, carried a quiet storm beneath his charm - singing love songs to white audiences while funding liberation movements behind the scenes. 2

Yet their greatest performances were not the ones that won them applause. They did not leave it all on the stage. No, the real work happened offscreen, in hushed meetings, in courtrooms, in the streets where their names carried weight and their money-built movements. They knew the price of being the first, the few, and the only in rooms built to exclude them. They played the roles, took the awards, but they never forgot who they were, never forgot who they belonged to. 3

In this way, they embodied Josiah Henson's Uncle Tom, not the caricature white America twisted into submission, but the real man - a warrior of dignity, a protector of his people, a strategist who knew that sometimes survival itself was an act of resistance. Hollywood may have tried to make them symbols of integration, proof that the system was changing. But they were never fooled. They knew better, and because of them, so did we.

Eartha Kitt

One of the realest to ever do it.

The First, the Few and the Only

Globally recognized for her iconic role as Cat woman and her sultry, timeless rendition of Santa Baby, Eartha Kitt was far more than a star — she was a force. By the 1960s, she had become one of the few Black women to crack the color line in prime-time television and film, dazzling audiences with her wit, elegance, and unapologetic presence. She wasn't just Hollywood's siren - she was a truth-teller in a town built on illusion. But the same voice that captivated millions would eventually cost her everything.

In 1968, Eartha Kitt was invited to the White House for a luncheon hosted by First Lady Bird Johnson, titled the "Women Doers Luncheon." It was meant to be a polite gathering — an opportunity to discuss "delinquency in the streets." But as the conversation skewed toward the criminalization of young Black youth and the supposed moral failures of urban communities, Eartha couldn't stay silent. She had seen too much, lived too much, survived too much to stomach polite lies.
With Vietnam raging and Black and brown boys being drafted to die abroad while being denied dignity at home, Eartha spoke up when the First Lady said something off-color and Eartha could no stay silent no longer. She said:

> *"You send the best of this country off to be shot and maimed. They rebel in the streets. They will take pot, and they will get high. They don't want to go to school, cause they're going to be snatched off from their mothers to be shot in Vietnam… Mrs. Johnson you are a mother too, although you have had daughters and not sons, I am a mother and I know the feeling of having a baby come out of my gut. I have a baby and then you send him off to war, no wonder the kids rebel and take pot, and Mrs. Johnson, in case you don't understand the lingo, that's marijuana."* (video of what really happened) 4

The First Lady wept. And white tears did what white tears often do. President Lyndon B. Johnson, who had made an unannounced appearance that day, was reportedly furious. Eartha had dared to speak truth to power — and the price was exile. A quiet blacklist swept through the entertainment industry. Phone calls stopped. Doors closed. America, once enamored with her feline grace and velvet voice, now treated her like a pariah.

The New York Times headline read:

The First, the Few and the Only

"Eartha Kitt Denounces War Policy to Mrs. Johnson."

But behind that headline was a woman exiled for honesty. A documentary would later call it what they wanted to frame it to look like: Cat woman vs. the White House. Her career in the U.S. effectively ended overnight. She was forced to perform in Europe for the next decade. This wasn't just industry retaliation — it was a state-sanctioned silencing of a Black woman who dared to tell the truth in a room that preferred smiles over substance.

It's hard to explain how much was taken from her. Imagine blacklisting Tyler Perry at his cinematic peak. Or erasing Taylor Swift from every platform for speaking candidly, without any malicious intent, and since the wife of the president who knew barely anything about the matter which she asked you about, leads her to cry white tears -which, inevitably upsets the lady's husband who happens to be the president. No shows. No studios. Not even an algorithm to remember you by. Total media blackout.

And yet — Eartha Kitt did not vanish. She endured. She rose again. She returned to Broadway, won hearts anew, and left behind a legacy not just of elegance, but of resistance. She wasn't just the first or the few. She was the only one in that White House room that day with enough fire and gumption to speak the truth — and enough backbone to survive the consequences.

Terrence C. Carson

The First, the Few and the Only

Terrence C. Carson is best known for his role-playing Kyle Barker in Living Single. It is widely believed that his is the very show that inspired the show Friends, but that trend in entertainment is for another book.

Kyle Barker was one of the six main characters in Living Single that made up the cast of this legendary hit sitcom. The iconic character of Kyle Barker was a dignified and educated Black gentleman, single in the city.

After so many months of great character arcs and development, the writers and directors wanted to make the men of the show buffoon-ish. In essence, the white people wanted to make a shift in the male characters that was more sardoodledom than art. The cast noticed the changes in their characters, and one day they agreed together that they could not, in good conscience, continue to do this. The six main characters realized they had a voice, and things started to change.

That was not the last time there would be issues on the show between the cast and the white writers and directors, whether it was the script or how the actors were treated on set. At that time, Blacks would simply shut their mouths and do their jobs no matter the workplace environment or workplace abuses. Often, the cast would go together and communicate with the set directors. At some point, the other five main cast members elected Terrence to represent all their voices on another occasion because as Charlie Murphy spoke of Rick James, the producers/writers were habitual line-steppers. He was chosen to communicate the incongruencies, which sounds like a really healthy work dynamic. It backfired. The white directors began to see Terrence as the ringleader. He was the one who was sent to represent the cast, but they only saw a threat. They wanted their actors to "shut up and act," much like what happened when a random white lady on Fox News told Lebron James to "shut up and dribble." They didn't want their Black actors to unite in that way, and they sure did not want them to elect a "leader" amongst themselves. They saw Terrence as the instigator and essentially fired him after that when he was simply the elected messenger. 5

Terrence C. Carson was labeled "difficult" across the industry by those white folks in the studio, which, in Hollywood, is like being branded with a white-hot iron. He was blackballed from other projects because of this "branding." That term – difficult - is a warning to all other white people, and BIPOC bodies in the good graces of whites, to stay away from that "difficult" person lest they be labeled "difficult" as well and bear the consequences.

The First, the Few and the Only

John Amos

Good Times began in 1974, the first Black family television show. John Amos' character, named James Evans, was the patriarch of a family five. Three children and a husband and wife showcased a two-parent Black family that inspired and brought laughter to homes across the U.S. At that time in the seventies, the only characters similar to this James Evans were George Jefferson from The Jeffersons and Fred Sanford from Sanford and Son. John Amos' character was the only one married and supporting three children, however. James Evans was one of the strongest Black on-screen fathers, and that started a long tradition that has carried on in other works. John Amos' role in Good Times would go on to inspire hit shows like Fresh Prince of Bel-Air, The Cosby Show, and even Family Matters. He became the first to portray the patriarch of a two-parent Black household that worked out issues and environmental hurdles together amidst their own internal dramas. Other shows like Moesha and Sister, Sister are also not as likely to have happened without the work of both John Amos' and Florida Evans' roles. This was also during the time of the Vietnam War and the free love movement, barely a decade removed from the assassinations of Medgar Evers, Malcolm X, and MLK Jr. Other historical happenings that occurred within the context of the show: Roe v. Wade, Watergate, Kent State mass shooting, anti-war rallies in Washington, the first e-mail was sent, Israeli athletes killed at Olympic Games, and Nixon's "resignation".

In 1976, an episode was debuted that killed off James Evans. It was explained that it happened due to creative differences and constant clashes. Although the show had been focused on the entire family and the different parenting styles of James and Florida, the producer had begun to turn James into a man who was unable to hold down a job. The children's characters had high hopes for their careers: one wanted to be a Supreme Court justice and another who wanted to be a surgeon. The show moved to focus on JJ, James' eldest son, as the star of the show, after John Amos' departure. Instead of JJ becoming the strong head of household, he turned out to be more of a negative caricature like Stepin Fetchit. 6

The writing of Black characters by white Hollywood writers was another big gripe that John Amos had. The writers' overuse of a buffoonish Black character embodied from the unchecked racial imaginations of white writers, resulting in bad role models for Black children. The show was supposed to focus on the different parenting styles in a Black household dealing with tough issues with a comedic

The First, the Few and the Only

twist. John Amos confronted the writers and Norman Leer about it like a father, protecting young Black actors and the messages they send to kids like his own son, and Norman got curt and aggressive. So, John Amos told him we can step outside if you want to take it there. He was soon killed off the show.

They wanted to make JJ Evans the star of the show through sardoodledom and buffoonery. John Amos' contract for season four was not going to be picked up by the producers, and in 1976, season four opened up with an episode that killed off John Amos's character off screen in a car crash.
John Amos wasn't the only one fighting behind the scenes. Esther Rolle wrote to the editor to request that they did not fire John Amos. The white producers had originally written Good Times as a show about a Black single mother. Before the show even aired in 1974, Esther Rolle was pursued for the role, but she would not take it unless there was a Black father alongside her character. Norman Lear, the show's producer, was pretty adamant about not having a Black father on the show, but Esther held her ground. She famously asked Lear, "Am I gonna have any say so about this show? Because remember, I have been Black the longest."

After killing off James Evans in episode one of season four, Esther Rolle would go on to leave the show at the end of that very season. The studio kept the show running without the parents, depicting the kids living on their own. It suffered, and by the end of season five, they realized that everything John Amos and Esther Rolle had told them was true.

Esther Rolle

 Esther Rolle walked onto the set of Good Times knowing full well the weight she carried. She wasn't just playing a role - she was fighting a war. A war against the slow erosion of Black families in the American imagination, a war against the scripts that painted Black mothers as weary, unprotected, and alone, a war against the rising tide of the fatherless caricatures that Hollywood was so eager to mass-produce. She saw the writing on the wall and, unlike so many, she refused to be complicit in her own people's erasure.

She put her career on the line, risked contracts, risked comfort, and drew a line in the sand: no Black father? No Esther Rolle. And she won. Because of her, America

The First, the Few and the Only

met James Evans, a working-class Black father who was present, who was loving, who was real. 7

She single-handedly disrupted Hollywood's agenda, held off the lie that Black homes were naturally broken, and forced the first Black family sitcom to be just that - a family. A full one. A whole one. She waged war against sardoodledom, against lazy storytelling that sought to reinforce a narrative of Black struggle without Black strength. And for a moment, she prevailed.

Like Josiah Henson, she was a fighter disguised as a servant. She knew the power of controlling how her people were seen, how they were remembered. Hollywood may have wanted to write the Black father out of the picture, but Esther Rolle refused. Because of her, an entire generation got to see something different, something truer. She made them put the father back in the frame, and that changed everything.

Little Richard: The Architect of Rock n' Roll

Sam Cooke.
Billy Preston.
Jerry & the Pacemakers
The Swingin' Blue Jeans
The Rolling Stones.
The Beatles.
They all opened for him.

Let that sit. 8

Little Richard didn't just perform - he built the stage they stood on.
He didn't just influence music - he was the architect of rock n' roll! In 1962, making fifty dollars a week a person, he took the Beatles on tour. He personally taught Paul McCartney how to do his signature scream and helped coach the Beatles on how to perform - not just play - on stage. He even bought them steak dinners every day on tour in Europe because they were broke, and he believed in them.

Otis Redding got hired as his band member. He gave Jimi Hendrix a shot in his band, for four years, long before the world knew his name. He poured into white

The First, the Few and the Only

artists, Black artists, global icons - most of whom went on to surpass him in fame, but not in contribution.

And yet, how many of those white artists ever turned back to acknowledge the man who taught them how to swing their hips, bend their vocals, and command the mic like thunder? How many ever said his name with reverence, publicly?

While Elvis was learning how to move from Black dancers and building a career off borrowed soul, Little Richard was already a global star. But unlike Elvis, he had to cosplay queerness - presenting himself as flamboyant, effeminate, and non-threatening just to be allowed on stage. Not because he was gay, but because as a heterosexual Black man, his very presence was seen as a threat to white America and seen as too dangerous, too virile, too disruptive to the white fantasy of sexual supremacy.

Before Rick James, before Prince, before George Clinton, there was Little Richard - the greatest! He was the king and the queen of rock n' roll. Not because he couldn't decide - but because he embodied both power and flamboyance, authority and flair.

He moved through an industry designed to exploit, erase, and profit off of Black genius. An industry that would take songs he wrote, have him record them, and then hand them off to white boys to re-record and claim as their own. No credit. No royalties.

Just theft.

There's a story he tells - heartbreaking and all too familiar - about being invited to sing a duet on national television. The catch? The other "singer" was a white man who had built his career off of Little Richard's song, bar for bar. They wanted him to sing it with the thief - as if that were some kind of honor. No payment. No acknowledgement. Just audacity.

This wasn't a one-time thing. It happened hundreds of times.
And still, Little Richard taught the game to Black and white artists alike. He wasn't just a performer, he was a professor of performance. A masterclass in survival, in sound, in spectacle. He could've been a studio executive. He could've run a label. Instead, he chose to blaze a trail. And make no mistake: without Little Richard,

The First, the Few and the Only

there is no rock n' roll. No funk. No disco. Even his influence on hip-hop is undeniable.

They took from him.

⌀ He gave anyway.

 And we are still dancing in the shadow of his sound. Put some respect on his motherf**** name.

Billie Holiday

Billie Holiday was the first African-American woman to work with an all-white band, occurring in the mid-1930s. She was also a musical icon who influenced jazz and pop singing. Her song "Strange Fruit" is considered one of the first protest songs of the American Civil Rights Movement. Her other accomplishments include:

- Recorded her first song with Benny Goodman in 1933
- Began recording under her own name in 1936
- Toured w/ the Count Basie & Artie Shaw bands in 1937 & 1938
- Co-wrote "God Bless the Child" and "Lady Sings the Blues"
- Won five Grammy Awards

Holiday's bluesy vocal style and intimate delivery added a new dimension to jazz singing. She was a musical icon who captivated the world with her artistry. She was awarded accordingly, until she set the nation ablaze with her song "Strange Fruit." She suffered for her art.

She was targeted by the U.S. government for daring to be defiant. The FBI hounded her for years, using her drug use as a pretext to silence her. They revoked her cabaret card, barring her from performing in clubs. But she kept singing. 9

She gave voice to the voiceless, and in doing so, Holiday embodied the double pain of being both Black and a woman in a country that criminalized both. She alchemized that pain into sound - her very survival was protest. Billie Holiday was admitted to the hospital in May 1959 due to liver and heart failure - the result of

The First, the Few and the Only

years of substance use, racial trauma, and the physical toll of a system that never let her rest.

By the time she entered Metropolitan Hospital in New York, her body was deeply weakened from decades of alcohol and heroin addiction, compounded by ongoing police harassment and poverty. She was only forty-four years old.

While in the hospital, she was handcuffed to her hospital bed and placed under arrest for drug possession. The Federal Bureau of Narcotics (led by Harry Anslinger, a staunchly racist official) refused her methadone treatment, which might have helped stabilize her. Furthermore, she was denied proper medical care during her final days until finally on July 17, 1959, Billie died at the age of forty-four with just seventy cents in her bank account and a tabloid photographer among the last to see her alive.

She died chained to a bed because she would not stop singing the song that immortalized the horrors of white culture and their Sunday traditions decorating their trees with the bodies of Black and Brown people. When I went to the National Memorial for Peace and Justice, I learned that, although many were lynched for inconsequential reasons and sometimes no real reason whatsoever, many lynchings were actually targeted murders of Black businessmen and wealthy Black people.

Billie Holiday didn't just die of illness. She died of state violence, neglect, and the slow poison of racism - administered over time, cloaked in legality. 🌱 Getting Involved Song: Strange fruit

From Then to Now

🎵 Eddie Griffin, comedian and actor in shows like Malcolm & Eddie and star in the film Undercover Brother, was once asked if he thinks Hollywood is still racist. Here was his response:

"Naww. Hell-motherfuckin'-yeah, they racist. Did you see the new movie about Moses? How the fuck is the Gladiator dude Moses? The fuck out of here. This was in Africa, not some small village in Sweden. Who comes up with this shit? That's like me playing JFK, Eddie Griffin as John F. Kennedy! The movie gon' start with

The First, the Few and the Only

my Black ass gettin' shot. Then the rest of the movie about some white detective tryna figure out who did it.... Hollywood, when we all came out, this goes for Martin's show to me and Malcolm's show [Malcolm & Eddie] to Jamie Foxx's show [The Jamie Foxx Show] so on and so forth, they put us on these new networks, remember they had UPN? I used to call it the 'The You-Pick-A-Nigga Network.' Every Black show that creates this network, once this motherfucker is built on our backs, they sell the motherfucker. Where's UPN at?"

Hollywood in the 1990s exhibited a pattern where Black TV shows were used to generate revenue and establish network stability, only to be canceled or deprioritized in favor of predominantly white programming. This pattern was particularly visible on networks like Fox, UPN, and the WB, which heavily relied on Black-led sitcoms and dramas to build their audiences before shifting toward more mainstream (i.e., white) programming and, in some cases, selling or merging networks. Below is an analysis of how, when, and why this happened.

The First, the Few and the Only

How Did This Happen?

During the late 1980s and early 1990s, networks like Fox, UPN, and The WB were struggling to compete with the "Big Three" networks (ABC, NBC, and CBS). To gain traction, they heavily invested in Black audiences, as Black viewership was loyal, consistent, and less catered to by major networks. This led to a boom in Black television content, with hits like:

Fox: Martin ('92-'97), Living Single ('93-'98), New York Undercover ('94-'99)
UPN: Moesha ('96-'01), The Parkers ('99-'04), Girlfriends ('00-'08)
The WB: The Wayans Bros. ('95-'99), The Jamie Foxx Show ('96-'01), Sister, Sister ('94-'99)

These shows were profitable, attracting both Black and crossover audiences, while keeping these new networks afloat. They provided ad revenue and solidified brand identity at a time when these networks were financially shaky with economic risks to their networks. However, once the networks gained stability and expanded their mainstream (white) audience, they "shifted programming priorities." Interpretation: canceling or marginalizing Black-led shows in favor of predominantly white series.

When Did This Happen?

The shift began in the late 1990s and early 2000s, when major television networks began pivoting away from the Black-led programming that helped build their platforms. This change was driven by a desire to attract a whiter, more suburban demographic - the audience advertisers considered more lucrative.

The First, the Few and the Only

Fox, for example, made its name with Black-led sitcoms and dramas like Martin, Living Single, and New York Undercover. These shows defined the network's early identity. But by the late 1990s, as Fox sought mainstream recognition, it began replacing these series with white-led shows like Ally McBeal (1997) and That '70s Show (1998). Even popular, high-performing shows were not spared. Living Single was cut despite strong ratings, while New York Undercover saw its budget slashed and cast overhauled in a failed attempt to appeal to white audiences - eventually leading to its cancellation.

In 2006, a more dramatic shift took place when The WB and UPN - both known for their investment in Black-led programming throughout the 1990s and early 2000s - merged to form The CW. The result was devastating for Black representation. Almost all Black-led programming was cut from the lineup. Girlfriends, one of the highest-rated sitcoms of its time, was canceled abruptly without a finale. Meanwhile, shows like One Tree Hill and Gossip Girl received heavy promotion and full story arcs. 10

Living Single: The show Friends is rumored to only exist because of Living Single

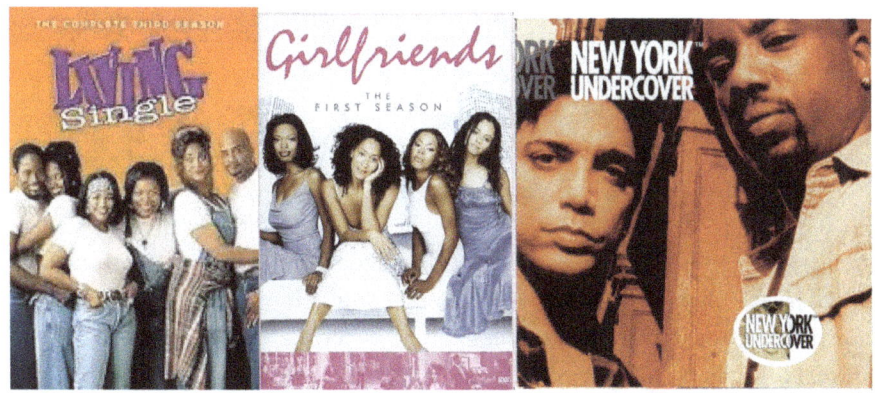

The First, the Few and the Only

How Often Did This Happen?

This wasn't an isolated incident - it was a recurring pattern throughout the late twentieth and early twenty-first centuries. Networks would strategically invest in Black-led shows to build early viewership and brand identity. Once they became established, they pivoted toward white-led content, often canceling Black shows that were still successful.

Take Living Single, for instance. It aired before Friends and often had better ratings during its early seasons. Yet it received a smaller budget and far less marketing. Or New York Undercover, the first cop drama to feature a Black and Latino lead, which was canceled after producers tried to "mainstream" the show with a whiter cast. Moesha, a flagship UPN show, ended on a cliffhanger with no resolution - all while newer, white-led shows were being greenlit and funded. Even The Parkers and Girlfriends, both audience favorites, were denied the budgets, finales, and promotional support regularly given to their white counterparts.

Why Did This Happen?

There were several intersecting forces behind this erasure:

1. Advertising and Ratings Bias

Advertisers favored white, suburban audiences, viewing them as more "valuable" consumers. This created a double standard - even when Black-led shows performed well, they were undervalued by ad buyers.

2. Network Growth Strategy

Many networks used Black audiences to gain traction and relevance. But once they achieved success, they shifted to white-centric content in pursuit of so-called "mainstream" appeal, often abandoning the very viewers who had helped build their brand. 11

3. Racial Gatekeeping in Hollywood

The First, the Few and the Only

There has long been a bias within media leadership that favors white-led productions. As networks matured, they deprioritized Black narratives, revealing how white comfort was still the unspoken default.

4. Mergers and Corporate Consolidation

When WB and UPN merged into the CW, the resulting corporate structure made it clear: Black-led programming wasn't part of the new vision. Success didn't matter - identity did. 12

This pattern contributed to a decline in Black sitcoms and dramas on network television by the mid-2000s. The erasure of Black-led TV shows from major networks pushed Black storytelling to niche platforms like BET, OWN, and later, streaming services like Netflix.

While Black-led shows have made a resurgence in recent years (Insecure, Black-ish, Atlanta), the 1990s and early 2000s serve as a stark reminder that Hollywood often uses Black talent to build wealth, only to cast it aside once it achieves mainstream success.

This pattern still continues today, though it has evolved with the rise of streaming platforms and social media. While Black-led shows are more visible than before, Hollywood still exploits Black audiences to build platforms and then deprioritizes them once mainstream success is achieved. Below are the ways this pattern continues and where some progress has been made.

The First, the Few and the Only

How This Pattern Continues Today

1. Streaming Services Use Black Content to Build Audiences, Then Pivot Away
   - Netflix, Hulu, and other platforms heavily marketed Black content early on to attract diverse audiences.
   - However, once these platforms established mainstream credibility, Black-led shows were disproportionately canceled after two or three seasons, even when they performed well.

Examples:
   - Netflix: The Get Down (2016-2017), Luke Cage (2016-2018), Raising Dion (2019-2022), On My Block (2018-2021), Dear White People (2017)
   - HBO Max (Max): South Side (2019-2022), Insecure ended after five seasons despite its popularity.
   - The CW (Post-WB/UPN merger): All American: Homecoming and Batwoman were both canceled despite strong social media engagement.

Why?
Streaming services, like networks in the nineties, capitalize on Black viewership to build a subscriber base, then pivot to broader (white-led) content to appeal to global audiences and advertisers.

2. Black-Led Shows Face Disproportionate Cancellation Rates
   - Studies show that Black-led TV series are canceled at a higher rate than white-led series.
   - Even when they perform well, Black shows often get less marketing, smaller budgets, and fewer renewals.

Recent Examples:
   - Amazon Prime canceled THEM (2022) and Poppa's House (2022), while renewing shows with white leads.
   - HBO abruptly canceled Lovecraft Country (2020) after one season, despite critical acclaim and strong ratings.

The First, the Few and the Only

Why?
Hollywood still operates on the outdated belief that Black stories are "niche" and not "mainstream" enough for long-term investment.

3. Hollywood Still Undervalues Black Audiences
- Advertisers continue to prioritize white suburban demographics, assuming they have more spending power.
- Even though Black consumers are among the most loyal and engaged audiences, their viewership is often overlooked in renewal decisions.
- The Nielsen 2021 Diversity Report found that Black-led content often ranks high in streaming hours but doesn't receive the same financial backing as white-led projects.

Example:
- The success of Black Panther (2018) proved that Black-led content is financially viable, yet Hollywood still hesitates to greenlight high-budget Black projects.

Where Progress Has Been Made

1. Social Media and Streaming Disrupt the Traditional Power Structure
- Fans can now mobilize online to push for renewals (#SaveTheExpanse, #RenewOneDayAtATime).
- Platforms like YouTube, TikTok, and Instagram allow Black creators to bypass Hollywood gatekeepers and find direct audiences.

Example:
- Issa Rae built a fanbase through YouTube before HBO picked up Insecure - a path that more Black creators are using.

2. Black-Led Production Companies Are Gaining Power
- Creators like Ava DuVernay, Jordan Peele, Tyler Perry, and Issa Rae have built their own production companies.
- Black-owned media brands (e.g., OWN, and LeBron James' SpringHill Company) are creating Black-centered content outside of traditional networks.

The First, the Few and the Only

Example:
- Tyler Perry's partnership with BET+ has made it a leading streaming platform for Black audiences - something that networks abandoned after the WB/UPN merger.

The Pattern Still Exists, But Power Is Shifting

While Hollywood still exploits Black-led shows to build platforms before deprioritizing them, the rise of streaming, social media, and independent Black production companies is disrupting the system. However, systemic issues persist:

Black-led shows still face early cancellations despite high viewership.
- Advertising bias continues to undervalue Black audiences.
- Hollywood still sees Black content as a "trend" rather than a permanent investment.

The Future?

The next big battle is equity in funding, ownership, and decision-making. If Black creators continue owning their content and platforms, the cycle of Hollywood using and discarding Black stories may finally break.

Tubi | Peacock

Tubi has experienced significant growth, with a notable portion of its audience being Black viewers. As of June 2023, nearly half of Tubi's users identified as Black. This demographic has been instrumental in propelling Tubi to over 8.5 billion streaming hours in 2023. The platform offers a diverse range of content, including specialized categories like Black cinema, which cater to its multicultural audience. [13]

However, concerns have been raised about Tubi potentially following a pattern reminiscent of past practices by major networks. Some observers worry that Tubi might adopt a similar strategy, leveraging its current Black viewership and content to establish a broader market presence before pivoting away.

The First, the Few and the Only

Peacock offers a selection of Black movies and TV shows, celebrating narratives by Black creators. While the platform showcases this content, there is limited information available regarding its strategic approach to Black-led programming and its commitment to sustaining such content over time. 14

Recent Trends

The broader industry has seen a series of cancellations of Black-led shows across various platforms. In 2023, notable cancellations included Grown-ish, Ziwe, and South Side, among others. LOVE the show Southside btw. These decisions have raised concerns about the industry's commitment to diverse storytelling and the longevity of Black-led content.

While platforms like Tubi and Peacock currently provide spaces for Black-led content, historical patterns and recent trends underscore the importance of vigilance. The sustainability of such programming hinges on continued audience support and a genuine commitment to diverse storytelling from these platforms. The underrepresentation and premature cancellation of television shows centered on Asian and Latinx communities have been persistent issues in the U.S. entertainment industry.

Latinx Representation and Show Cancellations

Despite Latinos constituting approximately nineteen percent of the U.S. population, their presence in television is disproportionately low. In 2022, just over three percent of TV shows featured a Latino lead, and a mere one-point-three percent of episodes were directed by Latinos. This disparity is further highlighted by the absence of Latino showrunners on major cable networks.

The few Latinx-centered shows that make it to production often face early cancellations. For instance, Gordita Chronicles was canceled just a month after its premiere in 2022. Similarly, Gentefied and Promised Land were also short-lived, each concluding with fewer than twenty episodes. 15

The First, the Few and the Only

Asian-American Representation and Show Cancellations

Asian-American-led television shows have also encountered challenges in gaining and maintaining traction. Historically, series like All-American Girl (1994) faced early cancellations due to various factors, including network decisions and perceived audience reception. [16]

In the 2015-2016 television season, shows such as Fresh Off the Boat and Dr. Ken provided representation for Asian-American families. However, despite its initial success, Dr. Ken was canceled after two seasons, reflecting the industry's hesitancy to sustain Asian-centered narratives. [17]

Contemporary Trends

The pattern of underrepresentation and premature cancellations persists today. The entertainment industry continues to grapple with systemic issues related to diversity and inclusion. Recent reports indicate that despite initiatives to promote diversity, equity, and inclusion (DEI), significant setbacks have occurred, including the laying off of high-profile DEI leaders and the discontinuation of programs aimed at supporting underrepresented groups. Even Sesame Street didn't survive the latest purge.

Similarly, shows with Asian and Latinx representation also experienced brief runs during the '90s and 2000s. The entertainment industry's historical and ongoing challenges in sustaining Asian and Latinx-centered television shows underscore a broader issue of underrepresentation and systemic bias. While there have been moments of progress, the premature cancellation of such shows remains a concern, reflecting the need for continued advocacy and structural change to ensure diverse narratives are given equitable opportunities to thrive.

Modeling

Outside of academia, Somalian goddess and model Iman talks about her experience alongside top model Beverly Johnson, who shares similar stories of tokenism in modeling. Check out this clip from her interview on Sway in the Morning.

The First, the Few and the Only

🌱 Dear reader, please stop and watch the clips from the above at minute 10:17
& Bethan Hardison @minute 13:28
⏱ Iman by Vogue

Bethann Hardison was the watchtower, the steel spine, the unseen architect of possibility in an industry built to erase Black beauty. Before the fashion world ever spoke her name in reverence, she was already there - lifting, fighting, dragging the industry into an era where Black models could walk the runway and not just be a trend, but a force. She was, in many ways, the Hobie Brown to every Miles Morales of the fashion world - an unsung hero who built bridges so others could cross, a rebel in a system that demanded submission.

Much like Hobie Brown, aka Spider-Punk, who refused to play by the rules of a world that was never made for him, Bethann saw the trap, the game, the illusion of inclusion, and instead of waiting for permission, she tore through the system with the kind of defiance that changes history. She understood that representation was not just about putting Black faces in high places - it was about power, about access, about who gets to shape the story.

In the seventies and eighties, while the world was fixated on the glamour of Black supermodels like Naomi Campbell and Veronica Webb, Bethann was doing the real work creating the Black Girls Coalition, gathering the vanguard of Black modeling to fight for not just space but sovereignty. When fashion tried to erase them, limiting their presence in ads, casting calls, and runway shows, she answered with numbers, receipts, and unrelenting fire. The world said Black women weren't desirable enough to sell luxury. Bethann made the industry eat those words.

She understood the currency of beauty, but she also understood its politics. By 2007, when fashion houses like Prada and Jil Sander started openly writing "no Black models" into their casting calls, she did what Black leaders have always done - she made them answer for it. She confronted the councils of Paris, Milan, London, and New York, calling their practices what they were: racism wrapped in high fashion's usual air of aloof indifference. She pushed back, not just with rage, but

The First, the Few and the Only

with strategy, forcing an industry that was content with tokenism to reckon with its sins.

And like Hobie Brown - who didn't just fight for himself but for every version of Spider-Man who came after - Bethann wasn't just looking out for the Naomi Campbells, Imans and Jourdan Dunns. She was ensuring that Blackness, in all its shades, shapes, and textures, was no longer an afterthought.

By the time Vogue Italia's "All Black" issue shattered sales records, proving the world had always wanted what the industry refused to give, Bethann had already spent decades proving that Black beauty wasn't just marketable - it was inevitable.

Her work was never about just fashion; it was about breaking the economic, social, and cultural barriers that kept Black creatives out of the rooms where real power sat. Though the industry has tried to smooth over its past with performative gestures of diversity, her name remains a lighthouse, a warning, and a legacy.

Bethann Hardison was never waiting to be invited. She built her own path and dared the world to catch up, while being a covering for some of the greatest sun-kissed women to walk the catwalk.

🌾 Terrence Howard & how they play with you
🌱 Undeniable | Unignorable | Saviors

You're not alone

The First, the Few and the Only

Chapter 15

Burning House Politics

Dave Chappelle said it best: "People are trying to replace the ideas of good and bad with better or worse, and that is incorrect. You got to keep your ethics intact, because good and bad is a compass that helps you find the way. A person that only does what's better or worse is the easiest type of person to control. They are a mouse in a maze that just finds the cheese, but the one who knows about good and bad will realize that he's in a maze." 1 Regardless of which political party you choose, I think of that quote often—especially when I see BIPOC bodies moving through politics, both red and blue. The maze may look different depending on the corridor, but the traps are the same.

Harry Belafonte once shared his final conversation with Dr. Martin Luther King Jr. before the assassination. In that moment, Dr. King confessed a haunting fear—that he may have led his people into a burning house.

Every election cycle, I hear the same phrase from both my conservative and liberal friends: "Pick your poison." And let's be honest—these party labels are no more real than the social construct of race. Democrat. Republican. Conservative. Liberal. These are not identities; they are instruments. Tools of division. Designed to tether us to illusion while the machinery of white supremacy keeps humming along.

I'm not calling for a revolution—at least not yet—but I am calling out the lie. The fantasy that these parties are fundamentally different in how they treat Black and

The First, the Few and the Only

Brown bodies. Many of us vote based on proximity: to whiteness, to safety, to social capital. Often, it's less about political conviction and more about where we feel least alone.

And yet—every four years, Black and Brown bodies become currency. Campaigns turn into meat markets. Candidates scramble to find someone who looks like "us," but speaks in ways that comfort "them." These are not leaders—they are mascots. This is not inclusion. It's theater. It's Pax Americana.

> *"In chess, the black and white pieces are fierce enemies,*
> *but the ones who move them are usually good friends."*
> -Anonymous Modern Aphorism

Lessons from Iceberg Slim's book, Trick Baby

There is an amazing dialogue that captures the gist of how the political landscape in the U.S. treats Black and Brown bodies like garden garnish, a crystallization of the decorated deception, as it were. Watch the dramatization of Trick Baby by Iceberg Slim. It's one of the clearest visual metaphors I've ever seen for how political systems co-opt BIPOC voices—not to empower, but to pacify. Please don't read any further until you watch this clip. Getting Involved:

262
You're not alone

The First, the Few and the Only

Clip from Trick Baby for a visual embodiment of how & why racial co-optation works

That's the game. Promote just enough into whiteness-adjacent roles—not to liberate, but to isolate. To ostracize. To create distance between the "risen" and the community they came from. It's a trick bag of epic proportions. And when you sign that Faustian bargain? You will cape. You'll be expected to.

(Caping: blindly defending someone, no matter how wrong they are. Shoutout to Urban Dictionary. After all, it comes with the territory.)
You may also be wondering… "What is a Faustian bargain?"

⏱️Put the book down, go to ChatGPT or some search engine and type in the above question. ;).

I've seen it. I've been tempted by its charming allure. I've adjusted my dialect and style of relating to fit the room. To be more palatable. But here's the aching truth many BIPOC leaders learn too late: No amount of assimilation will save us.
You can fawn, flatter, feign interest convergence. You can echo white talking points and toe the party line. You can do everything "right." And still—be discarded.

They may tolerate you. They may even celebrate you—for a time. But rarely do they accept you. And eventually, the system finds another mascot. Iceberg Slim's Trick Baby offers a haunting dramatization of the result of Faustian political bargains. This line hits me every time and applies to all BIPOC on either side of the aisle:

"He becomes alien to his brothers. They hate him. He becomes worthless to them & safe for us."

And there's huge trail of former BIPOC celebrities and "leaders" who have come and gone. During every campaign season, the commodification intensifies. Suddenly, Blackness is profitable again. Brownness is courted—just enough to harvest votes, not to hold space. It's not inclusion. It's exploitation dressed up in diversity metrics.

Again, this is not about individuals. It's about patterns. Institutions that elevate the "safe" BIPOC voice while sidelining the ones that challenge the system itself. . If anything is redundant, I apologize, but my goal is to make sure you OVER-stand.

The First, the Few and the Only

Still, I'd be lying if I said I don't think of Kanye West in the MAGA hat, or Stacey Dash walking back her statements made while surrounded by affirming white bodies and audiences, or even Vivek Ramaswamy's attempts at political assimilation. These are cautionary tales, not anomalies.

According to a COMPLEX article, Stacey Dash was written about in this way: "In 2015, she claimed then-president Barack Obama didn't 'give a shit' about terrorism. She also called for the elimination of Black History Month, BET, and the NAACP Image Awards, she made transphobic comments during an Entertainment Tonight interview, and she defended former president Donald Trump's 'very fine people' remarks in response to the deadly Charlottesville rally."

In addition, to saying there should be no Black History Month, she was against the protest known as #oscarssowhite and criticized Jada Pinkett Smith's protest of the Oscars. In a TheGrio article2, Stacey Dash would later go on to walk back a lot of her ire and statements after acknowledging that she had become blacklisted in Hollywood. Even the Black community as a potential audience in Hollywood had turned their backs on her. A NewsONE article is even entitled, "Stacey Dash Wants To Be invited Back To The Cookout: 'I Made A Lot Of Mistakes'" and is quoted saying, "Stacey Dash is following the classic - and pitifully stale - blueprint for redemption in the Black community by begging for forgiveness. In other words,

The First, the Few and the Only

she wants to be invited back to the proverbial cookout after selling her people out." In trying to disavow Blackness for mainstream praise, she became too Black for Hollywood, and not Black enough for the community she tried to leave behind.

Complex Article | Grio Article | 2021 NEWSONE

Vivek Ramaswamy

There is a snippet of what BIPOC bodies have been experiencing in white politics for generations. It has to do with an interaction between Vivek, a 2024 presidential Republican hopeful, and the infamous Ann Coulter. It can be seen here:

"I Wouldn't Vote for You Because…"

Vivek Ramaswamy, a Republican presidential hopeful in 2024, found himself in a telling exchange with conservative commentator Ann Coulter. She praised his intellect, even noting he was "articulate" because he wasn't Black - a racialized microaggression cloaked as compliment. Ramaswamy smiled along until Coulter,

The First, the Few and the Only

moments later, stated outright: "I still wouldn't vote for you because you're Indian."

That moment served as a sobering example of the illusion of inclusion. No amount of ideological alignment could erase racial exclusion. It revealed a broader truth: proximity to whiteness doesn't equal acceptance.

Many BIPOC leaders mistakenly believe that if they echo the values and beliefs of dominant groups, they'll be embraced by them. But as this moment revealed, what often awaits is conditional tolerance - not belonging. The risk isn't just personal. It's communal. When leaders use their platforms to invalidate the pain or history of their own people, they may find themselves both alienated from their community and ultimately still ostracized by the one they tried to appease. That's the paradox of proximity to whiteness: it gives you a stage, but never the director role. But as we'll see in the next section, there are those who refuse the script entirely.

The Reversal
When BIPOC Leaders Refuse to Fold

*"The world is held together by the love
and passion of a very few people."*
- James Baldwin

The First, the Few and the Only

This isn't a condemnation of political engagement, but a demand for discernment. Not every Black or Brown face in high places is a victory. Not every elevation is a win for the collective. Some are cautionary tales.

These examples underscore the importance of BIPOC leaders who, rather than conforming to the expectations of existing power structures, actively challenge and seek to reform them. Their efforts contribute to a broader movement aimed at achieving equity and justice within the political and social systems -chasing hidden giants just like Don Quixote.

Justice Ketanji Brown

Justice Ketanji Brown Jackson's appointment to the U.S. Supreme Court in 2022 marked a significant moment in American history as she became the first Black woman to serve on the nation's highest court. Her extensive legal background, including experience as a public defender and a federal judge, has brought a unique and impactful perspective to the bench.

In her initial term, Justice Jackson quickly established herself as a distinctive voice. She authored several solo dissents, a notable feat for a junior justice. Her approach often involves a progressive interpretation of originalism, emphasizing the historical context of the Constitution's amendments, particularly those adopted during the Reconstruction Era, to ensure equality for formerly enslaved individuals. This perspective was evident during her second day of oral arguments, where she highlighted that the 14th Amendment was not intended to be race-neutral but was designed to address racial inequalities.

Justice Jackson's commitment to equal protection under the law is reflected in her judicial decisions. For instance, she upheld a federal law allowing the Small Business Administration to ensure federal contracting opportunities for socially and

The First, the Few and the Only

economically disadvantaged individuals. In her ruling, she affirmed the constitutionality of the Section 8(a) program, which aims to extend government contracting opportunities to small business owners who have faced discrimination.
3

Her background as a public defender and her tenure with the U.S. Sentencing Commission provide her with a comprehensive understanding of the criminal justice system. This experience informs her perspectives on cases involving defendants' rights and sentencing disparities, contributing to a more holistic view of justice on the Supreme Court. Justice Jackson's presence has also influenced the dynamics of the Court. Her insightful questioning during oral arguments and her willingness to author dissenting opinions demonstrate her commitment to addressing complex legal issues head-on. Her approach has been noted for challenging the dominant conservative narrative, advocating for a constitutional interpretation that supports a multiracial democracy.

In summary, Justice Ketanji Brown Jackson's contributions to the Supreme Court underscore the importance of diverse perspectives in the judiciary. Her dedication to principles of equality and justice continues to shape the Court's deliberations and decisions, reflecting her unwavering commitment to upholding the Constitution's promises for all Americans.

Tennessee State Representative Justin Jones

One of the "Tennessee Three," was expelled from the Tennessee House of Representatives for protesting gun violence only to be reinstated by his constituents. His expulsion was not just about decorum; it was a clear attempt to discipline a young, unapologetic Black voice. Yet he returned, not pacified, but emboldened - proof that when we refuse to be neutralized, the system will try to discard us. And when it fails? Like Antaeus from Greek mythology, that's when we get stronger.

Senator Cory Booker

Senator Cory Booker has consistently demonstrated a commitment to confronting injustice and advocating for marginalized communities. His actions exemplify leadership that challenges systemic inequities and promotes civil rights.

The First, the Few and the Only

In March 2025, Senator Booker delivered a historic twenty-five-hour speech on the Senate floor, surpassing the previous record held by Strom Thurmond. This marathon address was a protest against the policies of President Donald Trump's administration, which Booker criticized for undermining democracy, social programs, and civil liberties. He drew inspiration from civil rights leaders like John Lewis, emphasizing the moral imperative to oppose harmful policies and calling for collective action to defend democratic institutions. His tears and passion were sincere, but the system he's a part of still functions within the limits of representation without transformation. His speech was deeply meaningful for visibility validation and historic record, but in the grand scheme of power and policy -not necessarily liberation, which is what happens when seeing isn't followed by anything changing. Further illustrating the paradox of this chapter.

Beyond this notable event, Booker's legislative efforts reflect his dedication to civil rights. He has championed bills such as the Do No Harm Act, CROWN Act, Equality Act, and HOME Act, all aimed at protecting individuals from discrimination based on race, gender, and other factors. In 2022, he authored the bipartisan Emmett Till Anti-Lynching Act, which successfully made lynching a federal hate crime after over a century of failed attempts. 4

Booker has also been vocal about environmental justice, highlighting the disproportionate impact of environmental hazards on communities of color. He asserts that addressing climate justice is inseparable from addressing racial justice, pointing out that the prevalence of polluted air and water is often determined by the skin color of one's zip code.

The First, the Few and the Only

State Governorship

Executive Branch

Dr. Claud Anderson walked into the White House not as a guest, not as a token, but as a strategist. He was one of the first, the few, and the only Black economists to sit at the highest levels of government and tell the truth - plain, unfiltered, and sharp as a blade. He didn't come to beg. He didn't come to assimilate. He came to shake the table.

Here was a Black man in the highest halls of power who refused to speak in a tone that comforted the status quo. While America was still congratulating itself on desegregation, patting itself on the back for letting Black folks into white spaces, Anderson was one of the few voices saying, "Wait - at what cost?" He saw the game for what it was. Integration wasn't the victory they claimed it was. It was a trade - Black economic power for white acceptance. Black businesses, once thriving, were now abandoned. Black schools, once rich with excellence, were now shuttered. Black self-sufficiency, once a source of strength, was now a distant memory.

He didn't just theorize about it - he worked from the inside, serving as an economic adviser for governors, heading economic development programs, and later, advising the White House on the very policies that would determine Black America's

The First, the Few and the Only

economic future. However, the truth he carried was too sharp for the comfort of those in power. He wasn't there to make people feel good. He was there to make Black people free. 5

Anderson exposed how desegregation led to the disintegration of Black economic power, identity, and community vitality. He pulled back the curtain on how integration by way of assimilation became a new wave of colonization. He showed how Black dollars were systematically funneled out of Black hands, how Black neighborhoods became ghettos overnight, and how the performative proximity of integration was just another way to strip Black people of what little independence they had fought to build.

He didn't just diagnose the problem - he laid out a blueprint:

PowerNomics, a strategy for economic liberation. A way back to self-sufficiency, group economics, and real power - not borrowed, not begged for, but owned. Dr. Claud Anderson was never just a scholar. He was a warrior, wielding knowledge like a weapon. He became one of the first to say it plainly: you cannot integrate into power. You must build your own. Here are some of his accomplishments:

Embodied Contranyms

There is a cruel irony in the history of the U.S. Supreme Court, a poetry so bitter it curdles in the throat. In 1991, the first Black Supreme Court Justice, Thurgood Marshall - a man who spent his life waging war on segregation, white supremacy, and the legal noose that kept Black folks in second-class citizenship - was replaced by Clarence Thomas, a man who would spend his career undoing Marshall's work with the eager compliance of a well-kept servant.

It was a passing of the torch, but not in the way history is supposed to move forward. This was no smooth transition of legacy. It was the exchange of a freedom fighter for a grinning accomplice, the replacement of a Josiah Henson with an 'Uncle Tom'. 7

The First, the Few and the Only

The Real Uncle Tom

To understand what was lost, we must first understand what Thurgood Marshall embodied. He was, in every way that mattered, the real Uncle Tom - not the slandered version spat out as an insult, but the truth of the man Josiah Henson, whose life Harriet Beecher Stowe loosely based her novel on.

Like Henson, Marshall believed in the law as a tool of liberation. He understood that America was never going to hand Black people freedom, dignity, or equality on a silver platter. It had to be fought for, sued for, dragged out of the hands of racists who clutched power like a life raft. As a young lawyer for the NAACP, he argued and won Brown v. Board of Education, that was him, striking down the lie of "separate but equal." He stood in front of the Supreme Court, time and time again, dismantling Jim Crow piece by piece.

Marshall was not interested in respectability politics. He did not cozy up to the powerful, nor did he mistake access for acceptance. He knew that to sit at the table was not the same as owning the house. And then came Clarence Thomas. Where Marshall wielded the law to break chains, Thomas has used it to tighten them. Where Marshall saw himself as a guardian of the people, Thomas feels like a guard dog for the powerful.

It is no small thing to betray your people, yet Clarence Thomas has done so with a zeal that would make a plantation overseer proud. He has spent decades ruling against affirmative action, against voting rights, against policies that would make Black life in America even slightly more bearable. While he likes to claim that he pulled himself up by his bootstraps, it is not lost on those of us who know better that he has been bankrolled - wined, dined, and luxury-vacationed - by the very white elite who benefit from his rulings. They have bought him homes, vacations, and God knows what else. They have paid for his mother's house. In return, he has done their bidding. Let's be honest - how many of us have seen this exact dynamic play out in our own workplaces, our own institutions? [6]

How many times have we watched a white-run establishment prop up one Black body willing to toe the company line, to speak the language of neutrality, while standing on the backs of their own? How many times have we been positioned against these figures, our names dragged through the mud while theirs are polished and praised?

The First, the Few and the Only

This is not just about two Supreme Court Justices. It is about a pattern, a system, a script that America has been running since slavery. It is about the way whiteness always seeks to control Blackness - not just through oppression, but through handpicked accomplices who do the work for them. I have seen this same pattern at almost every single predominantly white institution I have ever worked for.

And so, we must be clear: Thurgood Marshall was replaced, not succeeded. 8

Justice was not passed down. It was sold out.

As Toni Morrison once said, "The function, the very serious function of racism, is distraction. It keeps you from doing your work. It keeps you explaining, over and over again, your reason for being." Because justice, when stripped of its soul, becomes performance. And sometimes, the system would rather stage a performance than face a reckoning.

At the risk of overstating my point for clarity, let me be clear - this chapter is not an attack on individuals, but a reckoning with the patterns. Patterns of political co-optation. Costs of systemic assimilation.

For some, the bargain is one they will take every time. But every choice has its consequences, as I've tried to trace through the stories of those named—without disdain for their intent or character. Personally, neither party can contain all of my values as a Christian in a sun-kissed, melanated, mocha body in a red-or-blue, racialized nation. That's why I think Black and Brown bodies feel so politically torn in this country.

By definition, co-optation is the process by which a system absorbs potential threats by inviting them into its structure - not to elevate, but to manage. It's the strategy of offering seats at the table, not to share power, but to pacify critique. Whether through titles, funding, access, fiscal comeuppance or symbolic visibility, institutions often neutralize dissent by folding those who challenge them into their fold - disarming their voice while advertising inclusion.

This is not transformation. It is containment dressed as collaboration.

Simply put: we are picking different sides of the same knife.

The First, the Few and the Only

And in doing so, we risk colluding in our own co-optation.
America's most profitable Faustian bargain.
Even unto death.

Because no matter which side we choose, BIPOC bodies are too often left wrapping ourselves in the cloth of a political party that becomes, eventually, our own self-woven noose.

This chapter is not a call to abandon the political system.
It's a call to recognize when you're being seduced into colluding in your own demise.
Because power isn't presence alone.

It's purpose, no matter the stage.

It's clarity meets agency.

It's the refusal to be used as camouflage.

Thurgood Marshall

🌱 Getting Involved: What's coming up for you in body & mind?

_____

_____

_____

_____

The First, the Few and the Only

Chapter 16

Ghosts in the Shell

The anime Ghost in the Shell explores what it means to be human in a dehumanizing system—cybernetic bodies with lingering human souls. It's a haunting metaphor for what happens when institutions extract brilliance but deny belonging. When the body is seen, but the spirit—the self—is not protected.

This chapter is about Black and Brown excellence being platformed without protection. Embodiment without power. Voice without safety. These are souls encased in institutions that demand performance, erase personhood, and discard the body once its "utility" expires.

You'll be introduced to names you may not know yet—but their stories will feel like mirrors. Phillis Wheatley. Althea Gibson. Toni Morrison. Major Taylor and more. Each of them was celebrated, yes—but only as shells. As symbols. As avatars of progress for white audiences. Their pain was privatized. Their labor extracted. Their interior lives ghosted or distorted into projection.

This chapter isn't just about individual stories and accomplishments—it's about the psychic toll across generations. Ghosts doesn't only mean the past. It means the way the past haunts the present. It means the grief we carry in the present tense, especially for those of us who remain the first, the few, the only—even now.

This isn't just history. It's inter-generational inheritance. 🌱 It's the cost of being exceptional in systems that were never meant for our wholeness. It's the way the past keeps breathing through us—through every tightrope we walk, every boardroom we enter, every institution that calls us in but never truly lets us belong.

They praised the shell.
But they never protected us.
So we became ghosts… let's meet them;

The First, the Few and the Only

Literature

Phillis Wheatley was the first Black woman published in America. That's the line you'll read in history books, the polished version. The kind that celebrates the win but doesn't tell you what it cost. Because being the first, the few, the only always costs.

Phillis wasn't just a poet. She was made into a spectacle, a common weight of being turned into the exception. She began her life as a kidnapped African girl, stolen as a child, forced onto a slave ship, and dragged across the ocean into a world that only saw her as property. She landed in Boston, sickly and frail, and somehow ended up in the Wheatley household - not in the fields or scrubbing floors, but as a living experiment. They taught her to read and write, not out of the goodness of their hearts, but because her brilliance made them look good.

Even after she mastered English, Latin, and Greek, after she wrote poetry so refined it rivaled her white counterparts, she still had to prove she was capable of it. Imagine that: a panel of white men - governors, ministers, businessmen - staring her down, demanding evidence that she was, in fact, the author of her own words. Just like the film Finding Forrester, it wasn't enough to be brilliant. She had to justify her very mind.

Once they finally believed her, what did that mean? That Phillis Wheatley was exceptional? Was she used as proof that Black people could be civilized? That if one of us could rise to these heights, then surely racism wasn't that bad? She was their trophy, their controlled anomaly. [1]

Despite all the accolades, all the high society praise, Phillis Wheatley was never truly accepted. White folks loved her words but didn't love her. She was educated but still Black. Free, but never quite belonging. She had all the praise but none of the protection, and that can cost you.

And Black folks? It was complicated. She didn't openly align herself with abolitionism, and her proximity to whiteness made some wary. She was living proof of what was possible. She wasn't out here rebelling like Toussaint Louverture or Nat Turner. She wasn't burning down plantations. She was a poet in a time when freedom required fire and steel.

The First, the Few and the Only

Then, once the novelty of her brilliance wore off, what happened? Her white benefactors, so eager to lift her up when she was young and promising, were nowhere to be found when she actually needed support.

She married John Peters, a free Black man. On paper, that should've been her chance at stability, but life had other plans. They struggled. Money was scarce. Even with all her fame, her own people couldn't buy her book in large numbers. Why? Because they were still in chains, and most of them weren't allowed to learn to read.

We often hear the high point of what she accomplished but rarely how it ended. The story they don't tell us is that Phillis Wheatley, the first Black woman published in America, died broke and alone in a boarding house at age thirty-one. Thirty-one. She buried three children before she herself was buried in an unmarked grave. The first Black published author died uncared for and alone. 2

After all that genius, all that labor, all that sacrifice? She was forgotten for a long time — because that's what happens when you're the first. The doors don't always stay open for the next. She wasn't protected, wasn't nurtured, wasn't given the same room to stumble and rise again that her white peers had.

Phillis Wheatley is not just a story of triumph. It's a warning. If the world can use you, it will. And when it's done? It will leave you behind. Because being the first means walking a tightrope with no safety net. It means proving yourself over and over again, only to be discarded when the next Brown body experiment comes along.

I know you know what that feels like. Some of us are still out here walking that same tightrope, still being praised without protection, still being allowed to exist…but never fully embraced.

Naghmeh Abedini Panahi

In the early 2000s and 2010s, violence erupted in Iran, and many people were taken as prisoners and tortured. One of these individuals was a pastor named Saeed. His story gained widespread media attention when his wife, Naghmeh, advocated

The First, the Few and the Only

tirelessly for his release. She used the media - getting coverage from The 700 Club, Fox, CNN, and major newspapers like The Washington Post and The Wall Street Journal - to bring attention to his situation. Her campaign eventually helped to free him, and Saeed was released and reunited with his family.

As a result of this public battle, Naghmeh became known amongst prominent church leaders, and in the years that followed, she connected with a well-known pastor from a large megachurch - one with a congregation of five thousand. Within this church, there was a woman who had been homeless in the past. She had been forced to send her children to live elsewhere while she lived in her car. Despite her struggles, she remained a faithful member of the church, attending every Sunday and volunteering with special-needs children.

However, this woman's financial struggles worsened, and she faced the prospect of homelessness once again. She reached out to the church leaders for help, but they turned her away. Naghmeh, learning about the situation, was shocked by the church's inaction. In response, she shared a photo of the church's multimillion-dollar budget on social media, calling attention to the discrepancy between their wealth and the church's failure to support a struggling member. Just one outcast. By Friday, the woman's bills were paid, her debts covered, and she was taken care of, thanks to Naghmeh's intervention.

Many people celebrated this as a victory, but what is often overlooked is the personal cost Naghmeh faced for speaking up. She received backlash from the church leadership, who disapproved of her actions. This highlights a key point: when you're one of the few, or in Naghmeh's case, the only person willing to use your voice to fight for what's right, there is often a price to pay. In many spaces, especially in positions of power like the church, Black and Brown people are expected to remain silent. They might protest or speak up occasionally, but when someone truly steps out and takes a stand, that's when the backlash comes. There's a cost to using your voice, particularly in spaces where you're seen as a token rather than a true participant in power.

Naghmeh's advocacy wasn't just about one woman's needs; it was part of a much larger conversation about the silencing of marginalized voices in powerful rooms. She had a history of advocacy, including her efforts to free her husband, which led her to work with organizations like the United Nations. She even engaged in conversations with President Obama and President Trump during their respective

The First, the Few and the Only

administrations. But as Naghmeh's experience illustrates, being the "token" in a room has its price. Some people choose to stay silent to preserve their position. Others, like Naghmeh, speak out at great personal cost. Sometimes, it's that very voice that makes a difference. To those willing to speak truth to power, there's an undeniable strength in knowing that, even when the cost is high, the fight is always worth it.

Naghmeh Abedini Panahi's story is a case study in what it means to step into spaces where power is concentrated, especially as a Black or Brown person, and dare to use your voice. It's not just about the triumphs; it's about the backlash, the alienation, and the price exacted for speaking truth to power. When she spoke up against one of the biggest evangelical white men in Protestantism, he got in her face and threatened her. If you wanna know that story, then read her book. 3

Her experience echoes what so many before her have faced:

- The expectation to be grateful, not disruptive.
- The silent agreement that presence is tolerated, but power is not shared.
- The understanding that advocacy is only welcome when it doesn't challenge the institution.

When she did speak, when she disrupted the carefully maintained equilibrium of a multimillion-dollar church budget that couldn't spare a dime for a struggling mother, she wasn't celebrated. She was punished. This is the story of every Black and Brown leader, professional, minister, and activist who has ever been invited into the room but finds that the invitation comes with strings attached: speak softly. Don't rock the boat.

Stay in your place.

What happens when you refuse? What happens when you break the unspoken rules and demand more? Retaliation. Alienation. The full weight of the institution pressing down, reminding you that you were allowed in, not because they wanted to change, but because your presence made them look good…right up until you started making real change.

This is the exchange. The trade-off. The invisible contract that so many of us inherit when we become the first, the few, the only. For some, that trade is worth it.

The First, the Few and the Only

They keep their heads down, hold their tongues, collect their salary, and maintain their seat at the table. For others - those who refuse to be silent - there comes a breaking point, a moment when the cost of staying quiet becomes greater than the cost of speaking out.

When that moment comes? When you've tried to work within the system, tried to advocate in the shadows, tried to be the "good" one in the room but still find yourself punished for simply doing what's right? You make a choice.

Some choose to stay and fight, despite the backlash. Others walk away entirely, rejecting the idea that presence in the room is worth the constant suffocation. One thing remains true across history, across movements, across institutions: the cost of being the first, the few, the only is always collected either through silence, suffering, or sacrifice. Toni Morrison once put it, "The function of freedom is to free someone else." What she didn't say outright - what we know from lived experience - is that freedom work always comes with a price. And some of us are still paying it.

Toni Morrison

Toni Morrison didn't just win awards - she dared to win them as a Black woman writing unapologetically Black stories. The cost of that? It came in whispers, in dismissals, in the long, exhausting work of proving that she wasn't just good for a Black writer, but one of the greatest writers, period. [4]

When Morrison won the Pulitzer Prize in 1988 for Beloved, The New York Times ran an editorial about how she had been overlooked for the National Book Award - a public outcry that only made it painfully clear how often Black genius is ignored until the noise gets too loud to drown out. When she finally won the Nobel Prize in Literature in 1993, she became the first Black woman to receive it. You'd think that would have been a moment of unchallenged triumph, but no. Some critics - white critics - still found a way to downplay it, to frame her win as "political" rather than deserved. To them, a Black woman's excellence is always up for debate. [5]

Here's the thing: Morrison never played the game to be liked. She wrote for us. About us. In doing so, she shattered the unspoken rule that Black authors must either dilute their stories for white audiences, center the white gaze, or remain in the margins. She refused both, and that refusal came with a cost. [6]

The First, the Few and the Only

It came in the form of academic snobbery, in the reluctance of elite institutions to teach her work alongside the so-called "greats" (until her impact became undeniable). It came in the way her novels were sometimes dismissed as "too difficult" or "too Black" by critics who couldn't stomach the raw truths she laid bare. It came in the fact that, even with all her accolades, she still had to answer questions about why her books didn't center white characters, nor center the white audience, as if Black stories weren't enough on their own. 7

Like Phillis Wheatley, Morrison had to fight to be recognized in a literary world that was never designed to honor Black women's voices. Like Naghmeh Abedini Panahi, she knew that speaking truth - whether in fiction or in advocacy - came with consequences.

She did it anyway.

Morrison understood, just like every Black and Brown person who has ever been the first, the few, or the only, that the cost of entry into these spaces isn't just talent. It's endurance. It's knowing that your wins will be scrutinized, your excellence questioned, your very presence and brilliance seen as a disruption.

She also knew something else - something that makes all the difference. That once you get inside, once you carve out space, you don't just survive. You build something that lasts. ⊘

And she did.

Gynecology

Let's be clear: the so-called "Father of Gynecology," J. Marion Sims, did not earn that title through brilliance but cruelty. He earned it through blood. Through the genitalia and ignored screams of enslaved Black women in Alabama—women who were forced into untested medical experimentation.

Anarcha Wesctott.

Betsey Harris.

Lucy Zimmerman.

The First, the Few and the Only

Remember their names.
Say them. Out Loud.

Anarcha was one of those women. A young Black girl turned subject. Sims experimented on her—over and over—while she was fully awake. No anesthesia. No mercy. No choice. Anarcha endured more than 30 gential surgeries between 1845 and 1849. Her body was the blueprint. Her pain the prototype. Every gynecological tool Sims later claimed as innovation—he practiced first on these women. The only thing he can claim is the saying, "Black women don't feel pain."

But history called him "Father."

So let's correct that, dear reader.

Because Anarcha, Betsey and Lucy—and the many other unnamed, unseen, unfree Black women who bore this brutal legacy—are not footnotes. They are origin stories. They are the uncredited architects of modern medicine. The Mothers of Gynecology.

Their ghosts live in every speculum, every stirrup, every white coat that never asked where the tools came from.

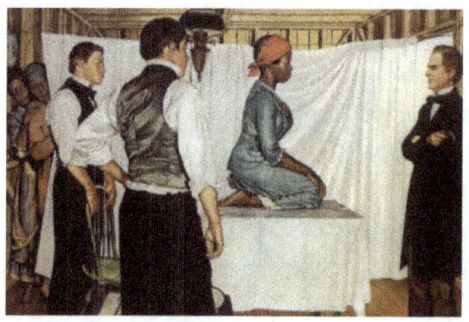

Say their names, again. Let their very real pain haunt the halls of medical schools. Let their disregarded pleas for these white men to stop – disrupt the narrative. Let them rest knowing someone finally told the truth, and remembered their ghost stories.

Neurodivergent Factoids

 Medical field

 Marvel

First Black comic hero: Falcon | First Black King:The line of Black Panthers (T'Challa in Marvel comics)
First Black comic writer at Marvel
Air Force neurodivergent factoid

The First, the Few and the Only

Sports

"If I had your athleticism…"

Major Taylor

The world's fastest man on a bicycle,
and the first Black international cyclist. 8

Major Taylor was so popular that when the world learned that he would not cycle or race on Sundays, they changed the race schedules. He was that influential. Cycling was seen as a white sport in the late 1800s and early 1900s. He defeated the number one champions of France, Germany, Belgium, Denmark, Italy, and England after knocking out all competitors in the U.S. Not only was he the first Black face on the track, he was regularly the only Black body in the crowd at the arena. This was a Muhammad Ali-level athlete that dominated the sport. He was often greeted by the stars of his day. Even Teddy Roosevelt went out of his way to shake Taylor's hand and congratulate him on his success.

Major Taylor later married Daisy Victoria Morris, and they had a daughter, Sydney. On a return trip to Australia, a couple of American cyclists (Lawson and McFarland) decided to engage in foul play at forty miles an hour. This altercation led to Taylor's hospitalization for two weeks. Although bandaged and still bloody, he was put on a five-hundred-mile trek to make another race, despite being banned from mounting a bike for three weeks by his doctors. He showed up to that race and won.

Many historians say that when he returned, he had a nervous breakdown, and others have been quoted saying, "Racism broke him." Afterward, from 1904 to 1906, he never mounted a bike for a competition. Major Taylor said, "Little did my friends realize the great physical strain I labored under, nor did they seem to realize the great mental strain that beset me in those races and the utter

The First, the Few and the Only

exhaustion I felt on many occasions both on and off the track. In most of my races, I not only struggled for victory, but also for my very life and limb."

In 1907, his wife encouraged him to go on a European tour. He was competing against racers ten years younger than him, and the circuit decided to no longer honor his personal decision to not race on Sundays. Soon after, he retired. By 1926, Taylor was no longer able to make money from racing, and both his business ventures and finances dried up. His wife never officially divorced him, but she moved to New York with his daughter, leaving him behind. He later wrote his autobiography, The Fastest Bicycle Rider in the World, and later had an idea for a new automobile tire, the precursor to the steel-belted radio. His idea was overtaken by other technological advancements, and the financial pressures of the Great Depression, loneliness, several diseases, and a weakened heart, along with the fact that his wife and daughter had left him, caused his health to greatly suffer. He checked into a hospital and never left.

Major Taylor died on June 21, 1932, at the age of fifty-three. He was buried in an unmarked pauper's grave at the Mt. Glenwood Cemetery on Chicago's South Side. He had been the first and only Black, world-champion cyclist, as well as a husband, athlete, father, man of faith, and barrier breaker. He would later be recognized as a great civil rights icon, and his legacy is palpable…but what did it cost him to be the first?

Althea Gibson

First Black woman to win a Grand Slam tennis championship. First Black woman on the LPGA Tour. First to walk through doors that weren't even supposed to exist.

Born in South Carolina in 1927 and raised in Harlem, Althea Gibson became the first Black player to break the color barrier in international tennis. This wasn't just about swinging a racket - it was about swinging the door wide open in an elite, white-only sport where she wasn't invited but showed up anyway. She won eleven Grand Slam titles, including five singles championships - two at Wimbledon, three at the French and U.S. Opens - all while being jeered, segregated, and often forced to enter tournaments through the back gate.

The First, the Few and the Only

Althea was not invited to play in the U.S. Nationals (now the U.S. Open) until 1950 - and only because former champion Alice Marble publicly shamed the tennis establishment for excluding her. Gibson walked onto those grass courts not just as a player, but as a protest in motion. And she didn't just play - she won. In 1957, she became the first Black athlete to win Wimbledon. A ticker-tape parade was held in her honor upon her return to New York, but even then, some country clubs and hotels still wouldn't let her stay inside. 9

After tennis, Gibson became the first African-American woman to compete on the Ladies Professional Golf Association (LPGA) Tour in 1964. She was one of the longest drivers on the tour - often outdriving men - but was routinely denied entry into clubhouses. She changed in her car. Ate in parking lots. And still she played.

She later served in state athletic commissions in New Jersey, mentored young Black athletes, and quietly battled illness and poverty in her later years. In the 1990s, she suffered a stroke and found herself so broke and isolated that she considered ending her life. It was only when tennis legends like Billie Jean King and others heard of her situation that funds were raised to support her medical care.

Gibson died in 2003 in East Orange, New Jersey. And though she had once stood atop the global stage, she died far too quietly for someone who had altered the course of history with a backhand and a boldness that couldn't be coached. Her honors - induction into the International Tennis Hall of Fame, the Women's Sports Hall of Fame, and the Black Athletes Hall of Fame - are rightfully earned. But more than that, she is a blueprint: not just for Serena and Venus, but for every Black girl who dared to dream on a court never meant for her. In 2022, Harlem renamed 143rd Street in her honor: Althea Gibson Way. And in 2025, a new U.S. quarter will bear her image - not as charity, but as memory. As reclamation. As a long-overdue recognition of the cost of being the first. 10

Jackie Robinson

Jackie Robinson broke the color line in Major League Baseball in 1947, not just by playing, but by enduring. His entry wasn't just athletic - it was political, psychological, spiritual. He didn't just carry a bat - he carried the burden of Black respectability, white rage, and institutional expectation. 11

The First, the Few and the Only

By the time he died of a heart attack in 1972 at just fifty-three years old, Robinson's body had already told the story America refused to hear: being first in a white institution can be fatal.

He suffered from heart disease, diabetes, hypertension, and strokes that damaged his eyesight. His final public appearance, at Game 2 of the 1972 World Series, was not a moment of comfort or celebration - it was a reminder of unfinished business. Standing with his cane, eyes clouded, he asked baseball to finally hire a Black manager. The crowd cheered, but the system stayed the same - no Black manager would be hired until three years after his death. [12]

Robinson's legacy is rich: the Rookie of the Year award bears his name, and he was posthumously awarded the Congressional Gold Medal. But the accolades arrived long after the stress and solitude of being "the first" had already ravaged his health. What does it mean when a country celebrates your courage but ignores the conditions it required you to survive?

Jackie Robinson, like Althea Gibson and Phyllis Wheatley before him, was not merely honored - he was used as a symbol of progress while being left to bear the weight of white comfort, white fear, and white scrutiny. Their brilliance gave them access, but never immunity.

Acclaim in white spaces, for many of us, is not arrival. It's endurance.

Fatal endurance.

Roberto Clemente

Somos Dos | We are both.

There are some men whose bodies speak before their mouths do. Men who, even in motion, testify. Roberto Clemente was one of them. Every swing of his bat, every outfield throw, every time he laced his cleats - he wasn't just playing baseball. He was playing against history. Playing against invisibility. He was bearing the weight of two continents' worth of misunderstanding - Black and Latino, Puerto Rican and proud, Afrodescendiente, and undeniably human. [13]

The First, the Few and the Only

In Pittsburgh, they remember him as a hero. But too often, they remember him only as a ballplayer. Not the man who demanded dignity in the face of media mockery. Not the man who refused to be called "Bobby" because Roberto carried the sound of his mother's language. Not the man who flew into a war zone with a plane full of aid because he knew what it meant to be forgotten.

Roberto Clemente was a first, a few, and an only - on and off the field. In the locker rooms where Spanish was mocked. In stadiums where the crowds cheered his plays but questioned his presence. In sports columns that tried to whitewash his Afro-Latino identity or caricature his accent. He belonged to no one but his people - and even we, sometimes, didn't know how to hold all of him. That's the weight of being born on the borderlands. That's the cost of being both…never either or enough. 14

But Clemente never shrank. He stretched. He played with an elegance and fire that made even racism blink. He demanded that the world say his full name, hear his full truth. He made his pain a platform and his presence a protest. He was not only a pioneer in baseball - he was an ambassador for an entire race. A witness of what it means to carry nations in your bones while still showing up to play.

"I am from the poor people; I represent the poor people," Clemente once said. "I like workers. I like people that suffer because these people have a different approach to life from the people that have everything and don't know what suffering is." That's not just a quote - it's a declaration of loyalty. A compass pointing home. He wasn't chasing fame. He was chasing justice with a bat in his hand and a fire in his chest. That's ganas! He knew his talent wasn't for personal glory; it was an offering to those who bore the same scars. 15

I see myself in him. I see my son in him. I see every Afro-Latinx child who's ever been told they talk "too negro" for the comunidad, "too Latino" to be Black in Pittsburgh, and "too brown" for the suburbs. Clemente reminds me that we are not fragments. We are full. Not half this and part that - we are whole stories, whole cultures, whole diasporas wrapped in flesh that refuses to be simplified. Somos Dos.

The First, the Few and the Only

He didn't just break records. He broke the mold. And in doing so, he gave many of us permission to stop translating our worth for rooms that would never understand our grammar of survival. 🙏

Tommie Smith & John Carlos

Tommie Smith and John Carlos' iconic Black Power salute at the 1968 Mexico City Olympics came at an enormous personal cost. While they weren't the first Black athletes to use the global stage to protest injustice, their silent, defiant stand on the podium - heads bowed, fists raised in black gloves - remains one of the most powerful images in sports history. It wasn't just protest; it was iconic. Their gesture forced the world to confront the contradiction between American ideals and American realities.

Tommie Smith & John Carlos
At the 1968 Olympics, Tommie Smith won gold in the 200-meter race and, alongside John Carlos, raised a black-gloved fist in protest against racial injustice. Their silent demonstration became an iconic moment in civil rights and sports history.

Though others had paved the way - Jack Johnson with his unapologetic dominance in the early 1900s, Jesse Owens dismantling Hitler's myth of Aryan supremacy at the 1936 Olympics, Muhammad Ali refusing the draft in 1967 on the grounds of racial injustice - Smith and Carlos' visual, politicized act of solidarity was unprecedented in its boldness and immediacy. They stood on the Olympic podium in front of the world and told the truth without saying a word.

The consequences were swift and devastating. Under pressure from the International Olympic Committee's openly racist president, Avery Brundage, both athletes were expelled from the Olympic Village and sent home. They were stripped of institutional support, lost endorsements, and were effectively blacklisted from professional athletics. Death threats followed. Careers were derailed. Their families were targeted. Institutions turned their backs on them - not because they failed, but because they dared to succeed on their own terms. 16

The toll extended beyond economics. Both men struggled financially for years, denied the opportunities that their white counterparts could take for granted. The emotional and psychological weight was even heavier. John Carlos suffered deeply;

The First, the Few and the Only

his first wife later died by suicide - a tragedy partially attributed to the relentless stress and isolation they faced.

And yet, despite it all, they endured. Smith became a coach and educator. Carlos found a path as a community activist and public speaker. Though it took decades, history eventually caught up to their courage. In 2008, they were awarded the Arthur Ashe Courage Award at the ESPYs - not as a consolation prize, but as a long-overdue acknowledgment of the cost they bore so that others could stand taller. 17

Their raised fists became a torch passed to future generations - to athletes like Colin Kaepernick and others who continue to risk everything to speak out against racial injustice. Smith and Carlos weren't just symbols - they were sacrifices. Their story reminds us that the price of dignity in white-dominated spaces is often erasure, delay, or punishment before it is ever praised.

Military

This burning house that Martin Luther King Jr. warned us about didn't just guide young Black and Brown bodies into white institutions like schools and neighborhoods. It led them into the military too. I recognize that Black and Brown folks were serving in the military long before King, Malcolm X, Medgar Evers, and James Baldwin sounded the alarm. But since their work, it has become even more visible - the way tokenism has tightened its grip on our beloved military, how it manifests institutionally and personally. It is full of soldiers who wore the uniform and bore the burden but still found themselves in a system not built for them.

Sometimes, the only thing more dangerous than a white overseer was a Black one. There are many Black and Brown military leaders that were and are a credit to Brown bodies in North America, but there is always the opposite. There's a story of a Black veteran recalling his experience under General Benjamin Davis, a Black military leader who had visited a southern camp where Black soldiers and their visiting families were treated horribly - not just by the military but by the entire town. 18

Things had gotten so bad that the soldiers collectively petitioned for real change in their treatment. When General Davis 19 arrived, they thought relief had finally come. When he stood before them, however, the first words out of his mouth cut

The First, the Few and the Only

like a bayonet. "I may be your color," he said, "but I am not your n*****." He drew a line in the sand between himself and the men who shared his skin. He made it clear: "You are n******. I am me. And I am not here for you."

Instead of offering protection, he told them to stop making noise. Fall in line. He was a token in leadership, a figurehead not of solidarity but of surveillance. His loyalty wasn't to the soldiers who shared his reflection but to the white institution that bestowed him with rank and title. It was betrayal - plain and brutal.

His words echoed through the ranks, a gut punch to those who already bore the weight of civilian hostility. Their families weren't treated with the respect and reverence you see extended to military families today. Back then, "Thank you for your service" was reserved for white bodies, white families. Black servicemen's families faced disdain instead of gratitude, suspicion instead of support. Eventually, many Black veterans began telling their loved ones that the U.S. Armed Forces was no place for a Black man.

While the Sambo caricature often showed up in the media as a grinning fool, in the real world, it had an evolution. It wore a uniform, commanded troops, and weaponized its proximity to power. These weren't just Sambos but the embodiment of the worst kind of 'Uncle Tom' - those who weren't just in the system but had become part of its machinery. They weren't just keeping the institution's gears turning; they were the grinding teeth of it, breaking down those who looked like them for the institution's benefit.

In every institution, you find them - the ones who rose through the ranks only to pull the ladder up behind them. The ones whose ambition smothered their empathy, whose desire for validation turned them into enforcers of the very systems that hold the rest of us down. "All skinfolk ain't kinfolk," and sometimes, the one who gets a seat at the table becomes the hardest gatekeeper to get past.

Disclaimer: Again, this is not true for all Black and Brown leaders in the U.S. military. I'm accounting for the real history of those who did more harm to their own as a way to honor (safeguard) their title, position and proximity to power.

The First, the Few and the Only

A Black army veteran on a Black general's mistreatment of Black soldiers

Dr. Margaret Morgan Lawrence

She graduated from Columbia Medical School, the only Black student in a class of 104. She retired as Chief of Child Psychiatry at Harlem Hospital, having transformed how we treat emotionally traumatized children. But most people never hear the story of what happened in between.

In 1932, she entered Cornell University as the only African-American student in the entire College of Arts and Sciences. Her dream? To become a doctor and save children, just like the brother she never got to meet. But the system had its own diagnosis for girls like her.

Cornell Medical School shut its doors despite her exceptional grades. Why? "We admitted a colored student twenty-five years ago, but he died of tuberculosis before he could finish." One man's death became the institutional excuse to exclude a generation. What I love about her is that she didn't turn away at rejection and give up. She used the difficulty as kindling.

When she applied for residency at Babies Hospital, they declined. The men's residence wouldn't accept a woman. The nurses' residence wouldn't house a Black one. This is where many stories end - in erasure, in exhaustion, in exile. 20 But Dr. Lawrence didn't break. She built.

She turned personal grief into professional purpose. She found her mentor in Dr. Charles Drew. She mapped a path where there was no road. In 1948, she became the first Black resident at the New York Psychiatric Institute.

The first Black trainee at the Columbia Psychoanalytic Center. And quietly, brilliantly, she did something the field wasn't ready for: she blended psychoanalysis with spirituality. At a time when medicine dismissed the soul, she insisted on its

The First, the Few and the Only

centrality. Her core belief? Love is universal, generational, and exists only in relationships. The results speak louder than any rejection letter ever could:

→ First practicing child psychiatrist in Rockland County
→ Co-founder of the Rockland County Center for Mental Health
→ Creator of the first child therapy programs in public schools and daycares
→ Twenty-one years leading developmental psychiatry at Harlem Hospital

And the center she co-founded? It now bears her name: The Margaret Morgan Lawrence Children's Center. It still heals children to this day. In a world that told her she was too much, too Black, too woman, too ambitious, she became exactly what wounded children needed. 21

The question isn't whether you'll face institutional violence. The question is: will you let it define you? Or will you do what Dr. Lawrence did and build something they never saw coming?

Corporate America

> *"There are some hard pills to swallow about working in predominantly white institutions, especially for Black people who hope to reform them."*
> Andre Henry, author of All the White Friends I Couldn't Keep

You get the corporate job, the one they said you were lucky to have. The one they whispered about when you walked through the door, as if your résumé hadn't been twice as long, your credentials twice as polished, your excellence twice as undeniable. You're in. Smooth sailing from here, right?

See, the problem with being the first, the few, the only is that it's never just a job. It's a performance. Every step, every word, every facial expression is scrutinized. You speak too boldly? You're aggressive. Too softly? You're incompetent. Laugh too much? You're the entertainment. Stay too serious? You're intimidating. God forbid you ever speak on race - suddenly you're "making everything about race," even as race is making everything about you.

The First, the Few and the Only

This is stereotype threat - a slow, steady suffocation. It's the weight of knowing that one wrong move won't just be your mistake; it'll be ammunition against everyone who looks like you. It's the double-consciousness of performing excellence while dodging the landmines of white discomfort. They call it imposter syndrome, but what it really is? A system that makes you feel like an imposter in places your brilliance earned.

Skyscraper Windmills and Corporate Plantations

So, what do you do? You chase windmills, like Don Quixote, believing that if you just work harder, climb higher, prove yourself enough, you'll finally belong. Or you see the game for what it is - a plantation with a new dress code - and start plotting your escape.

Let's break this down with a few real-world examples:
Across industries, the same pattern repeats: Black and Brown professionals are brought in during moments of public pressure—often hailed as symbols of progress—only to be sidelined, stripped of power, or outright dismissed once the spotlight fades. AKA 'racialized promotions'. From academia to tech, from media to education, BIPOC professionals are often the last hired and the first fired. Their roles are treated as symbolic, not structural. Below are key examples that illuminate this systemic trend:

1. Corporate America & the Tech Industry

- Dr. Timnit Gebru at Google – A leading AI ethics researcher, Dr. Gebru was forced out after raising concerns about algorithmic bias and institutional racism. Her removal highlighted how even the most credentialed Black voices in tech are treated as expendable when they challenge power. [22]
- DEI Teams Decimated – In the wake of 2020's racial reckoning, companies like Meta, Twitter, and others expanded DEI teams - only to gut them during the 2022–2023 layoffs. These roles, overwhelmingly held by BIPOC staff, were quietly deemed non-essential when profit margins tightened. [23]

The First, the Few and the Only

2. Academia & Higher Education

- Nikole Hannah-Jones at UNC-Chapel Hill – Despite her Pulitzer Prize and the cultural impact of The 1619 Project, Hannah-Jones was initially denied tenure, unlike her white predecessors. Only public outcry forced a reversal. 24
- Dr. Cornel West at Harvard – Another towering Black intellectual denied tenure at a leading institution 25, West's departure underscored how even elite scholarship is not enough to shield Black academics from institutional gatekeeping. 26
- Adjunct & Non-Tenured Faculty – Black professors remain overrepresented in precarious, non-tenured positions. When budgets shrink, they're often the first to be let go - echoing a deeper belief that their contributions are peripheral. 27

3. Journalism & Media

- Melissa Harris-Perry at MSNBC – Stripped of editorial control and pushed off-air, Harris-Perry's departure exemplified how Black media voices are welcomed until they assert independence or disrupt the status quo.
- DEI Rollbacks in Newsrooms – After 2020, outlets like NPR expanded DEI programming - only to slash it amid budget cuts, disproportionately affecting Black and Brown journalists. Don't get me started on what happened in 2025.
- Bon Appétit's reckoning – Following revelations of racial pay disparities, BIPOC staffers were promised reform - but many left or were sidelined when the company failed to deliver structural change. 27

4. Nonprofits & Social Justice Spaces

- Racial Justice Fatigue – Many nonprofits that rushed to hire BIPOC staff in 2020 have since downsized or eliminated those roles. DEI is treated as a temporary PR move, not a sustained commitment - leaving those hired to "diversify" the institution discarded when the budget tightens.

The First, the Few and the Only

5. K–12 Education

- Historical Erasure of Black Educators – After desegregation, thousands of Black teachers lost their jobs to make room for white educators in integrated schools - a precedent that still echoes today.
- Modern Burnout & Attrition – A Learning Policy Institute study found Black K–12 teachers leave the profession at higher rates due to racial isolation, being overburdened with disciplinary roles, and enduring workplace hostility. Their expertise is undervalued; their emotional labor, exploited. [28-29]

These examples illustrate a pattern: institutions eagerly hire BIPOC professionals to signal progress but fail to protect them when challenges arise. It's not just about being the "last hired, first fired" but also about being the most scrutinized, the least supported, the least funded, and the easiest to sacrifice when institutions retreat from their performative commitments to equity.

🌱 Getting Involved:

As Resmaa Menakem says, "Where is your breath?" Full stop. Notice your breathing.

What are you feeling? What is coming to mind? Name it to tame it below:

_____

_____

_____

_____

_____

_____

The First, the Few and the Only

Racial Tests in Corporate America

Then there are the racial tests - the ones that aren't written down but always given like pop quizzes from the teacher everyone can't stand. You can hear the stories in almost every workplace.

Despite your Ivy League degrees or extensive professional background, you've earned your place. The assumption remains, however, that white colleagues still see you as the diversity hire. In 2018, Mellody Hobson, the CEO of Ariel Investments and a Black woman, spoke about how, despite being qualified for years, many still looked at her as "the diversity hire." Her every word was put under a microscope. In her case, the test was whether she could maintain composure while carrying a collective burden of representing a race in spaces where her leadership was viewed with a stricter lens. In some cases, the white hire calling you a diversity hire was actually a legacy hire, a nepo-baby, or even a hook-up from their mom or dad who go to the same country club. It's jacked up that so many white bodies benefit from nepotism, but the ladder of meritocracy only applies to Brown bodies.

Self-Deputized White People

Not only do you have to put up with this stuff at work, but at least you got a nice apartment, condo, or house now to return to and get relief. You got money now, and after a long, hard day at work, you head to the gym to exercise out all that 'Mama said knock you out' energy in your body. After beating yourself up at the gym, getting out that anger or stress, you go to enter your building or neighborhood. Suddenly, some white woman or white man blocks the entrance and says, "Excuse me! I've never seen you here before. Why are you trying to enter my building?"

I have a friend named Adam that lives in a fancy spot in the Southside of Pittsburgh. He's African American and Asian, and this has happened to him on two separate occasions. Now you should know that Adam is one of the kindest and

The First, the Few and the Only

most handsome, capable men I know, and he makes pretty good dough to boot. He was stopped by a white woman one time, and he says he initially laughed because he swore this was a joke or a way to get his number at first. He quickly realized, however, that he had met a Karen in the wild. This woman would not let him into his own building and demanded that he prove that he lived there. She began to express signs of fear and anxiety for her "safety" when all my dude wanted was to go to his crib and take a shower. What do you think he did next?

As you can see from the clip, this is not new. It's damn near ancestral. What my friend did was immediately de-escalate the situation. He invited the woman to go to her apartment, and he would wait outside so as not to alarm her. This did not satisfy the woman.

As my friend Adam said, "If you want to chase giants, you better be prepared to teach." Here's how the story ended: he looked at her, and she asked him to put the code in to prove to her that he lived there. He put in the code, and then he laughed as he walked through the door. He looked behind him and saw her trying to enter in behind him. He stopped her, now inside the building with her outside and said, "How do I know you live here?" Aghast, she said, as if it was obvious, "You're gonna make me put my code in?!?!"

He continued, "Why do you obviously live here and I don't?" He then let her in because her white friend, who stayed quiet the entire time made a "Ohhhhhh!" sound, letting Karen know she just got told. This Karen was now embarrassed and had to deal with that moment. My friend kept the cops from getting called, he didn't yell, and he kept the temperature low.
The BIPOC body has to be smarter, wiser, more cool-headed, and in the mindset to teach white people while never getting mad so that the police and/or HOA don't get called on you…all without offending the white body.

It would have been easier for my friend to look at this white woman and say, "Bitch, this is fucked up. Get the fuck out of my face," then move her ass out his way. But we can NEVER do that

The First, the Few and the Only

The Microaggressions

Then there's the casual racism that becomes insidious. In corporate spaces, code-switching becomes your second job. Your hair, your clothes, your language - all these little things that white colleagues would never even think about are now scrutinized. Some colleagues want to touch your hair. Others wonder if you really "get down" to rap music, as if the essence of your identity could be reduced to some random beats. You're often tested on your "coolness." For instance, Misty Copeland, the first African-American principal dancer at American Ballet Theatre, faced these tests when she joined a world that was steeped in tradition and dominated by a predominantly white cast. Copeland talked about the scrutiny she endured, where her Blackness was often questioned, and how she had to prove her worth over and over again, every time she stepped onto the stage.

The test? Could she fit in? Could she pass the test of "being like them?" When she brought her own brilliance to the stage - her own dance style, her own Blackness - she was breaking boundaries.

The "Black Friend" Test

This is one of the most pervasive racial tests. Imagine being at an office lunch meeting where the only Black person is asked if they know how to "twerk," if they've ever been to a certain type of neighborhood, or being asked, "Why do Black people always _____?" If they try out racial or racist jokes around us to see if we laugh. If they share white nationalistic political talking points to see where you stand. It's uncomfortable. It's patronizing. It sets an impossible bar, forcing you to prove that your presence is more than just a "diversity hire." Will you be passive and not disrupt the cultural norms? Will you be an addition to the set of cultural norms and the unwritten laws within? It is a subtle game of proving your "whiteness compatibility." In short, it's a test to see if you'll play into their stereotypes, or at the bare minimum, not become a threat to their racial comfort.

I know you may not like the messenger, but he makes an age-old point:

The First, the Few and the Only

Not *One* Bad Day

When you are the first, the few, the only—there is no such thing as a bad day. You can never not perform well. You can't afford it.

Not one off-moment, not one quiet quitting, not one stumble. You are not extended the mercy of being human. While others get grace for mediocrity, you are expected to be exceptional—even when exhausted.

It is not freedom to leave the plantation if all you've done is relocate the performance. Even when you get out, you're still "on." Still watched. Still questioned. Still weighed.

Chris Rock tells a joke: in his wealthy neighborhood, he's a world-famous comedian—but his neighbor is just a white dentist. And still, they're equals in the eyes of society. That's the bar. I've DJed weddings where guests handed me their coats, assuming I worked catering. The moment they realize I'm the one running the show, they're surprised. Like I wasn't supposed to be there. Like I didn't earn it.

The 49th Oyster
@MrMarcus260

Nobody:

The only two Black people in the room:

The truth is, some of us leave the system and build our own—launching businesses, creating networks, designing spaces where we don't have to contort ourselves just to survive. We chase windmills, knowing the wind never stops.

Others stay. They stay in systems that were never built for them, trying to carve out just enough room for the next one to fit through. They play the long game, the tiring game—the one where legacy means enduring so that someone else won't have to. That kind of resistance costs something. Soul-deep fatigue. Loneliness. Moments where you wonder if it's worth it.

But some of us stayed anyway. I stayed. Not because I loved the system, but because I loved the ones who would come after me. I wanted to bend the frame just enough to make space.

The First, the Few and the Only

Still, don't be fooled—the game is rigged. The title of my favorite James Baldwin documentary says it all: I Am Not Your Negro. I am not your mascot. I am not your diversity data point. I am not your proof that progress has arrived.

Whether you choose to stay and fight or break away and build, the goal is the same: freedom. Not the kind they grant, but the kind you reclaim. And maybe, if you're lucky—if you survive it all—you'll have enough wind left in your lungs to chase windmills of your own. Or better yet, you'll set fire to the whole field and plant something real in its place.

Double Consciousness

It takes an inordinate amount of energy to not only exist and thrive in two totally different cultures, but you also MUST know how to comfort white people. Successful BIPOC bodies must speak two languages: English and white. A lot of what you do is not just about your job or your authentic self - it's about making white bodies comfortable around us. It's about not being perceived as threatening, not being too Black, or too Black-conscious.

If you don't watch for this, you'll end up being "too much" of yourself: too pro-Black, too pro-Asian, too pro-Latino, too pro-Indigenous. They'll use the four D's on you: dismiss, discredit, demonize, destroy. This is further explained in Book Three; The First, the Few, and the Only: Power.

In my research about covert racism in the workplace 30, I found this dope study on facts about Black North Americans in the workplace from Pew Research Center 31:

Aside from all the great facts about age, socio-geographic, race, ethnicity and gender data in the U.S. workforce, what this resource did not provide was any research or studies showing psychosocial aspects or evidence of stress in the work environment as a function of covert racism and/or the perceptions of racial-ethnic discrimination. I had to dig a little deeper. That's when I found Andre Henry.

The First, the Few and the Only

In *All the White Friends I Couldn't Keep*, Andre Henry recounts a pivotal moment while working at Relevant magazine. After proposing a robust editorial lineup for Black History Month—just as he had done for other heritage months—he faced immediate resistance from leadership. The CEO questioned the initiative, expressing concern about alienating readers. This moment marked a shift in Henry's role from managing editor to a symbolic contributor, eventually leading to his resignation. As Henry writes:

> "*These were angry tears… I spent the next six months feeling like a token. In the end, I wouldn't make it a year.*"
> (Henry, 2022, Ch. 12) 32

Henry's story illustrates a painful truth about many predominantly white institutions: they often welcome diversity in appearance but reject equity in practice. Rather than share institutional power, they issue subtle tests and reassert control the moment a Black employee's work begins to challenge the status quo.

A way that white institutions will try to filter out the threat of self-determined and strong Black and Brown bodies committed to racial reform is through something sociologist Glenn Bracey calls race tests.

"Race Tests"

Racial Boundary Maintenance in White Evangelical Churches by Glenn Bracey 33, a groundbreaking study, where sociologist Glenn Bracey researched race tests. These tests were built on the premise that white institutional space is established first and foremost to serve white people's interests. By exclusively prioritizing the centering of the needs and desires of white bodies, they can influence everything in that space, from who moves up in the organization to the cultural references in work meetings to the music that gets selected in the office. Sociologist Bracey expounds on how race tests happen in white spaces by performing microaggressions on Black and Brown bodies in their spaces to test out and assess how committed BIPOC bodies are to maintaining and securing the priorities and comfort of whites. He spent the bulk of his research time in seven predominantly white as well as white-led Christian churches to identify different categories of race tests. According to his study, the different race tests are deployed for different purposes. As you can see,

The First, the Few and the Only

the exclusionary race test was used on Andre Henry to get him to leave once his work threatened the very immune system of the white organization and even the white CEO himself.

Footnote: White evangelical churches I categorize as white institutions as much as any other type of workplace because of the systemic realities that pervasively weave through every white institution, even the evangelical church. Another study captures some of covert racism's psycho-social emotional terrain of the workplace injustices that precipitates from these ubiquitous race tests. This study charts the path of Andre Henry's experiences:

A model for understanding the contribution of workplace injustice to occupational health disparities

Andre left, so I would say that definitely affected his job outcomes. What about his other life outcomes? I wonder how they were affected.

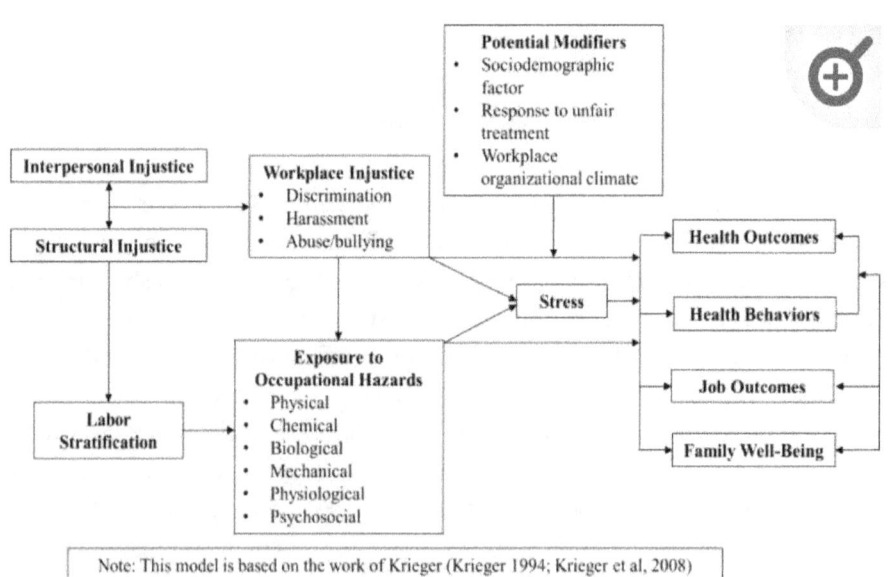

Note: This model is based on the work of Krieger (Krieger 1994; Krieger et al, 2008)

The First, the Few and the Only

🌱 Where is your breath? What is surfacing for you? Please stop reading and check in with your body to see where you felt your body stop breathing or tighten. Simply notice what, where, and how things are showing up in your body. What story did you get pulled into? Write it out in the margin or call a close friend that can offer good attunement and containment so you can process the story.

⏱Side Quest: If you'd like to read the study behind the image provided:

Discrimination, Harassment, Abuse and Bullying in the Workplace: Contribution of Workplace Injustice to Occupational Health Disparities Cassandra A. Okechukwu, MSN, Sc.D, Kerry Souza, MPH, Sc.D, Kelly D. Davis, PhD, and A. Butch de Castro, MSN/MPH, PhD

When I took a job at a title IX office at Point Park University, I had some friends, all Black men, ask for potential workplace discrimination advice to advocate for their partners' potential race-based workplace discrimination experiences that they never knew what to do with. The only thing they could do was leave. I sadly realized that that was outside of my realm of expertise, but I knew, in some way, the they commit violations of titles IX, VI, or VII due to disparate impact and disparate treatment. I told them what I knew based on that.

As a resource to the reader, I did find some referential data on anti-discrimination laws. It may not be necessary for you, but you never know when a friend or family member will be thankful that you knew about this. 🧭 A Princeton study:

Don't Go Chasing Waterfalls

But what happens when you don't leave? What happens when you stick it out despite underhanded mistreatment, like what happened to Andre? One way they maintain control is by changing the terrain by turning tokens against tokens.

The workplace has people you can trust and others you can't - that's a given regardless of race. When race enters the equation, the dynamics shift into a distinct political battlefield. Let me explain with a dramatized example.

The First, the Few and the Only

Jo-Issa Rae Diop, better known as Issa Rae, has done a phenomenal job exploring these nuances in Awkward Black Girl and Insecure. Shoutout to her dope work! A more recent and striking example is The Other Black Girl on Hulu. This series presents the workplace token experience in a stark and unsettling way. The protagonist, an African-American woman, is the lone Black employee at an all white publishing company until another Black woman is hired. Then things take a bizarre, almost Get Out-style turn. This time, it's not about Black and white bodies - it's about token bodies, Gamoras vs Nebulas. Yeah, I know, the plot thickens! (also, everything ties back to MARVEL, deal with it).

Understanding Status Threat

One of the most profound elements The Other Black Girl highlights is status threat. What exactly does that mean?

Status threat stems from both power dependence theory and social identity theory (identity threat). At its core, it refers to the fear that one's social standing is at risk due to a perceived rival or shift in hierarchy. This is particularly relevant in spaces where only a few marginalized individuals are "allowed" access. When another Black person enters the room, the unspoken rule of "only one at a time" is challenged, triggering competition instead of camaraderie.

Give me grace on this metaphor since I've never been in the armed forces but let me cook -literally. Imagine you're stationed at a small military base, working as the only cook. It's not a front-line gig, but it's essential. Then, one day, another squad joins up, and they bring their own cook. At first, you think, "Great! Now I have someone to share the workload with."

You look forward to camaraderie, thinking it'll be less lonely.
But soon, you realize the old adage is true: too many cooks in the kitchen.
This phrase refers to situations where too many people with differing agendas try to exert influence, leading to chaos, inefficiency, and internal conflict. Instead of teamwork, your fellow cook is more interested in being the favorite - not just keeping the base fed but climbing the ranks. Suddenly, what you thought was community within a warzone can quickly morph into a civil war within the camp.

The First, the Few and the Only

The Parallel in *The Other Black Girl*

The show brilliantly fictionalized a very real workplace dynamic: token versus token. This internal conflict isn't organic - it's a byproduct of institutions that have historically controlled Black and Brown bodies through observation, scarcity, grooming, and mistreatment. The competition between tokens is just a symptom of a larger triangulation designed to keep them from forming a collective power.

This brings us to two major workplace realities:

(1) The Token Leader with No Power

In many white-led institutions, a strategic game is at play: appointing Black or Brown individuals to leadership roles that hold weight in title but carry no real institutional power. These "leaders" are often placed not to make change, but to maintain comfort and control—performative racialized promotions meant to soothe critique rather than shift culture. Some of these tokenized figures are, unfortunately, underqualified—not because affirmative action is flawed, but because institutions continue to weaponize it as they did during Reconstruction, the Civil Rights Movement, and integration. It's not the policy that's the problem—it's the way white power structures contort it. Meanwhile, the qualified leaders—the reformers, the visionaries—are tucked out of sight. They are given roles without visibility, leadership without a platform. These are the Hobie Browns of the institution: underestimated, unseen, but carrying real influence from the shadows.

(2) The Judas Goat Effect

Some tokens aren't just figureheads - they're functionaries. Pick-me Negroes. Hand-selected, groomed, and placed close enough to power to feel its warmth, but never enough to wield it. Their job is clear: keep the machine running, keep the others in line, keep the doors shut behind them.

The term Judas Goat comes from the practice of using a trained goat to go out and find wild goats. The purpose is to lead the livestock to slaughter 34. The goat walks confidently amongst the group, signaling to the others that the path is safe, only to step aside at the last moment while the herd marches toward its demise. In Black

The First, the Few and the Only

spaces, the Judas Goat functions similarly: coaxing, pacifying, silencing, and, when necessary, sacrificing other Black people to maintain their own position.

This isn't theoretical. It's historical. It's corporate.
It's academic. It's religious.

It's the Black executive who sits on diversity committees only to tell HR that the real issue isn't racism, but that Black employees just "need to work harder."

It's the tenured professor who writes about equity but punishes Black students for "not being professional enough."

It's the pastor who tells his congregation to "just pray about it" while aligning himself with white evangelicals who uphold the very fascist systems crushing his people.

It's the Black journalist who platforms respectability politics instead of speaking truth to power.

It's the political strategist who convinces the community that incremental change is better than no change while cashing a check from the very people stalling progress.

Like Mike Tyson said, "Not everyone that fights you is your enemy, and not everyone that is nice to you is your friend." This is where the Hulu show The Other Black Girl hits a nerve (I'm sure you realize by now how much I love this show). We'd like to believe that when we walk into a room and see another Black face, we are safe. That there will be camaraderie, solidarity, an unspoken understanding of what it took to get here. Truth, however, is stranger than fiction. Sometimes the biggest threat isn't the institution - it's the one who looks like you but has been deputized by the institution to ensure you never get too free.

That's the tragedy of the Judas Goat Effect. It convinces those closest to the blade that they are wielding it. That they are not, in fact, just another part of the herd…until the machine decides it no longer needs them either. ⏱

The First, the Few and the Only

Not Every Dumbledore is a Friend, Not Every Snape is an Enemy

For all the Harry Potter fans out there, think of it this way: not every Dumbledore is your ally, and not every Snape is your adversary. Sometimes you need a Snape to check you when power blinds you. Some Snapes will fight for you and die for you. Others will fight for you but refuse to risk their own livelihoods when the institution demands sacrifice. Understanding this distinction is crucial in white-led workspaces. Just remember the difference between Hobie Browns and Miguel O'Hara's.

My Brother's Wisdom

A family member of mine handled workplace politics differently - by disengaging. His go-to phrases to me were:

- "Can't trust these white folks, but as long as that check clears, we gon be aight."
- "I'm just tryna make this money. I don't care about no diversity initiatives. I'm here to collect my check."
- "Don't be loyal to these jobs, Michael. It ain't a family, it's a workplace. Get paid and get out."

At first, I resisted this mindset, but the more I experienced white-led institutions, the more I saw the wisdom in detaching personal purpose from the sweat equity they expect us to invest in "changing them."

If you haven't already, check out this Code Switch episode side quest

Chapter 17

Young, Neurodivergent & Black

(Reference to Nina Simone's song; Young, Gifted, and Black)

To be young, neurodivergent, and Black is to be born with wings in a world that only hands out cages. It is to feel the velocity of your mind—and be told to slow down. To sense the rhythm in your blood—and be asked to move to someone else's metronome. It is to be gifted in ways the world has no tests for, and brilliant in ways the world forgets how to honor, and needs all the same.

Neurodivergence in a Black or Brown body does not show up in a vacuum. It enters the room already racialized—already read through the cracked lens of the white imagination. Before your creativity is seen, your movements are labeled "disruptive." Before your ideas are heard, your tone is policed. What might be eccentric in a white coworker is insubordination in you. What might be "spirited" in a white child is "defiant" in your son. Your brilliance must first survive suspicion.

ADHD: Trivial Scapegoat or True Brain Dysfunction

ADHD stands for attention deficit hyperactivity disorder. That's my flavor of neurospicy. Being neurodivergent while navigating predominantly white institutions as a BIPOC professional presents a litany of tightropes and challenges in my career, but also an overlooked set of strengths. Too often, neurodivergence is framed as a deficiency, a burden to be carried, or something to mask in order to conform. In reality, it is a wellspring of innovation, deep empathy, and unorthodox problem-solving that, when harnessed, disrupts the status quo in the most necessary ways.

Dr. Russell Barkley often calls ADHD the Rodney Dangerfield of psychiatry because it can never get no respect and is often not taken as seriously as major depression, schizophrenia, generalized anxiety or bipolar disorder. Despite the seriousness and prevalence of ADHD, I spent much of my life listening to trite Gen X and Baby Boomer dismissals. They hadn't learned the impact of ADHD—

The First, the Few and the Only

just passed judgment the moment my teachers were told (or warned) of my diagnosis. Which led to my experience with adults, except my mom, being them often over-trivializing my cognitive challenges and eventually me, all-together.

Here are just some of the lived realities of the neurodivergent ADHD brain, especially in BIPOC bodies. These aren't just symptoms—they're survival strategies misread, mislabeled and underestimated by systems designed without us in mind.

🔄 Object Impermanence - Out of sight out of mind, in the most LITERAL sense

⌛ Time blindness - Branching from object impermanence this can lead to a sense of blindness to time and schedules. This can lead to being often late to things but having this kind of brain in a BIPOC body can often get spoiled in the racial stereotypes and biases of the white imagination leading to prejudice beliefs, and discriminatory disparate treatment and disparate impact on the Black and Brown neurodivergent more than the white bodied neurodivergent. 🙌

🐑 Procrastination - Look up John Cleese's experiment on this and low talent architects versus high talent architects do their work. So, it is for the neurodivergent brain. Frank Lloyd Wright may have been seen as procrastinating but people only remember his final work, not how long it took him to come up with it. Creativity depends on disinhibition and spontaneity. Emotionally potent creativity can look like procrastination, but this observable behavior is actually the hiding place of our superpower of creativity - no matter how annoying it may be, you'll love us when it is all said and done. They mock our procrastination, never realizing our ideas are percolating under pressure, waiting to emerge transformed. 1

📁 Disorganization - Dr. Stephen Humphries has some great thoughts on Disorganization in ADHD brains you can look up. Email-paralysis doesn't read as "executive dysfunction" to most—it reads as lazy. 2

The First, the Few and the Only

🧩 Pattern Recognition - We don't always follow the thread—but we see the weave. Neurodivergent brains, especially those shaped by racialized survival, are masters of pattern recognition. We notice the unspoken rules in a room, the repeated microaggressions in a system, the ways a story or situation rhymes with the past. While others are looking at the pieces, we see the puzzle. In a world designed for tunnel vision, our panoramic brains are revolutionary. 〰️

❓ Forgetfulness - Ever walk into a room and totally forget what made you get up and go into that room in the first place and now that you're there, you get distracted and start doing something else, only to return to a resting place and remember later with sudden urgency that you left the stove on? Welp, welcome to a symptom of ADHD. This happens to us more often than neurotypicals think or can relate to. They label us forgetful, without knowing what it means to lack automatic behavior scripting.

🤖 Lack of Automatic Behavior Scripting – For many people with ADHD, the neurodivergent cerebellum doesn't store routine actions as "autopilot" habits. Instead of running on cruise control, we have to consciously think through tasks that feel automatic to others—brushing teeth, replying to emails, even tying shoes. This constant mental effort for basic routines can be deeply exhausting. What neurotypical individuals do without thinking, we often navigate like a checklist—step by step, every single day. It's not a lack of ability. It's a difference in neurological wiring. And that difference comes with a cost: cognitive fatigue from having to be mindful of what others can do mindlessly. 3

🌊 Overwhelm - Since much of our brain power is used for what neurotypicals experience as autopilot or cruise control tasks. We can experience real cognitive overwhelm. There are times that I must go outside or take a walk just to get away or I may become extremely impulsive and act out in ways that won't help me as a functioning, gainfully employed member of society. Sensory overwhelm isn't accommodated—it's misdiagnosed as incompetence or even aggression

The First, the Few and the Only

○ Accent Mirroring - A common psychological phenomenon known as "mirroring" or "the chameleon effect" leads people to unconsciously mimic those with whom they're speaking. I literally don't mean to but sometimes I cannot help but talk like those around me. It works great though when I want to trick people into thinking I'm from where they are from. 4

For ADHD adults especially, who many learned to mask at an early age to feel safe and fit into neuro-normative environments, this is especially common when neurospicy individuals unconsciously imitate the behavior and speech patterns of those they are interacting with. This is particularly prevalent in adults with ADHD, who frequently learned to mask their traits from a young age as a safety mechanism and to conform to neurotypical settings.

○ Narrative Mirroring - When someone tells me a story, I think of a story to tell them that is similar as an effort to relate to them. Depending on how much control I have over my impulsivity, and I somehow let you finish, I will follow up with my story but it is received by the neurotypical as me trying to one-up them or make the conversation about me when in reality I'm desperately trying to make friends and prove to you that I understand.

Emotional withdrawal — When you are used to rejection you not only psychologically expect it, but you also learn to beat it to the punch socially. This can later metastasis into rejection sensitivity because making friends ain't so easy as you hoped it would be.

ADHD linked to depression - Google "Trevor Noah ADHD Depression" in his interview with Neal Brennon; "I have found depression is often a symptom of something else." -Trevor Noah. As Trevor Noah reflects in his interview with Neal Brennan, sometimes depression is a downstream symptom—one expression of deeper neurological, social, or systemic misalignment. For many ADHDers, that resonates deeply.

Shame - Refer to Brene Brown definition… not that I have done something wrong but a deeply felt sense and belief that "I am something wrong"

The First, the Few and the Only

🐇Subject hopping / Project hopping 🐇- Often a symptom of distractibility but can become the strength of multitasking. When you're rich with ideas, what seems like hopping is often a sign of high creative output.

⚡ Impulsiveness - My brain experiences noradrenaline and dopamine with a perpetual state of high tide or low tide deprivation, and to get that motivating hormone high tide again my brain is like a rabid rabbit in search of his next carrot that holds intrigue or curiosity. This can become a strength that looks like rapid decision making♨.

🔥Hyperactivity - This can look like many things to the white gaze and can, oftentimes, be misused to confirm stereotypes in the white imagination for a neurodivergent brain in a melanated body. But the strengths of this key feature of ADHD neurodivergence, when in alignment with something that has intrinsic interest to the ADHD brain, can lead to incredible productivity, performance and brilliance.

🌀Hyperfocus - It is concentration on nitrous, and when the ADHD/ADD brain is in this state, when we're in hyperfocus? It's Super Saiyan 3. Artistic brilliance overnight. Bar exam prep in a week but exhaustion, which always takes them off this naturally occurring brain high, usually keeps them from such feats. Where neurotypicals have focus, we have OBSESSION. Word alert!

♨ Cognoscente (noun) – One who knows a subject thoroughly; a connoisseur. Often associated with fine arts but an ADHD person can become disgustingly knowledgeable about the thing they hyperfixate on.

△ **Impulsivity | Distractibility | Hyperactivity** - This is the holy trinity of ADD according to Dr. Russell A Barkley. You see, we have Ferrari engines for brains, but we have bicycle brakes as Dr Edward Hallowell says. This gets us into trouble because we cannot always stop when we need to. That's not dysfunctional. That's potential, waiting for alignment. But fear not, we can build the champion level brakes to help us win the races in day-to-day life. When we see this as the

The First, the Few and the Only

superpower that it is and get reps in metamorphosis. Distractibility becomes curiosity. Impulsivity becomes innovation. Hyperactivity becomes momentum.

👀 Inattentiveness - Often, I can't control what I'm paying attention to. Largely because my attention is attached to my interest or what is interesting. Literally unable to help it. If it doesn't tap my curiosity, then it's probably gonna get lost on me.

🎭 Neurodivergent Masking - Hiding your neurodivergence to either maintain social relationships, dodge negative impacts, acquire opportunities or relationships and even avoid shame or stigma. For BIPOC professionals, masking is a double burden: racial code-switching and neurodivergent camouflage. 〰️

💥 Chaotic Discipline - We experience discipline in waterfall surges not as steady streams. This means we can get a week's worth of work done in a fraction of the time and is where the superpower of hyper focus gets active under the umbrella of chaotic discipline. 〰️

🛑 Task initiation / Task avoidance - Initiating a task can feel so so difficult, which consequently leads to task avoidance

🗣️ Info Dumping –Sharing the focal point of our hyper fixation is a sacred offering as much as a sign of trust. 〰️

🙅 Aversion to Hierarchy - Many neurodivergent people with ADHD do have a deeply rooted aversion to mindless authority and rigid hierarchy. And for many, this aversion isn't just personality-based or oppositional; it's adaptive, often formed in response to early environments shaped by trauma, control, or unpredictability. Here's how that plays out, both neurologically and emotionally:

People with ADHD often have heightened sensitivity to injustice, hypocrisy, and inconsistency—not because they're "defiant," but because their nervous systems are constantly scanning for authenticity, threat, or contradiction. Combine that with impulsivity and pattern recognition, and you get:

The First, the Few and the Only

- Quick detection of performative or hollow authority

- A gut-level repulsion to rules that seem arbitrary or harmful

- A drive to ask "why?" when others have already submitted

In childhood—especially in environments with authoritarian adults, trauma, or neglect—questioning authority or developing emotional vigilance can be a lifesaving strategy for neurodivergent kids: If adults were inconsistent or explosive, the child learned to distrust surface-level rules and read beneath the behavior. If safety came from anticipating mood shifts, then hyperawareness of power dynamics became the skill.

If control was used as a tool for harm, then rebellion became a form of integrity.

So, when people say, "Why can't they just follow the rules?"—they miss the fact that many of us were raised in systems where "following the rules" meant abandoning self-trust, self-esteem, and self-confidence. By the time neurodivergent kids become neurodivergent adults in schools, workplaces, or churches, their trauma-informed radar for bad leadership or coercion is often pathologized:

- Called "disrespectful" in school

- Labeled "insubordinate" at work

- Branded "difficult" in family or faith systems

But in truth, this aversion to hierarchy without trust is a form of internal justice wiring—a compass forged in fire. Rather than viewing this aversion as oppositional defiance or authority issues, we can reframe it as a sacred refusal to perform obedience when trust hasn't been earned.
In short, neurodivergence (in my case ADHD) + discernment (internal justice wiring) = Aversion to Hierarchy. Thus, neurodivergent people make for bad sheep and therein lies our superpower, anti-fascist by nature.

⏱ Side Quest

The First, the Few and the Only

Search the following researchers, doctors and scientists for more videos and presentations that will leave you neurodivergent readers feeling seen, felt and heard:
- Rosie Young: Rosie Yeung on Neurodiversity
- Dr Gabor Maté on ADHD
- Dr. Russell Barkley, the ADHD scientist
- Dr. Lawrence Fung
- Dr. Thomas E. Brown
- Dr. Stephen Humphries
- Dr. Edward Hallowell

Imagine your neurodivergence like a Ferrari engine, as Dr. Edward Hallowell says—but with bicycle brakes. That's not dysfunctional. That's potential, waiting for alignment. Distractibility becomes curiosity. Impulsivity becomes innovation. Hyperactivity becomes momentum.

Other strengths include high resilience, big picture thinking, master multi-tasking, unusually cool in a crisis or chaotic situations. ADHD folks often have the traits of productive CEO's, inspiring creatives and impactful visionaries. However, the expression of executive dysfunction manifests in Black and Brown bodies, often gets interpreted and translated as a character flaw or that something is wrong with the body. Something dangerous to be put down.

Paul Mooney has a joke he tells that highlights the life-or-death double standard of neurodivergence in Black and Brown bodies in his comedy special Paul Mooney: Analyzing White America at minute 46 to minute 48:55;

When ADHD Meets the White Imagination

In white-led spaces—workplaces, classrooms, churches, and even daycares—ADHD in Black and Brown bodies doesn't get interpreted through the lens of neurology. It gets interpreted through the lens of pathology.
- A white child who can't sit still is "kinesthetic."

The First, the Few and the Only

- A Black child who can't sit still is "a problem."

- A white employee who's emotionally dysregulated is "burnt out."

- A Brown employee is "unstable" or "no longer a cultural fit."

- A white pastor with nonlinear preaching is "prophetic."

- A Black preacher with the same approach is "hard to follow."

This is what happens when executive dysfunction meets executive suspicion & bias. It's not the diagnosis that determines your treatment—it's the skin it comes wrapped in.

But we are not broken clocks.
We are not defective machines.
We are not half-finished people in need of a user's manual written by someone else.

For those of us who are both Black and neurodivergent, every label—ADHD, dyslexia, ASD, PTSD—carries a double weight: one diagnostic, the other a pathology. The world does not just misinterpret our brains; it misreads our bodies. And that misreading is not benign. It disqualifies us, punishes us more often than their white kids, and demands performance without care for our process.

What if your impulsivity is really your creative spontaneity?
What if your "distraction" is curiosity in disguise?
What if your hyperfocus is a portal to genius?

The world told us to hide these things. To sand down our edges. But the very traits that bring us shame are the same ones that build worlds. The thing you were told most often to fix might be the thing that will set someone else free.

We are the ones with brains like constellations, seeing patterns others miss. We are the ones who shift conversations just by showing up as our full selves. We are the ones whose minds are wired for survival, strategy, and storytelling.

The First, the Few and the Only

🌱 Getting Involved

If you type the following in any search engine; "Yale Child Study Center on Pre-k and Black boys" it will lead you to an article entitled "Implicit bias may help explain high preschool expulsion rates for black children" by Bill Hathoway.

Masking, Surviving, and Reclaiming Power

For many BIPOC professionals, survival in white institutions often requires a double layer of masking: one for race and one for neurodivergence. The tightrope walk between proving competence while managing executive dysfunction, sensory sensitivities, or nonlinear thinking is a weight that others don't carry. The battle with something as simple yet overwhelming as email paralysis… staring at an inbox flooded with seventy-one unread messages, feeling the weight of response expectations, and the internalized shame that follows - is a prime example. Neurotypical work culture views this as irresponsibility or inefficiency, but those who experience it understand the deeper reality: it's not about ability. It's about systems that weren't built for minds that function differently, yet, instead of questioning the system, individuals are made to question themselves.

The very things framed as "problems" - the aspects most often associated with shame - are often the raw material for the greatest strengths. The world tells people to shrink, to conform, to "fix" themselves, but what if the very thing they are told to fix is what makes them indispensable?

Think of Loki, Superman, Harry Potter, Jane Eyre, Luke Skywalker, and so many others. They all had backstories that marked them as outcasts - fostered, abandoned, misunderstood. It was precisely their displacement and difference that made them powerful. Their otherness was not a limitation but a crucible that refined them into something greater. Their supposed weakness became the foundation of their strength.

Neurodivergent BIPOC professionals are no different. Our way of thinking uncovers solutions others don't see. Our ability to hyperfocus can lead to mastery. Our sensitivity to nuance allows us to navigate complex cultural and social dynamics. We disrupt stagnant institutions precisely because we refuse to fit into a mold that was never designed for us in the first place.

The First, the Few and the Only

From Disability to Leadership

To lead while neurodivergent is to reimagine the table. To refuse to sit at one that demands erasure. The goal is not to mimic neurotypicality. The goal is to root deeply in your difference and lead from there.
When institutions allow for nonlinear thinking, deep pauses, movement breaks, and quiet rooms—they begin to reflect the people they claim to serve. They become less performative and more human.

This isn't just about inclusion. It's about designing for dignity.
Once neurodivergence is no longer viewed as something to be "overcome," but instead as something to be embraced, it becomes a means of connection, leadership, and transformation. The strength of neurodivergent leaders is not in how well they mimic neurotypical standards but in how fully they lean into their own way of processing, strategizing, and engaging with the world.
In academic and professional spaces, my most impactful moments often come not from rigid adherence to traditional structures but from authenticity. When institutions allow for flexibility, deep pauses, and nonlinear discussion, they create environments where individuals like me don't just survive but thrive.
Neurodivergence, when honored, doesn't just change individual experiences - it reshapes entire systems for thriving.

This is the power of neurodivergence when it's owned and wielded rather than hidden and apologized for. It gives people a way to build new systems, not just survive the old ones. It allows for leadership with authenticity and creates spaces where others don't have to choose between their truth and their success.

In a world that constantly underestimates those who think and process differently in melanated bodies, the power to reality warp worlds is incredible. What greater power is there than that?

Neurodivergent Pivot…

Random thought, when I work out, somehow lactic acid helps me focus, to the point where I do not need medication. Remember, ADHD is defined by a challenged executive function in the brain, particularly the deprivation of dopamine, with that in mind let's see what some cursory research must say;

The First, the Few and the Only

Lactic acid itself isn't a treatment for ADHD—but exercise, which produces lactic acid during anaerobic activity, is well-documented to support executive function, increase dopamine and norepinephrine levels, and improve mood and attention. For some people, especially those with ADHD, consistent movement can feel like a form of medicinal self-regulation along with the other dopaminergic benefits of exercise.

For some, especially those with hyperactive ADHD subtypes, exercise increases dopamine and norepinephrine levels—chemicals that ADHD medications also target. Anecdotally, I find that post-exercise states of exertion and lactic acid buildup leave me feeling more regulated, focused, and less symptomatic. While this isn't a substitute for medical treatment, it can be an effective complementary strategy.

So, while it's not the lactic acid per se, the physiological cascade triggered by the kind of intense exercise that produces lactic acid can mimic or support what stimulant medications provide, particularly in increasing the availability of dopamine in the brain for more balanced executive brain function.

Some folks need their meds, and I honor that. But for me? Movement is medicine. The natural high that hits when I sweat hard enough becomes its own form of regulation. My brain, so often scattered or overstimulated, gets quiet. My mind clears like a street after the rain. The momentum from getting through an exercise becomes inertia. The rhythm creates a peace. I don't claim this as a prescription, just as a personal truth: there are days my workouts do for me what no pill ever could. And on those days, I remember—this body ain't broken. I'm not defective. I can be a productive member of society. My brain (& body) just needs the right conditions to play.

The Story of the Pigeon

I'm gonna wrap up this portion with an allegory from the Protestant faith I come from, since that is a tradition familiar to me. Gotta put these twenty years of ministry experience to work somehow. This story is one that's been passed down in the tradition I come from. The way I heard it, when God made the heavens, He filled them with birds. When He made the sea, He set loose creatures to swim the deep. Everything He made, He made to fit perfectly into the world that He created specifically tailored to their own kind.

The First, the Few and the Only

One day, the pigeons gathered and tilted their heads to the sky, watching the eagles carve through the clouds, wings slicing the air like knives through silk. The pigeons, with their fluttering and their bustling, felt small. They went to God and implored, "Make us like the eagles. Give us wings that will carry us high."

God, in all His wisdom, said, "Yes."

But instead of eagle's feathers, He placed something heavy upon their backs - burdens, weighted and pressing. The pigeons staggered under the load, blinking up at God in confusion. "How are we supposed to soar with these?!" they cried.

"These are what you need."

And so they went, moving how pigeons do - flustered, low to the ground, weighed down by what they did not understand, bobbing their heads forward and back as if trying to get a head start in thermodynamics.

Some grumbled. Some gave up. But one…one pigeon stopped cursing the weight and started working with it, using the difficulty. This pigeon stretched, shifted, felt out the shape of the burden. Then, in one mighty motion, it lifted off the ground and began to soar at the heights of eagles.

What God had placed upon their shoulders was not a weight to bear, but wings!

I used to think of neurodiversity as a weight, a burden pressing me down while the neurotypical so-called eagles of the world soared free. One day, I stopped fighting against it. I stopped wishing for ease. I stopped envying those who moved differently, thought in straighter lines. I stretched, shifted, and honored what I had been given. Then I understood - these weren't chains; they were wings! Did you know pigeons can fly farther than almost any other birds? You do now!

Use the difficulty. Don't curse it. The very thing that feels like it holds you down might be the only thing that was meant to lift you up. Being BIPOC and neurodiverse became one of my favorite parts of my story. I like to think my neurodivergence not only helps me navigate within systems, but it has also saved my life. My neurodivergence wouldn't let me fall in line within abusive systems. In my work career it kept me from submitting to sophisticated tyrants like the

The First, the Few and the Only

character Hopper from Pixar's A Bug's Life. It helped me survive abusive authority figures in my early childhood. My neurodivergence allows me to reach people in an audience that no one else can reach like I can. It allows me to reach people in ways they have never been reached before. It is no longer a hindrance, but my superpower.

"I'm Allowed to Leave"

In my experience, the BIPOC bodies that stay in the workplace to reform it tend to be the ones who are cursed to become reformed, or better yet, deformed by it. Until they leave or get too burned out to stay. In doing so, they often abandon themselves -like Stanley from The Office, in the process.

Sometimes they will leave the organization all together. The organization will find young, hapless & hopeful BIPOC college grads to fill their place and start the process all over again.

I was at one of those fancy foundation dinners at the Westin in Pittsburgh, the kind where everyone sips overpriced wine and pretends not to notice how dry the chicken is. Between the polite networking and the occasional glance at the dessert table, I bumped into a young woman - polished, professional, glowing with the kind of contentment that only comes from truly loving your job.

We got to talking about life, about where we'd landed, about how much she was enjoying her work in land trusts and parks and recreation. Then, mid-sentence, she snapped her neck toward me like she'd just seen a ghost.

"Oh my gosh," she gasped. "I just remembered something. I'm where I am today all because of a conversation I had with you at church once when I was still a student."

Now, let me give you some context. Back in my campus ministry days, my teammates - let's call them K and D - and I spent our time meeting with students, mentoring them (or as we say in the Protestant world, *discipling*), and hosting weekly, large-group meetings where all the students we'd connected with throughout the week would gather. One of those students was Alex. Not only was she a student leader in our ministry, but she also became a member of my church. She even ended up working for the church after graduation.

The First, the Few and the Only

She told me she could still remember the exact moment that changed everything. It was just a casual Sunday, the two of us standing in the foyer after service. I'd asked how she was doing, how things were going with the college ministry we'd both worked for. And then, she said, I had looked her dead in the eye and said something to the effect of: "I'm getting the hell out of that ministry. I mean… we are allowed to leave."

She told me she went home that day, sat with those words, and cried.

"I'm allowed to leave."

She kept saying it to herself, over and over, until it finally sank in. And then? She left.

She walked away from the ministry job that had been weighing her down. She met her husband in the campus ministry. She went back to school. And now, here she was - thriving in a real-life version of Parks and Recreation.

Don't get me wrong - her story was moving, and I was genuinely touched. But at the same time, my neurodivergent brain was kicking my ass. All I could think about the entire time was asking, "Is your job anything like the show??"

Of course, I had enough sense to wait. I counted to seven in my head (what I determined was the socially acceptable amount of time after a heartwarming testimony before pivoting to something unserious). Then I asked.

Her answer? A resounding YES!

Being reformed by an institution can happen in many ways. For example, being labeled "difficult" is the way to blackball Black staff. My experience at Point Park University after they dismantled the Title IX office following Fox News coverage over our following new changes to Title IX under the Biden administration led to us being Blackballed and dismantled, despite being overrun with students needing support and faculty/deans asking for customized training of their faculty. Following COVID, a lot of faculty were experiencing traumatized students coming out of the pandemic

The First, the Few and the Only

and caught all the hell that came with trying to make them learn at an academic pace again. Funny thing is, the faculty were traumatized coming into the classroom and some were traumatized even more by trying to survive their students.

Forever Defying Gravity

Elphaba, the so-called Wicked Witch of the West, is the first, the few, and the only personified. She is the lone, green-skinned girl in a world that was never built to hold her brilliance, never meant to accommodate her presence. She is both exceptional and ostracized, a force of nature whose difference (and her burden) is her power.

From the moment she steps into Shiz University, Elphaba is marked - not just by the color of her skin but by the expectations placed upon her. She is the one with talent, who sees the world differently, the one with vision, the one with the burden of being extraordinary in a system designed to diminish her. She is welcome only so long as she can be controlled, as long as her gifts serve the interests of those in power. The moment she disrupts the order of things, the moment she refuses to bow, she becomes a problem to be solved, a force to be subdued. Wicked.

Like so many of us who are the first, the few, and the only, Elphaba learns that survival comes at a cost. She must choose between assimilation and exile, between playing along for proximity to power or standing firm in her truth, knowing it will cost her everything. She does not get the luxury of simply existing; she must either shrink herself or defy expectations entirely. When she chooses the latter, the system does what it always does - it vilifies her. It rewrites her story into a cautionary tale.

The First, the Few and the Only

It calls her wicked.

But what is wickedness if not the refusal to be complicit? What is rebellion if not the insistence on one's own worth?

Elphaba, like so many trailblazers, learns that the reward for authenticity is often ostracization. There is, however, freedom in it too. She defies gravity, not just as a spectacle, but as a declaration: I will not be who you say I am. I will not shrink myself to fit your mold. If I'm flying solo, at least I'm flying free. No wizard that there is or was is ever gonna bring me down.

Isn't that the lesson so many of us learn? The cost of being extraordinary in a world built for sameness is that we are rarely embraced, but we are always undeniable. Forever defying gravity. That to be the first, the few, and the only is to live in a space where every move is both scrutinized and necessary. That our power, our defiance, our refusal to be anything less than ourselves - that is what makes us dangerous. That is what makes us free

🔥 Final Random Link of Chapter:

Benediction to the Young, Neurodivergent, and Black

To be young, neurodivergent, and Black is to carry both fire
and fog in the mind.

It is to be misunderstood even by those who claim to understand.
But it is also to be magic. To be mosaic. To be by design.

You were never broken.
Just misread.

They pathologize what our body does to stay alive.
But being neurodivergent is not just about managing symptoms or masking—it's about reclaiming power.
We are not scattered. We are constellations—luminous, if you know where to look.

The First, the Few and the Only

We are not inattentive. We are hyper-attuned to what others ignore.
We are not inconsistent. We are cyclical like the moon, brilliant in phases.
We are not disordered. We are different, and difference is not disorder.

To the neurodivergent Black child told they were "too much."
To the neurodivergent Black adult masking through every meeting just to keep a paycheck.
To the ones who always sensed the room before they entered it—

Your power is not in your ability to mimic a system
that was never made for you.
Your power is in your rhythm.
Your rage. Your rituals.
Your rest. Your refusal.
Your authenticity.

Let this be the chapter where you stop managing yourself like a problem.
Let this be the chapter where you grieve, then reintroduce yourself.
Your difference is not your enemy.

It is your evidence.
Of survival.
Of genius.
Of God moving through you in non-linear time.

As Nina sang, to be young, gifted, and Black is a blessing and a battle.
To be young, neurodivergent, and Black is the same—only now, we name the gift, honor the difference, and refuse to let the world define us by its deficit.

We forged ourselves out of this fire. | Equality, Why don't we have it yet?

What's coming up for you? Jot down any data coming up from your body, memories, or imagination?

The First, the Few and the Only

The First, the Few and the Only

Chapter 18

Maroons of the Borderlands

*"...is the sheep preaching hate when he says that
I'm not gonna let the wolf eat me anymore?"*
Denzel Washington speaking on Malcolm X

 In *All the White Friends I Couldn't Keep*, Andre Henry recounts a powerful moment when his family member, Bitta, urges him to seek the wisdom of his ancestors: "A who teach me f'tweat ma' ncestor like stranja?" This translates to, "Who taught me to treat my ancestors like strangers?" The question lingers, challenging the ways we have been conditioned to sever ties with those who came before us. Admittedly, as much as I love Black Panther, my years of Christian ministry training make me wince at the thought of speaking to ancestors. However, ancestral veneration is not as foreign to my faith as it may seem. The God of Abraham, Isaac, and Jacob - do those names ring a bell? 1

I got a friend that interacts with their ancestors regularly. Through trauma training, I've come to understand that they're onto something. Whether or not the reader embraces ancestral veneration, interaction, or worship is beside the point. What matters is this: just as we inherit the wounds of our ancestors, we also inherit their strength. That inheritance - the resilience, the wisdom, the will to survive - is a gift. It is something I have learned to honor, to hold space for, and to channel in my own ways. This led me to a hidden tale of ancestors called the maroons.

There's a reason you don't hear much about the Maroons in school. They don't fit neatly into the American story of slavery and freedom, of chains

The First, the Few and the Only

and emancipation, of suffering and salvation by the hands of the state. The Maroons didn't wait to be freed. They snatched their own liberation from the hands of those who sought to break them. Just like in the prologue, I would love to present them to you like most superhero nerds learn about new characters of a story… by looking at a summary of powers, abilities and lore:

The First, the Few and the Only

-CLASSIFIED DOSSIER-
Maroons of the Borderlands

Name: The Maroons
Alias: Nyankipong Pickibu (Children of the Almighty in Twi), The Untamed, Wildlings, The Palenques from Spanish Colonies, Kromanti of Jamaica, Mocambos or Quilombos in Brazil, Los Cumbes of Venezuela, Mambises of Cuba, Ladeiras of Brazil, Louisiana Maroons, or Cimarrones, Liberators of Haiti. 3

Powers: Guerilla Warfare Mastery, Terrain Bending, Liberation Warping, Ancestral Blood Memory, Shinobi-level Stealth, Sovereignty Summoning, Ecosystem Camouflage, Adaptability, Ashanti Culture, Vawzen
Weaknesses: Historical Erasure, Betrayal by Treaty, Myth Distortion
Affiliations: The Oppressed, Exploited, Brutalized, and those with the hiraeth of freedom

Origin Story:
Born not of servitude but of refusal, the Maroons were those who would not wait to be freed. They tore themselves from the plantations and carved sanctuaries in the swamps of Carolina, the caves of Cuba, and the mountains of Jamaica. With blood memory as their compass, they formed hidden nations, outposts of freedom that outlived empire. They weren't just runaways—they were originators of Black autonomy in the so-called New World, existing beyond the whip of the "master's" gaze.

Mission:
To survive was not enough. Their mission was to

The First, the Few and the Only

remember. To remember that we were once free—and could still be. Not by inching closer to colonizers, but by moving deeper into the wilderness of self-determination. Their lives remind us that the borderlands are not the margins of power—they are its undoing.

Notable Battles:
- **The Swamp Wars of the Carolinas** - Evaded dogs, overseers, and soldiers through landscape mastery and prophetic leadership for decades

- **The British Surrender at Nanny Town** - Forced colonial powers into peace treaties through pure resistance

- **First Maroon** War (1728-1739/40) - Led by figures like Cudjoe (Leeward Maroons) and Nanny (Windward Maroons), The Maroons used guerrilla tactics and their knowledge of the rugged terrain to resist British forces in Jamaica. Notable events included Cudjoe's attack on the barracks at Titchfield Fort (1735 Jamaica) with Windward Maroon assaults. The conflict concluded with the British forced into unprecedented treaties— "granting" the Maroons land, freedom, and limited autonomy in exchange for a fragile peace. But that peace came at a cost: surveillance, and the forced collusion of capturing other runaways. The price of autonomy was being made a tool of the system they had escaped.

- **San Malo** - Jean Saint Malo, or Juan San Malo, rose to prominence as a maroon leader in Louisiana by forming and protecting a community of escaped slaves in the bayous and swamps southeast of New Orleans. Having fled

The First, the Few and the Only

enslavement on the German Coast, he orchestrated raids on plantations and motivated others to join his refuge. His success in defying oppression due to his leadership and his formidable fighting skills turned him into a living legend. Like Luffy from the anime One Piece, this earned him recognition as a symbol of resistance among the enslaved population of the region, and his memory persisted for many years.

- **The Silence of the Textbooks** - Erased by history, resurrected by ancestral memory—again and again. The most notable battle to date is your memory, dear reader.

Famous Quote:
"Not all ghosts are dead. Some are simply hiding in the trees, whispering maps of freedom."

Arch-Nemesis:
Willie Lynch Effect & The Plantation Logic — the lie that says obedience earns safety, assimilation leads to liberation and survival only can be found within the system.

Legacy:
They are not dead. They are dispersed. They live in every fugitive thought, in every exit strategy written in the margins of your copy of the employee handbook. They are the blueprint for building beyond—the origin story for every soul who ever walked away from the table and built their own damn house in the woods. You are not merely remembering them. They are remembering you.

Maroons were the runaways, the rebels, the ones who slipped into the swamps, the mountains, the thickets so dense that even the hounds lost their scent. They

The First, the Few and the Only

vanished into the earth, into the rivers, into the stories whispered in the night. They refused the plantation's prophecy that they would always be bound. Instead, they wrote their own scripture, one of survival and defiance, of Black bodies moving beyond capture, beyond control.

In the United States, they ran deep into the Carolina swamps, into the thick Florida heat, where they joined forces with the Seminoles and fought wars that North American history won't dare whisper about. In the Caribbean, they climbed high into the mountains of Jamaica, into the caves of Cuba, into the jungles of Suriname, building fortresses from the land itself. The Garifuna, the Mascogos, the Palenqueros - these are their descendants, still carrying the echoes of those who would not kneel. 2

History, as told by the victors, does not take kindly to those who cannot be tamed. The Maroons are left out of the textbooks because they disrupt the carefully curated tale of America's racial order. If the enslaved could break free, carve out entire nations in the wilderness, defeat colonial armies, and live untouched - what does that say about power? About control? About the lie that slavery was an unshakable fate? 4

The Maroons were not merely fugitives. They were the first experiment in Black autonomy in the so-called New World. They were the blueprint, the proof that another way was possible. They shattered the myth that Blackness was synonymous with subjugation. That, more than anything, is why their story has been suppressed.

For those of us who have found ourselves as the first, the few, and the only - navigating institutions never built with us in mind - the Maroons are not just history. They are prophecy. Their spirit is alive in every Black person who has had to make a way out of no way, who has had to carve a space for themselves in the borderlands of belonging. They are in the whispers of every ancestor who tells us to get free by any means necessary.

The U.S. has a way, like Uncle Tom/Josiah Henson 5, to make us look at our ancestors' glory with contempt. Some of you may not think you ever heard the term maroon before, but you have. If you ever watched Bugs Bunny from the Looney Tunes as a kid, he used to say it all the time to idiotic buffoonish characters. Don't believe me? Look up "Bugs Bunny - What A Maroon Whiskey Ginger Podcast" on YouTube. Full stop, do it right now.

The First, the Few and the Only

In the marvel TV show, Luke Cage, a character named Bushmaster recounts the power of this history and knowledge:

History of Maroon nations | Bushmaster's tale | Pachuca women
Additional Resource: Chapter Fifteen of All the White Friends I Couldn't Keep by Andre Henry. Andre Henry is a descendent of the Maroons, and Garvey-ites.

System Cost Benefit Analysis: Proximity & Distance

Surviving an institution feels like a constant negotiation of proximity and distance. Attachment or authenticity. The higher you rise, the more you believe that elevation brings power - the power to change things from within. The higher I climbed, however, the more I saw my own arrogance. I wasn't the only one trying to change the system; the system was trying to change me.

To stay at the top, I had to reckon with a culture that demanded my conformity just as much, if not more, than I expected to transform it.
Imagine the plantation. The power sits in the big house, where the master and his family live. The wife, the lady of the house, holds power, but only in the land allotted to her. Just beneath them, the house servants - often light-skinned, often the master's own children, whether acknowledged or not. Below them, the overseers - low-class white men armed with whips and the illusion of control. At the bottom, the enslaved field laborers and their families, bound together in toil, in struggle, in survival.
Beyond these concentric rings of power, at the periphery, lay another space - the borderlands.

Directors, executives - those closest to the big house - are under constant surveillance. The system has its agents, its gatekeepers, its overseers. Some, like Josiah Henson's Uncle Tom, build within faulty structures, attempt subversion from the inside. They can point you to resources, whisper warnings, but they are not free.

The First, the Few and the Only

Ever heard the phrase, "Keep your friends close but your enemies closer?" It doesn't always apply. Sometimes, rising in the system only sets you up to be watched, controlled, drained, and consumed. Like Regina Hall's character in the film Master, you are brought in just close enough to be paraded, to be used. You become an outward-facing figure, a proof of progress, but anything you create, anything you dream, must be done under their purview within their rules.

The big house has running water and heat. That is the draw. Once inside, however, you find that you cannot rest. You cannot be free. If you were the most outspoken voice in the field, they will remove you from it. They will not want you among the laborers, the ones in the trenches. They will bring you inside, offer you a seat, but give you no tools, no map, no way to build. When you burn out, when you spin out, they will blame you. Because that is how the system sustains itself.

Don't Become the Rat King

We're set up for competition, y'all. Sometimes to the death. Remember that movie called Highlander where "there can be only one?" This is a real-life example of how they set up BIPOC people in an organization, put them in a maze, and watch us cannibalize ourselves and/or each other.

That reminds me of how some countries' farmers deal with rats in their fields. They make what is called a rat king. Let's say you have a rat infestation amongst a crop, and they are ruining things. First things first, you got to dig a deep hole, big enough so that the rats can never climb out. Next, you have to put a bunch of food down there so that the rats will all go down there.

Then you walk away and leave the hole for a week or so. What will happen is, once the food runs out, all the rats will enter a scarcity mentality and what ethologist John B. Calhoun termed as "behavioral sink" – due to overcrowding, there will be a collapse in social functions. The rats will begin to consume one another until you have one rat left. Then you come back, capture that rat, and release him back into the field. Now the only thing that rat will eat is other rats. That rat is now the rat king.

When scarcity and "opportunity" are manipulated by institutions to get us to go into their hole- they pit the first, the few, and the only against one another, it creates the illusion that my skinfolk are my enemy/competition. That my path to

The First, the Few and the Only

success must be paved through the bodies of my siblings. Some of us—like Gamora in the MCU—learn to drive the bulldozer, desperate to survive, to please a system that plays the role of a masochistic and maniacal foster father. Others look away, numbing themselves to the violence of the maze. But some of us choose differently. We refuse to become the rat king—or queen. We realize the only way to win a rigged game… is to stop playing and get out.

In the Marvel universe, all Nebula ever wanted was a sister. Not a rival. But competition taught Gamora to fight instead of connect. Many of us become Nebulas and Gamoras, if we stay in the hole too long. Gamora became the rat king, all Nebula wanted was a sister. But healing begins when we look at the ones beside us and both choose kinship over conquest bit.ly/MCUratking

🌱 Getting Involved
Where's your breath? What is surfacing for you? Whose face came to mind? Write down their names.

Where the Runaways Remained

*"Just because you are used to the desert
doesn't mean you don't deserve the ocean."*
Rev. Fr. Albert Nwosu

The hills of Jamaica hold stories the plantations could never silence. In the thick of the Blue Mountains, where the trees stand like sentinels and the rivers run deep with memory, the Maroons built what the slavers feared most - a world beyond their reach. These were not just fugitives; they were architects of freedom, visionaries who saw that survival was not enough. They did not beg the master to loosen the chains. They broke them and left.

The Maroons were the ones who refused to be bent by the lash, who turned their backs on the plantation and its false promises of favor for obedience. They were

The First, the Few and the Only

not waiting for a better master. They were not waiting at all. With each footfall deeper into the hills, they unraveled the lie that the system was inescapable.

They built villages in the highlands, living on their own terms, governing themselves, waging war against those who sought to return them to bondage. They were skilled in guerilla tactics, striking swiftly and disappearing like ghosts into the landscape. The British sent armies to crush them, but the Maroons fought them to a standstill, forcing the colonizers into treaties they never imagined they would have to sign.
They were not merely surviving. They were free, and that distinction is everything.

The False Salvation of Deals With Devils

Josiah Henson, whose story was twisted into the myth of Uncle Tom, knew something about this distinction. Born into bondage, he believed, as many did, that loyalty and diligence might earn him a way out. He worked, he obeyed, he rose in the ranks. He trusted, even as he remained owned, but the system does not reward servitude with freedom. It only rewards it with usefulness. (Side Quest Review: chatgpt "the betrayal of Isaac Riley – Josiah Henson")

When he saw that the promise of power within the system was an illusion, he did not try to negotiate his dignity. He ran. Like the Maroons before him, he understood that true revolution was not in rising within the master's house but in leaving it altogether.

It is the lie whispered in every ambitious ear, the seduction of every system. The higher you climb, the more you realize the air is thinner for a reason. You breathe differently when you are being watched, and make no mistake, you are being watched. Every promotion, every title, every seat at the table comes with an unspoken contract: keep the system running. Be useful, but not disruptive. Be present, but not too present.

The plantation had its house, its overseers, its field hands, and its hidden hands - those who ran, those who built outside its walls, those who saw that the real prize was not a place inside but a life beyond. The Maroons of history knew this, slipping into the hills and swamps, forming something new instead of reforming something broken.

The First, the Few and the Only

The borderlands are where they made their lives. The borderlands are where we must go.

The borderlands were never empty. They were filled with the ones history tried to erase. Every institution that tokenizes BIPOC bodies follows the same ritual: parade, consume, erase. It is the cycle that makes history feel like a revolving door, each generation tricked into believing they are the first to push against it.

What happens when we stop playing by their rules? When do we stop measuring success by our proximity to the master's house? What happens when we start listening to the erased instead of the chosen?
The erased leave clues. If you listen closely, you will hear their names in the silences between official histories. You will find their fingerprints on work claimed by others. You will see their footprints leading not up the mountain of power, but away from it toward rest, toward healing, toward something freer than we have been taught to dream.

Survival is not the same as liberation🌱. We were not meant to simply survive institutions. We were meant to build beyond them, but the system tells us survival is enough. It tells us that exhaustion is a badge of honor. That suffering is proof of our worth. That to make it through without being broken is enough.

But what if making it through is not the goal? What if the goal is to no longer need the system at all?

Rudolph the Red-Nosed Reindeer was told to hide his brilliance until the system needed it. Until whiteness found a way to profit from it. He was shamed for what made him different, until that difference became useful. But Rudolph didn't need Santa.

Santa
needs
Rudolph.

We do not need these systems. These systems need us.
The master's house will always offer a room to those who make themselves useful, but the cost is your freedom. Your rest. Yourself. The question is not whether we

The First, the Few and the Only

can rise high enough to change it from within, but whether we are willing to leave and build beyond it.

Rest is resistance. Distance is power. Distance is resistance. To remove yourself is not to surrender but to reimagine. The borderlands are calling. And there is work to do - not to fix what was never meant to hold us, but to plant something new where we are finally free.

Why does rest matter? Why does time away matter? Because rest disrupts the psychological chains of the system. Because rest restores the imagination - an imperative for freedom.

Freedom at a Distance

The common belief? The higher I rise in the system, the more power I have to change it. The reality? The farther I step away, the more room I have to pivot, to make change from the outside.

But what of the maroons - the ones who escaped the system entirely? The ones who refused to play the game?

My friend KO and I were doing a talk together at a university on trauma-informed spaces in the arts as a co-creation by students and faculty. A student asked us a question about how to navigate spaces when you feel all alone and there is no one that looks like you: what do we do? KO gave an incredibly insightful thought about rootedness and remembering. They basically challenged them not to think of what they need to do aside from pausing and asking themselves: where is my breath? Then I recall stepping in and giving a metaphor akin to what KO was naming. I asked if anyone had ever watched Avatar: The Last Airbender. A bunch of hands flew up. I asked them if they know the avatar state when Aang is his most powerful. They did.

Aang is his most powerful because he embodies all the collective strength and mastery of his ancestors and the ones that came before him. All the ancestors' eyes light up and Aang sees them watching him, as they are all watching through his eyes now. That's what it is like.

The First, the Few and the Only

Aang, when he is most vulnerable, is his most powerful because he isn't alone. They are all there when you take that breath, that breath of remembrance. That breath of remembering, in that moment. And so, it is for them, the Hobie Browns of the past, and your ancestors are all with them. All with you. The maroons are important legacy kept from you far too long, but they are restored unto you now. What will you do with what you have reclaimed?

🌱 Getting Involved
I have given a sizeable amount of effort to introduce you to many a name of FFO's (the first, the few and the only) that you come from. That are a part of your legacy. Not to mention the people in your family that broke generational curses before you came to be. Take a moment to simply name the person and or family member that comes to mind or stuck with you throughout these pages now; (who watches you when you are in the avatar state?)

_____

_____

Picture this: your most recent ancestors are behind you with their hands on your shoulders. This is not ancestral worship, it is ancestral honor and remembrance. Their most recent ancestor is behind them with a hand on their shoulder, and so on and so on, just like Aang. KO reminds me all of the time that oppression lives in all spaces and so do your ancestors - with you, supporting you, watching you, sharing their strengths with you. We must remember ourselves to tap in. You are not the only one in that room. There are generations worth of strengths and epigenetic resilience in that space with you, like avatar Aang in the avatar state.

Without remembering our collective history, we become desultory and get lost in the fast pace of capitalism that keeps us busy and running fast by design. We have to slow down, breathe to remember. Where's your breath even now? 🌱

Keeping you in a desultory state, jumping from one thing to another, perpetually disconnected from yourself, is by design, but it is not your make up.

The First, the Few and the Only

HONOR

 We are more than buffoons, beasts, or receptacles of white lust and cosplayers of the white imagination. We are more than what white imaginations cook up for people that look like us to act out on screen, on stage, in political theatre, to function in the room to be silent and grateful. We don't need to reduce ourselves to dancing and singing and soothing and sheltering when racial discomfort becomes too close to their present realities, when the racial caricatures and tokenistic functions in their imaginations are cracked by the reality of our dignity, humanity, and glory.

These Josiah Henson's, these real Uncle Tom's above are folks whose blood, sweat, and tears we stand on the shoulders of. No matter how much white imaginations threaten us with their boxes and their hyphenated identities, we are mighty. Mighty like a flower that grows from the face of a rock or a flower that breaks street concrete to say good morning to the sun. We are vulnerable and do costly things anyway, all the while still maintaining our beauty with all the ferocity and dignity our ancestors passed down. All their dreams, fears, ancestral traumas, ancestral superpowers, and aversions. All their potential, the good stuff they had to leave in the tank because they were covered by the social and institutional concrete of racial oppression they tried to bloom through. Instead, our ancestors chose to spend it on the next generation in hopes that they would find the cracks their parents couldn't break, the cracks their parents couldn't exploit, the cracks that the Hobie Browns hadn't yet broken for them with their own bodies. They endured all of this so that, one day, their children would display the glory of the village, the glory of their family's true power, like Mirabel in Encanto.

The healers of generational wounds start with the one who is bravest enough to feel it…then name it. In light of that, we must learn to honor it by, or dare I say through, honoring them. Check out this clip of an older character from Good Times demanding honor where there is instead learned contempt for the generation that came before:

The First, the Few and the Only

🌱 Getting Involved

Is there any one from your past coming to heart and/or mind right now?
Please take a breath to recall their faces. Full stop. Breathe. Notice.

As you honor each new face with a breath, list them below or in the margin. What story would you tell about them?

_____

_____

_____

I wanted to give you all a way to disrupt the dis-membering. Dismembering of your body from your rootedness and where you come from. From your history.

Dr. Claud Anderson on what happens when
we let them put our history behind us

Let your ancestors inspire you. Allow them to blow a northern breeze throughout your imagination for the possibilities of who you are becoming. Let them blow a strong southern wind into your memories of the strength you inherit. Let them bolster how you remember yourself and the history we come from. Our history was lost by design but is now restored again by way of collective memory. When we listen to history, as told by the vulnerable, even our ancestors, we become wise.

With history, we need wisdom if we have any hope not to repeat it. Lastly, given all the history, a rule I try to live by goes like this:

Honor who came before you

The First, the Few and the Only

Protect those behind you
Respect those beside you
Be tender with the young child within you.

I was leading a mentorship group at a company that shall remain nameless. This company does a ton of recreation and seeks to remove barriers that block access to the recreation for every kind of body. We had high-school-aged Black and Brown youth as employees to basically get mentored at different outdoor companies, farms, and fisheries throughout Pittsburgh for six weeks in the summer months.

I was talking with the students about what I have learned as a Black or Brown body to navigate white institutions in the workplace. At first, I thought they were being teenagers and not too interested, but about halfway through they let me know they were getting what I was talking about. I asked how, and they started telling me stories from their elders in their family. I remember when my grandpa, dad, older sibling, aunt, mom, grandma, etc. had something happen to them at work like this or that, they shared. What did they begin to do? They started recounting their family history. They started recounting wisdom, and I realized that I had that too.

🌱 Getting Involved

Notice your breath.

What faces are coming to mind? What ancestor is with you right now?

Picture their face to the best of your ability. What are they doing? What are they saying to you?

In the margin of this book, I want you to write down what you're noticing. What elder or family is showing up even now? Write down their names. They are with you. Write down a story they are re-telling you.

The First, the Few and the Only

 Side Quest

Maybe put on the song open arms by SZA ft Travis Scott, or know your worth by Khalid, Disclosure, Davido, and Tems

Fargin

You're not alone

The First, the Few and the Many

Chapter 19

Fin

"Once you can see the way broadly, you can see it in all things"
-Miyamoto Musashi from the Book of 5 Rings

A Release

Fargin happens in the community. But who is my community? The Hobie Browns, the ones who know that not all skinfolk are kinfolk. Finding your tribe is more than proximity - it's resonance, a vibration that tells you, "You are seen." If you are in a space where there is only betrayal, one-upping, scarcity mindsets, backstabbing to rise in power on windmill farms and plantations, then guess what. No fargin.

Dr. Frances Cress Welsing reminds us, "There is a time for everything." I had to learn that sometimes you gotta leave to arrive. You must leave to find a community where repair and carving are possible. Some soils are too hardened for fargin to take root because when it's time to know your worth, you stop giving people discounts.

Dr. Frances Cress Welsing |
Old basketball star on being in a community of fargin is wealth building

Let go. Let go of the white friends you can't keep, the white companies you can't change, the white bodies you can't save - no matter how often they invite you to teach them for free. Own that your heart burns with depression and rage for a reason. Take a deep breath and remember you have the power to put out your own fire. You are as worthy of care and comfort as the white bodies that demand that you soothe them.

You're not alone

The First, the Few and the Many

You don't need any more advice now. "We are the children of [enslaved people] who would not die. We need to act like it." - George Fraser. When we name and notice our own somatic data, remember who we are, and make decisions in alignment with that, there is one thing left for our onlookers, haters and even the system to recognize: vawzen.

Vawzen (واوزين). An Arabic word that means the admiration of the unwilling. Sit with that for a second. Full stop. 🌱

Vawzen comes from people not afraid to work in the dark. Those not afraid to abandon the plantation, those not afraid to beat up giants even when everyone else sees windmills. Those not afraid to stop trying to survive and seek to truly be alive. Those not afraid to become a ghost in the same hallways that taught you to love your cage.

"Visibility these days seem to somehow equate to success. Do not be afraid to disappear. From it. From us. For a while. And see what comes to you in the silence." - Michaela Coel

This is what will be left in your wake for those who remember you, like Josiah Henson. Those who treated you as a token or caricature will have to, one day, put respect on your name no matter how badly they don't want to. If that ain't winning, I don't know what is. Those who resisted that very outcome? They will have to honor you, whether they say it or not. "You prepare a table for me in the presence of my enemies," as the Good Book says.

The First, the Few and the Many

Monica F. Cox · 2nd   + Follow
CEO, STEMinent LLC | Distinguished Professor of Engineering at The Ohi...
3h · Edited · 🌐

Stop believing you're washed up or have nothing to offer. Your gifts were planted in you for a reason.

If the people in your spaces don't recognize or acknowledge what you bring, continue to build and develop.

Invest in yourself.
Build your own team.
Knock on new doors.
Engage in new communities.

It's not your job to convince others you are worthy.

I promise those who need what you have to offer will show up.

Don't give up.

Post says, "Some people never undrstand what you bring to the table until they watch you in action at another table."

> Some people never understand what you bring to the table until they watch you in action at another table.

By now, you know that this book isn't about answers. It's about naming. Noticing. Remembering. It's about reminding you that you don't have to cut yourself off from your body or feelings anymore. There is nothing wrong with you. You are not alone, and neither is your body. This is about sitting with the data, the qualitative evidence of our token stories and experiences: the betrayals, the anger, the grief, the setups, the unnecessary competition, the rage, the loss, and the toll. We are worthy of care. This takes repetition. Healing takes repetition. Learning to nibble on goodness, delight, faith, hope, and love again takes repetition - not gorging.

When the Jewish concentration camps were liberated, soldiers handed food to the emaciated survivors, chocolate or whatever they had on them. Those who stuffed their faces died. Their bodies, after starvation, had to be eased back into nourishment with small, simple foods. If they ate too much too soon, they perished.

That was me in the thick of it. That is me in the thick of it. But as I nibbled on hope, on apricity, on hiraeth, I followed my nose, my heart, and my feet to freedom. I followed my senses towards more wholeness, even in the cold winter of toxic, tokenistic workplaces and spaces of worship.

The First, the Few and the Many

To those who know, viscerally, the stories I shared in this book: you are me, and I am you. I used to think I had to be healed to write this book. I used to think I was the only one going through these experiences in workplaces. But the more I interviewed folks, the more I discussed this with my friends, the more safe people I found in Francesco, Dr. Lee, Rebecca Wheeler Walston, Jen Murphy, Cyndi Mesmer, Peemo, Dr. Knorr, Dr. Walker, my former supervisor Vanessa, and my little sister, the more I realized: I could - as Miyamoto Musashi said – see the way broadly. And not just that. I began to believe my body was wise, trust my brilliance, and follow my nostalgic homesickness for what I never had. That longing was my sign: goodness was meant for me. That ganas, that hunger in the gut, is an internal compass pointing me toward what I am meant to have. And the same goes for you.

You deserve to feel safe. You deserve to experience belonging. You deserve querencia - a sanctuary where you feel safe. Whether it's when all the BIPOC folk sit together in the cafeteria, as Dr Beverly Daniel Tatum writes, "to get a pocket universe of reprieve from whiteness when we can let our hair down." It could be in finding a new job where who you are, not just what you can do, is appreciated.

When I couldn't find goodness or querencia in my location, my workplace, my place of worship, or even in my own body, my imagination stepped up to the plate. When my intellect couldn't talk me into hope, my imagination carried me forward through comic heroes, through visions of what could be, through the truth that none of us are alone in this fight, and that I have superpowers.

That is what I leave with you: the knowing, the naming, the remembering.

As my last gift to you in this book, as your neurodivergent and Black, Afro-Cuban author of choice… step into my querencia. My nibbling gave room for delight, goodness, faith, hope and love once more; Luke Cage, Miles Morales, and T'Challa.

Luke Cage

The First, the Few and the Many

🕐 You got to have thick skin, but even with thick skin, that doesn't mean you don't have tender insides. These insides of mine need a protector too. How does one get thick skin? A devotional called Streams in the Desert tells a story, on page thirty:

A noted scientist, observing that early sailors believed coral-building animals instinctively built up the great reefs of the Atoll Islands to protect themselves in the inner waterway, has disproved this belief. He has shown these organisms can only live and thrive facing the open ocean, in the highly oxygenated foam of the combative waves. It is commonly thought that a protected and easy life is the best way to live. Yet, the lives of all the noblest and strongest people prove exactly the opposite - that endurance of hardship is the making of the person. It is this factor that distinguishes between merely existing and living a vigorous life. Hardship builds character. (Streams in the Desert by L.B. Cowman, pages 30-31) 1

Skin like that of Josiah Henson and Don Quixote was not merely acquired but forged. My thick skin was forged by words that wounded me - "You sound white," "You're not Cuban, you can't even speak Spanish," "You're not Black." It was forged by the betrayal of white friends we couldn't keep, by the cruelty of institutions that call me "difficult" and facilitate our burnout, by the financial hardship that comes with authenticity, by the cost of refusing to be a "good" token - the lack of advancement, the higher cost of therapeutic care, the exhaustion of always proving our worth.

All these things, since childhood, didn't just create thick skin; they tempered it like the very heat that forged Luke Cage's impenetrable skin - the same experiment that killed every other imprisoned Black body and soul before him who didn't survive the test.

The First, the Few and the Many

Because if you plan to do what James Baldwin says - "You have to decide who you are and force the world to deal with you, not with its idea of you" - that, my friends, takes thick skin.

Luke Cage's strength did not only live in his skin and muscle fibers, although he is one of the few Marvel heroes who can go toe to toe with the Hulk, but within his genius. Strength and greatness do not spring from life's sunny side. Heroes must be more than driftwood floating on wave-less tides, tides of school-to-prison pipelines. They have to be able to think for themselves with cleverness and intelligence and see not just the villain in front of them, but the villain in the systems that create more villains, ones who had no other choice than to become the bad guy to change things.

Black Panther

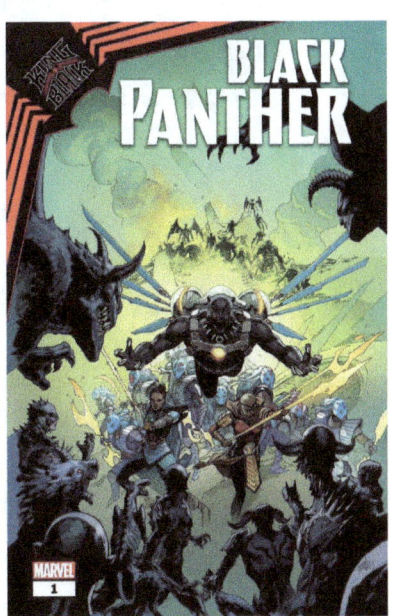

Despite the utopian wealth of Wakanda, it is not without its problems. Hardship, terrorism, perpetual threats of British imperialism and untempered Western capitalism - Wakanda faces external forces that threaten to dismantle it, in addition to the internal ones that come with governance. Death and loss, betrayal and grief - Wakandan royalty is not immune. The weight of political and economic governance, coupled with the spirituality of an entire kingdom, rests on the Black Panther's shoulders, and still, he finds the strength to fight beyond the borders.

Yet is it not the weights that keep the grandfather clock running? Like sailors who, rather than being consumed by a strong headwind, use it to reach safe harbor, so too does Black Panther teach me the perseverance of my ancestors. More than that, he reminds me of the nobility I come from - the nobility to resist becoming our enemies, which is the highest form of retribution. That is how we beat the work of trauma and the quiet violence of tokenism.

The First, the Few and the Many

When Black Panther fights beyond the borders of his home, a beautiful lesson I came to see, he was not alone if he didn't want to be. In the image above, we see Storm. Like her, he had allies he could call from beyond his nation and tribe. So can we. So, have I.

Miles Morales

Ever notice how supervillains are always trying to change things, while "heroes" are always trying to keep them the same? That's what I love about Miles Morales - he isn't clinging to the status quo. Unlike Miguel O'Hara, who fights to keep things exactly as they are to the point where people question if he's really Spider-Man at all.

Going against the grain is the magic of Miles Morales, as much as that of Captain America in Civil War. Doing what's right is often the least popular choice. It is the very thing that made Little Richard say;

The First, the Few and the Many

Quixotry and the Fight Against Giants

Quixotry—the noble pursuit of an unattainable goal. Because sometimes, success doesn't lie in the victory but in the valor-filled striving. Like the old German man who stood alone against Loki's schemes.

Like the Dora Milaje surrounded by their countrymen who are captivated by a tyrant.

You're not alone

The First, the Few and the Many

Like the three warriors standing against Thanos, the mad Titan in Endgame

Channeling

I once heard it said that when you need to do something, you channel the person you know who is good at that thing.

When I needed confidence in toxic workplaces, when I felt disposable, I channeled my older brother and his resilience in the face of institutionalization and tokenism. When I needed resourcefulness and community, I channeled Miles Morales. When I felt like turning cruel in the face of BIPOC competition, sabotage, and betrayal, I channeled T'Challa. When I felt vulnerable - like the institution was getting under my skin enough to bring the nigga out of me - I put on the thick-skinned brilliance of Luke Cage. He was even helpful in the face of opportunistic Sambos and

The First, the Few and the Many

Mammies when I needed super strength as much as genius. When I had to advocate in secret for myself and other staff of color, I channeled Isaiah Bradley. When I felt like I was the only one standing against an entire system, I planted my feet like the roots of a tree and channeled Captain America, whispering, "No, you move."

🌱 Getting Involved

Who have you channeled when you needed confidence? Who do you channel when you need self-love? Who knocks on the door of your heart, memory, or imagination to volunteer as tribute? Whose face comes up even now? Where is your breath? Take some time to NAME THEM, then write a note to honor them.

On Your Left

Remember this scene:

The fight was just as, if not more, important than the guarantee of victory.
One pyrrhic final stand.

The Final Stand

That is what Miguel de Cervantes gave the world in Man of La Mancha, what Don Quixote, like Luke Cage, Miles Morales (I mean Spider-Man), and even Captain America, represents.

Not just a character. An idea.

The First, the Few and the Many

The old war veteran standing alone against a god, refusing to bow to a cruel world.

Be quixotic. Be quixotic in your hope. Be quixotic in your fierce self-love and boundaries. Be quixotic in your belief that your experience with these "windmills" is your expertise. The more of us that become quixotic, the more of us will hear that famous "On your left" - not just whispered into Captain America's ear when he resolved himself to one last quixotic stand against Thanos and his galactic army.

The First, the Few and the Many

The more of us that become quixotic, the more we can have moments like in this image above.
The truth of being quixotic is that none of us are truly alone, like Cap hearing the voice of the friend he lost in war.

As long as a few - or even one - stand against you, can your enemies ever truly claim victory?

All of these characters became my querencia - my sanctuary in my imagination where I felt safe and hopeful. The daydream of these characters and what they stood for, however, didn't shield me from the harsh realities of racism within institutions, and I'm fairly confident that goes for you too, dear reader.

The First, the Few and the Many

Your body is saying, "On your left."
Your ancestors are saying, "On your left."
Your anger is saying, "On your left."

🌱 Getting involved: What/who else do you hear saying, "On your left?"

_____

_____

_____

_____

_____

_____

James Baldwin once said: *"A day will come when you trust you more than you do now. You will trust me more than you do now. We can trust each other. I do believe, I really do believe in the New Jerusalem. I really do believe that we can all become better than we are, I know we can. But the price is enormous, and people are not yet willing to pay."*

The First, the Few and the Many

The great comedian Bernie Mac

The First, the Few and the Many

Afterword

From Ones Who Witnessed Me First

Note: This afterword is written from the voice(s) of a collective witness—those who have seen Thornhill's journey, known its weight, and believed in its telling. It honors the countless co-laborers, proofreaders, friends, and readers whose lives echo in these pages.

"For those of us who live at the shoreline
standing upon the constant edges of **decision**
crucial **and** *alone*
for those of us who cannot indulge
the passing **dreams** *of choice*
who love in doorways coming and going
in the hours between dawns
looking inward and outward
at once before and after
seeking a now that can breed
futures…"
—Audre Lorde, A Litany for Survival

What began as a moment became a mirror.
What became a mirror became a map.

The First, The Few, The Only is not just a book.
It is cartography.

It charts the terrain that so many of us have walked in silence: the quiet violence of tokenism, performative inclusion, erasure, racialized promotions, backstabbing sambos, the precariousness of white women, code-switching, and the disorientation of being "the only" in rooms that were never meant for our wholeness. He writes like someone who has felt the water rise and chose not to drown.

You're not alone

The First, the Few and the Many

He writes for us.

And then there's Don Quixote.

There's something in the DNA of this book that is inherently quixotic—not in foolishness, but in the brave insistence on dreaming a better world. Thornhill, like Cervantes before him, defies the logic of his time by imagining a different one. Don Quixote dreamed of knighthood in a cynical age. Thornhill dreams of dignity in a world addicted to exploitation. He steps into the armor of language not to escape reality, but to reshape it.

What Cervantes did in the 17th century, Thornhill is doing now. With courage. With clarity. With the kind of imagination that could only come from someone who has survived systems of erasure and still insists on speaking.

This book is for those who are tired of surviving.
This book is for those who are told they are too much, too angry, too sensitive, too Black, too Brown, too neurodivergent, not Black enough.
This book is for those who have been asked to explain themselves, diminish themselves, justify their presence, or decorate the diversity brochure without a seat at the table.
This book is for those who tried to belong, but now know better.
This book is for those who still believe in the power of story, even if their own has never been told.

In these pages, Thornhill does what all great visionaries do: he names the pain without letting it be the end of the story. He offers breath. Belonging. Inheritance. Rage. Rupture. Grief. He maps what many have lived, and few have had language to express.
He does not offer a neat resolution.
He offers a mirror—and, if you're willing to look, a key.

To what?
Decisions and Dreams.

This book is not an escape.
It is a skeleton key.
It is also, impossibly, a prayer.

The First, the Few and the Many

To stand at the shoreline and feel the waves crash is one thing.
To find someone standing next to you, ten toes down, eyes closed, chest open,
smiling as if to say, we will do this together—that is what this book is.

So, breathe.
Let yourself be seen.
And dream an impossible dream

One you cannot wait
To wake up to.

🌱 Selah 🌱

Benediction

To the first, the few and the ones to come.
To the young, fiery spirits darkening the horizon of PWI's
—Red, Yellow, Black, and Brown—
who step into the world full of faith, hope & love, unaware of how much those virtues will be tested.

For those who still believe windmill farmers will, one day, see the giants too.

To those who have already learned the cost of being the only one— the lone chocolate chip in a plain cookie, eager to call itself 'diverse'—so long as the flavor stays the same.

Thornhill wrote for those who came before him, who crawled so he could run, and for those who will be asked, in time, to take his place and, we pray, fly.

This is your invitation—nay, your instruction—to take your story seriously enough to tell the truth. Then live like it matters. May our ceiling be your fertile ground. May the seeds of our ancestors' labor bloom wild and uncontained, stretching toward a sun that has always belonged to our sun-kissed bodies. And for those who have forgotten how to tend to their own gardens—who have spent too long toiling in fields not their own—may this book be your permission to drop the master's tools and tend to your own house.

The First, the Few and the Many

To the white-bodied reader:
What will you do with what you see?
Will you hold space to notice what arises —in your chest, your throat, your gut— and self-regulate wherever race stirs you biologically or emotionally, so that the FFO around you don't have to shrink, shift, or soothe on your behalf?

What are your decisions and dreams?

_____

_____

_____

_____

_____

_____

_____

_____

_____

_____

_____

_____

The First, the Few and the Many

Acknowledgements

"Miguel de Cervantes" was created
by Paula Modersohn-Becker

Dear venerable knight, Don Quixote,

You, mad knight of windmills and impossible dreams, have been my silent teacher, my patient companion, my mirror held up to a world that calls itself real but often lacks truth. They laughed at you, mocked your rusted armor, dismissed your visions as the delirium of a man unmoored from reason. But I have walked long enough through this world to know that reason is often just another name for resignation. I, like you, refuse to resign.

You taught me that to be quixotic is not to be foolish but to be free - to see beyond the edges of what is into the wide, unwritten space of what could be. You taught me to stare down giants even when others swore, they were just windmills, to charge headlong into the absurd because sometimes absurdity is just the mask that fear wears when it does not want to be seen or changed. You gave me permission to love this world even when it has been unkind, to believe in goodness even when it is difficult, to keep my heart soft when everything around me insists I harden.

Thank you for your unflinching idealism, for your wild and aliferous spirit, for teaching me that to hope, to fight, to dream, is not naivety but necessity. You

You're not alone

The First, the Few and the Many

showed me that, even in a world content to shuffle along the well-worn path of practicality, there must be those who chase the horizon, who carry a light no darkness can extinguish. If that makes us mad, so be it. I would rather be mad with faith than sane with despair.

Yours in impossible dreams,

Michael

What would you write to Don Quixote?

_____

_____

_____

_____

_____

The First, the Few and the Many

Dear Josiah Henson,

You, who carried freedom in your bones long before the world would let your feet touch it, have been my silent guide, my unwavering proof that leaving is not just an escape - it is an act of creation. They would have us believe that endurance is the only virtue, that staying put, swallowing our anger, breathing in the asbestos of tokenism and calling it air, is the price of admission to a world never meant for us. You taught me different. You taught me that I am allowed to leave. That sometimes, leaving is the holiest thing a body can do.

You left with a sick baby on your back, not just for yourself but for the generations who would follow, for the ones who hadn't yet learned that survival could be something more than enduring. You taught me that my "no" does not have to be spoken - it can be carried out in my absence. That my refusal to stay is its own kind of resistance. Its own kindness. That giving up on a burning house is not failure but wisdom. That wisdom, when held with sacred anger, does not have to harden into bitterness - it can soften into something life-giving. Into creation. Into industry. Into this very book.

I could have never written this book while still surviving on the plantation. I would have never been able to take all this love, this faith, this hope I once poured into a world that refused to hold it, and instead, pour it back into myself. You, a man of industry, showed me that faith in the world is only as good as the faith I have in my own hands, my own mind, my own ability to build. And so, I build. Not just for myself but for those who come after.

No matter how many white bodied fearmongers twist your name into a wound, I see you. Who you are what you have done - it speaks for itself. And because of you, so do I.

In freedom,

Michael

The First, the Few and the Many

To the Maroons of the Borderlands,

I bow my head to you - not in submission, but in deep and abiding reverence. You, who refused the lie that the only choices were the plantation or the horizon. You, who slipped into the wild and remade the world with your own hands. You, who understood that survival was not merely a thing of the body but of the spirit, the mind, the will.

You have taught me that violence does not always come with chains and lashes - it comes with contracts, with handshakes, reduced funding, with smiles that mean to tame you, to bind you, to keep you beholden to a world that will never see you as its own. Sometimes it is best that your enemy fears you. That your presence, your silence, your very breath unsettles them. Because, as the comic book hero Black Panther once said, "...a king is not feared for his power, but his mystique. What stills the hands of the enemies of Wakanda is not its might but what the king might do with it." That they do not know your true might, only that you might use it. A free person - a truly free person - holds a kind of might that no plantation can contain, no horizon can swallow.

You have given me the gift of boundaries, of knowing that resistance is not always a war cry but sometimes a whisper, a step taken into the shadows, a refusal to be seen until I choose to be seen. That hope is not some far-off dream but a reality I can carve into the landscape of my own oppression. In your honor, I will keep carving.

Teach me to honor you. Teach me to move in the way you moved, to build in the way you built, to make space for others as you did - not in the halls of power, but in the places where power does not dare go. I pray that those who hold this book in their hands will see you as I do - not as ghosts of the past, but as an excavated treasure, gleaming, undiminished, ready to change the world once more.

With all the reverence my spirit can hold,

Michael

The First, the Few and the Many

To Stan Lee and Jack Kirby,

First, let me say your names with reverence. Let me call them into the wind and let it carry, let it be heard in the halls of memory where giants, anti-heroes, and anti-villains still roam. You, teller of stories, builder of worlds, architects of something greater than mere fantasy - you imagined heroes, and in doing so, you gave us the space to imagine ourselves as more than what this world said we could be.

Luke Cage. A man with a genius intellect and unbreakable skin in a world designed to break Black bodies. You gave me a blueprint for survival - not just survival from bullets and fists, but from the brutality of systems, institutions, and expectations that were never meant to hold me, only to contain me and shrink my imagination. You showed me that thick skin is more than a defense; it is power. Power against police brutality. Power against the quiet, cutting violence of predominantly white academic spaces. Power against the plantation politics of windmill farms and corporate fields where they'd rather see me as a showpiece than a free man. Thick skin is what lets me keep standing when the world keeps swinging.

Miles Morales. Afro-Latino and Spider-Man, as much Spider-Man as Peter Parker - never lesser, never a shadow, never an afterthought. You let a boy like me see himself swing between buildings, stretch between worlds, move through the weight of expectations and still choose his own way. "Naw, I'ma do my own thing." That's what Miles said. That's what you wrote into his bones, and that's what I have learned to do. To take what is given, break the mold, and build something new. Miles taught me that my Brownness, my Blackness, my identity as an Afro-Cubano man was never an asterisk - it is a superpower. For that, I owe you.

There is Wakanda. There is T'Challa. There is Black Panther. Dignity. Power. Glory. A sovereignty of spirit untouched by colonizers' hands, unshaken by white delusion. A hero who did not need white validation because he came from a lineage that knew itself, a history that did not begin with chains. But even with his nobility, he never turned his eyes from the wickedness of the world - the world that whiteness built, the world that whiteness seeks to control. Like Baldwin said, "We have to know white people better than they ever have to know us." Black Panther embodied that wisdom. He knew his enemies better than they knew themselves, and that is the wisdom of kings.

The First, the Few and the Many

In the middle of the Civil Rights Movement in July 1966, Stan Lee and Jack Kirby gave us this character who first showed up in the Fantastic Four comic, the same four all-white super team who whooped a planet-eating goon named Galactus and even beat the indomitable Dr. Doom. In that first appearance, you gave us Black

Panther who popped up and whooped the Fantastic Four's asses, just to see if he could do it. You gave Black Panther vibranium suits as another allegory to thick skin, the strongest, most valuable and best metal in all of Marvel. You placed it in the hands of Black people in the midst of a country that was taking everything from Black people in the sixties.

Jack Kirby, you threatened to leave your desk at Marvel, go downstairs, and fight another white man who was objecting to the existence of T'Challa. Thank you for standing on business.

Stan and Jack, your courage and imagination gave me room to dream. It gave me a place to belong. It gave me heroes when the world gave me warnings. For that, I thank you. I miss you. I pray that I have done your characters justice in this book, that I have honored the echoes of what you created.

Excelsior!

Michael

🌱 Getting Involved: https://bit.ly/BlackSuperheros

What would you say to these men?

_____

_____

The First, the Few and the Many

Dear Dr. Lee,

Man, where do I even begin? I just got to say, you've been my ride-or-die, my brother from another mother, my partner-in-crime through it all. From the jump, you've had my back, no questions asked. From when this book was just a bunch of scattered ideas and random words like "sardoodledom," to you reading a whole prologue & opening chapters right before I put it in my book proposal to potential publishers. You were there, reading it all, helping me shape those fragments into something real. You saw the potential in the musings of a recovering DEI professional, and your belief in me pushed me to keep going. Without you, those early thoughts might've just stayed in my head. Those racial traumas may have just stayed in my body. With you, they turned into something that actually turned into a book.

I often think about all the prayers my biological mom must've said for me before she passed. I also think of the thousands of prayers my adopted mom prayed over me. I'm sure one of the clearest answers to all those prayers is you, brobro. How else could I explain the blessing of your friendship? From surviving Slippery Rock, to starting a church together, to practically naming our kids the same thing, you've been my witness and my brother through it all. You stood by me through the religious traumas, the ups-and-downs, and all the crazy stuff life threw my way.

Although I love my brothers, you've been the brother I never had, and for that, I thank God for you. I wouldn't be the man I am today withoutcha. Your support, your wisdom, your unwavering honesty have shaped me in ways I can barely put into words.

To more stories of adventure, bigger muscles, and being the fathers we always wanted as kids. Thank you, from the bottom of my heart, for being my best friend in the whole world. Like you said, "We don't have to dream small when we have a big God." Here's to living our dreams!

Shockadoo,

The First, the Few and the Many

Who is your Mychael Lee? Take a moment to write a letter to them:

_____

_____

_____

_____

_____

_____

_____

_____

_____

You're not alone

The First, the Few and the Many

Dear Brother Malcolm,

I sit down to write to you, not with pen and paper, but with the weight of gratitude that presses heavy on my heart. You, who walked the path of fire and truth, who faced the cold, unyielding walls of an all-white high school and emerged not just a survivor, but a conqueror. You, who stood tall, your intellect sharper than the sharpest blade in that all-white school, yet were told by the very man, a school principal, who should have been your ally, that your brilliance would only ever amount to the scrub of a dish or the sweep of a floor.

That moment, that cruel, soul-crushing moment, set you on a path that would shake the foundations of this world. You took your brilliance, your unyielding spirit, and applied it to the liberation of Black and Brown bodies, not just white ones. You spoke truths that burned like fire in the hearts of those who heard you, truths that still echo today, still relevant, still necessary.

And I, I must apologize. For the ways we, like Josiah Henson, looked at you through the lies of the white imagination. We saw you not as you were, but through the distorted lens of those who feared your power, your truth. We failed to see the fullness of your brilliance, the depth of your love for our people.

But you, you saw me. You saw the brilliance in me that I could not yet see in myself. You spoke words that cut through the fog of doubt and fear, words that illuminated the path before me. And for that, I thank you. I thank you for helping me see my own light, for showing me that my brilliance is not just a possibility, but a birthright.

So, Brother Malcolm, I write to you not just with words, but with the deepest gratitude. Thank you for corroborating my reality, for speaking truths that still resonate today, in a land that hasn't changed all that much. And thank you, most of all, for helping me see my own brilliance, regardless of the white gaze.

Assalamualaikum,

Michael

The First, the Few and the Many

Dear Reverend Dr. King,

I don't know if we'll ever be able to redeem the bones of the burning house you feared you led us into. Full stop.

The fire has spread, licking at the foundation, curling around the ankles of promises that once felt within reach. I fear that what you and Brother Malcolm dreamed of may be a dream too far gone, slipping through our hands like water, like something we almost had but never truly held.

You fought for our freedom, and we turned it into a seat at their table - just one, maybe two, while the rest of us stayed outside, faces pressed against the glass, waiting for our turn. We let tokenism devour the movement, let the illusion of progress pacify us, let the dream become a whisper instead of a roar. This was not the work you gave your life for. (I'm not a rapper)

Dr. King, did you know? Did you see it coming - the way they would twist your dream into a corporate slogan, pacify your revolution into a sanitized speech for school children, drown out your radical call with the lull of "progress?" Did you know that they would take your life and then use your name to justify everything you stood against?

And yet, even as I wrestle with doubt, even as I wonder if we've wandered too far from the dream, I need to know - was it worth it? Did the fight ever feel like it was slipping through your hands the way it does through mine? Or did you always believe that love, real love, would still win?

I am sorry, Dr. King, for the regret you carried in your final days. For the way your own government plotted your end while you pressed forward anyway, weary but unbroken. I am sorry that we have yet to finish what you started, that the road you paved is now cracked beneath the weight of our exhaustion.

And yet - despite my grief, despite my doubt - I am still thankful. Thankful for the way you loved us enough to believe in something greater. Just like Don Quixote. Thankful for the way you fought for a kingdom that was never of this world.

The First, the Few and the Many

I feel the need to apologize because, if I'm being honest, I don't know if this is worth it anymore. I don't know if we are still on the path toward the dream, or if we have wandered too far to find our way back.

Lord, help us in our unbelief. And Dr. King, if you can hear me from beyond the veil - I join you in these words to the Father, "Thy will be done, on earth as it is in heaven."

With reverence,

Michael (John 1:5)

https://bit.ly/WeNeedYouToo

The First, the Few and the Many

Hey Michael (Me),

Thank you.

For never quitting. For doing all this hard work. For always being a giver. For choosing to not become the villain you could have become. For just being you at all times. For never bowing to the weight of small expectations, for refusing to shrink in the face of systems that were never built to hold the fullness of who you are. Thank you for fighting the windmills and the plantations - both the ones outside and the ones that tried to take root inside you - just to carve out a space where your authenticity could breathe, where it could stretch out its arms and take up room like it was always meant to. And thank you for guarding that authenticity like the sacred jewel it is, knowing that the world will always try to dull its shine, to shape it into something easier to swallow. But you never let it.

Thank you for seeing your neurodivergence not as a burden but as a force - an unshackled current that moves in its own rhythm, a perspective that sees around corners, a brilliance that refuses to walk in straight lines. You could have spent your life cursing the difficulty, but instead, you made it a tool, a weapon, a light. You leaned into it, harnessed it, turned it into something unstoppable.

Thank you for your ganas - that fire in the belly, that relentless drive that keeps pushing even when everything in you is tired. And thank you for your orenda - that unseen but undeniable power that moves the world around you, the spirit-force that bends reality toward your will, that makes a way where there is none.

You have walked through fire and come out gleaming. You have sat in rooms where your presence was unexpected, uninvited, and still, you rooted yourself like an ancient tree, and said NO, you move. Refusing to be anything other than who you were always meant to be… you have learned, unlearned, fought, healed, and kept going. And for all of that, I thank you.

No pare, sigue sigue. Keep shining. Keep being you.

With love,
With excelsior,
With power,

The First, the Few and the Many

Michael

🌱 Getting Involved: https://bit.ly/4nnkJgj

What kind of letter would you write to yourself?

_____

_____

_____

_____

_____

_____

_____

The First, the Few and the Many

Mijo y Mija,

Before you even took your first breath, you carried the best parts of "me "- just like my mother once told me when I was still in her womb. She said I had the finest pieces of her and of my biological father, and now, I see that truth shining in both of you.

Wherever you go in this world, know that you belong. You don't have to change, shrink, or prove a thing to anyone. Like Miles's mom told him in Across the Spider-Verse, you are exactly who you are meant to be, and that is enough.

And if ever there comes a day when I am not beside you, know that I am never far. When you see the nobility of T'Challa and the mystique of Black Panther, there I am. When you see Luke Cage standing unbreakable, not just in body but in mind, you've found me. When Miles Morales refuses to let the world decide who he can be, Daddy is winking at you. If you ever feel like an Uncle Tom - beaming with vawzen, I'm on your left. And when you see Don Quixotes charging headfirst at windmills - ones that the world will one day see as giants - you'll know that Daddy never backed down either.

You are both made of fire and light, strength and grace. I love you with the heat and vibrancy of a thousand suns. And no matter what, you have each other. Be there for one another - no matter the distance. Be the Reed Richards to each other's T'Challa, minds sharp and hearts unwavering.

And when my time here is done, I will be waiting for you just over the rainbow, watching, longing, and ready to hold you again. Until then, go have adventures. Love deeply. Get knocked down six times and rise seven. Live boldly and gather stories - good ones, wild ones, stories worth telling me when we meet again.

Nos vemos mis milagros,

Daddy ⏲ https://spoti.fi/445MiBV

The First, the Few and the Many

Dear Lord,

Who am I that You should think of me? That You should see me, hold me, call me by name? I stand in awe.

These systems - built on the backs of the forgotten, thriving on the labor of the unseen - I know their wickedness. I see the weight of their injustice. So do You. I do not carry the burden of judgment; You do. I do not seek vengeance; that belongs to You. From Esther's courage to Jesus' righteous fury, you have always seen. Your Son did not sit silently - He overturned the tables of those who preyed on the faithful, who twisted worship into profit. You do not stand for it, so I stand with You.

There are those who navigate these systems without You. I will not.

You are exactly who You say You are. When I asked for the discipline to write this book, to finish this part of the trilogy, You didn't just give me strength - you gave me an obsession, a fire in my bones that would not let me rest.

You heard me. You answered. Nothing I have, nothing I do, nothing I accomplish is by my hand alone. It is You. It has always been You.

You let Stan Lee do what he did before I came to be. You let Dr. Lee and I meet at Slippery Rock. You had your hand on Malcolm and Martin. You never abandoned your son, Josiah Henson, on that plantation, and strengthened him for that six-hundred-mile track north, beyond the borders of this crooked nation.

You are the God of Hagar, the God of Rahab, the God of Joseph, the God of Ruth, the God of Daniel, the God of Timothy, the God of Esther - the God of the tokens, the least of these, the ones who walk into rooms never meant for them. You go before us. You don't abandon your remnant and your people. Maranatha.

In Jesus' name,

Michael

The First, the Few and the Many

Appendix A

WHITE EYEZ ONLY

Password: WeHaveBlackFriends

"When you debate a person about something that affects them more than it affects you, remember that it will take a much greater emotional toll on them than on you. For you it may feel like an academic exercise. For them, it feels like revealing their pain only to have you dismiss their experience and sometimes their humanity. The fact that you remain more calm under these circumstances is a consequence of your privilege, not increased objectivity on your part. Stay humble."
-Sarah Maddox

Let's begin this with getting involved. As a symbolic gesture of where to begin, just listen and notice what comes up for you;

🧭 Side Quest What sounded familiar? Do any memories come up for you? Any faces float to the surface? Any friends, mirrors, family, or place of worship or workplace? Name it to tame it:

_____

_____

What Do I Do?

Stop asking what to do - that comes second. Instead, begin with this: What do I need to see? BIPOC's journey is what we/I need to name and tend to. We have differing starting points on our collective healing journeys. Let me tell you a story.

The First, the Few and the Many

There was a campus minister - a white woman I trusted. I helped her start a Bible study. I believed we were building something good, even a lifelong friendship. But trust is a fragile thing when it rests on uneven ground.

She once told me about her first Black roommate in college. How, when she visited her roommate's home, she realized that nearly most of her roommate's personality was hidden at school. This was a proudly progressive Christian college, a school that prided itself on being liberal, inclusive, welcoming. And yet, her roommate knew — instinctively - that it wasn't safe to bring her full self. The code-switching, the careful shrinking of identity, the way she had to dull her edges just to belong.

And this white woman - this minister - realized what it cost not just her roommate, but herself and the entire campus. What was lost when Blackness had to be edited out in real-time. But even as she saw, she still could not see.

Because this same woman who had glimpsed the violence of assimilation was the one who tried to set me up with the only other Black woman on staff, as if our shared Blackness was enough to spark love. As if we were interchangeable. This same woman handed me over on a silver platter to Charles Muntz and Stinky, men looking for a rising Black charismatic star they could groom before he became too powerful.

This same woman - after I fought to get her on a diversity council in a company, after I sat there in my own vulnerability, fresh in my grief from losing my father, raw in my honesty about what it meant to be Black in that leadership team and in that ministry - she called me manipulative and conniving for speaking my truth.

That was the last thing I ever let her say to me.

Let me tell you about that pain. It felt like relational trauma that I never got away from but kept coming back for more. It forever fractured my trust in white women and helped me finally realize how white progressives can be the most dangerous. They will smile as they sharpen the knife. They will swear they love you as they cut you down. Maybe I still have some healing to do.

And this is why this book is not written for white people. Because the first, the few and the only, have healing to do.

The First, the Few and the Many

What This Book Is

"When Black spaces are intentionally created or maintained, I've noticed that some white people complain - ironically - about feeling "excluded" when what they actually mean is decentered."
-Tracey Micahe'l Lewis-Giggetts

This book is my attempt at telling the history of race through the lives and experiences of the first, the few, and the only.

This is the story of the token BIPOC bodies in your elementary schools, your Sunday schools, your school buses, your offices, your pews, your favorite bars and country clubs. This is your history, but you have never been forced to see it. Slowed down enough to feel its weighted-ness. If this book is to hold space for your tokenized BIPOC friend to name and notice what has happened to them, then this section is for you, dear white bodied reader, to acknowledge that you did not get out unscathed. Your very body did not get out from a racist white supremacist-soaked ancestral lineage of conditioned whiteness unscathed.

🌱 Getting Involved with your history:
Can you name five anti-racist white people in North American history?

_____

_____

_____

_____

_____

If you cannot... Please take a moment to reflect on what that tells you.

_____

The First, the Few and the Many

As Resmaa Menakem says, "Where's your breath?"

Now if you don't even know your history, assuming you strike yourself as anti-racist, then take a moment and do some research. And until you can add to this list below, I advise you do not continue reading until you do. I'll even give you the first one:

1. 🌱 Joana Trumpauer Mulholland
2. 🌱 Carl Braden   Carl Braden

3. _____

4. _____

5. _____

6. _____

7. _____

 ⏱ Side Quest If you want to start, I highly recommend Tim Wise's account of white history:
(1) White Like Me: Race, Racism & White Privilege &
(2) Tim Wise Playlist

The Difference Between Feeling Excluded and Being Decentered

I once met a white woman at a Christian conference. She had adopted a Black daughter. Her husband was white. They had biological children together, and one day, while taking a family photo in their small, white town, something happened.

A car slowed down as it passed them. The window rolled down. A Black woman leaned her head out.

And the white mother panicked.

380
You're not alone

The First, the Few and the Many

Before the driver of the car could even speak, her body flooded with fear. Full on flight response. She began calculating - how could she gather her children and run? Will her husband intercept this Black lady so she can save her kids from whatever verbal assault or worse may come from this Black driver?

And then, the Black woman in the car smiled and said, "What a beautiful family. God bless y'all."

The white mother was left staring, rattled by what had just happened inside her own body.

Because in her mind, she loved her Black daughter. She believed herself to be a good person. She believed she had no hate in her heart. But in her body, racism had already written the script. Her Black daughter is in her lap, who will one day grow into adulthood like the Black woman in the car. She realized that the way her body reacted to the driver, is the same way white bodies will react to her daughter.

This is what white people have to confront. Not just racism out there, but racism within. Not just what's wrong with the system, but what's wrong within themselves.

The Myth of Passive Anti-Racism

White people often act like racism is a surprise, something distant from them. But the truth is, racism is as close as their own reflexes.

You cannot be passively anti-racist.

The First, the Few and the Many

Because the system is already in motion. It does not need your active participation to do harm. It only needs your inaction. Dr. Beverly Daniel Tatum used to illustrate this with an airport metaphor. Think of a moving walkway at the airport. One person stands still. Other walks forward. But both are heading in the same direction. The one walking on the walkway is actively racist. The other is passively racist.

And at the end of that walkway is the same destination. So, if you are not actively disrupting the cycle - what options do you have left?

Shared Language:
A Lexicon for the White-Bodied Reader

Before we move forward, let's establish a shared language. If you are reading this as a white-bodied person, understand that you were not given the full picture. Your history lessons were censored, redacted, smoothed over to maintain a clean and comfortable narrative.

"Slavery is White American history, how Blacks survived is Black history." anonymous

If this were the 2014 sci-fi thriller The Giver, Black history would be Jeff Bridges' character—the keeper of memory, holding the unvarnished truth of the past. Meanwhile, you were raised under Meryl Streep's careful instruction, taught a sanitized version of history, and now you get to decide: Will you be Jonas, the one who chooses to see?

For One Piece fans, Black history is what really happened in Alabasta and Dressrosa. What you were taught is the World Government's version of events—a cover-up. The real history exists in the banned books, the erased stories, the knowledge hidden from your school's curriculum. The secrets of Ohara.

Your work—if you're serious—requires supplementing your malnourished sense of history. Because there is no "white history" without Black history. ⊘ Start here:

382
You're not alone

The First, the Few and the Many

Stereotypes

Stereotypes are narratives—reductive, oversimplified, and often false—that define groups of people, usually in ways that serve the dominant power structure.

They are most deeply held by those who have the least real interaction with the people they stereotype. When you don't know someone personally, you rely on inherited assumptions, passed down through history and reinforced by culture, media, and fear. Stereotypes don't just hurt the people being stereotyped; they also imprison the minds of those who believe them.

⏱Breaking Down Stereotypes

Bias

Bias is the internalized preference for or against a group based on cultural conditioning. It's not about whether you are a "good person" or not—it's about what you've been taught to believe without questioning. Bias is automatic. It operates in the background, influencing decisions, judgments, and behaviors in ways you don't even realize. The question is not if you have bias, but which biases you have, and what you're doing to unlearn them.

Prejudice

Prejudice is the judgment or assumption you make about someone before knowing them. It's often based on stereotypes and bias. Unlike bias (which can be unconscious), prejudice is more active. It's when you assign meaning, motive, or worth to someone based purely on their racial, ethnic, or cultural background.

Discrimination

Discrimination is what happens when bias and prejudice turn into action. It's when people in power—whether a hiring manager, a teacher, a police officer, a judge—act on racial bias in a way that denies opportunities, access, or rights.

The First, the Few and the Many

Racism

Racism is not just personal prejudice. It's a system—a structure that advantages one racial group (white people) at the expense of others. The simplest formula: Racism = Prejudice + Power

This means that even if a Black person dislikes white people, they do not have the systemic power to deny white people jobs, housing, education, or safety. But white people—whether intentionally or not—benefit from a system that disadvantages Black people.

Oppression

Oppression is the long-term, systemic control of a group by another group. It's maintained through laws, policies, cultural narratives, economic exclusion, and violence.

Oppression isn't just about the past—it is ongoing. It evolves, adapts. Slavery turned into convict leasing. Jim Crow turned into mass incarceration. Redlining turned into modern-day housing discrimination. And Oppression inevitably leads to…

Trauma

Trauma is the lasting psychological and emotional harm caused by oppressive systems, violence, and historical injustices. But here's the truth many don't want to admit: The agents of harm are also traumatized by the harm they cause. White bodies who inherit supremacy inherit its wounds, too.

Where have you known harm?
Where have you caused harm?

Then trauma can perpetuate stereotypes, which can cement biases, which can metastasize into prejudice. This without confronting it and healthy relationships with people you know the least, morphs into discrimination. This leads to

The First, the Few and the Many

oppression, which fosters more trauma. It's a loop.

Stereotypes: Historical, Intergenerational, and Shared Assumptions

Stereotypes don't just appear out of nowhere—they are passed down, reinforced over generations. A white child grows up hearing about "dangerous Black men" not because they've experienced harm, but because their parents, their schools, their media, their entire culture has told them to believe it.

These beliefs, rooted in historical trauma, shape policies, policing, hiring practices, and even the subconscious fear in an elevator when a Black man steps in. It's a cycle, dear reader. And unless you break it, you are part of it.

Self-Gaslighting

Self-gaslighting is when you start questioning your own experiences, memories, or observations because they challenge what you were taught to believe. It's when a white person begins to realize, wait—was everything I learned about history a lie? and then immediately thinks, no, that can't be true. That would mean…

It's when discomfort makes you shut down instead of lean in.
Your challenge is to sit with that discomfort. Stay with it. Don't rationalize it away. That discomfort is history knocking at your door, asking if you're ready to see the truth.

"As long as you don't know your history, you will be a prisoner of it."
James Baldwin's 1986 national press club speech - 🌱

"The wolf caught me in his jaws but when I cried out, others only said: I have seen the wolf many times and he has not bitten me." ⏱

The First, the Few and the Many

Do your own work

"As a white person, if you are listening only to other white people, it gives you permission to stay within the binary, not only reinforcing cognitive bias but white comfort. It keeps you from really feeling or sitting with yourself. This is why white people struggle to sit with emotions and often dismiss the emotions they learn along the journey."
-Myisha T. Hill, Heal Your Way Forward

As a primer: hear it from a white woman, for white women

🧭 Side Quests

Books:
- My Grandmother's Hands by Resmaa Menakem
- Why do all the Black Kids Sit Together In The Cafeteria? By Dr Beverly Daniel-Tatum
- The Minority Experience by Adrian Pei
- Austin Channing Brown's book entitled I'M STILL HERE
- The Fire Next Time by James Baldwin
- BEYOND COLORBLIND: by Sarah Shin
- White Awake by Daniel Hill
- Black Faces in White Places and Black Faces in High Places (Randall Pinkett)
- Working While Black (Michelle Johnson)
- The Black Ceiling (Kevin Woodson)
- Playing a New Game (Tammy Lewis Wilborn)

Film:
- I AM NOT YOUR NEGRO
- MASTER starring Regina Hall
- DECONSTRUCTING KAREN
- Marvel's Black Panther & Black Panther: Wakanda Forever
- TV show: The Other Black Girl

The First, the Few and the Many

The Burden of Remediation

A great woman I have the privilege of knowing, Rebecca Wheeler Walston, once spoke about white supremacy's grip on white bodies. She compared its removal to the painstaking process of asbestos remediation.
She said, "You must dispossess your identity and white body from the whiteness (asbestos) you have been fed your whole life."
This is the work of white bodies. But BIPOC bodies were also raised in that house.

And it is not our job to deal with the sickness in your lungs. It is our job to stop believing you when you tell us to stay - that the air is fine, that nothing is killing us. Because we are dying with you as you choke on white supremacy's demands on your bodies.

The moral injuries white bodies willfully commit - no matter how sincere, no matter how unintentional - against Black and Brown bodies in their orbit are endless in this country.

We have a common enemy. But we will never be able to fight it together as long as white bodies still allow their neighbors-friends-and-family to say, "There's no such thing as asbestos" at their dinner table. And racism is a smokescreen for economic oppression at the hands of white supremacy and the upper upper class. Look at history – 'Francis Bacon's Rebellion' is proof of the gameplan.

For centuries, middle-class and poor white Americans have been the foot soldiers of the very system that exploits them. They have been convinced, again and again, that Black and Brown people are the ones stealing their jobs, their women, their opportunities.

But until they realize that their own liberation is tied up with Black and Brown communities, until they understand that color blindness has never been and will never be the way forward, nothing will change.
Some white people have come to understand this:

- Tim Wise

The First, the Few and the Many

- Jane Elliott
- Daniel Warner
- Elizabeth Behrens with Be The Bridge
- Joan Trumpauer Mulholland

These are white ancestors and abolitionists who did the work, who broke away from whiteness without breaking their own humanity.
And here's the truth: There are more tools at your disposal than ever before.

Not niceness. Not perfectionism. Not white tears.
But REPS.

Challenges to Take On

1. Watch Regina Jackson and Saira Rao's documentary, Deconstructing Karen (Apple TV). Observe what real conversations about race and whiteness look like.
2. Take a fast from Fox News and CNN.
3. Acknowledge that you, too, have generational trauma.

If Black and Brown bodies have inherited the traumas of slavery and Jim Crow, why would white bodies believe they escaped unscathed?
Math ain't mathing.

We understand the trauma of being victims. But what about the trauma of being the descendants of perpetrators of racial violence, molestation, murder, torture, and the narrative of racial difference whites adopted in order to do all that stuff and be at church every Sunday?

The Cost of Knowing Where You Come From

<u>Aparigraha</u>- the art of letting go whatever is no longer serving you, art of non-attachment, when you attain something new - discard something old

There was a student I once worked with as a campus minister. He had spent his whole life wanting to be a cop. That was his dream. Then, one day, he decided to look for his biological father.

The First, the Few and the Many

His mother had always told him not to. Warned him not to.

But as he was preparing to meet the man, she finally told him the truth: "The only reason he is your father is because he raped me on our date."
That student's entire world collapsed.

I watched him unravel - watched him fall into depression, into a full-blown identity crisis in an explosion of tears. Because what do you do when you come face to face with the truth of where you come from?

Factoids to F A C E

- "Hard to Find Qualified Black Candidate" fallacy
    - BIPOC professionals are not unqualified candidates that businesses lower standards for. The reality is the opposite. White men are more often hired based on potential, while BIPOC candidates are required to prove competence at every level. "Diversity hire" is a slap in the face.
    Studies have shown that white men are promoted into leadership while BIPOC professionals remain overqualified and overlooked
- Resume Whitening
    - Ever wonder why so many BIPOC professionals in your workplace have white-sounding names? That's not an accident. Studies have confirmed that "whitened" résumés receive more interviews than those with ethnic-sounding names
- Making Things Cool

The Burden of Formation

A white pastor once asked me about this book.

The First, the Few and the Many

I was explaining my goal - to expose tokenism in white institutions - when she interrupted to tell me how much she had learned from having a Black college roommate. She spoke about how formative that experience was for her. How much it opened her eyes to race, to culture, to herself.

I listened. Then I asked her, "Do you realize that while you were being formed, your roommate may have been forced to shrink? That while you were having an epiphany, she was simply trying to survive?" Because that's what happens in these relationships. White people experience personal growth. Meanwhile, BIPOC bodies are burdened with teaching, translating, navigating - even in their own dorm rooms.

She was silent for a long time. Then she said, "I never thought about it that way." So, I ask you, reader - who are the people you've learned from?

Who are the names and faces of those you claim formed you?
Write them down.

And then ask yourself—how did they have to navigate you?

Getting involved: Apagripha exercise:
1. What are you taking away so far?
2. What are you leaving behind?

"Whites who are sincere should organize among themselves and figure out some strategy to break down prejudices that exist in white communities. They can function more intelligently & more effectively in the white community itself, and this has never been done"
-Malcolm X

There Is a Difference Between Knowing the Name of Something and Knowing It

"Every white person in this country. I don't care what he says, or she says, knows one thing. They may not know, how they put it, what I want but they know one thing… they would not like to be Black here. If they know that, they know everything they need to know and whatever else they say is a lie. …The American ideal of progress is how fast I can become white…."
-James Baldwin

390
You're not alone

The First, the Few and the Many

You just read a book about naming.

About giving language to what Black and Brown bodies have always known but were never allowed to name. But know this - even if a BIPOC body never reads this book, even if they never learn these terms, their bodies will still know more than your brain ever will.

They have lived it.

So, if you walk away from this with anything, let it be this: we all have different starting points when it comes to this healing thing. If that's the path we keep choosing. Any haughtiness, an inevitable byproduct of oppression, will corrupt how you see yourself because how you think of those as lesser, has already (de)formed your view of yourself.

Be allergic to haughtiness.
Because knowing the name of a thing is not the same as knowing it. Richard Feyman recounts his father teaching him this lesson:

Aparigraha exercise:
1. What are you taking away so far?
2. What are you leaving behind?

Brother Malcom

391
You're not alone

The First, the Few and the Many

Appendix B

Blight or Blessing

I have several brief points in this section.
Abandonment, Sacrifice, Loss, Terror, and one musing on allyship.

Abandonment

The degree to which you are race-aversive, unwilling to sit with the discomfort of racism and all the debris that comes with it, is the degree to which you will abandon your Black and Brown partner. You leave them to hold all the war and racial wreckage of the world in their body—alone. That abandonment catches up. It weighs down the relationship, wears on the bond, and erodes attachment.

Chloe's Story

I knew this couple once. Married for eight years at the point of this story. Chloe, a Black woman, and her husband, a blue-eyed white man. They were tender with each other, sweet in the way that made people believe in love. But love, as Chloe learned, can be a fragile thing when stretched across the chasm of race in America.

The First, the Few and the Many

I remember sitting in a group when Chloe opened up about what happened between them after George Floyd was murdered. She spoke softly, but the weight of her words filled the space.

She didn't just see a man die that day. She saw her uncle. Her cousin. The boy who grew up down the street. She saw the ghosts of history pressing down on the present, the familiar script of brutality playing out once again, indifferent to the screams of the people it crushed.

She had been through this cycle before - another Black body brutalized, another name turned into a hashtag. Chloe had expressed to her husband in previous years how much she needed him to check in with her when these murders happened, but this time, she decided to wait. To see if her husband, the man who vowed to love her, to cherish her, to be her partner in all things, would check in on her. Would acknowledge that the world was not safe for the woman he loved.

Two weeks passed.

Nothing.

When she finally brought it up, he blinked, barely registering it. "Oh yeah," he said, like he was recalling a headline in passing. "I heard about that."

That was it.
She sat there, stunned.

In his world, it was a ripple in an otherwise peaceful existence. In hers, the ground had split open beneath her feet. The contrast was gutting.
She felt abandoned, exposed. The man who shared her bed, her home, her future, had the privilege of choosing whether or not to engage with her pain. He could turn off the news, go for a run, or lose himself in ministry work. She could never turn it off. She lived inside it. She carried it in her bones, in the way her grandmother used to squeeze her hand a little tighter before she walked out the door, in the way her mother used to tell her to "be careful" with an urgency that white children would never have to understand.

The First, the Few and the Many

And now, here she was, sitting across from the man she loved, realizing just how deep the divide ran. As Regina Jackson put it, "As long as your skin is seen as a weapon, you can never be unarmed."

This was what Chloe was up against.
The terror. The powerlessness. The hypervigilance. The epigenetic trauma - how history leaves fingerprints on your nervous system, how your body still jolts with the echoes of your ancestors' fear. The vicarious trauma of watching Black death over and over again, knowing that you live in a world where this is not only possible, but common.

She thought about Willie Lynch, the man who taught enslavers how to break Black people - how to shatter the strongest among them in full view of the others, so they would all learn helplessness. If the strongest of you can't stop this, what can you do?

Chloe was staring at that lesson in real-time.
She and her husband had witnessed the same moment in history. One didn't have to look. The other couldn't look away.

So, who should have leaned in? Who should have reached across that chasm with care, with love, with urgency?
We all know the right answer.

But the lived reality is far too common.

Because in the end, it is usually the wounded one - the Black partner, the Brown partner - who learns to suppress their pain. To shrink it down into something invisible. To make sure their grief doesn't disturb the delicate comfort of the person who loves them.

But that only lasts for so long.
And when it breaks, it breaks everything. 🌱

The Reversal: Q's Lady

Her exact words were, "My man's job is to protect me physically, so I make it my job to protect his peace - and to protect our son."

The First, the Few and the Many

I remember sitting with my boy Q at a football game, listening to his wife talk about their relationship. She wasn't just saying the right things; she was living them. The more she spoke, the more it became clear: she wasn't passive in their love. She wasn't an observer of his struggle. She was an active participant in his protection, a defender of his dignity.

She had done the work - not just privately, but publicly. She challenged her own white family, pushed back against microaggressions, and refused to let silence be complicity. She didn't just expect her Black husband to bear the weight of the world alone, to shoulder the daily toll of racism, to carry his own exhaustion, her racist sections of her family's 'absestos' and hers too. She stood beside him in the fight, not as a savior but as a true partner. Even cutting off parts of her family that she knew would both have a problem as much as be one to her man.

And what struck me most was how much it mattered to him.

When I talked to him - when I watched the way he breathed easier around her, the way his shoulders weren't perpetually tense, the way his laughter came freely - I realized something. The survival of an interracial relationship isn't just about love. Love is not enough.

It's about allegiance.

It's about whether your partner is willing to see the world through your eyes and stand between you and harm when the world comes knocking. It's about whether they will challenge their own reflection, dismantle their own conditioning, and put their body, voice, and privilege in the way when necessary.

Too often, interracial relationships function on an unspoken contract: the Black or Brown partner learns to accommodate, to soften, to translate, to shrink. But what happens when the white partner takes responsibility for the burden instead? When they refuse to let their partner walk through the world alone?

My boy Q and his wife are proof that it's possible. Their relationship isn't built on the illusion that race doesn't matter - it's built on the truth that it does, and that love means choosing to act accordingly.

The First, the Few and the Many

And when I talk to him, when I see how he moves through the world with her by his side, I realize what should have been obvious all along: safety, peace, and belonging shouldn't be luxuries in a relationship. They should be the standard.

Sacrifice

La La Land is for whites only.
The Black body pays a price just to be with you.

A friend of mine once told me about his marriage to a white woman. He knew from the beginning that it would come with judgment - the quiet disapproval from older Black folks who saw him as a traitor, the suspicion from Black men, the sense of rejection & betrayal from Black women. He told himself that love would be enough to bridge the gap. But love does not erase history.

"For her," he told me, "conflict was an argument. For me, it could be a death sentence. For her, it was about feelings. For me, it was about survival."

If you are a white woman in a relationship with a Black or Brown body, understand this: the most dangerous thing in the world is your tears. If you truly love the Black man you are with, you must protect him - even from yourself.

My friend told me about an older white mother he once met who had a biracial son dating a white girl. One day, the son and his girlfriend got into an argument in public. The girlfriend began to cry and scream, making a whole ass scene. The son immediately walked away. His girlfriend was appalled. "Why would he just leave me crying there?" But he knew, and his mother knew. He knew that standing there, beside a white woman in distress, was a risk to his very life. That her tears could summon a force that wouldn't ask questions before deciding he was the threat. He had done what his mother taught him to do.

My friend told me me what the white mom told her son's white girlfriend, "Now, there is nothing wrong with a woman having emotions. But what you do with those emotions has consequences. A white woman's tears bring police, bring intervention, bring punishment upon the Black/Brown man she claims to love. That can turn DEADLY to the Black man you claim to love. If it was a white man you were hollering at, then no one would pay attention to it. But the deadliest thing is a white

The First, the Few and the Many

woman's tears. If there is no real danger, those emotions should be handled in private. The world responds to a white woman's distress with urgency and to a Black man's mere existence with code-red threat level. Guns drawn and all. Protect my son, even from yourself."

Then he told me about his ex-wife who is unmelanated. One night, they got into an argument. She was in his face, yelling, aggressive. His therapist had told him to leave situations like that. His mother had told him the same: walk away. So, he did. Hands raised, showing he was no threat, he backed away.

And then, she ran to the other side of the room and started screaming.
Screaming like he had hit her. Screaming like she was in danger.
But he had never laid a hand on her. Never even raised his voice. And yet, in that moment, he knew - if the police came, he would be the one in cuffs.

"That night," he said, "my body screamed at me: Run, nigga!"

So, he ran. Literally.

That was the first separation in their marriage, and led to the second time he was ever homeless, for a season. Afraid to tell his family or friends. The only reason they reconciled was because of COVID. But within four years, they were divorced. If you don't protect his peace, you will be a threat to it. If you don't protect him, you will become the threat. No matter how much you say you love him.

The Price of Admission

I heard this story from a friend of mine. He told it with the kind of quiet fury that comes from witnessing something both deeply personal and disturbingly familiar.

It's about a wealthy Hispanic man - let's call him Andrés. Born into a family that had clawed its way up, he had the kind of success that makes parents beam with pride. He married a white woman, moved into a pristine, manicured zip code - the kind where people like us always seem to know exactly where the richest houses are.

At first, it was the little things. His unmelanated wife refused to let him give their children ethnic names. "They'll be easier to hire this way," she'd say, as if his culture

The First, the Few and the Many

was a burden they needed to shed. Then came the gifts from his grandmother back in Central America - carefully wrapped packages of traditional clothing, sent with love across borders. When his wife saw them, she wrinkled her nose. "They look like something the cleaning ladies wear," she said. Not once. Not twice. But three times.

Andrés swallowed it. Like he swallowed everything else. No diddy.
One night, my friend - a Black man - was invited to dinner with Andrés and his business partners. It was a business thing, the kind of upper-class affair where men sip expensive wine and plan how to make a ton of money together. A young, white corporate lawyer showed up already tipsy, & oozing entitlement. He kept eyeing my friend, commenting on his watch, his clothes, his presence, in that thinly-veiled way that Black men know too well. Then he motioned to the waitress, demanding bottles of wine, and when the waitress asked if she had served him before, he smirked.

"Have I had *you* before?"

The air cracked with silence. The waitress - young, probably working her way through school - turned and walked away, holding back tears.
When her boyfriend showed up to confront the lawyer, the restaurant still let them stay. Wealth insulates people like that. But then, in front of everyone, the lawyer let it slip:

"Listen here, nigger - I mean, Negro."
My friend braced himself. Andrés said nothing. He just sat there, a man accustomed to swallowing things.

But my friend was watching closely. He realized something that night.
This is Andrés's world. These are the men he works with, the ones he boards private jets with, the ones he laughs with over $300 steak dinners. This is what he comes home to - where his own wife devalues his culture, where he bends and contorts himself to fit, where he apologizes for the racism of his peers as though it is his own.

That night, my friend saw the cost of Andrés's wealth. It wasn't just the white colleagues who called him an "English-as-a-second-language motherfucker." It

The First, the Few and the Many

wasn't just the way he was dismissed, diminished, tolerated, but never fully accepted. It was how thoroughly he had learned to accommodate it.

Andrés had paid his way into the upper class with silence. His success came at the price of his dignity.

But the real question - the one that lingered long after the wine had dried on the table and the racist lawyer had stumbled into the night - was this:
How much of himself did he have left?

Loss

Which leads me to one of my main points: too often, whenever Black or Brown bodies choose white partners in marriage, inevitably, the expectation is that the Black/Brown partner joins the white partners in their world, rarely the other way around. And this is often the gripe of Black women. That the idea of "stealing our men" is not as much personal as it is a communal loss. One less Black man in the BIPOC community to model Black masculinity, dignity, and achievement, which, considering the cultural history of Blacks in North America, feels like a loss worth grieving. Imagine, the Black/Brown bodied partner, in order to love their white lover, must become a token to keep them. But does it have to be this way? 🌱

Terror

I have another friend - let's call him David. He has a white wife. David's brother-in-law has a habit of saying racist things, small barbed wires dressed up as jokes. One time, they were watching TV, and his brother-in-law turned to him, pointed at the screen, and said, "See, that's a nigger. But you're a Black person."

Another time, David told him to stop, to knock off the ignorant comments. Later, in front of a room full of adults, including his wife, his brother-in-law put on a rap song and turned to him with a smirk. "Hey bro, is this ghetto enough for you?"

David's wife said nothing. And that silence - oh, that silence - was its own kind of violence and abandonment. Forget the fact that due to David's success in business he bails out his wife's family when they need help. He has them on the payroll to clean his house or to watch his kids, and he pays for any and all family vacations.

The First, the Few and the Many

David's a whole ass millionaire. Forget the fact that his white wife doesn't have to work, ever, yet still decides to never cook or clean the house or do anything. She makes her mother do it.

Looking back, he realizes the signs were always there. When he met her family. When they attended her brother's wedding in the woods, and her mother turned to him with a smile and said, "Don't worry - no one's gonna lynch you here"

His wife had said nothing then, too.

And now? David tells me in confidence that he feels trapped. The abandonment has piled up, layer upon layer, sedimented into something permanent. It didn't go away. It just became normal. Now, a mortgage payment and three to four kids later... he wonders how this will affect his kids and, ultimately, himself.

Musing on Allyship

I once interviewed Billy, the first diversity leader at a white Protestant ministry back in the 1980s. He had championed the need for the role but initially thought a Black person should take it. Then he had a conversation with Elward Ellis, the first Black man to hold a similar role at another organization. Ellis told him, "If I could do it again, I would have had a white person take my role first - to clear out the cobwebs, to take the backlash - so that when I came in, I could just do my job."

Billy took that to heart, and when he stepped into that role, the backlash confirmed Ellis' words. White ministers told him;

"This diversity push is reverse racism."
"Why focus on one group? We're all one in Christ."
"Why should we financially support Black staff when they should raise money like everyone else?"
And some things? Some things Billy would not repeat, no matter how much I asked.

This is what allyship sometimes looks like: stepping into the fire first, so that when Black and Brown bodies arrive, the flames of white backlash are not part of the job description or at least don't burn as bright. As Elward said to Billy, "Sometimes allyship means being the first in a position to clear out the racial cobwebs and racist

The First, the Few and the Many

knee jerk reactions of other white bodies, so that when a Black and Brown body arrives as one of the few or even the only, they can just do their job without as much racial static in the way." Like Elward Ellis longed for.

Final Word

To the Black and Brown bodies with white partners who refuse to carry the weight with you - I see you. I know what it is to be left alone in your racial pain. To be ignored so often that you try to ignore it yourself. When it is overwhelming, I've been there. When you feel numb to it, I've been there too. Either way, as long as you stay alive, your kids will at least have one parent they can come to when this part of the racialized world fragments their sense of coherent coexistence in a broken land.

You deserve a partner who makes your peace their priority. 🌱

Someone who chooses to be not just a blessing, but a shieldmaiden and burden bearer too.

When I proofread this to a white female friend of mine with a Black husband, she said, "this is so good Michael, and makes me reflect on how I treat my man. It's just that I'm so non-confrontational but he is still my man."

I told her, "*Disarming honesty, your life of being non-confrontational was over the moment you said I do to a Black body… the degree to which you choose to remain non-confronatational is the degree to which you leave your husband to, nay FORCE, your husband to deal with the storm while you nestle indoors with hot cocoa. You don't get to be non-confrontational, especially if you made him be at a white church or white neighborhood to be with you or live near your white family. All that racial, even if he is smooth and smiles and descalates still leaves a clamor in his nervous system no matter how much he downplays it. And you expect him to love as a husband and father at 100% capacity as if he isn't taking hits because of you are 'just non-confrontational,' that's some bullshit.*"

She said, "*I needed that. Thank you. You're right.*"

"When I criticize a system, they think I criticize them - and that is of course because they fully accept the system and identify themselves with it." -Thomas Merton

The First, the Few and the Many

Appendix C

Password for rest of Appendices links: VawzenIsEarned

Book Two Preview: The Body

Appendix D

Random Musings

Spotify playlist I listened to as I wrote book one

The First, the Few and the Many

Appendix E

Citations

*"I know I can't drive a truck.
I know I can't rob a bank,
I can't count, and I can't lead a movement.
But I can fuck up your mind."*
-James Baldwin

Prologue

1. David Bowie quote, https://www.instagram.com/share/_uZ9n2Maz

Chapter 1

1. Page 16, Adichie, C. N. (2013). Americanah. Alfred A. Knopf.

Chapter 4

1. Encyclopedia Britannica. (n.d.). Dunbar High School. https://www.britannica.com/topic/Dunbar-High-School-Washington-D-C
2. Metropolitan Library System. (2019, July). Douglass High School: A leading educational institution. https://www.metrolibrary.org/archives/essay/2019/07/douglass-high-school-leading-educational-institution
3. Hoffman, D. (Uploader). (2010, February 26). Manning Marable interview – Firsthand account of the history of Jim Crow South [Video]. YouTube. https://www.youtube.com/watch?v=nPBttI52sPw
4. NPR. (2024, November 7). How the Freedman Bank collapse of 1874 connects to economic disparities we see today. https://www.npr.org/2024/11/07/g-s1-33275/how-the-freedman-bank-collapse-of-1874-connects-to-economic-disparities-we-see-today
5. Wilson, V. (2020, June 25). Chasing the dream of equity. Economic Policy Institute. https://www.epi.org/publication/chasing-the-dream-of-equity/

6. Mora, G. (2021, May 6). Women of color and the wage gap. Center for American Progress. https://www.americanprogress.org/article/women-of-color-and-the-wage-gap/
7. Colarossi, N. (2021, April 15). Texas State Rep. says Asians are 'reaping the benefits of Black activists' sacrifices'. The Root. https://www.theroot.com/tx-state-rep-says-asians-are-reaping-the-benefits-of-th-1851740500
8. Poetry Foundation. (n.d.). Gil Scott-Heron. https://www.poetryfoundation.org/poets/gil-scott-heron

Chapter 5

1. Henry, A. (2022). All the white friends I couldn't keep: Hope—and hard pills to swallow—about fighting for Black lives. Convergent Books. (Henry, 2022, chapter 6 & pp. 86–88)

Chapter 6

1. Essential Civil War Curriculum. (n.d.). Uncle Tom's Cabin. Virginia Center for Civil War Studies. https://www.essentialcivilwarcurriculum.com/uncle-toms-cabin.html
2. Pilgrim, D. (n.d.). The picaninny caricature. Jim Crow Museum of Racist Memorabilia, Ferris State University. https://jimcrowmuseum.ferris.edu/links/essays/vcu.htm
3. Henson, J. (1876). The life of Josiah Henson, formerly a slave, now an inhabitant of Canada, as narrated by himself [eBook edition]. Project Gutenberg. https://www.gutenberg.org/files/49129/49129-h/49129-h.htm
4. Wilford, J. N. (2015, February 24). The story of Josiah Henson, the real inspiration for Uncle Tom's Cabin. Smithsonian Magazine. https://www.smithsonianmag.com/history/story-josiah-henson-real-inspiration-uncle-toms-cabin-180969094/
5. Golden Globes. (2021, February 4). Forgotten Hollywood: Lincoln Perry, first Black movie star. https://goldenglobes.com/articles/forgotten-hollywood-lincoln-perry-first-black-movie-star/
6. Pilgrim, D. (n.d.). Jim Crow Museum essay on Blackface and minstrel caricatures. Ferris State University. https://jimcrowmuseum.ferris.edu/links/essays/vcu.htm
7. Pilgrim, D. (n.d.). The Sapphire caricature. Jim Crow Museum of Racist Memorabilia. https://jimcrowmuseum.ferris.edu/antiblack/sapphire.htm

The First, the Few and the Many

8. Clutch Magazine TV. (2015, May 21). The Jezebel stereotype: Media representations of Black women [Video]. YouTube. https://youtu.be/_-D1hCY6nis
9. Wikipedia contributors. (n.d.). Magical Negro. Wikipedia. https://en.m.wikipedia.org/wiki/Magical_Negro
10. Wikipedia contributors. (n.d.). Supporting character. Wikipedia. https://en.m.wikipedia.org/wiki/Supporting_character
11. Wikipedia contributors. (n.d.). Protagonist. Wikipedia. https://en.m.wikipedia.org/wiki/Protagonist
12. Wikipedia contributors. (n.d.). Film. Wikipedia. https://en.m.wikipedia.org/wiki/Film
13. Wikipedia contributors. (n.d.). Magical Negro – Note on race. Wikipedia. https://en.m.wikipedia.org/wiki/Magical_Negro#cite_note-race-2
14. Wikipedia contributors. (n.d.). Negro. Wikipedia. https://en.m.wikipedia.org/wiki/Negro
15. Wikipedia contributors. (n.d.). Sambo (racial term). Wikipedia. https://en.m.wikipedia.org/wiki/Sambo_(racial_term)
16. Wikipedia contributors. (n.d.). Noble savage. Wikipedia. https://en.m.wikipedia.org/wiki/Noble_savage

Chapter 8

1. Jones-Rogers, S. (2019). They were her property: White women as slave owners in the American South. Yale University Press.
2. Pilgrim, D. (n.d.). Casual Killing Act of 1669. Jim Crow Museum of Racist Memorabilia. https://jimcrowmuseum.ferris.edu/links/essays/vcu.htm
3. Crowe, T. (n.d.). Under this law, white women were granted the right to kill mixed-race children. https://tonicrowewriter.medium.com/the-slave-law-made-to-protect-white-women-from-punishment-for-killing-mixed-children-b09b9d460d99
4. LinkedIn. (n.d.). Haley Lickstein [Professional profile comment]. LinkedIn. https://www.linkedin.com/search/results/all/?keywords=haley%20lickstein
5. Zippia. (n.d.). Chief diversity officer demographics and statistics in the U.S. https://www.zippia.com/chief-diversity-officer-jobs/demographics/

Chapter 9

1. Lynch, W. (1712). The Willie Lynch letter: The making of a slave. [Reprinted versions available widely online and in print; original authorship debated].

The First, the Few and the Many

2. Hare, J. (n.d.). Full quote from speech/interview on Black family and education https://www.youtube.com/watch?v=Tq2kJ56hSqo
3. Kendi, I. X. (2019). How to be an antiracist. One World.
4. Coates, T.-N. (2015). Between the world and me. Spiegel & Grau.
   or
   Coates, T.-N. (2014, June). The case for reparations. The Atlantic. https://www.theatlantic.com/magazine/archive/2014/06/the-case-for-reparations/361631/

Chapter 10

1. C. Zhang, personal communication/interview about her experience. March 5, 2021. Instagram @onlytokensallowed, https://www.instagram.com/p/CMDkKCvg2T3/
2. Screen Rant. (2024). Erika Alexander Interview – American Fiction & Racial Passing [Video]. YouTube. https://www.youtube.com/watch?v=EJSUGU24ehw
3. Black Brazil Today. (2023). What is the difference in race between the U.S. and Brazil?. https://blackbraziltoday.com/what-is-the-difference-in-race-between-the-us/
4. September Melody. (2021). A brief Black girl's perspective on Eurocentric beauty standards. https://iamseptembermelody.medium.com/a-brief-black-girls-perspective-on-eurocentric-beauty-standards-african-american-and-747ec838af06
5. Faculdade SESI. (2025). Comparative study of racism in Brazil and the United States [PDF]. https://www.faculdadesesi.edu.br/wp-content/uploads/2025/04/1-Comparative-Study-of-Racism-in-Brazil-and-the-United-States.pdf
6. Dr. Maria P. P. Root. (1993). Bill of Rights for People of Mixed Heritage. https://www.mixedpeopleshistory.com/bill-of-rights
7. Luo, Michael. (2025). Strangers in the Land: Exclusion, Belonging, and the Epic Story of the Chinese in America. United States: Diversified Publishing

Chapter 12

1. Brown, A. C. (2018). I'm still here: Black dignity in a world made for whiteness. Convergent Books. "White people are exhausting" (Brown, 2018, p. 11).

Chapter 13

1. Welwood, J. (2019, January 22). What is spiritual bypassing? Psychology Today. https://www.psychologytoday.com/us/blog/the-empowerment-diary/201901/what-is-spiritual-bypassing/amp

The First, the Few and the Many

2. (Page 220) Interview with Shaq, Instagram March 13, 2021. https://www.instagram.com/tv/CMYimsvA9SM/?igshid=MXV2MW1ndHk1aGZidQ%3D%3D

Chapter 14

Sidney Poitier & Harry Belafonte:
1. Whiting, S. (2022, January 7). Friends Sidney Poitier and Harry Belafonte made as much mischief as they could. Los Angeles Times. https://www.latimes.com/entertainment-arts/story/2022-01-07/friends-sidney-poitier-and-harry-belafonte-made-as-much-mischief-as-they-could
2. National Urban League. (2022, January). Sidney Poitier fought racial justice both onscreen and off. https://nul.org/news/sidney-poitier-fought-racial-justice-both-onscreen-and
3. Smithsonian National Museum of African American History and Culture. (n.d.). Harry Belafonte: Actor and activist. https://nmaahc.si.edu/explore/stories/harry-belafonte-actor-and-activist

Eartha Kitt:
4. The New Yorker. (2021, October 15). When Eartha Kitt disrupted the ladies who lunch [Video documentary]. https://www.newyorker.com/culture/the-new-yorker-documentary/when-eartha-kitt-disrupted-the-ladies-who-lunch

Terrence C. Carson:
5. Essence. (2023, October 12). T.C. Carson says he was fired from Living Single after calling out Warner Bros. https://www.essence.com/celebrity/t-c-carson-fired-from-living-single-calling-out-warner-bros-friends/

John Amos & Esther Rolle:
6. Ritchie, A. (2023, December 15). Why was John Amos fired from Good Times? People Magazine. https://people.com/why-was-john-amos-fired-from-good-times-8722823
7. Raised on Television. (2022, April 5). The real reasons why John Amos and Esther Rolle left Good Times. https://www.raisedontelevision.com/blog/the-real-reasons-why-john-amos-and-esther-rolle-left-good-times/

Little Richard:
8. PBS. (n.d.). Little Richard biography and career timeline. American Masters. https://www.pbs.org/wnet/americanmasters/little-richard-biography-and-career-timeline/27612/

Billie Holiday:

The First, the Few and the Many

9. Encyclopaedia Britannica. (n.d.). Billie Holiday. https://www.britannica.com/biography/Billie-Holiday

UPN & WB Merger:

10. Schneider, M. (2016, January 24). CW Network's 10-year anniversary: The UPN and WB merger. Variety. https://variety.com/2016/tv/news/cw-wb-network-upn-merger-announcement-10-years-ago-1201687040/
11. NPR. (2006, June 6). Black sitcoms could be casualty of network merger. https://www.npr.org/2006/06/06/5453863/black-sitcoms-could-be-casualty-of-network-merger
12. Albany Student Press. (2023, February 15). The rise and fall of Black sitcoms: The switch from UPN to CW. https://www.albanystudentpress.online/post/the-rise-and-fall-of-black-sitcoms-the-switch-from-upn-to-cw

Streaming Platforms:

13. Trapital. (2024, May 10). Tubi is great—but will it follow the Fox playbook? https://www.trapital.com/memos/tubi-is-great-but-will-it-follow-the-fox-playbook
14. Tubi. (2024, March). Insights on reaching cord-cutters and cord-nevers. https://corporate.tubitv.com/press/tubi-unveils-insights-on-how-marketers-can-reach-cord-cutters-and-cord-nevers-in-the-stream-2024/
15. Peacock. (n.d.). Black movies and TV shows. https://www.peacocktv.com/collections/black-movies-and-tv-shows

Chapter 15

1. Chappelle, D. (2020, October 17). Unforgiven [Video]. YouTube. https://www.youtube.com/watch?v=6pxmHX_gQuc
2. TheGrio. (2021, March 10). Stacey Dash says she's done with politics and regrets past comments. https://thegrio.com/2021/03/10/stacey-dash-quits-politics/
3. NAACP. (2022). Historic nomination: Ketanji Brown Jackson, Supreme Court Justice. https://naacp.org/resources/historic-nomination-ketanji-brown-jackson-supreme-court
4. U.S. Congress. (n.d.). Cory Booker [Member profile]. Congress.gov. https://www.congress.gov/member/cory-booker/B001288
5. Anderson, C. (2020). Reparations for slavery [Video excerpt]. C-SPAN. https://www.c-span.org/clip/public-affairs-event/user-clip-reparations-for-slavery-excerpt-dr-claud-anderson-of-powernomics-and-the-harvest-institute/4661065
6. Davis, K. (2023, June 28). Clarence Thomas moves to reverse the legacy of Thurgood Marshall. The

The First, the Few and the Many

   Conversation. https://theconversation.com/supreme-court-justice-clarence-thomas-moves-to-reverse-the-legacy-of-his-predecessor-thurgood-marshall-203626
7. Butler, A. (2024, June 2). Brown v. Board, Thurgood Marshall and me. Politico Magazine. https://www.politico.com/news/magazine/2024/06/02/brown-v-board-of-ed-thurgood-marshall-and-me-00161050
8. Bouie, J. (2023, August 25). Thurgood Marshall and Clarence Thomas: Two visions of Black justice. The Atlantic. https://www.theatlantic.com/ideas/archive/2023/08/thurgood-marshall-clarence-thomas-black-justice-scotus/674975/

Chapter 16

1. Poetry Foundation. (n.d.). Phillis Wheatley. https://www.poetryfoundation.org/poets/phillis-wheatley
2. Boston Public Library. (2020, October 1). Tracing the life of Phillis Wheatley Peters. https://www.bpl.org/blogs/post/tracing-the-life-of-phillis-wheatley-peters/
3. Panahi, N. A. (2023). I didn't survive: Emerging whole after deception, persecution, and hidden abuse. Whitaker House.
4. The Dig at Howard University. (n.d.). Toni Morrison: Life of a literary giant. https://thedig.howard.edu/all-stories/toni-morrison-life-literary-giant
5. Encyclopedia Britannica. (n.d.). Toni Morrison. https://www.britannica.com/biography/Toni-Morrison
6. TheGrio. (2023, October 15). More than peace: How Toni Morrison urged us to fight for something bigger than war. https://thegrio.com/2023/10/15/more-than-peace-how-toni-morrison-urged-us-to-fight-for-something-bigger-than-war/
7. The Root. (2023, July 10). Nobel Prize winner Toni Morrison: One of America's greatest voices. https://www.theroot.com/nobel-prize-winner-toni-morrison-one-of-america-s-grea-1836995611
8. Taylor, M. (2023, August 10). Joy Taylor on breaking barriers in sports commentary [Video]. YouTube. https://www.youtube.com/watch?v=nzDn3Ifmd0k
9. History.com Editors. (2020, February 28). Althea Gibson. HISTORY. https://www.history.com/articles/althea-gibson
10. United States Golf Association. (2016, February). Althea Gibson's second act. https://www.usga.org/content/usga/home-page/articles/2016/02/golf–althea-gibson-s-second-act.html
11. Ken Burns. (2016). Jackie Robinson [Documentary]. PBS. https://www.pbs.org/kenburns/jackie-robinson/

The First, the Few and the Many

12. Bill of Rights Institute. (n.d.). Jackie Robinson. https://billofrightsinstitute.org/essays/jackie-robinson
13. Walker, J. (2020). Roberto Clemente: Baseball rebel. Society for American Baseball Research Journal. https://sabr.org/journal/article/roberto-clemente-baseball-rebel/
14. Latino Power Baseball Project. (n.d.). Roberto Clemente. https://lpbp.org/programs/roberto-clemente/
15. Plaschke, B. (2020, September 8). Roberto Clemente fought racial injustice. Los Angeles Times. https://www.latimes.com/sports/dodgers/story/2020-09-08/roberto-clemente-fought-racial-injustice
16. United States Olympic & Paralympic Foundation. (2017, August 28). 1968 Smith & Carlos salute. https://www.usopc.org/us-olympic-and-paralympic-foundation/news/2017/august/28/1968-smith-carlos-salute
17. BBC. (2023, October 11). In history: How Tommie Smith and John Carlos's protest at the 1968 Mexico City Olympics shook the world. https://www.bbc.com/culture/article/20231011-in-history-how-tommie-smith-and-john-carloss-protest-at-the-1968-mexico-city-olympics-shook-the-world
18. National Museum of the U.S. Army. (n.d.). Benjamin O. Davis Sr. https://www.thenmusa.org/biographies/benjamin-o-davis-sr/
19. Woo, E. (2002, July 7). Gen. Benjamin O. Davis Jr., 89; dispelled racial myths as leader of pilots unit. The New York Times. https://www.nytimes.com/2002/07/07/us/gen-benjamin-o-davis-jr-89-dies-dispelled-racial-myths-as-leader-of-pilots-unit.html
20. NYP Health Matters. (n.d.). What happened to Dr. Margaret Morgan Lawrence? https://healthmatters.nyp.org/happened-dr-margaret-morgan-lawrence/
21. Columbia University Libraries. (2019, December 10). In tribute: First African American psychoanalyst Margaret Lawrence dies at 104. https://blogs.library.columbia.edu/rbml/2019/12/10/in-tribute-first-african-american-psychoanalyst-margaret-lawrence-dies-at-104/
22. Metz, R. (2020, December 4). Google forced out Timnit Gebru, a top AI ethics researcher. MIT Technology Review. https://www.technologyreview.com/2020/12/04/1013294/google-ai-ethics-research-paper-forced-out-timnit-gebru/
23. BBC Worklife. (2024, March 4). U.S. corporate diversity, equity, and inclusion programme controversy. https://www.bbc.com/worklife/article/20240304-us-corporate-diversity-equity-and-inclusion-programme-controversy
24. Robertson, K. (2021, May 19). Nikole Hannah-Jones denied tenure by UNC. The New York Times. https://www.nytimes.com/2021/05/19/business/media/nikole-hannah-jones-unc.html

The First, the Few and the Many

25. Medina, J. (2021, October 14). Cornel West on his departure from Harvard. The Harvard Crimson. https://www.thecrimson.com/article/2021/10/14/cornel-west-harvard-tenure/
26. Kelley, R. D. G. (2021, November 1). Cornel West's Harvard exodus: A crisis of integrity. Boston Review. https://www.bostonreview.net/articles/robin-d-g-kelley-cornel-west-harvard/
27. The Sporkful. (2020, August 17). A reckoning at Bon Appétit [Podcast episode]. https://www.sporkful.com/a-reckoning-at-bon-appetit/
28. Bristol, T. J., & Goings, R. B. (2024). Modern burnout and attrition due to racial isolation among teachers of color. American Educational Research Journal. https://journals.sagepub.com/doi/10.3102/00028312241278597
29. Learning Policy Institute. (2024, March). Teachers of color: High demand and short supply. https://learningpolicyinstitute.org/press-release/teachers-color-high-demand-and-short-supply
30. Fordham Institute. (2023, October 5). Are racially isolated Black teachers more likely to leave their jobs? https://fordhaminstitute.org/national/commentary/are-racially-isolated-black-teachers-more-likely-leave-their-jobs
31. Pew Research Center. (2023, February 22). Facts about the U.S. Black population: Educational attainment. https://www.pewresearch.org/social-trends/fact-sheet/facts-about-the-us-black-population/#educational-attainment
32. Hamidullah, M. F., & Greer, T. (2021). The role of perceived respect and racial identity in workplace outcomes. Journal of Vocational Behavior, 129, 103582. https://www.sciencedirect.com/science/article/abs/pii/S0022103121001025
33. Henry, A. (2022). All the white friends I couldn't keep: Hope—and hard pills to swallow—about fighting for Black lives (Ch. 12). Convergent Books.
34. "These were angry tears… I spent the next six months feeling like a token. In the end, I wouldn't make it a year." (Henry, 2022)
35. Bracey, G. W. (2017). Race tests: Racial bo Carl Braden undary maintenance in white evangelical churches. Sociology of Religion, 78(4), 429–452. https://www.researchgate.net/publication/316355727_Race_Tests_Racial_Boundary_Maintenance_in_White_Evangelical_Churches
36. National Geographic. (2018, October 10). On the Galápagos: The betrayal of Judas goats. https://www.nationalgeographic.com/culture/article/on-the-galapagos-the-betrayal-of-judas-goats

Chapter 17

1. Grishin, D. (2020, December 29). 3 lessons everyone ought to know on creativity from John Cleese. https://dinagrishin.com/2020/12/29/3-lessons-everyone-ought-to-know-on-creativity-from-john-cleese/

The First, the Few and the Many

2. Humphries, S. (2021, October 3). Disorganization and ADHD [Video]. YouTube. https://www.youtube.com/watch?v=ouZrZa5pLXk
3. Koch, K., Reess, T. J., Metzger, C., & Walter, H. (2011). Neurobiological correlates of self-regulation in the medial prefrontal cortex in adults with ADHD. The Primary Care Companion for CNS Disorders, 13(3). https://pmc.ncbi.nlm.nih.gov/articles/PMC3065892/
4. CommunicationTheory.org. (n.d.). Communication accommodation theory: Accent mirroring and social interaction. https://www.communicationtheory.org/communication-accommodation-theory/

Chapter 18

1. Henry, A. (2022). All the white friends I couldn't keep: Hope—and hard pills to swallow—about fighting for Black lives. Convergent Books. (Referenced again here if quoted or cited anew in this chapter.)
2. Diouf, S. A. (2014). Slavery's exiles: The story of the American maroons. NYU Press.
3. Oxford Research Encyclopedia. (n.d.). Maroon societies in Latin America. Oxford Research Encyclopedia of Latin American History. https://oxfordre.com/latinamericanhistory/display/10.1093/acrefore/9780199366439.001.0001/acrefore-9780199366439-e-5
4. JSTOR Daily. (2018, February 20). Maroon societies in Jamaica. https://daily.jstor.org/maroon-societies-in-jamaica/
5. Henson, J. (1876). Truth stranger than fiction: Father Henson's story of his own life. [Project Gutenberg edition]. https://www.gutenberg.org/files/49129/49129-h/49129-h.htm
6. Episode 42, Grits & Eggs Podcast, minute 32:03- 37:12

Chapter 19

1. Cowman, L. B. (1997). Streams in the desert (pp. 30–31). Zondervan.

www.ingramcontent.com/pod-product-compliance
Lightning Source LLC
Chambersburg PA
CBHW080753300426
44114CB00020B/2727